(Re)Presenting Wilma Rudolph

Other titles from Sports and Entertainment

(Re)Presenting Wilma Rudolph

*Rita Liberti &
Maureen M. Smith*

SYRACUSE UNIVERSITY PRESS

BIOGRAPHY
Wilma
RUDOLPH

For a listing of books published and distributed by Syracuse University Press,
visit www.SyracuseUniversityPress.syr.edu.

ISBN: 978-0-8156-3384-6 (pbk.)   978-0-8156-5307-3 (e-book)

Library of Congress Cataloging-in-Publication Data
Liberti, Rita.
   (Re)presenting Wilma Rudolph / Rita Liberti and Maureen M. Smith. —
First edition.
      pages cm. — (Sports and entertainment)
   Includes bibliographical references and index.
   ISBN 978-0-8156-3384-6 (pbk. : alk. paper) — ISBN 978-0-8156-5307-3
(e-book) 1. Rudolph, Wilma, 1940–1994.   2. Runners (Sports)—United
States—Biography.   3. Women runners—United States—Biography.
4. Memory.   5. Collective memory.   I. Smith, Maureen Margaret, 1967–
II. Title.
   GV1061.15.R83L53 2015
   796.42092—dc23
   [B]   2015006735

Manufactured in the United States of America

Rita Liberti is a professor in the Department of Kinesiology at California State University, East Bay, in Hayward, California. She also directs the Center for Sport and Social Justice at the university. Liberti earned her PhD from the University of Iowa. An emphasis of her research is the study of African American women's sport history across the twentieth century.

Maureen M. Smith is a professor at California State University, Sacramento, in the Department of Kinesiology and Health Science. Smith earned degrees from Ithaca College and The Ohio State University. She is a member of the North American Society of Sport History (NASSH), of which she is a past president; the North American Society for the Sociology of Sport (NASSS); and the International Society for the History of Physical Education and Sport (ISHPES).

Contents

Illustrations

Acknowledgments

THIS PROJECT began seven years ago, and since that time a number of people and institutions have assisted us in moving the book forward to its completion. Florence Planells-Benjumea's translation skills enabled us to gain a perspective on Wilma Rudolph as described in the newspapers of several French speaking African nations. Amber Wiest was especially helpful in accessing Wilma Rudolph's deposition from the Claude Pepper Library at Florida State University. Kay Parsons's assistance with several of the photographs was greatly appreciated. Grants awarded to us by the Western Society for the Physical Education of College Women and the Ken Doherty Memorial Fellowship through USA Track & Field and the Amateur Athletic Foundation of Los Angeles in support of this project were invaluable. Wayne Wilson, archivist at LA84, was generous with his time and expertise during our stay at the LA84 library.

We want to thank Harcourt Children's Books for allowing us to reprint the image from Kathleen Krull's children's book *Wilma Unlimited*. Nancy Beffa, of Cappy Productions, was generous in allowing us to quote from the Bud Greenspan film *Wilma*.

At California State University, East Bay, Glenn Brewster and Terry Smith's technical expertise, with the images and photos in the book, was matched by their endless supply of patience. Jared Mariconi of the university library solved every dilemma we brought his way, including any number of issues with microfilm readers. We appreciate the financial support provided by the Department of Kinesiology and the efforts made on our behalf by Associate Provost Linda Dobb. At California State University, Sacramento, Robin Carter, Associate Dean of the College of Health and Human Services, generously provided financial support in the indexing of this book.

Portions of this book were presented at several conferences, including the North American Society of Sport History, the North American Society for the Sociology of Sport, the Western Society for the Physical Education of College Women, and the American Academy in Rome, celebrating the fiftieth anniversary of the 1960 Olympic Games. We're grateful for the helpful comments and feedback of our colleagues in these organizations, as well as their continued support during the project. Thanks to the two anonymous reviewers who provided helpful feedback on the manuscript. Many thanks to our manuscript editor, Maria Hosmer-Briggs, for her perceptive comments and diligent attention to the small details.
R.L. and M.M.S.

My thanks to Maureen, who invited me to take this intellectual journey with her several years ago. It has been quite a ride. I am grateful to Susan Birrell and Tina Parratt for accepting me into the PhD program at the University of Iowa twenty-five years ago. Sitting in their classrooms was a privilege that transformed my world. Their influence runs throughout my contribution to this book. Finally, to Trudy, whose selflessness, quick mind, and limitless curiosity strengthened this book . . . and has added so much richness to our lives together.
R.L.

Any time something takes seven years to complete, one is certain to accumulate a lengthy list of indebtedness. I am no different, and recognize that the work I do and the life I live is a result of great partnerships, collaborative efforts, and good fortune. I knew Wilma Rudolph merited serious academic treatment, though I also knew I could not attempt to tackle this project on my own. To that end, my thanks to Rita for her willingness to take on this challenge with me. I am especially grateful to a group of friends who provided tremendous support and sage guidance throughout this process, from phone calls, emails, and supper clubs to the occasional baseball game or hike: Becky Beal,

Nancy Bouchier, Sarah Fields, Steve Gietschier, Kathy Jamieson, Dana Kivel, Dan Nathan, Tina Parratt, Sam Regalado, Joel Nathan Rosen, Alison Wrynn, and Patricia Vertinsky. Further, I am fortunate to have friends and colleagues whose encouragements and friendships provide great sustenance: Carly Adams, Mary Louise Adams, Mel Adelman, Bob Barney, Susan Birrell, Laura Chase, Cheryl Cooky, Dick Crepeau, Heather Diaz, Russell Field, Larry Gerlach, Virginia Goggin, Annette Hadjimarkos, Diane Higgs, Matt Hodler, Annette Hofmann, Pauline Kajiura, Kimberly Kernen, Shelley Lucas, Malcolm MacLean, Mary McDonald, Joan Neide, Timi Poeppelman, Jaime Schultz, Jennifer Sexton, Jane Stangl, Craig Tacla, Jan Todd, David Wiggins, Claire Williams, and Mike Wright—among many. I am beyond grateful for the unending support of my sister Steph, my first friend in life, and to my Grandma Floss Tully, whose pride in her oldest grandchild has no boundaries. Ellen Carlton is simply my favorite doubles partner. She is a great strategist, helps me to focus on my side of the net, sees the long game, and coaches me and challenges me to be my best self. Dog walks with Roxy and Che helped with many a wording and idea, as well as the gift of perspective. Three friends and mentors, Catherine Cauffield, John Maxwell, and Nick Trujillo, passed before this book was complete, but left their fingerprints in important and meaningful ways that extend beyond this book.

M.M.S.

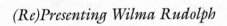

(Re)Presenting Wilma Rudolph

Introduction

"THE WILMA RUDOLPH STORY is the stuff of fairy tales, only in her case the fairy tale came true," so proclaimed *Sports Illustrated* one week after Rudolph's untimely death at fifty-four years old on November 12, 1994. The sports weekly followed up with their evidence, noting that the Olympic champion, "the 20th of her railroad porter father's 22 children from two marriages, . . . was a frail and sickly child. Stricken with double pneumonia and scarlet fever when she was four and later diagnosed with polio, she went through childhood with a crippled right leg."[1] The day after Rudolph's death, Ira Berkow, writing for *New York Times*, offered a similar framing of the athlete's early life. Berkow told his readers, "She became America's black Cinderella. But her early dreams were not to find Prince Charming, or to be Queen of the Debutante's Ball. Or even to be adored, as she would be, and cheered lustily and mobbed around the world, with her fans sometimes even stealing off her shoes—while she wore them. . . ." Berkow continues, "Wilma Rudolph's life, however, became the stuff of fairy tales, the crippled girl at age eleven who became an Olympic sprint champion at age twenty, whose charm and elegance captivated millions."[2] Both remembrances cover similar ground, and in doing so are illustrative of the shared narratives upon which Rudolph's obituaries and her life's story rest. The end of Rudolph's life serves as the starting point for our book because her obituaries provide an introduction to the often-told narratives of her life, while acting as a site for the construction of particular stories about the Olympian.

In exploring the meanings attached to the stories we have told, and continue to tell ourselves, about Wilma Rudolph, our book takes

1

its theoretical and methodological cues from the relatively recent "cultural turn" in sport history. The field of sport history has taken many turns in recent years and our hope is that *(Re)Presenting Wilma Rudolph* joins with other work around the discipline's latest pivot, the move toward a new cultural history. Relatively few sport historians have taken the "turn" toward culture, leading Mike Cronin to argue that the perspective is a "rare and delicate flower" in the field (pun intended).[3] This newer emphasis on discourse, ideology, and power, at least among sport historians, underscores a shift from "examining causality and context" (a social history paradigm) "to analyzing meaning" (a cultural history paradigm). The nascent trend in sport history (too slow for some and much too quick for others) from social to cultural history moves us from an "*explanation* and an excavation for causes, to that of *interpretation* and an interrogation of meaning" and attendant relationships of power.[4]

The most recent directional change in sport history rests upon a couple of epistemological assumptions about the past and our ability to "know" it in the present. These assumptive starting points inform *(Re)Presenting Wilma Rudolph*, and are thus worthy of note here. First, the book troubles the notion of a single, knowable account of Rudolph's life, one in which the past is retrievable, given sufficient time and energy devoted to digging around in the archives. Instead, we acknowledge that historical knowledge is partial, filtered, and ideological. This is not to say that retellings of the past are "made up," but it is to recognize that they are indeed "made."[5] Our close reading of various texts and sites of memory is meant to explore the various meanings attached to Rudolph over time and place. Examining the spaces in which these narratives were constructed is crucial to this project: as Daniel A. Nathan reminds us, "history is always an account by someone for someone."[6]

This perspective directs us to another major assumption on which the cultural turn is based, and to the second driving theoretical force of our work. What "really" happened within and across various episodes of Wilma Rudolph's life is less of our concern in this book. Rather, we are more interested in interrogating why certain stories and remembrances of Rudolph remain center-stage, while others have far less purchase, and are forgotten. Wilma Rudolph's past, like that of all others, comes to us through some representational means, which are ultimately reconstructions in a present moment. We caution however, that interpretations of the past are, by no means, exclusively and unfailingly presentist. To say that the present moment shapes our understanding of the past is not to obliterate conceptualizations of continuity in history. To be sure, while we may "never step into the same river . . . it still has persistent characteristics, qualities that are not shared by any other river."[7]

Thus, the expansive field of memory studies, with its attention to present influences on historical retellings, informs this text, as well. Cultural or collective memory studies, which have occupied the discipline of history in recent decades and sport history in much more recent years, guide *(Re)Presenting Wilma Rudolph*. The perspective is invested in examining the shared pasts constructed by groups within a society via "media, institutions, and practices."[8] These shared memories become a kind of "common cultural currency" that when enacted enable us to communicate with others about a communal past.[9] In Rudolph's case, the collective remembrances of the athlete and her life rest on a narrow range of tales that continually re-circulate around the former track superstar. The stories have been disseminated on countless occasions throughout her life, after her death, and beyond. It is, after all, according to Wulf Kansteiner, within these "repetitive representations" that the "backbone of collective memories" is formed.[10] Thus, our interest and analysis rests within these stories and various sites of memory as we explore representations and remembrances over more than half a century.

These pages, then, do not provide a biographical rendering of the former track great or an attempt to "recover" the facts of Rudolph's life and present them as truth tales for the reader. This presented a conundrum for us when it was suggested by the book's reviewers that we offer a biographical sketch of Rudolph to orient readers who may not be familiar with the "facts" of her life. The extent to which it is even possible to retrieve facts of a life, and retell them as such, is precisely what we trouble in *(Re)Presenting Wilma Rudolph*. Thus you see our dilemma. Without question, there are some certainties attached to Rudolph's life story that could be communicated to readers. The facts include, for example, Rudolph's birth in 1940; her winning three gold medals in track at the 1960 Olympic Games; that she was the mother of four who had her first child out of wedlock as a high school student; that the former Olympian died in 1994; and so forth. This, and any portrait of her life, even one that claims to distill the facts and only the facts, is still subjective in its selectivity. What "facts" should we provide; which do we ultimately include, and which have we chosen to leave out? The objective in narrating our ambivalence is not a pretentious dismissal of the reviewers' reasonable suggestions. It is done, instead, to illustrate that biographical entries are constructions, inevitably edited by the teller/writer; and in this case, that is the primary point we emphasize in *(Re)Presenting Wilma Rudolph*. Our concern is not "with [Rudolph's] past as such," but instead with her "past as it is remembered."[11]

Clearly then, we understand retellings, including those associated with Rudolph, as being far from ideologically neutral. We also remain mindful that collective memories should not be conceived of as "passive storage" recalled for us in any number of present moments.[12] We are quick to note the plurality of collective memories surrounding the former Olympian, as well. While there may be preferred memories that are recreated and retold, they are far from singular or uncontested. There are sites in which the dominant tale of Rudolph's life is troubled, including the athlete's own voice and the black press, among other spaces, and we seek to explore those in this book. Collective remembrances of Wilma Rudolph, we note, are fluid, dynamic, and imbued with power, offering us a window onto historical representations that are "negotiated, selective, present-oriented, and relative."[13]

Wilma Rudolph's obituaries, similar to the other episodes we share in this book, contour our remembrances of Rudolph, marking the parameters of her life. The obituary's significance, according to Bridget Fowler, rests on two levels, because it is one of the "material and symbolic rewards for lives considered well lived," and it stands as the "first step towards posthumous memory." More importantly, she suggests that the obituary is not "just a *store of value*, it is also a *measure* of value."[14] Far from merely a passive receptacle of narratives about a life, obituaries are politicized remembrances and commemorations in which an existence is deemed worthy of note. Fowler contends that obituaries belong in the category of Pierre Nora's "lieux de memories"; like other sites, such as museums, films, novels, and libraries, the obituary is an important "cultural product" that molds collective memory.[15]

Building on the concept of obituaries as collective memory, Janice Hume explains that obituaries "combine past and present, public and private," legitimizing "characteristics of individual Americans to a collective audience," and as a result, "adding to cultural values and memory."[16] Andreas Huyssen contends, "The past is not simply there in memory, but it must be articulated to become memory."[17] Thus, narrative is core to the creation of memory, as "once a moment is gone the past must be reconstructed."[18] Accordingly, Hume views obituaries published in newspapers as providing a mechanism which "articulates virtues of private citizens for assimilation by a society," introducing readers to individuals they may never have known of before and contributing to "individual and generational memories an element of public consciousness through the mass media."[19]

When Wilma Rudolph died of brain cancer in late 1994, the nation mourned her passing, and the former Olympian's achievements on the track nearly thirty-five years prior were the hallmark of the remembrances. Rudolph's obituaries serve, in this introductory chapter and previously to newspaper readers in 1994, as the entry point into the athlete's storied life and the multiple narratives that have been told about her, both in life and death. The athlete's premature death was front-page news for some newspapers, with standard obituaries in the following pages, most serving as tributes to the athlete and some accompanied by a photograph of Rudolph in her twenties. Rudolph's death as national news, and the subsequent prominence of her obituary, signify her fame. According to Fowler, "one characteristic of the *obituary* is that these lives are *selected* [Fowler's emphasis] as particularly memorable, distinguished or newsworthy."[20] In writing his version of Rudolph's obituary, Philip Hersch concluded that "[b]y the time brain cancer caught Rudolph . . . she had achieved a stature that made her legend and her sport greater in the long run."[21]

As reflected by the prominent obituaries of several newspapers notifying their readers of her untimely death and her accomplishments, Rudolph's life and early death were deemed worthy of recognition. For many readers, perhaps non-sports fans and younger people, Rudolph's obituary serves as their first introduction to her life. Hume, in writing about obituaries, sees them as summarizing "the essence of the citizen's life," and as a form of both "commemoration" and "a life chronicle." The obituary, Hume continues, "reflects . . . what society values and wants to remember about that person's history."[22] Obituaries as a form of collective memory are subjective and selective as they "revalorize a certain view of the past."[23] Specifically, the obituaries tell Rudolph's life story, in a brief format, highlighting the stories, the "facts," for which she is worth being remembered and mourned. In considering narratives, collective memory, and representation, we ask: what do these obituaries and the other remembrances of Rudolph tell the reader? What stories do they retell from her life, which are forgotten, and why? And which accomplishments do the obituaries and other sites of memory emphasize? Finally, who is served by particular representations of Rudolph?

The "facts" according to the numerous obituaries published about Rudolph recycle several stories previously featured in newspaper and magazine articles throughout her running career, in children's books, and in a made-for-television movie about her life. Every obituary takes note of Rudolph's early childhood illnesses, reiterating pneumonia, scarlet fever, and polio as the culprits. These remembrances upon her death were certain to include mention of doctors' early cautions to Rudolph's mother that her child would never walk, making her later accomplishments all the more incredible. Most of the obituaries mention Rudolph being one of her parents' twenty-two children, further marking the track star as "other." All of the obituaries highlight Rudolph's triple gold-medal success at the 1960 Olympic Games in

Rome, with fewer referencing her less-than-successful post-retirement activities and struggles.[24] To include this material would lessen the "mountain climb" image and meteoric route of Rudolph's biographical narrative as it was re-imagined for readers.[25] When life's obstacles are included in the narrative, they are only present to illustrate the omnipresent power of agency. The local Nashville paper, the *Tennessean*, made note of Rudolph's ability to overcome a number of challenges throughout her life. In doing so, the paper carried forth in death the recurring story lines popular throughout her life:

> As a little girl, Wilma Rudolph battled polio, double pneumonia and scarlet fever. She was poor and from a large family. Her first baby was born when she was unmarried and still in school. She grew up at a time when black women had precious few opportunities. Instead of being detoured [sic] by those adversities, Ms. Rudolph seemed to gain momentum from them. Both on the track and off, Wilma Rudolph personified determination, strength of character, and the will to win.[26]

Two tropes, constructed as a binary, dominate the obituaries of African American athletes: sport participation as "salvation or a poisonous gift."[27] Remembrances of Rudolph trend quite clearly toward the former and remain far distant from the latter.

The "facts" of Rudolph's life as outlined in the obituaries, including her three gold medal performance in Rome, become the foundation upon which the politics of memory are played out. A couple of processes within collective remembering are thrown into sharp relief across the obituaries, as well as through the other sites of memory included in (*Re)Presenting Wilma Rudolph*. Inaccuracies and exaggerations, for example, about Rudolph and her experiences are threaded throughout historical retellings of the athlete. Nowhere is this more evident than in remembrances of Rudolph as the first American woman to win three gold medals in one Olympic Games, despite the fact that she was not the first. Why is she remembered this way? What value/narrative does it serve? And importantly, how does this remembrance play, relationally, on the process of forgetting?

Errors and embellishments are "embedded in American public memory," and this is, we argue, the case with retellings of Rudolph's life, including within the obituaries and well beyond them.[28] Inaccuracies combined with the limited range of stories told about the Olympian produce a life void of dimension. Accounts about Rudolph are exaggerated, and certain aspects highlighted while others are left off the page. On another level, the tales remain stable in their interest in making us feel comfortable with the facts of Rudolph's life. However, the result is a symbolic Rudolph, rendered more compelling and influential than the actual person ever could be. Moreover, the "solidification of the fictions" constructed around and about historical figures, including Rudolph, diminishes their legacy: the complexity of an individual's life is reduced to a handful of actions, statements, or events.[29]

Errors are lodged seamlessly and passed on as truth within the narrative accounts of Rudolph's life as told through her obituaries, adding even greater appeal to a story already deemed fascinating. According to one obituary:

> Rudolph fought not only to win gold medals, she fought scarlet fever, pneumonia, and polio just to walk. In a day where racial barriers in Tennessee could have held her down, she fought to get her education and break the shackles of her physical disabilities. Her triumph at the Rome Olympics of 1960 made her a legend. She became the first woman to win three gold medals (100, 200 and 4x100 meter relay) during one Olympiad.[30]

This account, similar to a number of other Rudolph obituaries, is noteworthy on at least two levels. First, it provides "cultural continuity" as it clearly relates to the reader the most valued pieces of Rudolph's fifty-four years.[31] Filled with agency, in a classic rags-to-riches schema, Rudolph is said to have "overcome" obstacles around race and disability. Importantly, the obituary, specifically its assertion of Rudolph's place in Olympic history, is factually inaccurate. Rudolph was not the first woman to win three gold medals during a single Olympiad; several other women accomplished that prior to 1960. Moreover, these claims are especially interesting considering that US athlete and Rudolph teammate, Chris von Saltza, is overlooked, despite having won four medals in Rome: three golds and one silver. In other Rudolph obituaries, even after acknowledgment of the error, efforts to correct it were not always successful. For example, the *New York Times* mistakenly reported, "Over seven days, she became the first woman to win three gold medals in track and field in one Olympics." Twelve days later, the newspaper printed a correction, stating that Rudolph was "the first American woman to win three or more medals in one Olympics, not the first woman; Fanny Blankers-Koen of the Netherlands won four gold medals at the 1948 London Games." While the correction is partially accurate (Blankers-Koen did win four gold medals at the 1948 Games), the amendment identifies Rudolph as the first *American* woman to achieve the feat of winning three gold medals at one Olympiad; this is still an error.[32]

To recall Rudolph and her accomplishments in this way is to fail to remember the numerous other athletes, including several US women, whose accomplishments were as spectacular as Rudolph's. As Aleida Assmann reminds us, "When thinking about memory, we must start with forgetting."[33] "Forgotten" athletes include three US female athletes who were triple gold medalists within a single Olympiad. Ethelda Bleibtrey won three gold medals in swimming at the 1920 Antwerp Olympic Games.[34] Helene Madison, at the L.A. Games in 1932, also won three gold medals in swimming.[35] There are some interesting similarities in the biographies of Bleibtrey, Madison, and Rudolph. For example, Bleibtrey began swimming to deal with her polio. Madison, after winning three gold medals, was welcomed home with a parade in Seattle, dealt with financial problems in her adult life, and died a premature death. All three women were unable to financially capitalize on their athletic success, with Madison losing her amateur status after appearing in a film. Finally, as Rudolph ran to three golds in Rome, teammate Chris von Saltza medaled four times, taking three gold medals and one silver.[36] In addition, international athletes including Fanny Blankers-Koen in track and Larissa Latynina in gymnastics each won four gold medals, in 1948 and 1956, respectively. Astonishingly, Latynina finished first three more times in 1960. Lastly,

Rudolph's accomplishments on the track were matched four years earlier, in 1956, by Betty Cuthbert of Australia. What is safe to say is that Rudolph was the first American woman to win three gold medals in track and field in a single Olympiad. She is also the first African American woman to win three gold medals in a single Olympiad.[37]

The fictive heralding of Rudolph's triple-gold achievement is largely facilitated by a news media, and a society, more generally, that collectively forgets about these earlier champions. Barry Schwartz employs the concept of "oneness" to further interrogate the recognition of one individual, while ignoring others who may well have "performed as well as or better than the one acclaimed."[38] He argues that "commemoration" is the central way in which "oneness" is perpetuated. While history, according to Schwartz, "chronicles" the past, commemoration "publicly celebrates it." Further distinguishing the two, he notes that history is "inclusive of every significant facet of an event." Commemoration, on the other hand, is "selective, highlighting an event's most significant moral feature."[39] Commemoration, conceptualized in this way, is the central element of Rudolph's obituaries and the other sites of memory we feature in *(Re)Presenting Wilma Rudolph*. For Schwartz, commemoration, not history, upholds "oneness," given commemoration's tendency towards glorification and romanticization. At each commemoration we are reminded of "who is worth remembering and why."[40] In its absence we are left to forget, despite the many grand achievements of those not celebrated. Rudolph's obituaries, similar to other forms of tribute, offer a consistent barrage of hyperbolic praise, with little if any room for others to share the frame. As one obituary declared, "Hardly anyone was more of an inspiration to youngsters—not only in the United States but throughout the world—encouraging them to improve their lives, especially through the healthy form of athletics, than Rudolph."[41] There is no mention in the many obituaries we surveyed of any of the aforementioned female athletes whose accomplishments in athletics reached or exceeded Rudolph's greatness.

The decision to "remember" Rudolph's accomplishment as a first tells us much about the news media at the time, as well as about subsequent authors who repeated the error (including in Rudolph's own obituary in the *New York Times*). The fact that these authors forgot Bleibtrey, Madison, von Saltza, and others to instead trumpet Rudolph leads us to think about questions that echo throughout this book. How have the wide-ranging commemorative sites in tribute to Rudolph sustained and magnified her memory? Or do we hope that in retelling Rudolph's tale we will cement our belief that an (or any) African American girl, born poor, and disabled for years of her young life, can be successful in the United States? How do Rudolph's triumphs, in that case, serve American ideals and in ways that Bleibtrey's, Madison's, and von Saltza's do not? Rudolph's victories occurred in the early years of the civil rights movement, and her success provided much-needed evidence to trumpet the greatness of America and served to highlight the promise of democracy, in ways that Bleibtrey, Madison, and von Saltza simply could not exemplify.

Wilma Rudolph's obituaries are but one site in which the track star has been represented and remembered. That site serves as a springboard to other locations of memory, which are explored throughout the book. In the days just after Wilma Rudolph's remarkable performance at the 1960 Olympics, and in the half-century since, she has been the focus in scores of written materials, as well as being talked about and remembered in a variety of ways: newspaper and magazine accounts, a made-for-television movie, almost two dozen children's books, a postage stamp, a statue, a street, and a college dormitory created and named in her honor. With these sites in mind, we offer seven content chapters woven around particular events, themes, or specific source materials. The topics are not meant to be all-inclusive but are selective, to highlight the range of ways meaning was constructed around Wilma Rudolph and her achievements on the track. The chapters move in a loosely chronological order, beginning in the fall 1960. In some ways the book is less about Rudolph than it is about how we have made and remade her across a variety of settings over the past half-century. Wilma Rudolph, like many celebrities and athletes, was and continues to be constantly interpreted for us. Thus, it is the ways in which Wilma Rudolph has been represented and remembered across time and place that drives *(Re)Presenting Wilma Rudolph.*

As an African America female who was disabled for much of her youth as well as born into poverty in the Jim Crow South in 1940, Rudolph's experiences and achievements were and often are framed as a classic "rags-to-riches" story. This particular tale of Rudolph's life is made possible by suspending her in that 1960 moment, as a twenty-year-old with the world's attention and awestruck gaze upon her. In moving beyond a biography and hagiographic rendering of Wilma Rudolph, we ask the following in a close reading of the discourses constructed around the track great: what meanings are generated from the narratives surrounding Rudolph? Who or what is privileged by particular retellings and representations of Wilma Rudolph? Importantly, what voices, perspectives, and identities are marginalized or even silenced in the process of constructing these narratives? How do these discourses shape historical and contemporary constructions of race, gender, and class? The book aims to privilege and interrogate the narratives upon which representations of Wilma Rudolph have been built by examining who is served by continually romanticizing the track star and her achievements for the past half-century. In critically engaging with discourse, we hope that *(Re)Presenting Wilma Rudolph* will further theoretical trends within sport history and the field of history more generally by illustrating that the many representations of the track champion cannot be separated from the ideological baggage that the writer brings to the source.

In chapter one, "'Wilma's Home Town Win'?: Race on Parade in Clarksville," we examine newspaper reports about Rudolph's hometown victory parade and banquet just weeks after the Rome Olympics. At the time and in the decades since, the integrated parade is often invoked in remembering Rudolph; thus our interest in it here. With the nation and the world watching, the local press in and around Rudolph's hometown of Clarksville, Tennessee, was quick to use the occasion (and Rudolph) to tout the integrated parade as evidence of the municipality's racial progressiveness and tolerance. However, we interrogate the sources and position Clarksville's mythical representation of itself against the stark reality of continuing racist power arrangements that disenfranchised the town's African American citizens, including Wilma Rudolph. In this chapter, as in the rest of the book, our aim is to trouble the dominant narratives that are constructed around Rudolph and ask who is served by telling a particular story at a particular moment in time.

Wilma Rudolph's three gold-medal-winning performances at the 1960 Olympics in Rome, Italy, propelled her to become one of the most highly visible black women across the United States and around the world. Journalists, both locally and globally, were enchanted with the three-time gold medalist, often as preoccupied with Rudolph's personal appearance as with her athleticism. Comments about Rudolph's attractiveness and graceful presence signaled a change in dominant (white) constructions of African American womanhood. Racist characterizations, grounded in myths and stereotypes, cast black female bodies as the antithesis of femininity and beauty. How do we make sense, then, of this apparent shift in the dominant discourse as it relates to Rudolph? In chapter two, "'She Isn't Colored, She Is Gold': The Politics of Race and Beauty," we argue that constructing Rudolph as an American beauty was dependent on viewing her in juxtaposition to Earlene Brown, a dark skinned, heavy-set African American female shot putter, and Chris von Saltza, a young, blond, white American swimmer. Amid white responses to Rudolph, we are equally interested in how media accounts from black sources framed the track star. Discourses surrounding the three athletes expose the way their multiple subjectivities were constantly in flux, yet arrangements of power around race, gender, and size remained firmly entrenched.

In chapter three, "Running With a Story: From Cold War Icon to Civil Rights Rebel," we continue to examine the American and international press coverage, including the publications of the American government, in their development and usage of Rudolph as a Cold War icon. Throughout the 1950s the Cold War was "fought" on the level of culture, with sport used as a weapon at the nation's disposal. For a nation eager to define itself to the world as open and democratic, African American athletes and Wilma Rudolph specifically were important characters to the United States in telling not just any story, but a particular story about racial progress possible within a color-blind democracy. This narrative was a powerful, very visible one, but was not the only story told by the press. The nation's black press troubled the tale told by the US government and dominant press reports. High-profile African American athletes, as presented by the black press, offered an opportunity to underscore race pride and the hypocrisy of continuing racial inequality. Though relatively marginal, the black press narratives are significant, we believe, because they produce different meanings and attach them to Rudolph's iconic status. In these meanings, we contend, dominant narratives are contested and even destabilized. This chapter culminates with Rudolph's 1963 US State Department visit to Africa and her return to the racial unrest in the American South and her hometown of Clarksville, where she participated in the desegregation of a local Shoney's restaurant. We position Rudolph's civil rights activism upon her return from Africa as troubling her status as a Cold War icon.

While countless narratives have been written about Wilma Rudolph, her autobiography, *Wilma: The Story of Wilma Rudolph*, penned in 1977, offers an important and valuable site through which the track star speaks for herself and is thus the focus of chapter four, "Examining the Autobiographical Self: Wilma Rudolph on Bookshelves." The text served as the foundation upon which subsequent narratives about Rudolph were told, including a number of children's books, making the autobiography an even more important cultural product to examine. Rudolph drew upon bodily discourses in relating her life story to readers, and this serves as the chapter's analytic perspective. Rudolph's admissions about her body and identity speak forcefully to broader cultural forces that informed her life and experiences. The spaces she occupied as a black female, born into poverty, and disabled for many years of her young life provide a unique lens through which to explore issues of corporeality, identity, and agency. With that said, we also understand that autobiographical writing, including that by Rudolph, is constructed. It, like other sites of memory, is selective and partial.

Chapter five, "*Wilma*: Biopics, Nostalgia, and Family in the 1970s," looks at the 1977 made-for-television movie, *Wilma*, which traces the track star's early life through age twenty and the winning of Olympic gold in Rome. A preoccupation with family is a common trope throughout the biopic and docudrama genres during this period, and *Wilma* is no exception. Her family, and particularly her relationship with her father, is prominent throughout the film. The importance of family, and the preservation of it, is central to *Wilma* and, we contend, is critical to perpetuating a mythical, nostalgic notion of family. Given the perceived threats to and encroachments on the family in the 1970s, the filmic representation and centrality of the institution in *Wilma* are particularly significant to us and to our analysis of the biopic.

One of the most popular forms of representation of Wilma Rudolph appears in the form of biography, specifically books aimed at juvenile readers. By 2014, there were at least twenty-one books focused on Rudolph and her athletic accomplishments for young readers in pre-school to junior high. Interestingly, despite numerous books for children, there remains no adult biography on Rudolph. This cannot be characterized as an innocent action, according to the historian Catherine Clinton, who charges that this inactivity is a form of "disremembering."[42] In chapter six, "Against All Odds: Reading Rudolph over Four Decades of Children's Literature," we examine representations of Rudolph as she is depicted in stories for young readers. We address the continued interest in her story for children and focus on several themes in the books, namely race, gender, poverty, and disability, as well as the myriad ways authors use Rudolph's life as inspiration for another generation. Ultimately, the collection fails to subvert or even challenge relationships of power along class, race, gender, and ability. Instead the books' focus on "overcoming" narratives fills the pages of text, obscuring the structural and ideological inequalities that shaped Rudolph's life and experiences.

Since her untimely death in 1994, Wilma Rudolph has been com-memorated in a variety of mediums, including a US postage stamp, two statues, a road race, a state historical marker, a residential center, an indoor track, and a stretch of highway. In chapter seven, "On the Margins of Memory: The Politics of Remembering and Forgetting Wilma Rudolph," we seek to interrogate the processes of memorializ-ing Rudolph and the subsequent ways in which she has been forgotten. We examine a number of Rudolph "memorials," such as markers on the campus of her alma mater, Tennessee State;[43] a US postage stamp; and several sites of memory within her hometown of Clarksville, Ten-nessee. This chapter reminds us of the central role played by Rudolph's hometown, beginning with her integrated parade discussed in chap-ter one, and culminating decades later with various monuments and markers celebrating Rudolph's origins in the city. Importantly, these material sites are reminders of the contested quality of memory and its politics.

In the book's conclusion, we highlight Wilma Rudolph's Decem-ber 5, 1960, appearance on the CBS television game show, *To Tell the Truth*. Our book is about various ways Rudolph's stories have been taken up as truth, and this game show offers to tell us the "truth" about the "real" Wilma Rudolph. Tellingly, Rudolph's own voice on the telecast is silenced, as her "truth" is left up to others on the game show. It is a fitting end to our book, which has addressed the ways the "real" Wilma Rudolph is unknowable. The often-repeated stories we are told about Rudolph, including those on *To Tell the Truth*, do little except reinforce the conventional narratives of triumph, individual agency, and success.

Wilma Rudolph was an outstanding athlete deserving of our attention. The content of *(Re)Presenting Wilma Rudolph* illustrates that the track great has, to be sure, been the focus of our gaze over the past half-century. Paid homage by her neighbors and strangers across the street and the world, respectively, Rudolph has been rep-resented and remembered throughout a wide range of locations since her triple gold medal performance in late 1960. A close examination of each of these spaces or events, whether it was a welcome parade in her hometown or a statue erected to honor the former Olympian, sheds light on the dynamic and deeply politicized process of pulling the past into the present. Each recognition or tribute to the athlete is ideologically coded and fundamentally grounded in "who wants whom to remember what."[44] We begin with remembrances of and at home: Wilma Rudolph's birthplace of Clarksville, Tennessee.

"Wilma's Home Town Win"?

Race on Parade in Clarksville

Which side you are on is all that matters in this place . . .
where White Only seemed in my lifetime,
an ordinary sign, like Entrance
or Welcome, which didn't mean everyone . . .
where I ran as a boy and pretended
I was Wilma Rudolph breaking
the finish-line tape,
ashamed to have such thoughts,
not because I was a boy
but because I was white,
proud of her just the same,
of the speed that carried her
down the world's ellipse,
out of our shared hometown.

     —Neal Bowers on his memories of Clarksville,
      Tennessee, in the 1950s and 1960s[1]

ON OCTOBER 4, 1960, Clarksville, Tennessee, welcomed home
Wilma Rudolph, its favorite daughter, on the heels of her triple gold-
medal-winning performance in the Rome Games. Local officials organized a whirlwind day of events that included a parade, a tour of the
nearby United States Army installation at Fort Campbell, and an evening banquet. Other Olympians joined Rudolph throughout the day's
events, including her Tennessee State and 4x100 relay gold-medalist

18

teammates Barbara Jones, Martha Hudson, and Lucinda Williams. Classmate and fellow gold medalist Ralph Boston, as well as Eddie Crook, stationed at Fort Campbell and winner of a gold medal in boxing's middleweight division, joined the festivities. However, as a native Clarksvillian, Rudolph was clearly the center of the town's attention. To pay tribute to the triple gold medalist, local businesses decorated their windows in anticipation of the event and flags were flown until after the parade's conclusion.[2] So supportive was local government that reportedly Clarksville school children were dismissed early from school so that they could attend and participate in the parade for Rudolph.[3] As the parade and Rudolph's motorcade moved through town, thousands of residents lined the streets of the Northern Tennessee municipality to catch a glimpse of "Clarksville's gift to the Olympics."[4] In addition, over eleven hundred people joined Rudolph in capping off the day's celebration by attending a dinner in her honor at the Armory.[5] The tickets, at $1.50 a plate, were so popular that the event sold out one day in advance of the occasion.[6]

The October fourth celebration was in some ways the culmination of a media frenzy, of sorts, in the weeks leading up to the event itself. In the days after Rudolph's superior performance in Rome, the local press, especially, began detailing Clarksville's plans for the champion's return. Regional and even national press accounts joined in the chorus of daily local accounts throughout mid- to late- September as the planning and activities took shape on the pages of the press.[7] Media attention, once half a world away in Rome, soon shifted to the American South and to northern Tennessee in anticipation of Rudolph's return. Excitement seemed to grow in the published reports through September and early October, as stories provided readers with reminders and updates about the city's plans for the Olympic champion.[8] It is largely within the published print accounts of the homecoming that our interest and analysis rests. Characterized in many of the press reports as the first racially integrated event in this Jim Crow South community, we ask ourselves how the Rudolph homecoming was represented at the time and how it has been remembered since. The homecoming occurred just at the historical moment that legalized racial segregation and white supremacy across the South began to fragment amid black resistance.[9] However, despite a wave of varied protests by African Americans and their allies, deeply entrenched ideas about race remained firm.[10]

Wilma Rudolph's Clarksville homecoming was a rare occurrence, but not the only one, around the midcentury mark, in which very public attention and praise were bestowed upon an African American athlete.[11] New York City, the nation's most prestigious promenade site, welcomed the 1936 four-time gold medalist Jesse Owens and Wimbledon champion Althea Gibson after she became the first African American to win the title in 1957. However, the location of Rudolph's hometown welcome, in the American South, sets it apart from that of Owens and Gibson. The homecoming events of two other African American Olympic champions provide opportunities to examine how and to what extent the Jim Crow South welcomed athletic stars whose second-class citizenship characterized their residency in the region. Mainstream press accounts of Mildred McDaniel's and Cassius Clay's returns to their hometowns of Atlanta, Georgia and Louisville, Kentucky, in 1956 and 1960, respectively, after their gold-medal-winning performances, shed light on the American South's enduring system of racial injustice. Similar threads to that of Rudolph's story weave across press accounts of the McDaniel and Clay homecomings, as racial tensions framed public discourse and white society's ability to pay homage to its black citizens. However, as is apparent with Rudolph's hometown welcome, a critical collection of voices occasionally countered these dominant narratives with their own, positioning athletic achievement among African Americans as a keen marker of individual and collective success. Thus we turn to a brief discussion of the McDaniel and Clay events, which offer valuable context to Clarksville's public embrace of Rudolph.

Clarksville's apparent eagerness to roll out the red carpet for its Olympic heroine was an orientation not employed by the city of Atlanta for Mildred McDaniel in 1956. Despite her gold medal winning performance in the high jump, the native Atlantan and Tuskegee (Alabama) Institute student was barely a footnote across the pages of the city's mainstream daily. The *Atlanta Constitution* ran two articles, buried deep in the paper, about McDaniel through December 1956, and in the first spent one-third of the account detailing fashion etiquette. The Russian athletes "may be mighty talented," the paper opined, "but they had to take a tip in comfort from some plain old American girls." McDaniel, one of the "plain old American girls," took off her high heels to minimize the discomfort of wearing the shoes at the Games' opening ceremony in the summer heat of Australia, resulting in the Russian athletes following suit.[12] The dismissal of McDaniel and her athleticism, by highlighting the shoe story, is as gendered as it is racialized, and the marginal space afforded the athlete is a product of both.

On one occasion, at least, the *Atlanta Constitution* offered up on its pages a voice in support of McDaniel, encouraging all Georgians to welcome the champion home just as they had the white Olympic gold medalist and Atlantan Paul Anderson. In a letter-to-the-editor, Noble Dixon acknowledged Anderson's achievements and also noted the Governor's recognition of the male athlete. But he cautioned, "can poor grace and calculated slight move us to overlook a no-less-remarkable feat" by McDaniel? He continued, "Does her color detract one whit from the acclaim due her?" It was, according to Dixon, not in spite of the fact, but *because* of the "uphill fight the Southern Negro is always forced to make to win such a championship, that the achievement ought to be proclaimed around the world."[13]

Georgia's white establishment pushed McDaniel to the margins, but the black press in the city did not. The *Atlanta Daily World's* editors proudly claimed that McDaniel "shows the spirit of her people," where in the South "grim patterns of race relations . . . chained [African American] progress but not their competitive spirit." In winning a gold medal, the world champion "refused to bow to the mandates of second class citizenship," according to the black newspaper.[14] Marion Jackson, the paper's sports editor, used the occasion to praise McDaniel and criticize Jim Crow and those who worked to sustain it. McDaniel, in Jackson's view, triumphed over "titanic odds" and in doing so represented a "new enlightenment." The athletic achievements of

McDaniel and Olympic teammate and fellow Atlantan Margaret Matthews of Tennessee State were an inspiration to all African Americans, according to the columnist. "Not all of us can race against time," but the track athletes' efforts give strength to help African Americans "hasten the day when there will be no imprisonment of hope."[15]

The city's Black press welcomed the Olympian home, using McDaniel's homecoming parade as an opportunity to pay homage to the athlete and take note of, as well as speak out against, the continuing racial injustice that permeated the South. Held at one of the city parks, the event attracted a few hundred African American well-wishers, some of whom in the "happy confusion" of the event spilled out into parts of the park normally off limits to them. According to Jackson, "[t]an welcomers forgetting the Interstate Commerce Commission ban against waiting room distinction surged into the jimcrow [sic] hovel which still remains a pungent and odorous reminder of separate but equal."[16] For Jackson and others in the community, even in the midst of joyous events such as this, reminders of the injustices of the South's racial hierarchy remained close and constant.

Few white dignitaries were present at McDaniel's celebration and this did not go unnoticed by Marion Jackson. Governor Marvin Griffin, characterized by a biographer as "one of the South's most outspoken supporters of racial separation," was invited to the event, but did not attend.[17] To which Jackson remarked that the "eloquence of [the Governor's] absence" made for the best speech of the day. Even when white elected officials did attend, the black daily was certain to use the occasion to indulge in tongue-in-cheek remarks about the realities of racial inequality in Georgia. Atlanta Mayor William B. Hartsfield, in his speech at the event, named the city the "home of champions and a championship town," Jackson noted. The columnist added, the mayor's "pitch for Atlanta and glad hand for its successful folks is a landmark of Deep South relations."[18] As these press accounts illustrate, McDaniel's return to her hometown was contested, and exposed the racial tensions that pervaded the South. Other African American Olympic champions upon their return to the American South endured similar homecomings.

Olympic boxing gold medalist Cassius Clay returned home to Louisville, Kentucky, in September 1960 to a town eager to claim the fighter as their "conquering hero," but apparently less willing on some levels to extend an official city-sponsored red-carpet welcome.[19] Local press reports seemed, at times, more preoccupied with the home-coming the Clay family had for its son than with the city's plans for the champion. On its editorial page, the *Louisville Courier-Journal* announced that the turkey dinner Clay's mother had planned for the champion upon his return from Rome "should be an immense tri-umphal success." The paper added that the homecoming "is expected [to] include outside civic festivities," almost as an afterthought to the turkey dinner held in the privacy of the Clay family home.[20] Louis-ville's public events for Clay included a greeting at the airport upon his return to the city and a program at Central High, the school from which he had graduated months earlier. Two hundred people, includ-ing "a heavy sprinkling of young friends," greeted Clay at the airport and joined in the twenty-five-car motorcade to Central High.[21] Ali, in his 1975 autobiography, remembers the "long police escort all the way downtown; black and white crowds on the streets and sidewalks."[22] Mayor Bruce Hoblitzell and representatives from the chamber of commerce were present at the airport welcome, though the chamber "didn't have time" to sponsor a dinner as part of a welcome for the Olympic champion. The mayor, in his remarks at the airport, used the occasion to comment on Clay's "manner and attitude," as much as the athletic achievement that gave rise to the event. The mayor noted, "He [Clay] acts like you would like a young American to act. . . . If all young people could handle themselves as well as he does, we wouldn't have any juvenile problems." Clay, the mayor assured those in atten-dance, was a "swell kid."[23] The mayor's comments about young Clay smack of the white paternalism that long pervaded American South race relations.

Not unique to the Louisville mayor's office, condescending atti-tudes from whites towards the heavyweight champion extended to the fledgling professional partnerships Clay formed with the Louis-ville Group soon after his victory in Rome.[24] Michael Ezra, relying on the *Louisville Defender*, which described Clay as "intensely happy," and "humble," views Clay in his welcome home celebration as "Louisville's favorite son, seemingly endorsed by the full city."[25] As Ali biographer David Remnick claims, "For a while, life was a parade for Cassius," but concedes, "The celebrations masked an underlying ambivalence about Clay in Louisville that would deepen with time."[26] Decades later Muhammad Ali (formerly Cassius Clay) recounted that he hoped and even anticipated that his Olympic achievements might translate to "something greater" for him—namely, the silencing of racist insults he suffered under Jim Crow. However, shortly after arriving home he was denied service at a segregated lunch counter in Louisville. Despite telling the waitress who he was and even showing her his gold medal, Clay was told to leave. The "key to the city" he was given upon returning from Rome symbolized nothing, according to Clay, as he remained defined by his blackness.[27]

Clay, like McDaniel and Rudolph, returned to the United States as Olympic champions, though the extent to which the South was willing to bestow honor upon them was mired in the racism that plagued the region. In addition, much as we will see with Rudolph's event, a close reading of the Clay and McDaniel homecomings exposes voices of resistance to those in the mainstream, troubling the dominant narrative's neatness. Thus, the athletes' homecoming parades and related public events, as reported in press accounts, offer up rich locations to examine narrative constructions of southern identity amid the swirl of these broader tensions and changes around race and civil rights.

Moreover, the parades themselves, in addition to the ways in which the events were represented in media reports, are incredibly valuable sites in understanding cultural negotiations of power. The study of events, including parades, once thought to be "anecdotal marginalia" among scholars, has in the past two decades become a central location to examine social relations as they are played out in public.[28] Far from mere entertainment, parades as public spectacles are sites of propaganda, political action, and powerful means of communication. These very public "messages in motion," despite their nonpermanence, carry with them ideological perspectives and meanings originating from those who created them.[29] Public dramas, such as parades, engage with and promote existing power structures, as well as discourses, which give license to those with power.[30] In Clarksville, Rudolph's parade worked to promote a particular image of the town that erased racial tension, conflict, and inequality. Town officials and event organizers used the parade to "appropriate public spaces and more permanently imbue these spaces" with their own particular agenda about the state of race relations in the town.[31] Parades and other public rituals can, and do, "present a view of society emphasizing consensus, harmony, the compatibility of constituent parts, an accepted hierarchical ordering and shared values."[32] Wilma Rudolph's homecoming celebration was exactly that.

As events that often occupy a town or city center, parades form a symbolic and literal hold on core, prime public space. Indeed, a parade's enchantment derives, at least in part, from the setting in which it takes place. The location of Rudolph's parade, for example, much of it through downtown Clarksville, is more than simply a "passive backcloth for the enactment of spectacle." Rather, the "materiality of the landscape," in this case the city's core, helps to form the locus of the parade's power.[33] Parading through public squares, occupying the space for the event, is a "powerful geographic strategy to control people and things by controlling area."[34] Clarksville's dominant message about racial harmony and the erasure of Jim Crow realities was enacted and transmitted through Rudolph's parade as it moved through town.

The event's importance was magnified by the uniqueness of the spectacle often attached to parades. As they advance through city centers, parades "[invade] the spaces of everyday life and [transform] ordinary streets into theaters of pomp."[35] Far from plain, parades impress through their pageantry. *LIFE* magazine's article and images on Rudolph's parade illustrate the event's distinctive drama. Taken at eye level, the article's leadoff photograph features Rudolph sitting atop a grand convertible car with a bouquet of roses and ribbons in her lap as she waves to crowds of people lining the streets. Streamers adorn the car, flags are draped across the roadway for parade participants to

Figure 1.1. Wilma Rudolph's hometown parade in Clarksville, October 1960. Original photo appeared in *LIFE* magazine. Reprinted with permission of Getty Images.

pass under, and military men march in formation as the town pays homage to the track star.[36] The image captures the spectacle, and in doing so moves the event beyond the ordinary or routine. Marching bands, military personnel in perfect synchronization and order, large crowds of both black and white onlookers, and other parade participants add aural and visual complexity to the spectacle, announcing the event and testifying to the expense and expanse of the production. It was this elaborate visual display that local and national press reports tapped into as they recounted the "Welcome Wilma Day" parade for interested parties around the country and world.

In examining the press accounts of the day's events, we follow Daniel A. Nathan's theoretical lead and agree that "although the news offers us privileged renditions of social reality, it does not offer us transparent, unproblematic versions of it."[37] The stories circulating in the press in the build-up to and shortly after the "Welcome Wilma Day" celebration serve as a fiction in many ways.[38] Clarksville's efforts to tell a particular story about itself and its racial past, as well as its present, are wrapped up in representations of Rudolph's welcome-home events. As a result of her Olympic victories, many around the world got to know Wilma Rudolph and the stories told about her. Many across the US and the globe admired and even adored the young track star. Her hometown of Clarksville, Tennessee, was eager to certify that it did, as well. To do so, however, Clarksville officials had to disentangle a widely held view across the rest of the nation and even the world, one that fastened Southern (white) identity to segregationist practices that included disenfranchisement and cruelty.[39]

Motivated to construct a counter-narrative that instead spoke to the town's harmonious racial present and its past, Clarksville officials worked to mold this story for observers as the homecoming drew near. The injustices of racism and the racial tensions that saturated the South and Clarksville were silenced on this day, and there seemed little space for anything other than glorifying Wilma Rudolph and the town from which she came. In this way, press accounts actively shaped not only the way the celebration and Clarksville were represented but also the contours of the ways both would be remembered from October 1960 forward.[40] Thus, we contend, the contemporary constructions of the narrative accounts as well as the remembrances of the day's events should be understood as purposeful and dynamic. They have as much to do with "identity, power, authority, cultural norms, and social interaction" as they do with the "simple act of conserving and recalling information."[41] In the homecoming's retelling in the days, weeks, and years afterward, "the beliefs, interests, and aspirations of the present shape[d] the various views of the past."[42] We position retellings of the 1960 homecoming, conceptualized in this fashion, as far from simple, static, and factual bits of information retrieved and innocently told in the present. Instead, the various stories of the event are understood as active, ever-evolving versions or constructions of the past to fit with the present.

In order for Clarksville, and the region more broadly, to acknowledge and honor Wilma Rudolph, they had to know of her. Though

Rudolph was a previous Olympic medal winner from the 1956 Melbourne Games, few Tennesseans seemed aware of her or of the track star's superior athleticism, outside of some Clarksville residents as well as peers and college officials at the historically black Tennessee State campus in Nashville, where she was a junior. Rudolph was "better known in Moscow rather than in her native state" of Tennessee, reported the *Clarksville Leaf-Chronicle* shortly after she stood atop the gold medal stand in Rome.[43] It is not surprising that as an African American female in the mid-twentieth-century rural South, Wilma Rudolph was not a household name. In addition, gender and racial dynamics marginalized virtually all female athletes, including and mainly African Americans.

However, the champion's anonymity was about to change as her achievements at the 1960 Games quickly thrust Rudolph into the national and international spotlight. Even for James Stahlman, the steadfast segregationist *Nashville Banner* publisher, Rudolph's accomplishments could not be ignored or minimized. For decades, under Stahlman's control, the paper's conservative leanings were evident; the publication served as a solid "guardian of southern racial customs."[44] In one of only a handful of reports about the track star, the *Banner* congratulated Rudolph, as well as her teammate and fellow Tennessee State classmate Ralph Boston, on their Olympic accomplishments. Stahlman concluded that champions "don't just happen," instead they are "products of natural ability, plus arduous training under expert hands—and, in track, the most punishing self-discipline of any program in the field of sports. Their achievements reflect credit on their school, their state, and their nation. They have honored all three," the editor proclaimed.[45] Though he lists "natural ability," Stahlman at least acknowledges that achieving world champion status required more than good genes.

By the early October homecoming in Clarksville, Tennesseans in her hometown and around the state had ample opportunity to become more familiar with Rudolph; newspaper accounts detailed her early life, as well as providing readers with the circumstances that gave rise to her athletic achievements. We argue, however, that the press reports by the *Clarksville Leaf-Chronicle*, as well as other regional and national publications, constructed a narrative of Wilma Rudolph and the homecoming that were intent upon fabricating a particular story about Clarksville and its relationship to Wilma Rudolph and other African Americans. In obscuring inequities and tensions, press accounts of the event reproduced dominant racial ideologies and thus perpetuated white supremacy.

In some instances, sustaining relationships of power rests as much with what does not appear on the pages of newsprint as with what does. In a relatively lengthy front-page article titled "A Life of Foot Deformity Once Faced Swift Wilma," in the *Nashville Tennessean*, for example, readers learned of Rudolph's childhood illnesses, which led the future track star to wear braces on her legs as a child. The article implies that Rudolph simply outgrew (with the assistance of a white Clarksville physician) her illness and the leg braces she wore as a result. Absent from the *Tennessean*'s account are the ways in which the Rudolph family sacrificed and suffered under the weight of a racist medical establishment in their efforts to find treatment for their daughter.[46] These omissions or silences "tell us a great deal about the workings of power and hegemony," according to Iwona Irwin-Zarecka.[47] With little or no medical care available to African American Clarksville residents in the 1940s, Rudolph's parents were forced to take their child on weekly visits to the historically black Fisk University Meharry Medical School in Nashville, over fifty miles away, for treatment. White press accounts chose to frame this story in a particular way, but the track star did not. In her autobiography, written years later, Rudolph remembers the humiliation and degradation of being told where to sit on the bus and where she and her mom could and could not eat as part of their frequent journeys to and from Nashville.[48] Taken together, the items that appear in the text and those that do not, the *Tennessean*'s account of Rudolph's experiences makes central a particular version of Clarksville and the South's racial past. Accounts such as this serve to "sanitize the past and unburden us of the messy, the unpleasant, and the inconvenient," and in doing so privilege whiteness while obscuring racial injustices.[49]

As the Rome Olympics drew to a close in the first week of September 1960, Nashville and Clarksville papers turned their attention to publicizing homecoming events for the Tennessee State athletes, within their respective cities. Far from being a point of omission, the issue of race and the intended integrated celebration was instead offered up as evidence of Clarksville's untroubled racial past and present. In the lead-up to the Clarksville homecoming, the *Clarksville Leaf-Chronicle*, as well as the two most prominent Nashville papers, the *Banner* and the *Tennessean*, were explicit and succinct in announcing the occasion. Clarksville mayor W. W. Barksdale expected "several hundred people of both races to honor the Negro speedster" by attending the evening banquet.[50] The *Leaf-Chronicle* seemed to recognize the significance of a city-sanctioned integrated gathering in Tennessee at the particular midcentury moment by "commend[ing]" the Clarksville mayor and the Chamber of Commerce president for "the lead they have taken in honoring Wilma Rudolph."[51] Our point is not to minimize what certainly was a historic event, since most areas of the South and Tennessee, including Clarksville, were years away from full or even partial racial integration. However, in interrogating the media accounts of the planned integrated homecoming for Wilma Rudolph and her African American teammates, we note that they conceal, rather than expose, the enduring racist practices and racial realities within Clarksville and neighboring Tennessee communities in 1960.

Clarksville's racial tensions did not begin in Wilma Rudolph's lifetime; a willful history of white supremacy and resultant African American disenfranchisement had deep roots. In the immediate post–Civil War era, white residents of Clarksville and Montgomery County worked to ensure their economic and political privilege.[52] The city's placement on the Cumberland River aided its recovery from the ravages of the Civil War. As a major port on the river way, Clarksville quickly re-established itself economically by 1880. To a great extent, the city's African American population did not share in late nineteenth- and early twentieth-century prosperity within the region. Nor was there much change in the day-to-day lives of African American residents when the military installation at Camp Campbell was constructed, just ten miles from Clarksville, in the early 1940s. Camp Campbell (later renamed Fort Campbell) helped to boost the region's vibrancy, nearly doubling Clarksville's population to over twenty-two thousand residents by 1960.[53]

Despite these changes, structural inequalities around race persisted throughout the region during the mid-twentieth century and could be seen, among other places, in employment, income, and educational opportunity and attainment for twenty-five percent of the city population that was African American. At the state level, as late as 1950, nearly a third of Tennessee counties offered no high school education for African American citizens.[54] When secondary educational opportunities were provided, African Americans completed far fewer years in school than whites. In urban settings across Tennessee, a category in which Clarksville was included, whites completed over eleven years of education, on average. Blacks, on the other hand, as reported in the 1960 census, trailed considerably, with less than eight years of schooling.[55] In addition, inequalities in public education continued well past the midcentury point as some cities and counties resisted the *Brown v. Board of Education of Topeka* decision of 1954 or were slow to comply with the federal law to desegregate schools. Unlike other communities in which white challenges to Brown resulted in demonstration and even violence, white Clarksville residents displayed no such action. However, this absence of drama should not be read as the community's acceptance of public school integration. Rudolph's hometown was sluggish at best in its response to comply with federal law, officially desegregating schools nearly twenty years after Brown, in the 1973–74 academic year.[56]

At the historical moment Clarksville planned, staged, and carried out Rudolph's homecoming events, African Americans in the town suffered the injustices of Jim Crow in public education and beyond. The median income for black families in Clarksville was roughly half of that of white families in the 1950s.[57] Ironically, as Clarksville celebrated its most famous African American woman in October of 1960, the realities of black women's lives in the city were anything but cause

for a parade. In addition to being restricted to a very few employment options, African American women's wages were extremely low.
Across the state's urban areas, including Clarksville's, African American women earned just thirteen percent of the income of white men.
At just $690 a year, African American female wages were less than
half of the $1,488 earned by white women. Income levels were held in
check by a myriad of constraints, including the very limited job pros-
pects for African American women. In 1959, a total of 1,270 African
American women were employed in Montgomery County, Tennessee,
the county in which Clarksville sits. Nearly six hundred or almost half
of that total were employed in white homes as domestics or "private
household workers."[58] African Americans in Clarksville were subjected
to segregationist policies and practices that extended to a variety of
locations in town through the early 1960s: some public and private
spaces, as well as access to services, remained restricted or off limits.
Clarksville leaders constructed a narrative around "Welcome Wilma
Day" that obscured the actualities of racial injustice that permeated
the town and negatively impacted the lives of African Americans.

Racialized arrangements of power, beyond those related to
Rudolph's homecoming, were evident on the pages of the local press
throughout the period. In one example from the editorial page of the
Clarksville Leaf-Chronicle in early 1962, white Clarksvillians' human-
ity toward local African Americans is underscored as evidence of the
town's racial amicability. The paper commended local residents for
stepping forward when an African American woman from Clarksville
needed blood for an upcoming surgical procedure. Two dozen citizens
responded to the call for blood and "there was no question of race,"
claimed a writer in the local press. The paper added, ". . . for five
of the donors were colored and the remainder were white." The act
"was an example of citizens of Clarksville, regardless of race, working
together . . . ," the *Leaf-Chronicle* concluded.[59] The story's exceptionality is marked in that it occupies column inches on the newspaper's
editorial page. In other words, a more mundane event might not have
captured the paper's attention, but this did, and in doing so provides

a glimpse of the realities around race that shaped Clarksville at the beginning of the 1960s.

Far from silent, African American residents of Clarksville, like their peers across the region, voiced within the local press a growing frustration with segregation and the inequality that resulted from those realities. In the weeks after Rudolph's homecoming, letter writers to the *Clarksville Leaf-Chronicle* were persistent in their questioning of Clarksville's racial status quo as the authors' emotions bubbled up and onto the paper's pages. The waves of civil rights protest and other activities by African Americans and their allies across the South and in Rudolph's hometown by early 1960 galvanized the movement, engendering even greater will toward action. Nashville's *Globe*, of the black press, captured the "new spirit," saying "no amount of jeering, spitting and smashing by sloppy, slack-jawed hoodlums, egged on by the dregs of the Southern past, will kill it." Speaking to the lunch counter sit-ins, as well as other acts of resistance, the paper noted that each becomes a "symbol" of an "unsegregated school, a decent home, a seat up front in a bus, a job without a broom, a desk in a state capitol."[60]

The *Globe* encouraged outspokenness and resistance in a range of ways, including local letter-writing, as each act represented meaningful contributions to eradicating Jim Crow. Clarksville residents answered and joined with the cause in letters to the editor published in the *Clarksville Leaf-Chronicle*, including concerns over access to the public library. In questioning why he was denied use of the public space, writer Ernest L. Woods asked in late 1960, "who constitutes the public?" Woods continued, "the quest for knowledge knows no racial barriers"; and yet Clarksville officials drew the color line. "[B]y birth right I am a citizen," Woods concluded, "therefore why should I not be treated as such?"[61] Just weeks earlier, another letter took issue with newly elected public officials in Clarksville over a host of concerns, library entry among them. "One wonders," the writer mused, "why some candidate doesn't propose to [sic] 'If I'm elected I'll make the Public Library really public.'"[62] Exposing the reach and scope of

Jim Crow within the town, the writer adds that there are a number of other areas that political candidates need to be mindful of, including "the fact that Clarksville needs at least one industry that would hire a man or woman according to his or her ability and not according to the color of his or her skin." Beyond denial of access to public facilities and services, as well as employment discrimination, the writer facetiously ponders "why some candidate doesn't appoint a committee to investigate the source of the water that runs into the fountains at the rear of one of our five and ten cent stores. I'm sure that would be quite some investigation. It would be interesting to know what the difference is."[63]

In similar ways, other letters pushed for change that demanded not only an end to the exclusionary practices by whites but the creation of ones that also afforded African Americans opportunities to make greater contributions to civic life. Less than a month after Rudolph's homecoming, African American veterans of Clarksville and Montgomery County asked "why is it every year the Negro Veterans are left out of the planning [for the Veterans' Day Celebration]?" Questioning the patriotism of those who planned the event, the African American veterans asked, "Is this the American Way? Are we Americans going to continue this policy of discrimination?"[64] The letter prompted a response to the African American veterans, published in the *Clarksville Leaf-Chronicle* three days later. William H. Rogers, commander of the American Legion Post that organized the Veterans' Day festivities, quipped, "If the writer of the letter desires to have more participation, then I suggest that he assist in planning some program for his organization similar to the program Post 7 plans."[65] Despite African American resistance, the Veterans' Day parade, held one month after Rudolph's homecoming festivities, remained segregated, as Rogers's retort makes clear. Importantly, this exchange in the *Leaf-Chronicle* and the other letters, highlighted here, call attention to African Americans' challenges to the racial status quo. Tellingly, the narratives also shed light on the unease among some of Clarksville's white citizens as threats to racialized structures of power and privilege were inscribed on pages of the press by African Americans.

Efforts by the town's white leaders to construct a mythical image of Clarksville for the track star's homecoming, one in which racial inequalities ceased to exist and where white and black citizens lived without incident, may well have been due to the fact that observers well beyond the local region watched as Rudolph came back to her home in the rural South. Just days after Rudolph won gold in Rome, the *Louisville (KY) Courier-Journal*, a publication of the city's mainstream press, ran a story on the Clarksville native. In it the paper reported details of the Rudolph family, including that they were "humble, hard-working" people. The paper acknowledged that despite the fact that the Rudolphs lived "in one of Clarksville's segregated sections," the town planned to spare little in welcoming home the champion. Rudolph will get the "red carpet" treatment, the paper assured readers, and will be "received by Clarksville folk like any returning hero" upon her return.[66]

Nonetheless, at times it was as though Clarksville had to be reminded of its place in paying tribute to Rudolph. "It would certainly be fitting," a Florida resident opined in a letter to the editor of the *Clarksville Leaf-Chronicle* in mid-September 1960, "if Clarksville gave Miss Rudolph the full honor and welcome which she highly deserves when she arrives home."[67] The *Leaf-Chronicle* reminded readers in a front-page article two weeks later that nationwide publicity was going to be given Clarksville's welcome to Wilma Rudolph and a host of national media would be present to cover all or part of the day's events. With attention directed toward the town and its planned activities, the paper assured readers that as the guest of honor, "Wilma . . . will be given the opportunity to speak as long as she cares to."[68]

Indeed these local, largely white declarations may well have been in response to Rudolph's own ambivalence about returning to the racial status quo of the United States and Clarksville. White leaders of Clarksville must have cringed (if they noticed) at the black *New York Amsterdam News*'s front-page story on the track great and her return home. The paper claimed Rudolph's "one worry" of her soon-to-be return to the country and to Clarksville was the injustice and hostility of the racial status quo. "It's going to all but kill me to have to go back home and face being denied this, that, and the other, because I'm a Black American," Rudolph told the black paper. She added, "In America, they push me around because I'm a Negro, here in Europe, they push me to the front."[69] The triple-gold-medalist was coming home, but would she be welcome, she wondered.

In many ways the homecoming events provided a stage on which white Clarksvillians with interest to do so could contest dominant (northern) narratives of the South as a region, and its white citizens, as "savagely racist, intellectually stunted, emotionally deranged," and full of "unhappy rednecks waving the Confederate flag and spewing contempt for national authority."[70] Wilma Rudolph's homecoming furnished an opportunity to reconstruct the image of the South as open and responsive, rather than intractable and static. "The people of America, and Tennessee in particular, will turn out," the Nashville *Tennessean* affirmed, "to honor a slim Negro as the fastest woman runner in the world." The event, the newspaper continued, "will be strictly local. We want to show Wilma what Clarksville thinks of her. The program calls for complete participation from the whole community."[71] The homecoming, the paper implied, afforded all citizens of Clarksville, both black and white, an opportunity to demonstrate their affection for and pay homage to the athlete while it bore witness to the town's unprejudiced orientation. On the morning of October 4, the Clarksville *Leaf-Chronicle* continued to publicize the event and encourage residents' involvement. "It is appropriate and fitting," the newspaper cajoled, "that members of both races that make up this community join, under the sponsorship of the City and Chamber of Commerce, in honoring" Wilma Rudolph.[72] The mayor's proclamation, announced October 4 as "Welcome Wilma Day," and in the same issue of the paper, the mayor "*urged*" [authors' emphasis] all citizens to participate in the day's activities, which the city leader said "will demonstrate to Wilma Rudolph and to people everywhere the gratitude and admiration of her own city."[73] In convincing the rest of the country and world of Clarksville's sincere commitment to Rudolph, the town seemed to first have to convince itself.

It is perhaps the *Leaf-Chronicle*'s account of the homecoming in the days after October 4 that present, most vividly, the dominant constructions of Rudolph's homecoming and of Clarksville. Rather than "the mere production of inherent historical truths," the *Leaf-Chronicle*'s preferred rendering of the day's events embodies a much more active process of "selecting, structuring, and imposing meaning on the past," according to W. Fitzhugh Brundage.[74] In describing the integrated homecoming, the *Leaf-Chronicle* related to readers that "there appeared not the least bit of friction or misunderstanding as members of both races assembled in the armory, or gathered on the sidewalks to watch the parade."[75] While on one level accurate, the statement distorts, obscures, and whitewashes the ways that racial tensions and inequalities continued to play themselves out in Clarksville and the surrounding community. The self-congratulatory remarks continued as the *Leaf-Chronicle* noted, "Of the many fine speeches made at the banquet . . . [County] Judge W. D. Hudson perhaps scored the best hit when he declared that to get the best music out of a piano one had to play both white and black keys." The paper continued, "The Community has long used both types of keys in a symphony of steady progress with a maximum of understanding and a minimum of friction. Let's hope that the national magazines represented at the Wilma Rudolph Day festivities will reflect the spirit that has long marked relations between the two races in a community that is south of the Mason-Dixon line."[76]

The *Leaf-Chronicle*'s hope not only that the national press be present but that they represent the town as it wished to be seen was confirmed when two weeks later *LIFE* magazine's article "Wilma's Home Town Win" was published. *LIFE* reported that the integrated Clarksville ceremony was Rudolph's hometown win as the town's black and white residents honored her. In confirming Rudolph's victory, the magazine included a photo whose headline read "New Local Admirers" and pictured the young athlete signing autographs for white fans.[77] The *LIFE* article provided powerful testimony in defense of Clarksville's desire to be seen as progressive with regard to race. Clarksville appeared to have accomplished what various other communities across the South could or would not, that being a post-racial space in which all citizens were treated equally.

Clearly the *Clarksville Leaf-Chronicle* thought Judge Hudson's piano keys quote to be significant, as it published the parable as part of two separate stories about the homecoming on subsequent days.[78] The quote is significant to us because it is attributed, through implication, to Hudson, despite the fact that the passage is not his. Rather, the original author was James Emman Kwegyir Aggrey, a black African educational leader in the late nineteenth and early twentieth centuries.[79] The *Leaf-Chronicle's* claim, although an implicit one, that the quote is that of a white judge, literally gives white voices a stage from which to legitimate a narrative about racial injustice and their place in it. In this example, Hudson, the white judge, is afforded a privileged position from which to speak and be heard, while Aggrey's life and place as a historical figure is erased. In a more general discussion about the civil rights movement, Renee Romano reminds us that whites have certainly been "active figures" in the fight for civil rights and racial equality, and as a result are deserving of attention and praise. However, a preoccupation with the words and actions of whites in the civil rights struggle minimizes and obscures black agency in bringing about justice.[80]

The power of racism, however, was never absolute in Clarksville in 1960 and across the Jim Crow South more generally, and to suggest so here is misguided. The black counter-discourse in relation to the ones constructed by whites remained largely at the margins, but nonetheless existed, and is evidence of black resistance to the racial status quo that permeated much of the South in the period.[81] In a letter to the editor of the *Clarksville Leaf-Chronicle* just a week prior to the Clarksville homecoming, a reader questioned why the football team from Burt High, the town's African American high school, was not invited to join other local teams at the Fort Campbell ceremony to honor Rudolph and her teammates. "It is true that Burt is a Negro school," the letter's author declared, adding "surely this cannot be an oversight because Burt High [is] the very first school in the entire U.S.A." to produce a three-time Olympic gold-medalist.[82]

The author calls attention to the hypocrisy in honoring Rudolph but excluding the school from which the track star graduated. Such an expression of resistance, like the sit-ins and other forms of protest happening around Tennessee and the South in October of 1960, enabled African Americans to contest the dominant narrative about the homecoming, specifically, and the racial status quo in the South more generally. At least in this instance, Wilma Rudolph became the symbol upon which that resistance was expressed.

In the half-century since the "Welcome Wilma Day" celebration in Clarksville, the event has been remembered across a variety of representations of Rudolph's life, from a story within numerous children's books to other occasions in which the track star is memorialized. In eulogizing Rudolph shortly after her death in 1994, the then Clarksville mayor, Don Trotter, recounted that the track star was not going to attend her own homecoming celebration if the town did not agree to an integrated parade and dinner. Trotter continued, saying of the integrated event, "Wilma brought Clarksville together that way in life. In her passing, she is still giving and bringing Clarksville closer together."[83] In 2003 at the unveiling of a roadside historical marker for Rudolph in Clarksville, the Reverend Robert Tramil said, "I'm so glad to see those piano keys out here for this occasion," referring to the crowd's racial diversity. "She [Rudolph] was a fighter," said Tramil, "she accomplished a whole lot, not just for herself, but for all of us."[84] In a 2007 *Leaf-Chronicle* article, Yvonne Prather, local professor and Rudolph biographer, suggested that Clarksville's original plan called for two separate homecoming celebrations—one for African Americans and the other for whites. "When she [Rudolph] demanded her parade be desegregated," Prather noted, "she made waves in her hometown and across Tennessee."[85] Finally, in 2008 writer David Maraniss in *Rome 1960: The Olympics That Changed the World* uses the Rudolph homecoming as the final story upon which to close his book. According to Maraniss, "The triumph of Wilma Rudolph temporarily transformed the racial landscape of her home turf, but the change did not come merely because of her grand accomplishments in Rome. It came because she insisted on it."[86]

Clarksville's original parade plans and any specific demands made by Rudolph for a single, desegregated celebration, as well as any subsequent negotiations between the track star and city officials, may never be known with certainty. Nearly three decades after the homecoming, Wilma Rudolph made what appears to be the only reference to her involvement in orchestrating the integrated parade. In the late 1980s Rudolph told interviewer and photographer Brian Lanker, "I told them [presumably Clarksville officials] I could not come to a parade that would be segregated. I sort of broke the barrier in my hometown. I probably did everything I wasn't supposed to do, but it was to pave the way for other blacks in the town."[87] While it has not been our aim to search for definitive answers concerning Clarksville's initial parade arrangements and Rudolph's response to the city's proposal, we are nonetheless intrigued by the athlete's agentic claim in the late 1980s after decades of public silence on the issue. Why, for example, did Rudolph, or others who were aware of Clarksville homecoming details, not make mention of the Olympian's involvement prior to this point in time?

In an effort to further explore that question we offer a reading of the "Welcome Wilma Day" descriptions made over the past two-and-a-half decades since Rudolph's statement in the late 1980s. We contend that these remembrances reconstitute a different understanding of the South, one different from the region into which Rudolph was welcomed home in late 1960. Over the course of the past decade or two the number of African Americans returning to the South has increased dramatically. In the last decade of the twentieth century, for example, the number of African Americans in the South grew by well over three million, doubling the previous decade's numbers.[88] Once "denied their regional identity," African Americans are moving back to the South and reclaiming the region and shaping its identity in a way that includes, rather than excluding them.[89] According to the *New York Times* in 1994, "blacks are staking claim to their vision of the South—not as background figures on the mythic landscape of moonlight and magnolias, not as victims of oppression dragged here from Africa, but as southerners, with as much stake in the region as any Mississippi planter or Virginia farmer."[90] Rather than simply and totally a nostalgic look back at Clarksville, the late twentieth and early twenty-first-century accounts of Wilma Rudolph's homecoming are each marked by black agency and a determination to reimagine the South and its identity. Read this way, the narratives force us to reconsider how southern whites were served by past constructions of the homecoming, and to simultaneously question how African Americans were erased from the pages of text.

In conclusion, Brundage argues, "groups secure broad recognition of their identities by colonizing public spaces with their version of the past."[91] If conceptualized broadly, we argue, "public spaces" can be understood as the narratives inscribed on and within the pages of the press. In the days surrounding Wilma Rudolph's homecoming celebration in Clarksville, Tennessee, in October 1960, local and regional news accounts offered up a version of the past that served to mark race relations in nostalgic and benign ways, legitimizing white hegemony as it minimized white culpability for a system of injustice and brutality. It is only in recent years that the largely white historical memory of Rudolph's homecoming in 1960 has been disrupted a bit, by positioning the track star not as absent or even as a passive historical actor, but rather as an agent of social change. This examination of Clarksville's homecoming for Wilma Rudolph reminds us that memory is never static. Memory is imbued with cultural power arrangements. But memories shift and can signal undercurrents of change in relation to cultural power, thus making the Wilma Rudolph homecoming and countless other events well worth interrogating.

"She Isn't Colored, She Is Gold"

The Politics of Race and Beauty

"THIS QUEEN OF THE 1960 OLYMPICS is a slender beauty whose eyes carry a perpetual twinkle," wrote sports columnist Jerry Footlick of Wilma Rudolph in the days after she won the second of three gold medals at the Rome Games. To which he added the Olympian's height, weight, and "Vital statistics: 34-24-26," concluding, "she has the legs of a showgirl."[1] Rudolph's multiple gold-medal winning performance at the Olympics catapulted her into the spotlight, making her one of the most highly visible African American women across the United States and around the world. Smitten with Rudolph, Jerry Footlick, and American media coverage more broadly, lauded her personal appearance and demeanor as much as her remarkable athletic feats. In doing so, coverage of Rudolph, on the surface at least, appeared to mark a departure from dominant representations of black female bodies as the antithesis of preferred [read white] notions of femininity and beauty. Far from transformative, however, we argue in this chapter that Rudolph's iconic status is, at least in part, conferred upon her by continually juxtaposing her against what she is not (at least from the dominant press's perspective): other African American women, and, of course, white women. Specifically, media accounts of her American teammates, 230-pound African American shot putter Earlene Brown and the blonde haired, blue-eyed white swimmer Chris von Saltza, serve as the backdrop against which our analysis of representations of Wilma Rudolph rests.

42

In explaining representational practices around difference and "otherness," Stuart Hall contends that "'difference' matters because it is essential to meaning; without it meaning would not exist." Meaning, according to Hall, "depends on the difference between opposites."[2] In other words, we are defined as "woman" or "black," for example, by what we are not: "man" or "white," respectively. Importantly, these poles, far from simply markers of identity, are imbued with power, because privilege is conferred upon one end of the binary and not the other. We find these basic explanations of identity construction and representation useful in this chapter as we explore mediated accounts of the three athletes. Also informing our analysis is Hall's caution that these binary codes of difference can be simplistic and reductionist, since they fail to speak to the more nuanced complexities of identity construction and the meanings associated with those processes. Mindful of this call, we contend that the meanings generated by and around Rudolph's, Brown's, and von Saltza's multiple identities create a much more dynamic, complex narrative. In looking beyond binaries then, we consider the multiple intersections in play as they are represented in media accounts of the three athletes. The athletes' identities are constructed in opposition, yet are simultaneously interdependent upon each other. Read collectively, representations that feature Rudolph, Brown, and von Saltza open up a discursive space in which to explore the construction and contestation of multiple subjectivities. Ultimately, we contend that these discourses reinforce rather than subvert or even de-stabilize dominant racialized, gendered, sized, nationalized, and other arrangements of difference throughout the late 1950s and early 1960s.[3]

Public perception of female athletes in general, and track and field competitors in particular, by the mid-twentieth century ranged from ambivalence to scorn. Fears of mannish or freakishly abnormal women continued to pervade the sport and its participants.[4] *New York Times* sports columnist Arthur Daley was one among a number of writers who took it upon themselves to toss insults and degrading comments at female track and field participants, making clear his views on both women in sport and broader gender arrangements within society. In making his standard case for women's exclusion from track and field events and the Olympics generally, Daley, in the lead up to the 1956 Games, opined, "Women really are wonderful. They make devoted mothers, charming wives, and delightful daughters. When they try to be athletes, however, they make misogynists out of sportswriters."[5] The profound stigma attached to the sport of track and field at the midcentury mark was impactful on all women, particularly African Americans.

By the early 1950s African American women were enormously successful within elite track and field competitions across the nation and the world. Despite minimal allocation of resources, community-sponsored teams and competitions as well as historically black colleges and universities served as the primary training sites for fostering the development of female athleticism. Though tensions existed around women's participation in sport within black communities, it was muted by a more expansive understanding of femininity that did not necessarily preclude athletic involvement.[6] African American female track and field athletes worked to navigate the sometimes ambivalent attitudes within their own communities toward their involvement, as well as the more general masculine stigma attached to the sport. As they did so, however, African American female dominance at the elite levels of track in the United States during this period risked furthering racist stereotypes, because rigorous physicality remained central to success in the activity's events. Conceptualizations of African American womanhood were continually framed by whites as beyond the bounds of the acceptable notions of femininity. Constructions of black and white womanhood were created in opposition, with the latter believed to hold a monopoly on conventional femininity. White women were believed to embody grace, refinement, and sophistication; black women on the other hand did not, or so the dominant narratives would have had us believe.[7] Thus, Wilma Rudolph's presence in the sport, and that of other African American women, had the potential to play on and play up long-established dominant ideologies around race and gender.

Figure 2.1. Wilma Rudolph at the Los Angeles Invitational, January 1961. Reprinted with permission of AP Photo.

Wilma Rudolph enjoyed considerable success in international track and field in the years leading up to the 1960 Games, though national media attention was not directed at her until her extraordinary performance in Rome. Few took notice when four years earlier Rudolph, as a sixteen year old, helped her team win a bronze medal in the 4x100 meter relay at the 1956 Games in Melbourne. Despite being an accomplished athlete, few expected Rudolph to win three gold medals at the 1960 Games. She was just one of the many Tennessee State Tigerbelles expected to perform well. Her three Olympic victories propelled her into the spotlight, albeit a marginal one, as a female athlete. Rudolph, in the weeks leading up to the 1960 Games, made appearances in the press, though it was her record-breaking performance in Rome that solidified her central place on the world stage. Press accounts soared in the days just after the Olympic Games, with Rudolph often featured across headlines, front-page stories, and above-the-fold photographs. Moreover, later appearances on television, including *To Tell The Truth* and *The Ed Sullivan Show* further promoted Rudolph's increasing bright-star status across the nation. As the United States moved to more securely position itself, at midcentury, as the world's economic, military, and moral leader among global powers, Rudolph's life history provided an especially compelling narrative to buttress the story the country wished to tell the world. Rudolph's identity as a black woman born into a poor family in the Jim Crow South serves as the foundational piece to the story's strength. This portrait of Rudolph, including the markers of her subjectivity, was promoted in earnest in the period after Rome 1960. Yet, as we argue, Rudolph's ascendency as one of the most visible and sought-after African American women in the country rested with situating her in contrast to other female athletes as well as distancing the track star from, ironically, the realities of her past and the contours of her own identity.

The press, both black and mainstream, was giddy with Wilma Rudolph in the days, weeks, and months following the Rome Olympic Games. The press and public's seemingly endless preoccupation with female athletes' femininity (and perceived lack thereof) continued, with Rudolph becoming the center of that attention. The triple gold-medalist from the Rome Games was America's athletic "leading lady" by late 1960, and the press worked to maintain and advance Rudolph in this starring role. Observers routinely emphasized Rudolph's beauty, charm, grace, and poise, and even attributed the adulation she received not to her running, but to "her good looks and charming ways."[8] Described as "tall," "willowy," "slim," "slender," "lissome," and the "long-legged lady from Clarksville," corporeality remained at the core of ways in which Rudolph was represented through press reports to the public.[9]

One read of the press's turn toward highlighting conventional notions of femininity and sexualizing Rudolph is as a progressive departure from depictions of female athletes as "muscle molls."[10] This interpretation warrants critical attention in that it fails to recognize how focus simply shifts from fears of mannishness to emphasized femininity among female athletes, who remain nonetheless under constant patriarchal gender surveillance. For example, *Newsweek* concluded that Rudolph's appeal was two-fold: "[U]nlike most American female sprinters," the weekly claimed, "she wins; and, unlike many American female athletes, she looks feminine."[11] Portrayed as the exception to a more general rule, Rudolph's distinction, in this case at least, was made possible by continually denigrating other female athletes. On the rare occasion, in the mainstream press, when racial terms were used to describe the track great, modifications made by the author were in order. As a light-skinned African American, Rudolph's skin color, as well as her thin, tall frame, were noteworthy markers observed in the media: *Sports Illustrated* identified the athlete as a "café au lait runner."[12] Similarly, *Mademoiselle* characterized Rudolph as the "very embodiment of black grace, a beautiful, flowing, lissome sight as she bounded over the track."[13] In both instances, Rudolph's beauty is qualified to mark her as African American. Eurocentric beauty standards remained the barometer against which black women were measured: Rudolph embodied many of the physical characteristics to enable her crossover appeal with white, male audiences.

Dorothy Dandridge was one among a handful of high-profile African American female actresses who achieved some level of mainstream success in the 1950s and 1960s and thus, we argue, offers a helpful point of analysis in understanding representations of Rudolph. Like Rudolph, Dandridge embodied many physical qualities that enabled her some degree of success in the white-dominated entertainment industry over the course of the 1950s. Her successful career in motion pictures was not, however, without trial, since Dandridge worked within a broader field that systematically marginalized, devalued, and erased black female talent. Indeed, Dandridge's career and even her life, according to Maguerite H. Rippy, were "destroyed by media obsession with reproducing the commodification of white femininity on a black body."[14] Dandridge's screen roles, usually as the "tragic mulatto," were, more often than not, narrow and confining. Constructed as uneasily occupying a middle ground between black and white worlds, Dandridge's characters are unable to navigate the intermediate space separating the two distinct poles. The "tragic mulatto" narrative positions failure squarely on the individual: Dandridge is portrayed as an ill-fated and unsatisfied character, who, in battling "the duality of [her] personalities," is cast as "nervous and vulnerable."[15]

Dandridge's race-based identity was, in some ways, everywhere in the creation of the characters she portrayed on screen, while it was simultaneously absent. Hollywood's reluctance to fully support African American women in leading roles in the late 1950s is epitomized in its attention to "diluting" Dandridge's blackness.[16] In order to promote her as a black star consumable for mass audiences, Dandridge's racial identity was obscured. Dandridge's wide appeal and more specifically her desirability to men, both black and white, rested on camouflaging her race; her leading roles included playing Polynesian and Italian characters.[17] Moreover, Dandridge's crossover allure with white audiences was as grounded in classed notions of respectability as it was firmly within patriarchal constructions of desire. Regardless of the setting, Dandridge's stylish dress and "manners" that "remained impeccable" were, according to biographer Daniel Bogle, crucial to the actress's favorability among whites. Media responses to and representations of her within the national press treated Dandridge "like a lady whom it perceived as being worthy of White male adoration."[18] Despite persistent efforts to sexualize the star throughout her career, observers were equally likely to distance Dandridge from classed and raced constructions of the actress as promiscuous. Dandridge "gave you a 'queen' feeling," according to Hollywood director John Peyser; "[s]he was a lady."[19] Dorothy Dandridge's and Wilma Rudolph's fame originated from vastly different talents, yet they shared a national stage, attracting attention and admiration across a broad range of American society in a period when few African American women could claim that reality. Like Dandridge, Rudolph's appearance fit fairly neatly within the established standards of white hegemonic beauty, and the press's fixation on her beauty continually reinforced these standards. Moreover, other comparisons can be drawn between the two public figures, including the ways in which media, at various points, distanced the women from the subjective spaces they occupied as black females.

In addition to Rudolph's beauty, newspapers and magazines focused a great deal on her grace and poise to describe both her actual running as well as her behavior off the track. Writing for *Sports Illustrated*, Jim Murray claimed that everyone was "quite in love with Wilma Rudolph," with the exception of the "girls she defeated."[20] [She is a] "5-foot-11-inch young lady of charm and poise," the *New York Times* declared.[21] No one could match the "incomparable Wilma Rudolph Ward for effortless grace and poise," according to *Sports Illustrated*.[22] When named one of the ten young women of 1960 by *Mademoiselle*, Rudolph was praised for her "dignity and poise and fine sportsmanship," which "earned her world-wide affection and respect."[23] Indeed her appeal, at times, rested firmly on a range of attributes, with Rudolph's superior athleticism buried among them. *Sports Illustrated* even bestowed royal standing upon the Olympic champion, to whom they ascribed a kind of graciousness that "suggests a duchess."[24] Rudolph was, to others, best described simply as "the Queen."[25] Amid throngs of adoring fans the weekly reported that "her [Rudolph's] manner is of a natural delicacy and sweetness as true as good weather."[26] Local newspapers also joined in the chorus of national reports in the days and months after Rome to highlight and confer preferred markers of femininity on the Olympian.

Los Angeles area press accounts of Rudolph and her participation in the city's second annual indoor invitational track meet in January 1961 bring into sharp relief the ways in which her celebrity status was tightly fastened to gender ideologies and tensions, which swirled around female athleticism during the period. The star power of the triple gold medalist gave an enormous boost to the indoor track circuit in the months following the Olympic Games in Rome, as tens of thousands of fans came to see "the magic that is Wilma Rudolph."[27]

Newspapers across Los Angeles eagerly anticipated Rudolph's appearance, and the female track great made headlines and filled column inches, moving other athletes, including male stars, to the margins of published reports. For at least one writer, male Olympic champions were barely an afterthought as Rudolph commanded center stage. In describing the meet, *Los Angeles Mirror* sports writer Harley Tinkham began his column, like other writers, with attention paid to Rudolph, who was to "head" the event. Following a short review of male participants, Tinkham was clear about his and presumably his readers' priorities, saying, "[b]ut let's get back to Wilma," as he continued discussion and completed the piece on the female star's preparation and competition.[28]

The sports writers were not the only southern Californians keen on seeing Rudolph: nearly fourteen thousand fans packed the arena in anticipation of the meet. Some of the five thousand people said to be without a seat were willing to pay three times the cost of a ticket for entrance and the opportunity to see Rudolph. There were, unfortunately for them, few sellers, according to James Murray, whose writing for *Sports Illustrated* brought national attention to the city invitational and to Rudolph as the country continued to eagerly follow her exploits in the months following Rome.[29] Sid Ziff, Sports Editor for the *Mirror*, was quick to add that Rudolph's presence not only stirred excitement but also increased revenues. The event, Ziff concedes, "probably would have laid an egg" in terms of gate receipts, not coming close to covering the estimated $24,000 in expenses. Fortunately, the writer declared, "Wilma will see 'em through."[30] Rudolph's on-the-track performance lasted less than seven seconds as she outdistanced her closest opponent by more than ten yards to win the sixty-yard dash at the Los Angeles Invitational. Despite her reservations and those of Coach Temple about running such a short distance indoors, Rudolph blew past the competition with seeming ease and few if any in the "massive sports arena" were disappointed in the star's lopsided victory. In fact, the lack of a serious opponent seemed to add to Rudolph's cachet among some observers, as "wonderful Wilma . . . won without removing her wristwatch, and there was some indication she could have carried her purse."[31] While Rudolph's athletic event elapsed in just seconds, the track star's total performance in Los Angeles lasted much longer. Rudolph's deportment off the track, both before and after the race, captivated reporters and fans as much as her achievements on it.

As soon as Rudolph stepped off the plane in the southern California city the press was quick to locate the Olympian securely within the boundaries of idealized notions of femininity. *L.A. Times* writer Jeanne Hoffman's article led the week-long obsession with the track great, reassuring readers in its title, "Speedy Wilma Rudolph Not Interested in Racing Men." According to Hoffman, the "pert-nosed 'reigning dear' of track," in the city for the invitational meet, "promptly" made it clear she would not be racing against men.[32] What remains unclear is whether Rudolph simply offered her perspective on competing against the opposite sex upon deplaning in Los Angeles, or was responding to a reporter's question. What is clear is the media's interest in the question and Rudolph's answer, and other sportswriters picked up the line of inquiry and continued to write on the angle throughout the week.[33] "The fastest woman in history hit Los Angeles Wednesday night," chirped Harley Tinkham of the *L.A. Mirror*, and she has no desire to compete against the "male animal."[34] Rudolph's response and its representation to us via the press was compelling. It not only stood to further distance her from any association with masculinity or mannishness; it also defined the parameters of her womanhood. Rudolph, according to reporters, "demurely" reminded those around her, "protest[ing] prettily" to the query that running against men was out of the question. With gender arrangements in place and in view, the champion told reporters, "I'm a young lady."[35]

The battle of the sexes theme created, seemingly, by the press continued throughout the week in advance of the invitational, with playful flirtation a central topic in captioned photographs of Rudolph and male competitors. The *L.A. Mirror* pictured Rudolph being carried around the sports arena by Olympians Dickie Howard and Don Bragg as they "inspect[ed]" the track prior to the meet. Rudolph's street clothes (blouse, skirt, and high heels) are set in explicit contrast to the sweats and running shoes worn by Howard and Bragg, further under-scoring gender difference established in narratives over the week.[36] The same day, the *L.A. Times* preserved the storyline and featured a large photo of the three athletes running on the track with Rudolph "out in front" of the two male athletes as the female track star "with high heels in hand outlegs" the competition.[37] Far from threatening, Rudolph's athleticism is situated safely within the confines of empha-sized femininity.

Wilma Rudolph outran opponents in Rome and elsewhere, and apparently also outran her history and identity, as Los Angeles report-ers' focus tended to highlight the ways in which they believed she had transformed into an improved version of a former self. The cham-pion's betterment, according to observers, revolved around and owed itself to a much more gracious, stylish, and sophisticated Rudolph. The gold medalist was a "different girl" from the one Sid Ziff claimed gave reporters the "cold brush off" in Rome after her 200-meter vic-tory. Despite having a "nice educated voice," Ziff noted during the Games, Rudolph refused to talk to newsmen, leaving him to conclude that the "fastest female of all time . . . is also one of the most untalk-ative." However, far from distant and cold, Rudolph was "friendly" and "obliging," as well as "autographing everything within reach," at the Los Angeles Invitational meet months later. The track star's comportment, not her athleticism, mattered more to Ziff, who con-cluded that Rudolph was "pleasant and patient" with fans and report-ers alike.[38] For others, Rudolph's graciousness, combined with a new, more sophisticated fashion sense, advanced her status as the "pretty, very feminine Queen of Track." In Rome, the three-time gold medal-ist "sported a funny straw lid," which unfortunately (according to this observer) became Rudolph's "trademark." Her Los Angeles arrival four months later was evidence of a dramatic shift, with Rudolph appearing in a "cool, feathered chapeau, and a stylish grey suit which accented her slender legs and made her look like a page out of *Vogue*."[39] The poor, rural, racially segregated and unequal reality from which Rudolph came was pushed into obscurity with barely a mention given in the press. Los Angeles's and the nation's enthusiasm for Wilma

Rudolph was driven, at least in part, by much more palatable identity markers, including her proximity to idealized femininity.

Those covering the Los Angeles Invitational event in the city's black press, like their mainstream counterparts, were equally enthralled with Rudolph's physical appearance and manners, though their reasons for being so were tightly bound to notions of racial pride, respect, and equality. Rudolph's presence in the city was a momentous event in the black community, even to those for whom athletics were not central in their lives. The track star's arrival at the Los Angeles airport signaled the significance of the affair, when Jessie Mae Brown, society editor for the *Los Angeles Sentinel,* and a host of other African American dignitaries greeted Rudolph as she deplaned. Representing diverse fields within the black community the "welcoming committee" was composed of those in law, politics, the military, community organizing, and athletics.[40] Similar to the white press's coverage, *Sentinel* sports editor Brad Pye Jr. was quick to note that Rudolph's athleticism was not the only draw, adding, "she wouldn't have any trouble in a beauty race either."[41] Rudolph's physical appearance in its proximity to hegemonic beauty standards provided the community with an opportunity to resist dominant ideologies, which dismissed black women as uncivilized and beyond the bounds of ladyhood.

L. I. Brockenbury's column in the *Sentinel* just days after the indoor meet provides some of the most striking narratives with regard to the momentousness of Rudolph's attendance at the invitational for the black community, as well as gendered threads woven throughout representations of the Olympic gold medalist. The evening, according to Brockenbury, was full of historic firsts for African Americans and their quest for equity and respect. Ed Temple's designation as the honorary referee of the Invitational was a commendation very much due, in Brockenbury's view, given the coach's contributions to the Olympic team as well as to the historically black Tennessee A&I University (now Tennessee State University). Compton College student Mary Mabson's singing of the national anthem to open the track meet was a first for an African American woman at a Los Angeles sports event, and thus another point of pride about which Brockenbury penned.

However, Wilma Rudolph was the evening's pièce de résistance for the *Sentinel* sports writer, who was clear about the track star's and the event's significance in achieving racial equality. The triple gold medalist's presence would "change the course of Negro history": the attention Rudolph received from those in the dominant media was unprecedented. Rudolph's celebrity status, according to Brockenbury, transcended that of Marian Anderson, Lena Horne, Dorothy Dandridge and Althea Gibson. The crowds in Los Angeles "drool[ed] over Wilma," Brockenbury opined, and her introduction stirred the thousands of fans into a thunderous frenzy. Rudolph moved through the arena before the race interacting with spectators, reporters, and photographers "with just enough sophistication to make her friendly manner seem oh so gracious."[42]

In doing so and in this moment, Rudolph re-scripted incredibly powerful images that persisted through mid-twentieth-century America portraying black women as crude, immoral, and uncivilized. According to Brockenbury, Rudolph had "[become] a lady" as evidenced in the crowd's enthusiasm for, and infatuation with, Rudolph, and affording the track star a level of admiration and respect from whites that heretofore was rarely granted to African American public figures. In these representations of Rudolph, the mainstream press moved beyond stereotypical images of black women that rested on their denigration, and this shift in newspaper coverage was as much cause for celebration as a victory in the sixty-yard dash would be. In Brockenbury's view, Rudolph was the change agent; as he added, "I was glad that she was able to make them [whites] stop talking about her as a 'colored girl from the sticks of Tennessee.'" The press, in referring to Rudolph as a "real American girl" and "a queen," stamped their approval on the track great and her transformative journey from the margins of society to royalty.[43] It seemed, for many observers, both black and white, that Wilma Rudolph's importance as a cultural icon stretched far beyond her ability to win track events.

Just days after leaving Los Angeles in early 1961, Rudolph participated in New York City's Millrose Games at Madison Square Garden. Normally a "stag" event, the Millrose Games created a sixty-yard

dash event for women, specifically to provide New York track followers an opportunity to see Rudolph.[44] Though she received far less
media attention than in Los Angeles, race organizers in New York
were nonetheless thrilled at Rudolph's presence. Fred Schmertz, Millrose's director, eagerly told the *New York Times* that Rudolph's image
graced the cover of the nearly one-hundred-page program, making her
the event's first "cover girl."[45] The national press picked up the story
and reiterated a number of the same gendered themes from the Los
Angeles Invitational just days earlier. According to *Time*, Rudolph's
gentle and patient demeanor made even racism's indignities seem like
mere inconveniences:

> The night of the meet, Wilma changed into her track suit in her
> hotel, pulled on a white leather coat, and tiptoed through the
> mounting snow of a blizzard while Temple [Coach Ed Temple]
> vainly flagged the empty cabs that cruised blandly by. Worse yet,
> when she did reach the Garden the guards refused to let her in the
> nearest entrance, brusquely directed her to a door a block away.[46]

Time added that these "foul-ups" would not have been handled
well by any other athlete. Rudolph, however, with "one of the most
remarkably relaxed personalities in all sport," entered the arena and
immediately greeted her fans with grace, signing autographs for those
who eagerly awaited her entrance. Just as the Los Angeles press had
done days earlier, *Time* devoted as many column inches to the details
of Rudolph's "charming" ways as they did attention to the superior
athleticism displayed by the Olympian in running the sixty yards in
6.9 seconds. For those New Yorkers who may not have been enamored with Rudolph's manner, her "long, floating stride" made them
"cheer like schoolboys," winning the race and winning over fans by
the event's conclusion. Despite successfully "storming the male citadel," Rudolph was well aware of her place, concluded *Time*. At the
race's end Rudolph hurriedly turned to a "friend" asking, according
to the weekly, "Quick, do you have a mirror [and] a comb?"[47] As is the
case in the previous examples, attention to Rudolph's physical appearance bolstered notions of heteronormativity.

For many observers, Wilma Rudolph's friendship with Olympic team member Ray Norton provided another pathway upon which the track star's normalcy, as female, was sustained. Across the African American and white press, reporters throughout the duration of the Games were intrigued with the status of the relationship between the two athletes. While other romances, real or imagined, from the Olympic village occasionally made headlines, it was Rudolph and Norton's bond that was the most widely reported.[48] The press's preoccupation with the liaison between the two Olympians competed with and sometimes overshadowed Rudolph's superb feats of athleticism on the track. After winning her first gold medal of the Games, *San Francisco Chronicle* headlines proclaimed, "Wilma, Ray Tell Secret: 'In Love.'" The storyline's main point was the "big secret" of their relationship, now broadcast to millions around the world. After Rudolph's gold medal winning race in the 100 meters, and "before 40,000 fans in the Olympic Stadium," the paper concluded, "the two entwined their arms around each other's waist and walked out the exit."[49] Which constituted the better of the two triumphs, winning gold medals or supposedly dating Ray Norton, was difficult to distinguish. The Olympics were a "glorious experience" for Rudolph, according to one account. The female champion not only "won everything in sight" but had also "grown extremely fond of Norton."[50]

Moreover, the press's reaction to Ray Norton's poor performance on the track in Rome fueled constructions and expectations of gendered performances off the track. Norton's last place finishes in the 100- and 200-meter races seemed to occupy as many column inches in the dailies as Rudolph's victories. Dejected after the losses, Norton reportedly was consoled by Rudolph, whose own emotional responses to his poor performances filled the pages of press reports. After winning her third gold medal, Rudolph, according to the news, "fled Olympic stadium in tears . . . because of Norton's shame."[51] Five months after the Olympics' end, as Rudolph prepared for the Millrose Games in New York City, the media's preoccupation with her romance forced a reaction from the track star. Rudolph queried, "I have noticed that a large majority of people I talk to are more interested in my love life, which is unknown to me, than my performances on the track."[52]

While Rudolph was continually the subject of the discourses constructed and circulated around her by others, she also was a contributor to the creation of a particular classed, raced, and gendered identity. Importantly, however, her efforts at self-representation were carried out in response to, and within the confines of, dominant understandings of black womanhood. Wilma Rudolph and other African Americans, over a period beginning in the late nineteenth century and lasting throughout the first several decades of the twentieth century, employed the "politics of respectability" as a strategy to counter racist ideologies and practices.[53] Good grooming, self-control, and graciousness among African American women were far from mere actions: they were duties and "obligations to the race," because respect was conferred upon those women who embodied Eurocentric markers of beauty and of graciousness and self-control.[54] Thus, hair straightening, for example, through the 1950s and early 1960s was one part of a much larger and more expansive tactical plan designed to signify a dignified self-presentation and thus warrant inclusion of African American women in dominant society.[55] Wilma Rudolph, as a high-profile African American woman involved in an activity (athletics) that was already believed to dislodge femininity, was well aware of her responsibility. As she recounts in her autobiography, in the days just after the Olympics in Rome the Tigerbelles were invited to participate in the British Empire Games in London. After an all-day meet in the rain, Rudolph had little time to get ready for an evening banquet and fix her hair, which, according to the gold medalist, was "a mess." Rudolph, "desperate" and "frantic" to set her hair, realized that her Tigerbelle teammates with whom she was having squabbles and disagreements had purposely hidden the curlers to make the athlete "look bad in public."[56]

The incident highlights agency's limits on Rudolph and other African American women whose bodies (and hair) were policed by dominant society. More than merely a faux pas, the hair incident was a racial transgression because "whites were not supposed to see nappy hair."[57] Good grooming, in this case straightened hair, was crucial in advancing a racial project intent on accentuating markers that were believed to symbolize dignified womanhood, thereby uplifting the entire race. The hot comb acted as a "tool for exerting self-control," and thus proof of good character among African Americans.[58] In calling attention to the episode and her anxiousness around it, Rudolph makes visible the dynamics of racism and sexism as these tensions played themselves out on African American women's bodies, including their hair.

Others, including Ed Temple, were well aware of the centrality and gravitas of respectability politics as it played out on black women's bodies. Speaking to the "stigma" attached to women's athletics, Temple disclosed his instructions to the Tigerbelles that they were "ladies first, students second, and athletes third." He added, "I don't want any pictures taken of them while they are all sweaty after a race." It is important, according to the Coach, that after a race they "comb their hair and put on some lipstick" before making themselves available to reporters and fans.[59] Throughout his career Temple persisted in advocating for girls' and women's elite track and field opportunities in the United States. Temple did so with an equally passionate insistence that his athletes adhere to rigid codes of femininity, claiming in a 1962 interview that he wanted "foxes not oxes [sic]."[60] On one level these narratives can be read as discourses of resistance in defense of black womanhood whose corporeality had long been constructed as deviant from that of whites. However, they simultaneously reinforce norms of racialized femininity and heterosexuality as well as classed subjectivities. These characterizations of Rudolph's beauty, poise, and graciousness, coupled at times with acknowledgment of her unprecedented success on the track, extended to her a high and thus unique praise rarely afforded an African American woman in 1960 by the mainstream press. However, when read against the narratives of her Olympic teammates shot putter Earlene Brown and swimmer Chris von Saltza, the rhetoric assigned to Rudolph reinforces, rather than disrupts, dominant constructions of idealized female bodies.

Figure 2.2. Earlene Brown, Rudolph's 1960 Olympics teammate, throwing the discus in Rome. Reprinted with permission of Getty Images.

Earlene Brown, 1960 US bronze medalist in the shot put, serves as the other brown body against which Rudolph is cast. Brown was darker-skinned, married, mother to a young son, and a large-size woman in the throws events (discus and shot put).[61] By the summer of 1960, Brown had established herself as America's top throws specialist. Finishing fourth in the discus throw and sixth in the shot put at the 1956 Games in Melbourne, Australia, Brown earned All-American honors in both events, winning the outdoor titles in 1957, 1958, and 1959. Brown also participated in two US-USSR dual meets with mixed results, winning the shot put and finishing second in the discus in 1958, and second in the shot put and third in the discus the next summer. At the 1960 outdoor championships, which also served as the Olympic Trials, Brown repeated as champion and cemented her status as a potential medalist in both events. In the months leading up to the Games, Brown was identified by the mainstream and black press, as well as *Amateur Athlete*, the monthly publication of the Amateur Athletic Union, as an American favorite, in part because of her consistent performances and previous outcomes against her Soviet competitors.[62]

Prior to and during the Olympic Games, newspaper and magazine descriptions of Brown emphasize her marital status, her outgoing personality, and her large size, with athletic accomplishments seeming to be secondary. In almost every mention of Brown, whether in black or mainstream publications, she is identified as Mrs. Earlene Brown, and often times referred to as a Los Angeles housewife, though there is no discussion of her husband and only brief references to her young son.[63] In sharp contrast to her teammate, Brown is marked both racially and in terms of her large size as the "colored foil" to Rudolph's light skin, thin frame, and calm demeanor.[64] Brown is the "big bundle of good humor" whose "huge hands" make the eight-pound shot look like a "pea." Rudolph, on the other hand, "actually looks like an athlete" because her "long slim legs," mark her exceptionality in "perfectly proportioned" ways.[65] Brown's high energy and her outgoing, friendly manner, often linked to her powerful 230 pound body, is the thread woven throughout mainstream publications' portrayals of the athlete. As a study in contrasts, Rudolph is made more appealing to white audiences *because of* Brown's ongoing presence in the media.

While all female athletes were under scrutiny for perceived gender transgressions, as a throws specialist Brown and her peers received particularly critical attention from observers. Given their size and muscularity, field event participants were mocked because their bodies and the actions performed on the field challenged dominant ideals of femininity with every turn, twist, or push. As a *New York Times* magazine article published at the start of the Games proclaimed, "Venus wasn't a shot-putter," and cautioned that women who participated in certain sports destroyed what the author, William Furlong, considered "The Image." Furlong closes by suggesting that when people think of women athletes, if they think of them at all, they do not instinctively think of shot-putters and hurdlers, sprinters, and discus-throwers, because these competitors do not "possess The Image."[66] Australian track coach Percy Cerutty, quoted in Glanville's *Mademoiselle* article, asserted, "The women's shot-put final is absurd. What a travesty of womanhood! Huge, overweight monstrosities of human malformation. These monstrosities—they interest me like the fat woman in a circus does, or the elephant. But you can never really love 'em, like you can the race horse or the giraffe." In underscoring a misogyny that seemed to have no limits, he concludes, "Freakishness is attractive. Everybody pays to see the two-headed cow. But we must give up lionizing and paying tribute to these freaks, who, by reason of being freaks, win at athletics."[67]

Moreover, Earlene Brown's events, the shot put and discus throw, were dominated by Soviet women and thus provided an added opportunity for critics, in the Cold War moment, to hurl callous insults at the "Amazons." The de-humanizing verbal assaults were tossed at individual athletes, including one of Brown's counterparts, Soviet shot putter Tamara Press. *The Nashville Banner*, a mainstream, conservative daily newspaper, described Press as "198 pounds with a strong, square face and legs like young oaks," and noted that the athlete was studying construction. Her sister, Irina, a hurdler, was described as having "close cropped curls" and bore a "striking resemblance to the late Babe Didrikson."[68] Another description of Tamara Press put her at 215 pounds, a gargantuan weight according to the women's magazine *Mademoiselle*, and sarcastically noted that her briefs showed off every pound. The magazine opined, "When she puts the shot, her mouth opens and she gasps like an expiring whale." British athlete Mary Rand claimed she admired the Soviet shot putter's bravery, stating, "If I were that size, I'd probably hide and not come out at all."[69]

Like many of her athletic peers, Earlene Brown was not spared the disparaging remarks aimed at trivializing her athletic accomplishments and maligning her person. As the "pudgy California strong girl," Brown's body is "triply removed from the West's conceptualization of normalcy and situated beyond the outskirts of normative boundaries," according to Andrea Shaw.[70] Gendered, racialized, and sized discourses converge on Brown's body, marking it as abnormal and problematic. Though we are cautious in not wanting to create a strict binary between the black and mainstream press around representations of Brown, there are nonetheless patterns that emerge in each. The dominant press used terms like "mammoth," and was more likely to identify Brown by her actual weight, which seemed to vary between 225 and 239 pounds, depending on the newspaper. *Sports Illustrated* described her as "Los Angeles's outsized ('I won't even tell you how much I weigh') Earlene Brown."[71] In the "They Said It" section of another *Sports Illustrated* piece "beautician and shot-put winner" Brown is quoted: "[M]y best weight is 196 pounds, but I've never made that."[72] Brown's poundage was the media's preoccupation, and the athlete's body remained a fascination. During the Games Sid Ziff of the *Los Angeles Mirror* related to readers that Brown, disillusioned with her performance in Rome, was on a hamburger binge in the Olympic city. According to Ziff, Brown gained six pounds, which he mockingly noted was "somewhat lost [on Brown] since she's built like a baby blimp."[73] Prior to the Rome Games, the *Atlanta Constitution* reported that Brown "tossed a big problem into the hands of Italian tailors." The paper recounted that the tailors had to rely on "special know-how and enough fabric to cover a sofa," to create the thrower's outfit for the Games' opening ceremony.[74] In these accounts Brown's size is cast as more than an observation about her weight; instead, the descriptions carry a scornful and humiliating tone, denoting her body as repulsive.

Black press accounts, on the other hand, were quick to acknowledge Brown's size as well, but were much more likely to connect her largeness and deportment to her athletic achievements or something far more significant than a sporting victory. Brown was said by members of the black press to be a "big doll" or "hefty," one whose weight and personality were factors influencing the greater good. The force of Brown's extrovert presence, according to some observers in the black press, had great import on her athletic peers and countless others far removed from sport. In the weeks leading up to the Games, the *Cleveland Call & Post,* as well as the *Pittsburgh Courier,* referred to Brown as "California's 200-pound-plus energy-laden, fun-loving, bundle" and noted her contributions to team spirit.[75] She was described as "one of the most jovial persons you ever met. As a dancer and party 'pepper upper' Mrs. Brown is tops."[76] More than simply the life of the party, her local black newspaper, the *Los Angeles Sentinel,* suggested that Brown had done more during the 1960 Games to "cement better international relations than any other single athlete on the team. Language was no barrier for this big doll . . . somehow she was quick to make friends and influence people."[77] Others, too, saw in Brown's jovialness a sense of purpose with potential to impact relationships between and among individuals as well as nations. The *Sentinel*, after Brown failed to win the gold medal in either event, celebrated her as "one of Uncle Sam's best goodwill ambassadors," claiming that everyone would remember the athlete.[78]

The black press was much more likely than mainstream publications to embrace Brown and her "plus-size" figure, which can partly be explained by the different attitudes of the African American community toward body size during this time period, as evidenced in the pages of the popular magazine *Ebony*. Peter N. Stearns explains the cultural differences as owing to several factors: religion (the idea that "God determined what size a person should be" and dieting was questioning the Lord's standards); and the general feeling that black women had enough to worry about without adding their weight to the list. Above all, according to Stearns, the African American "tolerance and embrace of large women reflects the distinctive power position women have held in African American families and the family economy. Unlike their white counterparts, black women have always worked, even when married; and in some physical labor, size was a positive advantage, associated with strength, not fat."[79] Athletics, then, and representing your nation in this realm, seemed a perfectly respectable means of using your body. We read these subtle differences within the narratives surrounding press accounts of Earlene Brown. While nearly all published reports, regardless of origin, commented on the athlete's weight and demeanor, the mainstream press was more likely to disapprove of her size as antithetical to an idealized (white) construction of femininity and womanhood.

We suggest that the overwhelming critical emphasis on Brown's large size and comportment invokes racist images of African American women, in this case, as mammies. The mammy/Aunt Jemima archetype utilizes the image of a black domestic servant, who is generally good-natured and overweight. Used to re-inscribe racial hierarchies, the mammy image persisted across the twentieth century as a tool to define black female bodies as the antithesis of dominant conceptions of beauty, femininity, and womanhood. Mammy/Aunt Jemima reminds us that the "ideology of slavery was based on an ever-refining set of hierarchies demonstrating the radical difference between black and white bodies."[80] According to Diane Roberts, and instructive in our analysis, "Blacks in a slave society were powerless and marginal yet the whites who owned them built their culture around *not* being black. The stories they subscribed to about the meaning of black skin shaped their construction of what whiteness meant."[81] Throughout the twentieth century, various images of the mammy/Aunt Jemima construct served as a "symbol of proper order, living proof of the racial and sexual harmony that results when blacks and whites occupy their separate and well-understood roles, and a denial of any conflict between masters and mistresses as well as blacks and whites."[82] The mammy depiction formed the basis on which Aunt Jemima was created, becoming so familiar in white imaginations that it rendered her "practically invisible, part of America's racial background noise."[83]

Throughout Earlene Brown's competitive career, Quaker Oats (who owned the Aunt Jemima image) "kept the nostalgia coming" through a deluge of advertisements and other promotions found in a variety of places and on numerous products.[84] So deep-seated and profitable was Aunt Jemima's image that Quaker Oats, in 1955, contracted with one of the "shrines of American popular culture, Disneyland" to operate Aunt Jemima's Pancake House in Disney's Anaheim, California theme park.[85] The restaurant, with its mammy character as marquee, served over 1.6 million customers in its first eight years of operation.[86] We believe Aunt Jemima's ubiquity as a cultural form influences how media constructed and represented one of the few other large-sized African American women with a public profile, Earlene Brown.

Like Aunt Jemima, emphasis on Brown's ever-present smile and warmth deflected the realities of racial inequality, as it simultaneously justified it in whites' minds. Whites in the United States believed the image to be an innocuous one, as Aunt Jemima pleased, comforted, and entertained them. According to press accounts, Earlene Brown entertained whites as well, by combining her naturally gregarious personality with freakish strength. As the AAU (Amateur Athletic Union) national track meet drew to a close in Corpus Christi in the summer of 1960, *Sports Illustrated* reported, "if gold medals were awarded for pecan harvesting, Earlene Brown would be a favorite. As she was telling and showing the Texas people before she left: 'First you take a hold of the tree trunk, see, you give it a good shake or two, and . . . '"[87] Brown's size served a comedic function, as did Aunt Jemima's, as she was either "perceived as humorous [or] expected to humor others."[88] In Brown's case her size served up humor, often in incredibly cruel ways.

Despite her athletic achievements, Earlene Brown's large, black, female body remained the point around which observers marked and evaluated her. Even in attempting to pay Brown a compliment, albeit a backhanded one, *Mademoiselle* illustrates the continuing unease around the thrower's body. Noting that the US athlete was even bigger than Soviet athlete Tamara Press at 250 pounds, the magazine asserted that Brown had "a fine, roly-poly, fish-fry quality about her that redeems her from all charges of non-femininity."[89] Brown is spared being denigrated as masculine, but remains beyond the boundaries of a beauty, thus is lodged in an uneasy tension with white constructions of femininity.[90] Like Aunt Jemima, Brown's large and strong black body is de-sexualized, yet remains linked to femininity, albeit loosely, through a maternal marker—nurturance. Doris Witt argues, "Aunt Jemima *prepares* and *is* food; she is the ever-smiling source of sustenance for infants and adults."[91] Likewise, Brown and her "roly-poly fish-fry quality" sustains whites, preserving gendered and racial hierarchies in the process.

While representations of Earlene Brown served as the "alter-ego" to Wilma Rudolph, they simultaneously "became a shadow against which white women's beauty [could be] contrasted."[92] We argue that Chris von Saltza provided that contrast. Years before US swimmer von Saltza dove into the pool in Rome, at age sixteen, she made her entrance into American living rooms and America's consciousness

Figure 2.3. Chris von Saltza, teen swimming sensation of the 1960 Olympic Games. Reprinted with permission of Getty Images.

with feature-length stories and covers in *LIFE* and *Sports Illustrated*, among other media accounts. Von Saltza's pre-Olympic coverage eclipsed that of virtually all other US female athletes. She was paid at least a mention in *Sports Illustrated* over two dozen times between 1957 and 1960. So popular and familiar, on a national level, was von Saltza that she was mentioned even if only to announce that another swimmer had broken one of her records.[93] Von Saltza swam for the storied Santa Clara (California) Swim Club, under the direction of legendary coach George Haines. She first appeared in the national press as a thirteen-year-old in 1957 after setting national records in the backstroke.[94] Among her many achievements were nineteen individual

AAU titles, five gold medals at the 1959 Pan American Games, and finally three gold and one silver medal at the Rome Olympics.[95]

Like Rudolph and Brown, media preoccupation with von Saltza rested as much with her appearance as her athleticism, yet, we argue, for reasons, and in ways, that highlighted a set of preferred subjectivities—namely, dominant notions of white femininity. Unlike Earlene Brown's field events, swimming was long defined and conceptualized as a "feminine" sport where aesthetic elements masked the physical rigors necessary to be successful. The physical demands of the activity were largely out of view, beneath the water's surface, which only cemented perceptions of the sport's appropriateness for female participants. Moreover, in the pre-Title IX era, competitive swim programs in the United States were most likely found in private clubs, whose restrictions and membership fees narrowed the range of individuals participating by race and class.[96] Thus, we read the cultural responses to swimming and to Chris von Saltza, in particular, bearing these aspects of the sport as a cultural construction in mind.

Like all other female athletes at this midcentury moment, the bodies of the mostly white young women who represented the US in elite swimming competition were the focus of media reports. In reference to the US team, one observer noted, "They are young and pretty—and can they swim!"[97] Infatuation with Chris von Saltza rested on any one of several subjectivities underscored by the media, including the swimmer's "pretty platinum blond" hair, which was largely the frame around which her beauty was cast.[98] In serving a "symbolic function," Marina Warner notes, blondeness was a ". . . guarantee of quality. It was the imaginary opposite of 'foul,' it connoted all that was pure, good, clean. Blondeness is less a descriptive term about hair pigmentation than a blazon in code, a piece of a value system."[99] Blondeness's value and privileged place is in its larger association with whiteness. Continual attention to von Saltza's blond hair does not simply further blondeness's centrality. Rather, it works to construct and reproduce whiteness and its concomitant hegemonic place.[100] The association between blondeness and beauty is also evident in the various media accounts of von Saltza. Given that the noun "fair" has its etymological roots in "beauty," the tendency to equate blonde hair with comeliness is made evident. As Warner suggests, in terms of desire, "Hair's power can bind" especially if that hair is fair.[101] Von Saltza's hair re-inscribed preferred (heteronormative) notions of femininity and beauty with whiteness; she was, as one observer noted, a "blond bombshell."[102]

While the swimmer's blonde hair was used as a marker to define whiteness and all that it was thought to embody, her locks were also used to distance von Saltza from what she was not. "When we think of women athletes—if we think of them at all," opined William Furlong in the *New York Times*, "we instinctively call to mind girls like . . . Chris von Saltza, . . . [the] cute young blonde swimmer . . . we do not think of shot-putters and hurdlers, sprinters and discus throwers."[103] Relative athletic respectability was extended to von Saltza in part by constructing her, and swimming more generally, in opposition to track and field athletes of the period who remained well beyond preferred notions of femininity and womanhood.[104] Indeed her good looks seemed to be *the reason for* her athletic achievement. "[Von Saltza's] shapely form is already cutting quite a swath through US records" noted *Sports Illustrated* in 1958.[105]

Just as representations of von Saltza played up and on discourses of preferred femininity and beauty, they were equally steeped in notions of white innocence and youth, as her fair-colored locks remained solidly in the frame. She was, as *Sports Illustrated* noted, "a water nymph with blonde hair."[106] *LIFE* magazine added, "she has almost as many swimming medals as she has freckles."[107] Media frequently reminded interested observers of the US female swimming cohort's youthfulness in making note, for example, that the athletes' braces were worn as "irksome badges of adolescence."[108] Moreover, von Saltza's blondeness and youth were fused within these discourses, producing a kind of teenage innocence around her and the athleticism she displayed. In describing the Santa Clara, California, Swim Club, of which von Saltza was a member, *Sports Illustrated* thought it important to highlight the team's plastic red-and-green toy frog mascot. The toy frog, noted the magazine, "observed most of the meet from the starting blocks, where he stood on his own two feet. Every bit as self-sufficient, the Santa Clara team set four American records and two world records."[109] A similar tack is taken in a feature on von Saltza, as *LIFE* magazine reassured readers that even after a very long day of school and training, before the swimmer sleeps she is sure to "[swap] telephone tidbits with girl friends on hairdos, clothes, and other vital matters."[110] Infantilizing von Saltza and her teammates undercuts the power embedded in their athletic achievements, as it confirms notions of racialized and gendered youthful innocence. The innocence, even playfulness, conjured up in these examples can be understood as evidence of pureness (whiteness), and thus distanced from dominant constructions of black female athletic bodies.

Representations of sixteen-year-old von Saltza were not without tension, however; unease was occasionally voiced by some. For one observer, the lack of enthusiasm in support of female swimmers was due to the athletes being "ridiculously young." Despite their work ethic and amazing times in the pool, the young swimmers "remain essentially schoolgirls, intriguing mainly to those with a Lolita penchant."[111] Their youth removes them, at least in this instance, from being the object of sexual gaze, and their worth, as athletes, diminishes along with it. At other times, von Saltza's young age did little to dissuade sexual innuendo and interest. In one instance, von Saltza's coach, George Haines, thought it best that male reporters distance themselves from the young swimmer in his charge. Haines observed a handful of media men snapping pictures and video of von Saltza as she and other members of the swim team relaxed at poolside near the Olympic Games' end. When one videographer asked von Saltza to walk down a path toward him Haines realized the camera's gaze was solely on the young woman's "shapely legs." To which Haines responded, "I think we've had enough picture taking for today," sending the "men unwillingly away." In these exchanges, although rare, dominant discourses about power, eroticism, and female athletes are troubled, given von Saltza's young age *and* her gender.[112] Von Saltza's femininity was clearly at issue in the press, moored as it was to whiteness and youth.

Media response to Wilma Rudolph's athletic success was unprecedented in 1960, both in terms of the amount of coverage and its favorable tone. Given the continuing tensions around gender and athleticism, as well as dominant constructions of black bodies as deviant and distanced from white corporeality, how do we make sense of Rudolph's welcome to the world stage? Important to us and our arguments in this chapter is the notion that the meanings attached to Rudolph's body by the media and the public were not made in isolation, but were rather constructed against, and in relation to, others. Earlene Brown and Chris von Saltza provided the contrast against which we understood Rudolph's place on the pages of the press. Similar to Rudolph's, Earlene Brown's and Chris von Saltza's narratives were also woven with gendered threads, but each woman's representations were constructed differently from the others.

In this chapter our point in examining the three athletes has been to explore the ways in which representations of Rudolph were dependent on the presence of both Earlene Brown and Chris von Saltza. Discourses surrounding the three athletes expose the way their multiple subjectivities were constantly in flux, yet arrangements of power around race, gender, and size remained firmly entrenched. Portrayals of Wilma Rudolph distanced her from other black women (as represented by Earlene Brown), because she was said to embody idealized markers of femininity—to date, a white women's club. Yet, media constructions of Chris von Saltza, with attention paid to her golden locks and youthful presence, negated Rudolph's secure place in this club. To put Rudolph in this space required that her blackness be dislodged. We see this in the words of Frances Kaszubski of the AAU, who, in what she may have considered high praise, said of Rudolph, "She isn't colored, she is gold," making explicit that Rudolph's blackness troubled her beauty.[113] Ultimately, in order to confer preferred status on Wilma Rudolph, she could not be black.

3

Running with the Story

From Cold War Icon to Civil Rights Rebel

JUST DAYS AFTER WILMA RUDOLPH won her first of three gold medals at the Rome Olympics in 1960, *Nashville Tennessean* writer Raymond Johnson detailed the event's significance and impact well beyond the athletic arena. "For one day, at least, the space race, the missile madness and all the rest, disappeared into the sub-conscious," according to Johnson, "as Wilma rocketed down the 100-meter straight-away in 11 seconds." For Johnson, Rudolph's gold medal winning performance erased, albeit temporarily, Cold War realities and anxieties. However, Johnson's implicit claim that the Olympics provided those in the United States with a needed apolitical arena around which they could cheer was as fleeting as the time it took Rudolph to break the tape in the 100 meters. Johnson continues, reminding readers, "[e]ach contestant represents a country, and each country has its pride and position resting on [the athlete's] effort."[1] Indeed, for Johnson and many other observers in this period, sport, especially international competitions like the Olympics, became enmeshed in, rather than distanced from, Cold War tensions.

Throughout the 1950s the United States expanded its Cold War arsenal to include sport as a weapon, of sorts, in a much broader propaganda campaign to assert its political and moral supremacy among nations, especially the Soviet Union. Among its many facets, the Cold War by the mid-1950s was also to be waged "on, and through, the terrain of culture."[2] Propagandizing popular culture became an important avenue for the United States in the overall strategy to win "hearts and minds" of many people around the globe, especially in light of the volatile risks involved in military engagement with the Soviets.[3] American sport and international athletic competitions became highly visible and important aspects of US strategy. Moreover, the athletes and not just the games they played became symbols of the expansive cultural Cold War between and among nations. As the 1960 Rome Olympics approached, *Newsweek* noted that whether the athletes liked it or not they were "pawn[s] in a hot athletic war that is a phase of this country's cold political war."[4] Far more than merely athletes and athletic contests on an international stage, the Games were thought to represent much more. For some, achievement and success in the athletic arena symbolized a set of values, a way of being, and as such became "the most immediate, confrontational and viscerally resonant points of nationalist engagement," according to Wagg and Andrews.[5] US athletic victories on the worldwide stage represented the strength and omnipotence of political and economic systems, namely democracy and capitalism, respectively.

Wilma Rudolph and other African American athletes' participation and success in sport, especially on an international stage, served additional and important functions as part of the larger US Cold War strategy. For the United States, a nation eager to define itself to the world as open and democratic, African American athletes were important characters in telling not just any story, but a particular story about racial progress possible within a democracy. The success stories of African American athletes, many of whom came from humble beginnings, perpetuated propaganda that athletic talent nurtured within a free society afforded opportunity for all. The presence of African American athletes served as a powerful symbol and the embodiment of a "color-blind American democracy" in action.[6] Importantly, African American achievement, including achievement in sport, was thought to pacify a "quintessentially American dilemma," the racist realities of Jim Crow against the nation's claims of equality and opportunity for all.[7] The world watched as tensions, sometimes violent, erupted across the Southern United States throughout the late 1950s and early 1960s, when white segregationists staunchly defended their privileged place and the racial status quo. Images and stories of successful African American athletes, including Rudolph, provided the US mainstream media and government with a narrative of opportunity contrasting with those that underscored racial inequality, oppression, and brutality. However, that narrative, albeit the dominant one, certainly was not the only story told to the public by the US media. The nation's black press had its own perspective on the achievements of Rudolph and other African American athletes, one that brought race pride and civil rights to the fore. Though relatively marginal, the black press narratives are significant in helping us frame and more deeply understand Rudolph's iconic status among Americans, both black and white.

This chapter examines the competing narratives of Wilma Rudolph as a Cold War icon, contextualizing her international track and field experiences and related activities within post-World War II America. Her international successes positioned her to be used as an exemplar of the American Dream. She was the subject of a United States Information Agency (USIA) video made in 1961 and distributed around the globe as evidence of America's racial tolerance. Our textual analysis of the USIA video, one of the government agency's "Negro Stars" series, pays close attention to the ways the film reifies the promise of American democracy, using Rudolph to do so.[8] Rudolph also traveled to Africa in 1963 as part of athletic goodwill tours, which were standard practice between 1945 and 1968.[9] However, even as Rudolph was used as part of an American global campaign to offer an image of African American success, as well as the goodwill tours there were the competing powerful images of the American civil rights movement, which challenged the very ideals promoted in the USIA series.

The chapter culminates in one such competing image, that of Rudolph participating in the desegregation of a local Clarksville restaurant in 1963, just weeks after her return from a government sponsored goodwill tour in Africa and the notable Birmingham, Alabama protests. The demonstration at the Shoney's restaurant in her hometown is significant because it provides an important counter-narrative to the US government's efforts to centrally position the track star as part of its cultural Cold War arsenal. Rudolph's participation is important, as well, because it signaled an early moment of public resistance and civil rights agitation by an African American athlete against racial injustice. A close reading of the protest, and of the silences that surrounded the event in subsequent decades, is in order for those reasons.

Sport as Cold War Weapon

With the Soviet Union participating in the 1952 Olympic Games, the international sport stage took on new meanings.[10] According to Jenifer Parks, "Soviet leaders saw Olympic participation as an opportunity to show the world the superior technique and training achieved by the Soviet system."[11] The Soviets were not alone in this regard: the United States also expanded its Cold War arsenal to include sport. Thus, sport competitions served as one vein of the "soft power of culture," according to Ban Wang, through which the two super powers faced off regularly.[12] Stephen Wagg and David Andrews clarify the relationship: "sporting contests regularly became high-profile public spectacles through which the respective merits of the competing social and political systems, ideologies, and moral order were contested in symbolic combat."[13]

Track and field quickly emerged as the sport of choice for the rivalry to be played out between Olympiads. After several years of negotiations, an annual dual meet between the two super powers was established, with Moscow's Lenin Stadium playing host to the inaugural meeting in July 1958. The sport's place as a Cold War weapon was made explicit by US coach George Eastment, who told his team before the matchup, "There are international tensions in the world and today is very important."[14] Track and field was well suited to take on the banner of the premier Cold War sport, according to Joseph Turrini, since "the USA-USSR track meets . . . easily captured more public and political attention in the 1950s and 1960s" than other sport competitions.[15] With only four competitors in each event, the track and field dual meets were "both tense and easy to follow, generated excitement, and encouraged patriotism." Two nations, one sport, and a small number of athletes created within the USA-USSR track and field meet structure "provided a direct and undiluted competition between the two countries that mirrored the bipolar perspective" that pervaded track and field and remained so entrenched throughout the period.[16] As a result of these dual meets, "unprecedented attention" was given to African Americans athletes, as well as female athletes, most of whom were African American.[17] Both groups were critical to the success of the United States in their matchups with the Soviet Union.

Even before the Soviets officially entered Olympic competition in 1952, it was obvious that American women were trailing their Soviet counterparts. It was believed by those charged with training American women, the Amateur Athletic Union, that with more competition, the US contingent of female athletes would be capable of matching their European opponents.[18] A year after the Soviets' Olympic debut, sports writer Jimmy Powers of the *New York Daily News* called for an increase in the number of competitions for American female athletes to help prepare them for their Russian opponents. His interest in women's athletics seemed narrowly conceived, stemming from a desire to meet cultural Cold War challenges rather than to further female participation in and empowerment through sport. If Russia was going to "compete in all events," Powers wondered why the Americans were not doing the same.[19] Importantly, the push, by Powers and others, as part of the larger cultural Cold War strategy, to advance female athletics throws into relief the myriad tensions at the intersections of nationalism, race, and gender at midcentury.

Historian Susan Cahn identified the "deficiencies of women's track and field" as being "a minor matter" until the Soviet domination of the Olympic Games, and the Soviets' immediate success "posed an acute problem for US politicians, sport leaders, and a patriotic public."[20] In 1956, high jumper Mildred McDaniel won the sole gold medal for American women. Two years later, the inaugural dual meet against the Soviet Union marked a "momentous turning point for women's track in the United States." The meet was dominated by the Soviets, whose success served notice to American sport leaders that the "egalitarian athletic programs" of the Soviet Union, designed to "develop fully the most talented, irrespective of gender," produced athletes who were far superior to the under-trained and under-supported American women.[21] The Soviet system also provided a clear distinction between the training programs of the two nations. Communist athletics were considered professional activities, whose support was subsidized by the government. This was constructed in sharp contrast to the American perspective on international sport where athletes' standing as 'amateur' was a repeated mantra. In addition, financial support for the enterprise was said to rely solely on "voluntary and private contributions in accordance with [American] concepts and . . . way of life."[22] Russian sport was considered a "big, grim, production-line business," with no expense spared in the obsessive pursuit of victory.[23] The need to frame US and Soviet society as being ideologically and structurally different in every respect extended to female athleticism.

The dual meets cast a rare spotlight on US female athletes who otherwise toiled, for the most part, in obscurity.[24] Their accomplishments were especially significant, given the nation's gross negligence in supporting elite female athletes in the first half of the twentieth century. With restrictive gender norms firmly entrenched throughout midcentury, femininity, physicality, and athleticism were largely conceptualized as contrasting rather than complementary markers of womanhood. As a result, women's sport, including international competition, was relegated to the margins. Despite occupying a peripheral space, Cold War rhetoric was nonetheless central to notions of womanhood and femininity. Even when observers did urge more support for female athletes, they did so by qualifying their endorsement around limited and exclusionary constructions of femininity. US attempts to define a nation and its people in opposition to the Russians extended to female athletes. Again Jimmy Powers makes the position clear: "[w]e have graceful and skilled lady athletes in this country," who are "superior to the ponderous, peasant-type Russian athletes, especially in track and field."[25] Powers's emphasis on Soviet female athletes and their success in international competitions excused American female athletes, alluding to the clear contrast in femininity between the Americans and the Soviets. The words of leading physical educator Eleanor Methany underscore this point. "Practices which may have value for the women of Russia may not interest girls in the United States, who are—and want to be—," she concluded, "essentially feminine human beings."[26] Indeed, casting Soviet female athletes as the "mannish" other served to dislodge similar accusations directed at the US women's team by critical observers during the period.[27]

Despite the gender tensions and ambivalence that continued to swirl around elite female athletes, especially within track and field, the nation's fears of being beaten by the Russians eclipsed anxieties of mannish women running around a track. Soviet track and field success and dominance was worrisome to various political and athletic leaders, as well as to other observers in the United States, and the issue demanded a fix.[28] The Ed Temple-led Tennessee State Tigerbelles provided much of the solution to the nation's problem. Soviet women's fiercest American opponents were African Americans, most of whom were students at Tennessee State University, coached by Ed Temple. By the mid-1950s the Tigerbelles were well established as the nation's premier squad of female athletes. Six out of the seventeen women on the American track team in 1956 were part of Temple's Tigerbelle program. The historically black college's preeminent position in women's track continued to 1960, when seven of the twenty-five female track athletes on the US team in Rome were connected to the Nashville campus. The Tigerbelles dominated AAU competition at the indoor and outdoor national championships in the 1950s.[29] The Tigerbelles' AAU titles "laid a firm unyielding grip" on women's track and field and "completely rewrote the record books" for the sport, wrote the school's student paper.[30] As early as 1955, *Ebony* magazine named African American women in track as "America's newest sports heroines."[31]

Like other media outlets, *Ebony* did not miss the opportunity to promote Cold War nationalism by constructing competing understandings of womanhood. *Ebony* editors opined that US black female athletes were "definite threats against the huskier, state-subsidized Russian women in next year's Olympic Games."[32] In the months leading up the 1956 Games, *Sports Illustrated* asked "Can the Soviet Girls be Stopped?" and identified the Tennessee State Tigerbelles as "the one and only Notre Dame of women's track," who could "match the Russians" if they were given "one-tenth the support the Russians give their women."[33] At those 1956 Games, Wendell Parris, writing for the *Negro History Bulletin*, claimed that "Negro athletes were real Olympic place-getters at Melbourne" in women's track and field.[34] The *Meter*, Tennessee State's school newspaper, considered the 1958 dual meet in Moscow to be "the greatest single amateur sports event, other than the Olympic Games."[35] The American women were defeated by the Russians in Philadelphia, by more than twenty points, and Hank Solomon, writing for *The Amateur Athlete*, suggested that "if it were not for 'Ed Temple's vaunted Tennessee State charges, we would be smarting from a great American tragedy—no women's track.'"[36] The Cold War rhetoric was entangled with praise for female athletes, particularly Wilma Rudolph, as the 1960 Games approached, with the Tennessee State star described as "America's big hope to break the Russian-Australian monopoly in women's track."[37]

The Tigerbelles and Wilma Rudolph were America's best hope against Russian track domination, but they were, to at least one reporter, still only women. In exposing the continued trivialization of female athletes, Braven Dyer of the *Los Angeles Times* used Rudolph's extraordinary performance as an opportunity to bring criticism to US Olympic efforts. When "that little known speedball from Clarksville, Tennessee" is the only multiple medal winner in the Games, it is time, according to Dyer, for US Olympic officials to alter their strategy. He urged the state department to spend more resources on the men's team, adding, "women's rights are one thing," but that American priorities are skewed "when a slim student from Tennessee State has to rescue our dashmen from oblivion."[38]

For many other observers, however, Rudolph's victories in Rome cemented her status as a Cold War icon in local Nashville papers, and those far from Tennessee as well. Described as a "jewel," Rudolph's "swift talents" were the reason why the "U.S. flag was [twice] flown at the tallest pole in the middle of the stadium," proclaimed the *Nashville Banner*.[39] The *Appleton (WI) Post-Crescent* joined the chorus, asking, "where would the United States be without . . . the amazingly fast team of Tigerbelles from Tennessee State with Wilma Rudolph the effective anchor girl."[40] On the heels of Olympic victory, Rudolph's standing was so powerful in the Cold War environment that on occasion the press even injected Rudolph into the 1960 Presidential race. Speaking in Portland, Oregon, vice president and presidential candidate Richard Nixon attributed the US success at the recent Games to African American athletes, making specific mention of gold medalist Rafer Johnson. To which Nixon's wife, Pat, added, "Don't forget my girl, Wilma Rudolph."[41] A few weeks later in early October 1960, Rudolph and her Tigerbelle teammates were present for a Nixon tour stop in Nashville. Newspapers around the country picked up the Associated Press photo of Rudolph and Nixon standing on the stage, in conversation.[42] New York's *Oneonta Star* featured the image of the two on the front page, with a caption that read: "TOP RUNNERS." Nixon, according to the paper, "talks things over with Wilma Rudolph who did her running at the Olympics. . . ."[43] Press reports were quick to praise Rudolph's achievements and that of other Americans as indications of the nation's presence and place on the world stage. As we will see, however, many within the nation's black press spoke of Rudolph's and other African Americans' athletic accomplishments with patriotic pride, but their narratives were equally intent on calling for racial justice and equality.

Sport, Racial (In)equality, and the Cold War

Soon after the closing ceremony marked the end of the Rome Olympics, the black press's *Atlanta Daily World* used the moment to comment on the realities of continuing racial injustice in the United States. In addition, the newspaper took the opportunity to remark on the potential of African American athletes in helping the nation win the Cold War. The Olympic team's performance would have been much stronger, argued the newspaper, if the United States "had a few more Rafer Johnsons and Wilma Rudolphs, Negro Americans." Russian superiority at these Olympics, according to the article, was best explained by the fact that contestants were recruited from the nation's entire populous, not ninety percent of its youth, as was the case in the United States. Thus, limiting opportunities for African Americans in sport and the broader society restricted the nation's potential and strength. "When we consider the Wilma Rudolphs and the Rafer Johnsons who might have run," opined the daily, it is then that "we get some notion of the difference between nine-tenths and ten-tenths." Pushing Cold War fears to the fore, the paper continued, "Just as she [the United States] gave Russia the advantage at Rome, she is giving Russia the advantage *all along the line* [italics added]. How late do the Negrophobes think it is? Russia is currently too strong to be outdone by our country's nine-tenths."[44]

As the *Atlanta Daily World* article attests, in addition to being an important source of racial pride, Wilma Rudolph's athletic success and that of her teammates was also a point around which civil rights were asserted in black newspapers.[45] Moreover, the black press used black athletic achievement to highlight the hypocrisy of US claims of moral superiority among nations against the continuing racial oppression perpetrated against African Americans throughout the nation and specifically in the South. Noting the many accomplishments of black Olympic athletes in Rome, Frances Walters of the *Baltimore Afro-American* pondered just how powerful African Americans, as a people, could be "if our brains and technical ability were trained as athletic directors train our bodies." Until that time, the writer continued, America would remain a "diplomatic cripple," adding, "we have a hard time telling the world how it should behave when we misbehave ourselves."[46]

At minimum, arguments employed and voiced by the black press created a discursive space in which more than one narrative about the cultural Cold War and sport was put into play. More significantly, perspectives on athletic achievement within the black press disrupted dominant discourses constructed and sustained, largely, by whites around nationhood and the racial status quo. Given their athletic success, Rudolph, other Tennessee State Tigerbelles, and African American track athletes more generally were often the subjects around which these narratives were spun.

As the civil rights movement grew in scope and intensity throughout the 1950s, African American athletic success served the cause in "richly symbolic" ways, in part by prompting and fortifying race pride.[47] The Tennessee State University student paper, *The Meter*, joined the chorus of black press accounts in paying homage to African American Olympians. Given that students enrolled at the University won seven gold medals at the Rome Games, there was much to praise. "Drawing forth the physical strength and mental cultivation from more than 300 years of Afro-American propagation in slavery and freedom, reaping the golden harvest of victories crowning the days, weeks, months, and years of physical conditioning and poise," declared the newspaper, "the Tennessee State University track stars approached the human ideal of the ancient Greeks, 'A strong mind in a strong body.'"[48]

Reporters for the black press were not always of one unchanging voice, however, and to suggest so here is misguided. Marion Jackson, a sports columnist for the *Atlanta Daily World*, is a good case in point. Initially the columnist viewed the presence and dominance of African American athletes in Cold War exchanges, including the Olympic Games and dual meets that rotated annually between the United States and the Soviet Union, as evidence in support of democracy and the result of the athletes' agency and hard work. With that said, even his writings that take a less critical stance toward the United States, penned in earlier columns, always considered sport within the broader political contexts, whether that included Cold War politics or the civil rights struggle. Prior to the 1956 Olympic Games, Jackson warned his readers that the Soviets would "try and make capital of the current school segregation controversy" in the United States. He suggested that the women's track team, which was dominated by African American sprinters from Tennessee A&I, would be "the target of cynical talk by the Reds who will try to exploit the shameful mobs which greeted Autherine Lucy at the University of Alabama." Jackson further noted other incidents the Soviets would exploit—the Montgomery bus boycott, the murders of two African American men in Mississippi, and the $100,000 fine against the NAACP. It was, according to Jackson, the task of the athletes to absorb the "grim spears and indignities," and to ignore the Communist "oracles who revive the failings" of the United States, as they "proudly hail [the] glory and greatness" of the millions of Americans who were on their side in the fight for "freedom and decency."[49]

Black press reports around athletic achievement were more than self-esteem stories for the black community; they were also keenly political. Importantly, the accounts were imbued with nationalist rhetoric intended to provide further evidence justifying full and unfettered participation of African Americans within the democracy. Wilma Rudolph's enormous success on the track in Rome often made her the feature character around which pride in community and nation were wound in black press reports. "The tan representation should be proud of their accomplishments," asserted the *Atlanta Daily World*, and "[a]ll Americans were proud of the achievements of Miss Rudolph."[50] The press routinely used black athletic success, in the context of the cultural Cold War, as an important tool against those within dominant society intent on continuing to deny or limit African Americans' full participation in civic life. According to the *Pittsburgh Courier*, "a blistering battery of Negro Stars [sic] got the United States off to a flying start" in a 1959 dual meet with the Soviets, adding, "Uncle Sam's tan contingent soared to five first place victories in a mighty show of strength."[51] Arguably, the language employed by the *Courier* was intensely purposeful and meant to tap into broader Cold War rhetoric of worldwide competition, power, and control.[52] The political significance of the global dominance of African American athletes within US track and field throughout the mid-twentieth century was not lost on the participants. The *Courier* quoted 1956 Olympic gold-medalist Greg Bell: "[W]ithout the Negro this country would be lost when it comes to competing against other nations of the world . . ."[53] The discursive boundaries of the black press's efforts to position African American athletes and their successes were built, at least in part, upon the nation's fears of weakness in the face of a Soviet challenge.

The stories also sought to underscore the power and potential of sport in creating a more equitable and just society within the United States, with African American athletes as the agents helping to prompt social change. Wendell Smith of the *Pittsburgh Courier* related to readers that Lee Calhoun, track star at North Carolina State for Negroes, and white hurdler Joel Shankle of nearby Duke, trained together in secrecy in the period leading up to the 1956 Melbourne Olympics. Their training represented something far greater than two athletes engaging each other to better themselves. "When some say that desegregation won't work . . . it can and will," declared Smith. "If you don't believe it, ask Calhoun and Shankle, they know!"[54]

Justifiably, the American South with its continued allegiance to a system of racial inequity and oppression drew some of the most severe criticism from the black press. "One of the most regrettable aspects of the mass Southern mind is its complete emphasis on channeling freedom instead of broadening it," concluded Marion Jackson in 1958.[55] A. S. "Doc" Young countered that the "restricted world of Jim Crow" could not and would not impede or slow the race toward equality and freedom for African Americans. The athletic performances of students enrolled at black colleges and universities across the South were, according to Young, one of the "great . . . unheralded sports stories of our time." African American athletes, many born and raised in the South, raised the profile of their academic institutions, while they earned the respect of the United States and the world. Wilma Rudolph and other students "are getting around, and they're making their presence felt—all the way from the NAIA to Rome, and on to Tokyo."[56] For "Doc" Young and many other members of the black press, the achievements of African American athletes at midcentury symbolized the nation's potential and its strength when all of its citizens were afforded equal opportunity.

Wilma Rudolph: Olympic Champion

Wilma Rudolph's status as a Cold War icon was constructed, sustained, and contested not only in the press but also by the US government. The United States Information Agency's 1961 film *Wilma Rudolph: Olympic Champion* serves as one of the best examples of direct, state-supported propaganda concerning the track star, and thus warrants our attention.[57] While the production centers on Rudolph and her experiences, the film provides an opportunity to explore the story the

United States chose to tell the international arena about itself, as much as about the track star. To be sure, the USIA film of the track champion helped to tell "America's story to the world," especially as that story concerned race.[58]

By the early- to mid-1950s, in the face of what appeared to be a protracted Cold War, the Eisenhower administration was especially eager to influence international opinion of the United States. Establishing the USIA in 1953 was a significant step in that direction. The USIA's practices included transmitting the symbols and values of the nation to those abroad, through film, cultural exchange programs, television and radio reports, libraries, books, and pamphlets. In just a couple of years beyond its formation, the USIA grew to be a significant and high-profile influence on US foreign policy.[59] The agency was "on the front line of the Cold War," quipped Eisenhower, as he underscored the agency's importance.[60] Far from peripheral or "adjunct," the USIA films and the ideological leanings embedded within them were seen as central to 'winning' the cultural Cold War through the "hearts and minds" of folks around the globe.[61]

In the late 1950s and early 1960s, African American athletes including Wilma Rudolph, Althea Gibson, and Rafer Johnson were offered up by the USIA as proof to the world of America's democratic principles in action, notably around race equality. The films "provided overseas audiences with visual evidence of this country not only coming to terms with its racial minorities but also fostering and celebrating their achievements."[62] Rudolph's extraordinary accomplishments on the track are lauded in the film, as is the track star herself. Employing a Horatio Alger mythology, USIA films on Rudolph and other African Americans highlight the athletes' moral fortitude, tenacity, and humility in achieving success.[63] *Wilma Rudolph: Olympic Champion* features the athlete's accomplishments on the track, as it simultaneously obscures the racial injustices she endured away from it. It was understood, according to the film's director Walter de Hoog, that a romanticized version of events was to be presented, not one that highlighted or even mentioned racial tensions.[64] The short film's total silence around race and racial inequality, while not surprising, given the USIA's orientation of whitewashing social tensions, is nonetheless conspicuous in its absence.

What *is* present in the ten-minute film is the attention paid to Wilma Rudolph's student status at Tennessee State, with nearly half of the production firmly situated on or about the campus. In fact, the film's opening narration makes this part of Rudolph's identity clear in stating, "This is Wilma Rudolph, a twenty-year-old American university student and track star." US propagandists, in remaking their own narrative emphasis on "slow and steady progress on race," according to Hixson, stressed the increasing numbers of African Americans in higher education.[65] College enrollment signaled the "most significant index" of African American advancement, and the film works to position Rudolph's student status and Tennessee State University (TSU) as democratic spaces that allow for greater opportunity.[66] American democracy afforded all citizens, including African Americans, access to material success—or so the USIA films would lead viewers to believe. Of course what viewers were not privy to was the severe limits placed on access to higher education, for Wilma Rudolph and other African Americans. Rudolph's attendance at, and even the need for, the historically black TSU are never raised in the film.[67] For USIA producers and directors to take note of TSU as an all-black university may have triggered larger, critical questions among viewers about the "separate but equal" doctrine that ruled the South. Instead, portraying Rudolph as a good, hardworking, well-liked student, taking advantage of the many opportunities available to her at TSU, stood in contrast to powerful violent images being circulated around the world of African Americans unable to gain full and unfettered access to higher education.

Even Rudolph's work-study employment in the University post-office is put forth as another piece of evidence in celebrating the American way of life, while denigrating communism. US propagandists cast labor within communist regimes as oppressive, offering workers meager pay and harsh working conditions.[68] Rudolph's employment, on the other hand, is portrayed as being far from stifling, and instead, work is imagined as an avenue to opportunity. According to the documentary, "Wilma has a part-time job at the student post office. Many American students hold part-time jobs to help finance their education." In the film, Rudolph's fellow students gather around as she sorts and delivers mail. Moreover, the narration, over the voice-less Rudolph, declares, "Working in the post office is a good way of meeting her fellow students. Wilma gets a lot of mail herself. She was a hit with the girls and boys in Rome. From friends all over the world she receives letters, postcards, pictures, and greetings. And yes, quite a few marriage proposals. She has become internationally famous." This becomes the standard, dominant narrative of labor within a democracy, where work is represented as anything but finite and repressive. Fostered within a democracy, labor is instead a path to greater material and social success.

The Nashville campus of Tennessee State University and the physical space it occupied became central to the film's construction of a narrative espousing freedom and the many opportunities that were said to arise from that. In *Wilma Rudolph: Olympic Champion,* viewers are introduced not only to the athlete, but also to her life at Tennessee State and in the United States. The campus is featured through multiple images of large, brick structures whose grounds are manicured and neatly kept. The University union, gymnasium, dormitories, the President's residence, and various other academic buildings with their sleek and modern lines convey a certain affluence, one free of struggle and austerity. However, what remains out of focus in *Wilma Rudolph: Olympic Champion* is the reality of a system of white supremacy that gave rise to a segregated and unequal existence for African Americans across the American South, including at the historically black institution, Tennessee State University.

The idealized representations of Rudolph's life USIA producers hoped to create extended to the music chosen for the film. Beginning with the Olympic Games in Rome, the film's producers attempted to capture the moment with martial style marching tunes playing over the narrative. At the nearly one-third mark, however, the film transitions from images of Rome and the Olympics to Nashville, "the city Wilma Rudolph came back to after her Olympic triumphs." Aerial video moves over the city skyline, capturing a landscape of tall, concrete buildings whose look appears neat, modern, and orderly. The musical score changes at this instant from militaristic music to an up-tempo beat and carefree sound that conjures up images of Ozzie-and-Harriet domestic bliss.[69] Over the course of the next several minutes of video, viewers are invited in to get an intimate view of Rudolph by being introduced to the track star's family, coaches, and classmates. We watch Rudolph move through her world, a place carefully constructed to highlight both the achievements of the track star and a system of American democracy. This all takes place in the film as the upbeat tone and charge of the musical score reminds us that all is good in Rudolph's life and the country in which she lives.

The American way of life is affirmed in still other ways as the documentary includes a clip of Rudolph attending religious services. The narration begins this particular episode in the film with "On Sunday the church beckons," as we see Rudolph enter the service. We should not conceive of this clip as random, given the fact that at midcentury, religion was "virtually synonymous with American nationalism."[70] Americans in the post-World War II era, through the 1950s, were reminded by national leaders that "recognition of the Supreme Being is the first, most basic expression of Americanism."[71] It appears the USIA was interested in promoting this belief not only to the nation but to the world, as well. The USIA film of Rudolph continued, "She has been all over the world and made friends everywhere but still there is no place like home, surrounded by the people she has known since childhood." Interestingly, the video shows Rudolph walking into church, with, according to the narrator, her "young niece." In all likelihood the child was actually Rudolph's daughter, Yolanda, and not her niece.[72] To make such an admission, however, would tarnish the account the USIA and others had constructed of Rudolph, and importantly, of the United States. These videos were crafted for an international audience, not other Americans, and the ideological intent for that population is clearly evident. The USIA's carefully crafted story of the Olympian was not the only narrative in circulation, however.

Rudolph's Transition from Cold War Icon to Civil Rights Soldier

In late May 1963, Rudolph's participation as part of a civil rights protest in her hometown of Clarksville served to advance other storylines besides that of a cultural "Cold Warrior" for the United States. Rudolph's efforts to desegregate one of the city's restaurants and the subsequent backlash throw into sharp relief ongoing white resistance to the changing racial landscape in Clarksville and across the American South. Black press reports about the incident sarcastically opined that the key to the city Rudolph had been given just three years earlier, upon her return from the 1960 Rome Games, did not work to unlock the realities of Jim Crow.[73] Interestingly, we believe, Rudolph's decision to involve herself in this Clarksville protest came just weeks after she returned from a month-long goodwill tour of several African nations. While we are cautious not to give undue causal importance in linking her trip to Africa and her civil rights agitation, we are nonetheless interested, in the remainder of this chapter, in exploring the role and place of the goodwill tours in relation to the politicization of African American athletes in the late 1950s and early 1960s. We draw upon Penny von Eschen's work on jazz as a cultural export during the Cold War, in which she asserts and re-inscribes the role of agency among the "ambassadors" sent abroad—particularly to nations in Africa.

In the post-World War II era, goodwill tours by athletes, entertainers, politicians, and others represented one of several propaganda ploys enlisted by the United States government in their attempt to frame and control discursive constructions of democracy in the face of perceived communist threats.[74] In this period, the United States strove to project itself as the politically, economically, and even morally superior nation, which all other countries should emulate. In 1950, the Truman administration, cognizant of the increasing assertiveness demonstrated by the Communist bloc, launched a "Campaign of Truth." Focused not only on intensifying rhetoric but also on enlisting a much more expansive group of foot soldiers, the Campaign underscored the point that "propaganda was no longer the preserve of government [alone]; now, spreading the truth and waging the Cold War became a national duty, and frequently a national obsession."[75]

As a number of scholars have noted, athletes and the sporting events and activities in which they participated became integral to the Cold War arsenal used, in particular, by the United States and the Soviet Union.[76] Throughout the Cold War period African American athletes, in particular, were represented by the United States as the embodiment of democracy in action. For a nation eager to define itself to the world as open, democratic, and humane, African American athletes were important characters in telling not just any story, but a particular story about racial progress and the triumph of democracy over totalitarianism, and (the moral equivalent to some) of good over evil. Hundreds of athletic goodwill tours were sponsored by the State Department in the two decades following World War II. The tours provided the government a platform from which to "showcas[e] African Americans as the preeminent citizens of the African Diaspora, rather than as victims of racism," according to Damion Thomas.[77] The USIA films on athletes, including Wilma Rudolph, join with the goodwill tours in celebrating African American achievement as a product of living in a democracy.

Cultural Cold War propagandistic images and narratives, such as those outlined above, were, however, "always several steps ahead of reality."[78] In actuality, Jim Crow permeated the Southern United States in the 1950s, as segregationists dug in their heels in defense of white supremacy and a racist worldview that upheld the racial status quo. Civil rights activists intensified their charge in pursuit of racial equality. The subsequent tensions, clashes, and violent confrontations spilled out as images onto a world stage, severely tarnishing narrative constructions by and of the United States as a nation predicated on freedom and individual liberty. In an effort to counter negative images, US officials recognized that African Americans might be best able to deliver the most powerful messages about racial progress, equality, and justice to world audiences, who remained less than convinced, given the images originating out of Montgomery, Little Rock, and numerous other locations across the South.[79]

Von Eschen, in *Satchmo Blows Up the World: Jazz Ambassadors Play the Cold War*, contends that for US officials, jazz music, performed largely by African Americans, had a very critical and potentially powerful role to play as a Cold War weapon. As a result, the United States sent African American jazz musicians, including Dizzy Gillespie, Louis Armstrong, and others, on high-profile tours to Africa and Asia to act as goodwill ambassadors to build relationships, in part, by promoting a "color-blind American democracy." Interestingly, as von Eschen concludes, "the State Department failed to anticipate that people would interact in unforeseen ways—that artists would bring their own perceptions, agendas, and aspirations to the tours and become transformed in the process."[80] Rather than being used as pawns in a Cold War battle between and among nations, jazz musicians held views that, according to von Eschen, were not always in step with the official government position on issues. This same perspective must be applied to African American athletes on goodwill tours. For example, Bill Russell, NBA star, went on a State Department-sponsored trip to Africa in 1959 "armed with basketballs and films of the Celtics," and returned with much more.[81] The basketball star felt "confronted with the deep emotional feeling of returning to a homeland."[82] Russell, as a result of his trip, invested in various businesses in Liberia. When asked about his trip, Russell spoke of a homecoming, saying he had "found a place where I was welcome because I was black instead of in spite of being black."[83]

Ironic on many levels, the opportunity to play to African audiences in newly independent nations across the continent provided the artists with a rare platform on which to promote a particular, sometimes oppositional, perspective to views held by the government that sent them on tour in the first place. By the mid-1950s jazz tours abroad and the musicians performing in those tours created enough of a stir to call Congress to act. Eventually, the Senate Appropriations Committee ruled that no additional funds were to be used to send jazz bands and ballet companies abroad, as they were "alarmed by the impression of the United States conveyed" by these groups. Instead, the committee urged "Government-aided travel for choral groups and miscellaneous sports projects," both assumed to be far less political.[84]

Africa, in the late 1950s and early 1960s, represented a contested terrain for the United States and their Soviet competitors. As African nations declared their independence, their new-nation status offered the United States and the Soviet Union new opportunities for cultural imperialism. Sport was not immune to these Cold War battles over the newly independent nations. Twenty-one new African nations emerged between 1956 and 1963, and many of these new countries sought entry into the Olympic movement.[85] The Soviet Union and their International Olympic Committee (IOC) member Constantin Andrianov were particularly interested in supporting these countries' admission into the Olympic movement.[86] Simultaneously, the United States was sending athletes as part of the goodwill tours to Africa, which represented another contested terrain for the United States and the Soviet Union, as they "battled" to influence the newly independent nations.

The value of female athletes as cultural icons increased dramatically as their athletic skills and achievements became necessities in the Cold War arsenal. Two African American female athletes were sent abroad by the US State Department prior to Rudolph's 1963 goodwill tour to West Africa. Althea Gibson, tennis champion, played a series of exhibition matches throughout Asia in the winter of 1955–56. According to Mary Jo Festle, Gibson "understood the program's goal and didn't mind helping achieve it," noting that the athlete jumped at the chance to earn money for traveling and playing tennis with capable opponents.[87] Gibson "downplayed racial problems" in the United States, and in an interview with *Time* replied, "Sure we have a problem in the States, as every country has its problems. But it's a problem that's solving itself, I believe."[88] Mae Faggs, Rudolph's teammate in Ed Temple's summer Tigerbelle program, was selected as the only female on a 1956 US State Department sponsored goodwill trip to Africa with six American male athletes. Faggs and the group traveled to Monrovia, Liberia, Accra in Ghana, and Lagos and Ibada in Nigeria.[89]

Rudolph was sent to Africa as an official representative of the United States at the 1963 Friendship Games held in Dakar, Senegal, the third such meeting of African nations, some of whom were newly independent. The Friendship Games at Dakar exceeded, in popularity and participation, the two previous events, with over twenty-four hundred athletes from two dozen African countries.[90] For some in Senegal, the Friendship Games symbolized Africa's growing movement away from colonial rule and a desire to reclaim the continent. Multi-nation sporting activities, such as the Friendship Games, were seen as a "powerful factor of unity," as well as a path to further "mutual understanding and love." Supporters argued that the Games provided a space for newly sovereign nations to "discover how deeply they resemble each other and how similar their ideals are."[91] Others, too, were interested in promoting sport on the continent, but for other reasons. As African nations claimed their independence, the IOC quickly used sport as a means of re-colonizing the emerging nations. These sporting contests worked to engage Africa into the Olympic movement, which included both the United States and the Soviet Union, making the Cold War play out in new ways on African soil as the two superpowers battled for the newly independent nations in their search for allies. The Games' political significance was matched by tremendous excitement among the Senegalese in anticipation of the event, with Rudolph's presence core to that emotion. The local press announced that "the beautiful, the unforgettable black gazelle" would be in attendance as the American Sports Ambassador at the Games.[92] Pictured in the company of and in private conversation with American diplomats and Senegal's president Leopold Sengha, Rudolph's important place at these Games was clearly evident.[93]

Senegal was not the only African nation to place the track star in royal standing. The Ghanaian press wrote extensively and enthusiastically of Rudolph's four-day visit to that nation in late April 1963. In advance of her arrival in Accra, press reports underscored that the athlete's visit was supported by the State as Mr. Ohene Djan, Ghana's Director of Sports, was scheduled to greet her at the airport.[94] Press reports continued to detail the Olympian's itinerary as she met with additional Ghanaian officials, toured girls' schools, and watched as well as commented on athletic events. Despite the royal treatment bestowed upon Rudolph, she was not paid an honorarium for her services, so she could retain her amateur status in hopes of competing in the 1964 Olympic Games in Tokyo.[95] In addition to attending the Friendship Games in Senegal, and her visit to Ghana, Rudolph also traveled to Guinea, Mali, and Upper Volta, attending school assemblies and soccer games, appearing on radio and television shows, and attending the premier of the USIA film on her life, *Wilma Rudolph, Championne Olympique.*[96] According to Davis, American diplomats were "eager to exploit" her "magical presence," and after the Friendship Games, a French embassy official told an American official "that America had won more prestige from the thousand or so dollars spent for Wilma Rudolph's travel expenses than France gained after paying the $4 million the games reportedly cost."[97]

The US government's agenda in using Rudolph to influence world opinion of the United States, however elaborate and well planned, could not diagram or foretell the trip's impact *on* the Olympic champion. Wilbert C. Petty, cultural affairs officer at the American Embassy in Dakar, suspected that Rudolph's goodwill tour to Africa was "her first time in an area where black rather than white is the color that counts. She seemed delighted to be among 'the folks.'" He believed her to be "intrigued by the everyday life of the people."[98] Of the trip, Rudolph echoed sentiments similar to those expressed earlier by the NBA's Bill Russell, saying she "just felt at home," and noting that there was something about the people that made her fall in love with them. She recalled visiting an area called the "Medina," which she explained was a "slum area." She said, "I just went out like I belonged there. They accepted me and that's what I wanted them to do. And whatever they wore, I wore."[99] This point is clearly illustrated in an image of Rudolph, in traditional African attire, featured on the front page of the Ghanaian paper the *Daily Graphic*, during the athlete's visit.[100] Rudolph was obviously touched by the reception she received across the tour and especially in Ghana, where her "brothers and sisters" welcomed her warmly.[101] Unquestionably afforded enormous respect, the depth of the attraction, between Rudolph and her hosts, was mutual as the female track great was said to be a "source of inspiration to the people of Africa."[102] The significance of their shared ancestry was illustrated in Djan's gift to Rudolph upon her departure from Ghana. A "replica of a drummer and two talking drums," presented on behalf of the nation's president, the gift was to "constantly" remind Rudolph of her "origin from mother Africa."[103]

Over the course of the month Rudolph traveled in Africa, the American civil rights struggle gained momentum. Daily newspaper coverage across the nation and around the world featured the protests, marches, legislation, and other efforts by African Americans and their allies to end racial apartheid in the American South. In the months before Rudolph left the United States, Rev. Dr. Martin Luther King Jr. led six weeks of daily demonstrations in Birmingham, Alabama, that included sit-ins at lunch counters and other public facilities. Televised images of African Americans being sprayed with a high-pressure fire hose in Birmingham were aired across the nation. These were the first racial demonstrations to be carried live over American television airwaves, and they took some in the nation by surprise.[104] King was arrested for demonstrating in defiance of a court order. In his jail cell, King penned his famous "Letter from a Birmingham Jail." By mid-May, the National Guard was ordered to Birmingham by President Kennedy.[105] These acts of civil disobedience, as well as thousands of others, prompted white responses, but also further energized African Americans and their allies in the fight for racial justice.

In the weeks following the Birmingham demonstrations, Charles Livingston, Associated Negro Press sports writer, "urged Negro athletes, like entertainers, to join the freedom struggle." Livingston credits the picketing of Washington Redskins games, and the efforts of the National Association for the Advancement of Colored People (NAACP), the Congress of Racial Equality (CORE), and other civil rights organizations with changing the Jim Crow policy of the Redskins. He asks, "Why then shouldn't Negro athletes show their gratitude by leading picket lines and other campaigns against racial bigotry on behalf of their less fortunate 'brothers?'" Livingston suggested that the involvement of famous athletes leading pickets and sit-ins would have a tremendous impact.[106] Weeks later, former baseball player Jackie Robinson and former heavyweight boxing champion Floyd Patterson flew to Birmingham to show their support for Dr. King and the protestors.[107]

Robinson penned two columns for the *Chicago Defender* addressing his involvement in the Birmingham protests. On the day he left for the southern city, Robinson claimed he and Patterson were going to "thank Dr. King and the heroic Birmingham youngsters who freedom-marched on to the world's front pages and into the world's conscience," suggesting it was the least he could do. He called on readers to donate "freedom dollars" to the Back Our Brothers Movement.[108] His call for funds resulted in $1,000 from Peter Ottley, president of the Local 144 Hospital and Hotel Union. Robinson, in his second guest column, reiterated his reasoning for the trip, telling readers that he and Patterson "felt that if Dr. King and those heroic marching kids could make the kind of sacrifices they made, the least that we can do in the North is to express our gratitude." He described the trip as "one of the most moving experiences of our lives."[109] Patterson echoed Robinson, saying, "It is the responsibility of outstanding Negroes to cooperate in the civil rights struggle, however or wherever they can."[110]

At least one critic of Robinson and Patterson's trip to Birmingham was former Olympic athlete Jesse Owens, who spoke out against his peers' using fame as leverage in the struggle for civil rights across the South. In response to the two athletes' trip to Birmingham, Owens expressed his concern. "I can't see where they're going to be of any great help," the former track great concluded. "They're not going to live there, and you've got to live there to understand the situation." Owens explained, "If it would be left to the people that live there, they might find the solution quicker. I feel we (Negroes) have capable leadership in the South. I'm a great believer in Martin Luther King. He is one of the smart men of this decade."[111] Livingston lambasted Owens in his column, writing, "The outmoded 'leave-it-to-the-local-people' philosophy is sheer malarkey. By mouthing this philosophy, Owens is playing right into the hands of the segregationists. They want 'local Negroes' left alone so they can continue to dominate them and bend them to their evil designs."[112] Robinson, in response to Owens's criticism, stated, "We must keep these youngsters aware—and especially we who have been fortunate like Floyd, Jesse, and myself—that no Negro has it made, regardless of fame, position, or money—until the most underprivileged Negro enjoys his rights as a free man."[113]

Owens's comments sparked a debate that expanded to include his former Olympic teammate, Ralph Metcalfe, who was a city councilman in Chicago. Metcalfe sided with Robinson and Patterson, and chastised Owens for his conservative approach. Also supportive of the visit was Edwin Berry, executive director of the Chicago Urban League, who commended the athletes for their action. Berry saluted "all persons of prestige no matter what their color or national origin, who support and encourage by their presence and action other people in their fight for equal rights. I think it is a great moral booster to the people of Birmingham, or any other community, to have their national heroes and other famous persons join them in their struggle."[114] This is the context into which Rudolph returned home from her month-long trip to Africa in May 1963.

Civil Rights Rebel

Just weeks removed from her goodwill tour and days after Charles Livingston's call, Rudolph, having graduated from Tennessee State, returned to Clarksville. It is within this historical moment that she participated in a civil rights protest to integrate the local Shoney's restaurant. Heeding the words of Robinson, Patterson, and others, Rudolph, albeit briefly, used her athletic celebrity as a force for change in the civil rights movement. Rudolph now made headlines of a different sort, beyond that of a former Olympic champion and Cold War icon, when her involvement in the protest was published in newspaper accounts, especially within the black press.[115] Critical comments in the black press were quick to highlight the hypocrisy, as the key to the city given the "all-conquering hometown hero" in the fall of 1960 could

NO KEY — Olympic sprint star Wilma Rudolph enters a drive-in restaurant in her hometown of Clarksville, Tenn., where she and 300 other Negroes were refused service. With her, left to right, are: Dr. F. D. Coleman, Dr. Paul Dumas and the Rev. Carl Liggin, chairman of the local Christian Leadership Council. Twelve other Clarksville restaurants have opened their doors to Negroes during the past two weeks.

Wilma Finds Key to City Doesn't Work

CLARKSVILLE, Tenn. (ANP) — The key which the city of Clarksville gave to Wilma Rudolph during a round of festivities when she returned as a all-conquering

Court OKs McDowell Order Miss. U. To Admit Negro

BILOXI, Miss. (ANP) — Casting aside state objections, a Federal judge ordered the University of Mississippi to admit a Negro to its law school for the summer semester that began June 5.

Figure 3.1. Wilma Rudolph attempting to enter Shoney's in Clarksville; appearing on page 3 of the *Pittsburgh Courier*, June 8, 1963. Reprinted with permission of *The New Pittsburgh Courier*.

not "unlock a restaurant that was shamefully padlocked in her face."[116] The papers also reported that the track star was "badly shaken" by the event because Rudolph "couldn't believe that the same city that had opened its heart to her in 1960 would bar her from dining in a restaurant because of her race."[117]

Local press accounts in the days leading up to the Shoney's incident are illustrative of the status of race relations in Clarksville, and throw into sharp relief the ongoing white resistance to changing the racial status quo. Contributions to "Letters to the Editor" underscored the tensions when townspeople, as they had done in 1960, drew attention to both the persistent racial inequities and their opposition to the broader civil rights struggle. In the days just before the Shoney's protest, one anonymous writer questioned the small fraction of nursing home beds for "Colored people of Montgomery County" when whites have "5 times the space."[118] Others expressed their angst at African Americans' and their allies' appeals and efforts for racial justice. In a rambling tome, one letter writer asked why "must we force the issue [of desegregation]?" African Americans were, after all, in his view, shiftless criminals who espoused anti-American views.[119] In a response, a Mrs. Wyatt called on Christian principles in advocating for racial equality, stating that God's concern lay in what folks held in their hearts, not the color of their skin. Wyatt chastised the previous writer, along with his power and privilege as white: "We still tell them [African Americans] what they can do. And a lot more of what they can't do."[120] These voices provide some hint as to the range of perspectives on civil rights and the racial climate within Clarksville as Wilma Rudolph joined with other protesters in attempting to integrate Shoney's.

The Shoney's protest occurred in the midst of sweeping changes, not only around desegregation of public facilities and restaurants within Clarksville, but transformation in Rudolph's life, as well. On Tuesday, May 28, 1963, the *Leaf-Chronicle*, picking up an Associated Press story, reported that Rudolph was coming home for an extended period of time to "rest and [re-establish] family ties." The track champion had graduated from Tennessee State the day before and divorced William Ward the previous week, according to the article. Rudolph's plans also included finding employment in the city, while using the time to decide on her future in track.[121] However, she wasted little time in attending to business that was not on her published 'to-do' list, as Rudolph and a few hundred other local African American residents "called" at the Shoney's drive-in restaurant at 9:00 a.m. the morning of her return to town. The protesters were "denied service" and despite being "heckled" by onlookers who also "tossed an egg or two into the crowd," peacefully dispersed in an hour's time.

The demonstration came on the day that several other restaurants in Clarksville desegregated, the paper reported.[122]

Not to be deterred, Rudolph and the others persisted, returning to the restaurant the following evening only to, again, be denied access. Naming Wilma Rudolph, once more, as a participant, the press also noted that the event was "peaceful" except for "heckling by white youths and one [white] youth on a motorcycle circled cars carrying the Negroes until City police dispersed the crowd." The African American leaders of the demonstration, encouraged by the fact that other restaurants had begun serving blacks earlier in the week, promised to return every day until Shoney's changed its policy.[123] Quite like cities and towns across the nation, tensions in Clarksville were building, as were more violent responses from whites. Hours after the second night of Shoney's protests, local white businessman Clyde Foust reported that several gunshots were fired into his home, narrowly missing one of his children. Foust was believed by some white residents to be an "organizer" of the Shoney's protests, and thus the target of the attack.[124] Bracing for a third night of protests at Shoney's, a "large crowd of white people" gathered in anticipation. In addition, several "youths hanged a dummy dabbed with red paint from the railroad overpass near the restaurant." Reportedly, however, the crowd dispersed when African American protestors did not appear.[125] Amid a climate of heightened hostility and violent action by and among Clarksville's white residents, it was announced that a temporary "truce" was reached until a meeting could take place among African American leaders, city officials, and Shoney's management. In the meantime, protesters vowed to promote job opportunities among African Americans rather than focusing on public protest, implying an end to demonstrations at the restaurant.[126] The next Monday, less than a week after the initial Shoney's protest, the press reported that a "Committee of nine business and professional men," appointed by high-ranking city officials, met and decided it would be best to desegregate all restaurants in Clarksville. The committee made the point to also admonish civil rights protesters, stating, "coercion by demonstration is not in the best interest of the community and is not to be condoned."[127] Within the week, the Clarksville City Council voted to integrate the city's public facilities, including dining establishments, public parks, and city swimming pools.[128] In a letter to the editor, T. W. Mayhew, despite being "moved by a deep sense of pride" in his city for voting to desegregate public facilities, nonetheless acknowledged that the city council's action "does point to a new way of life in Clarksville, and some, no doubt, have been reluctant to see it come, but all of us must know that it is a way to justice, decency, and brotherhood."[129]

As we mentioned at the start of this chapter, this may be the only example of Rudolph's engagement in collective civil agitation, leading us to wonder what prompted her involvement in this matter and what role her trip to Africa played in the decision to become publicly involved in the protest. Penny von Eschen, writing about jazz musicians as cultural ambassadors, argues that [US policymakers] failed to "anticipate" that musicians, and in this case, an athlete, "would interact, generating multiple meanings."[130] We contend that Rudolph's goodwill trip to Africa was, in the words of von Eschen, a "transformative experience."[131]

Rudolph, in the years following her triple gold-medal performance, had "willingly done her share for Americanism," according to Tennessee State's *Meter*.[132] Indeed, Wilma Rudolph was not only a good "Cold Warrior"; she also stood with other Americans in the fight against racial injustice. Her engagement, however brief, in civil action marks one of the few examples of African American athletes answering the 1963 call of Charles Livingston, echoed a year later by Olympic gold-medalist Mal Whitfield, who urged a boycott of the Olympics in Tokyo in 1964 by African American athletes.[133] While much has been written on the involvement of African American male athletes with the civil rights movement, primarily crediting Muhammad Ali and a number of college athletes in the late 1960s as the main characters, Rudolph's involvement has been largely ignored.[134]

The relative silence around this particular Wilma Rudolph story, at the time of its occurrence and in the decades since, is fascinating within this larger project concerning the tales told (and not told) about the former Olympian. Equally intriguing, and worth our review, are the rare instances when the protest does emerge in Rudolph's story-line, and the meanings that can be made from those moments. Omissions about the 1963 Shoney's incident may stem, at least in part, from Rudolph's own desire to delete the protest from her life story. Unlike her challenge to the segregated homecoming parade in her honor, Rudolph scarcely discussed the Shoney's event publicly, despite opportunities to do so. The track great's involvement in the civil rights protest is not mentioned in her autobiography, written in 1977 (see chapter four), for example, which includes frequent sections on racism and her responses to injustice.

The Shoney's protest did get a mention in a 1964 *Sports Illustrated* article, where the topic is raised, only to be dismissed as a relic of Rudolph's past. The article's focus in detailing Rudolph's "slight change of pace" from 1960 was to ensure that her current role as wife and mother eclipsed remnants of previous political action and even the former star's athletic history.[135] Rudolph seems to show little interest in either within this 1964 moment. Writer Anita Verschoth offers that when Rudolph is asked to show guests her Olympic medals, the track star "finds it difficult to remember where she put them last."[136] Readers are also told that the former track great uses the James E. Sullivan Trophy (for winning the US Amateur Athlete award of 1962) as a place to hang her car keys. The article's only photo further distanced Rudolph from her athletic past, showing husband Robert Eldridge pushing the former Olympian on a swing. "Wilma's Husband Gets Her Swinging," according to the caption.[137] Rudolph is characterized as a content and dutiful housewife, mother, and extended family caretaker.

Pleased with her domestic role, Rudolph notes that her civic engagement continues, but in ways different than in the past. In a reference to the Shoney's protest, Rudolph comments that monthly parent meetings to discuss their children's education have replaced "demonstration marches." Verschoth adds that Rudolph's apparent shift away from race and civil rights issues blends with the sprinter's other opinions on the topics. As an example, Rudolph, when asked, is not "bothered" by teaching in a segregated elementary school, according to Verschoth, who adds that the track great's comments are delivered "without any indication of bitterness." As if to defend segregation, Rudolph adds near the article's end, "I have seen mixed areas which are a lot worse."[138]

Decades later and just three years before her death in 1994, Wilma Rudolph spoke once more, and very differently, about racism and the events in May 1963 outside of Shoney's restaurant in Clarksville. In 1991, Rudolph provided a deposition in a case involving a charge of racial discrimination against the Shoney's restaurant chain. Rudolph's testimony was offered in an effort to prove a poor record of integration at Shoney's. Removed by the passage of time, as well as speaking in a different moment and to a different audience, Rudolph acknowledged how intensely painful the memory remained. With the event still "too vivid" in her mind, she recalled the "humiliation" felt and the physical pain of being tear-gassed on those evenings in late May 1963. Rudolph adds, in reference to the protest, "I cannot begin to impress upon you how I felt as a black American."[139]

In these accounts, Rudolph's memories of the Shoney's incident have shifted drastically over the decades. Reluctant to discuss the matter, let alone make a decisive claim to it, in 1964, Rudolph seems eager to remove herself from anything that positions her beyond the mainstream. Albeit just four years from her gold medal winning performance, Rudolph was already fading from public memory. As Verschoth quips, "not many strangers drive up the hill anymore to visit Wilma." We cannot "know" Rudolph's motivations in the *Sports Illustrated* piece (September 7, 1964), but if she still hoped to capitalize in some way on her achievements in Rome, a presentation that detached her from issues or behaviors perceived to be 'radical' best served that aim in 1964.[140] This detachment is in contrast to her presentation in the 1991 deposition, where Rudolph, in a keenly personal way, relates the trauma and impact on her being in the Shoney's protest, then and in the decades since. In constructing these stories, Rudolph's descriptions of the event underscore the shifting, changeable quality of memory.

With the exception of these two very brief references to the protest, silence on the topic pervades the multiple narrations of Rudolph's life over the past half-century. As certain stories about the track great replay with tenacity, the Shoney's protest, in juxtaposition, is all but forgotten. Rudolph pushes it to the margins of her story, and thus many after her fail to recount it in their own reconstructions of the Olympian's life, each having personal motives for selectively remembering the past. For Rudolph, to retell her participation in the Shoney's incident is to stir hurtful memories of racism. As Holloway suggests, writing about memory for those African Americans who lived under Jim Crow, it is "wiser to edit the reality of the past to protect [the] present."[141] Wilma Rudolph clearly remembers the Shoney's event, but chooses to "forget" it as a means of self-preservation. For others writing of Rudolph's life, the silence surrounding the Shoney's protest signals something different. To engage and retell it is to encourage a specific, much less common and endorsed, memory of Rudolph. Thus, the many silences that surround the few narrative clips of Rudolph's participation in the Shoney's protest tell us a good deal about the politics of memory-making and the selectiveness of historical accounts. Ultimately, the narrow storylines around Rudolph's participation in the Shoney's civil rights protest help to sustain Rudolph's iconization as a Cold War icon.

Conclusion

Our aim in this chapter was to examine the multiple ways Wilma Rudolph has been represented to the public as a Cold War icon, rather than as a civil rights soldier (though the two are not mutually exclusive roles). The various representations of Rudolph, whether in mainstream American newspapers, the Black press, or the US government's USIA film, all reveal narratives that use Rudolph as a symbol for various agents. The stories of Rudolph are about advancing particular American agendas; each is politicized and none are free from ideological leanings. Working from that assumption, it is worth asking ourselves how each of the representations privileges or obscures particular perspectives. Who is best served by each story, and who is least served, if served at all? In asking these questions our intent is in no way to discount Wilma Rudolph's accomplishments, those of her Tigerbelle teammates, and other African American Olympians. Instead, we contend that we best honor the memory and achievements of these individuals by critically interrogating how and why media and the US government ran with their stories in the ways they did.

Examining the Autobiographical Self

Wilma Rudolph on Bookshelves

IN THE OPENING PARAGRAPHS OF HER AUTOBIOGRAPHY, *Wilma: The Story of Wilma Rudolph*, the author and former track great writes, "When I was four or five, just starting to become aware that I was a human being, almost all of my brothers and sisters were grown up. . . ."[1] Rudolph draws on bodily discourses in this sentence and at a number of points throughout the text as she constructs her identity in recounting memories of her past. It is through this lens of embodiment that we have chosen to read Rudolph's autobiography. Situated at the crossroads of sport autobiography and African American female life narratives, *Wilma: The Story of Wilma Rudolph* presents us with a unique space to explore: as Sidonie Smith and Julia Watson suggest, when and where the "body becomes visible," and what that visibility means in autobiographical texts.[2]

As an athlete, Rudolph's body is central to her life story, as it is in many sport autobiographies.[3] G. T. Couser reminds us that life narratives that make the body central have historically been written "mostly by movie stars (about their sex lives) or by sports stars (about their athletic feats)."[4] Moreover, as a female, Rudolph's body is principal to the telling of her story because, according to Kristi Siegel, women are "socially constructed as bodies."[5] In many ways, women's stories tend to be much more and differently embodied than male narratives.[6] Such is the case with Rudolph as she constructs an account in which her identity as female, an African American, born poor, who is temporarily disabled in young life, greatly informs her life story. How Rudolph's "body becomes visible" and "the meanings of this visibility" serve as important texts and illustrate the ways in which Rudolph "is both differently embodied over time and shaped by the cultural stories available" to her.[7] Importantly, we believe, it is Rudolph's admissions about her body and identity that speak forcefully to broader cultural forces that informed her life and experiences. We agree with Rosi Braidotti in arguing that the body's surface is a site where "multiple codes of power and knowledge are inscribed" and thus worthy of our attention. Indeed, bodies are "integral" to better understanding the "politics of [a] period" but must be "rescued from the amnesia of traditionally conceived life narratives."[8]

Written in 1977, seventeen years after her remarkable triple Olympic gold-medal performance, Wilma Rudolph authored her autobiography with the editorial assistance of Martin Rabolvsky. In writing *Wilma: The Story of Wilma Rudolph*, she joined the exclusive club of the handful of female athletes who had written their life histories.[9] While many others have spoken for and about Wilma Rudolph in the half-century since her triumphs in Rome, she too represented herself, remembered her past, and constructed a life narrative via this autobiographical rendering. Her narrative's significance is grounded not just in the fact that it offers us insight into political dimensions of identity and subjectivity, but also that the autobiography has served as the framework for a majority of the biographies written about the triple gold medalist. We contend, in this chapter, that Rudolph's autobiography is an important piece of evidence because of its influence on subsequent representations, including a made-for-television movie and nearly twenty-one children's books written over the past three decades. Moreover, Rudolph's stories of her experiences growing up as an African American female athlete tell an unfamiliar tale, both in 1977 and today, when there continues to be an absence of autobiographical writings by African American female athletes, as well as female athletes in general.[10] Lastly, Rudolph's autobiographical perspective on moments in her life which may or may not have been documented in other written sources is valuable in understanding her life story, as well as her own agency in telling her stories. Autobiographical texts, including Rudolph's, offer a distinct perspective on a life and thus become a "valuable document through which to connect with the past."[11] Other authors mark autobiographies' importance as historical material even more forcefully. Life stories, according to Jennifer Jensen Wallach, are made even more powerful as historical documents precisely because of their "subjective, firsthand character."[12]

Thus, we read Rudolph's autobiography as an important cultural product, understanding that it is much more than a simple or elemental, descriptively driven, narrative account of her life. Far from a "transparent record of a life lived," an autobiography, according to Michael Oriard, is instead a "consciously crafted self-presentation of an individual framed by certain social, economic, and political contexts and guided by any number of personal motives."[13] Rudolph's efforts to produce "the self" are in constant negotiation with any number of cultural assumptions about blackness, femaleness, and other forms of identity. Hence, the process of remembering in autobiography, and in other spaces as well, does not just happen in some "splendid isolation" but is always in conversation with society more broadly.[14] As a production and construction of the self, autobiography is ceaselessly in relationship with, and never free from, the cultural assumptions that surround the subject.[15] Despite autobiography's assumed position with regard to individual agency and autonomy, "we do not invent our identities out of whole cloth. Instead, we draw on the resources of the cultures we inhabit to shape them."[16] Consequently, we take Rudolph's autobiography seriously because it offers us a unique perspective on subjectivity, identity, and agency, as well as an important site of memory. After all, "[m]emory is the raison d'être of autobiography."[17]

In *(Re)Presenting Wilma Rudolph* more generally and in this specific chapter on autobiography, our aim rests less with determining the falseness or truthfulness of specific "facts" and more with examining the strategies the track great uses to tell her story. Even if the veracity of Rudolph's life story could be confirmed or rejected, we argue, to what greater end does that path take us? Similarly, Sidonie Smith and Julia Watson encourage us to ask "for whom and for what" we seek to truth-test any autobiographical narrative.[18] Instead, we begin from the presumption, as we do across various sites in *(Re)Presenting Wilma Rudolph*, that the track star's memories are constructions, selective and framed to tell not just any story, but a particular story. Though Rudolph fashions her own story, as opposed to using tales created by others of her, we do not believe that this produces a stronger bond with "truth." Those who narrate their lives, including Rudolph, draw upon "imaginative acts of remembering" in an effort to sway us toward a particular understanding of the past.[19] With this in mind, Rudolph's narrative is a valuable document through which to interrogate how one of the twentieth century's greatest female athletes recounted her life and experiences.

Because the public consumed, valued, and viewed her as an athlete, we situate Rudolph's writing, on a primary level, as a sport autobiography, and briefly survey, here, the major tenets of that specific genre. Sport autobiographies follow a traditional arc, one in which the "rags to riches" motif is usually tightly woven into the stories' fabric.[20] Speaking more narrowly to African American sport autobiographies, Oriard argues that athletics serves as an escape for those born into poverty. African American athletes recount the central, guiding influences of parents and black or white mentors in assisting them through setbacks on their way, usually, to triumph by books' end. This narrative model creates a "pattern of the American success story . . . its appeal to readers [is] in its utter familiarity, as well as its reassurances that talent and hard work can defeat all obstacles, even racial ones."[21] These are the classic American tales of Horatio Alger and rags to riches with a racial element to the story. Despite this overarching theme of success, which is critical to sport, African American athletes writing their stories bring, according to Oriard, "an inescapable political dimension, whether or not the author chooses to acknowledge that reality."[22] Wilma Rudolph's story shares this stage as "inescapabl[y] political," despite not being created as an overtly political text by its author.

Wilma Rudolph's autobiography joins with hundreds of other life narratives that have an athlete at center stage. Men dominate athletics in the United States and thus it is not surprising that the sport auto-biography genre is populated with more titles authored by men than by women, with achievement and success tropes tightly woven across the class of books. As a genre, sporting autobiographies have their critics and are typically not celebrated as literary triumphs, with one author claiming that athlete memoirs reveal that "pro athletes have brutally repetitious, uninteresting lives. . . . Sports memoirs may be intended as post-retirement victory laps, but many of them read like a cry for help."[23] While Rudolph's writing does not rise to literary great-ness, it nonetheless remains an important document to examine and interrogate.

Rudolph's narrative is driven by some of the same elements dis-cussed by Oriard as reflective of African American autobiography and found more generally in the category, as described above.[24] Yet, far from the rags-to-riches arc, it is clear that the issues, around race for example, that Rudolph was forced to confront at an early age con-tinue to be part of the larger narrative to which she speaks long after Olympic glory. Rudolph's narrative departs from conventional tales, sequenced to climax in triumph, showing the years following her Olympic gold as being filled with frustration and disappoint-ment. Born into a large family, Rudolph acknowledges her family's poverty in segregated Clarksville, Tennessee, as she recounts her par-ents' various jobs to support the family. Rudolph, like many of the subsequent narrators of her story, recounts that her young life was marked by a number of debilitating illnesses requiring her, as a result, to wear a leg brace during childhood. Moreover, she documents the assistance she received from her parents throughout her young life, with her mother taking her to Nashville regularly for treatments and both parents providing support to her when she was pregnant in high school. In addition, Rudolph writes throughout her autobiography of the mentorship received from Burt High School coach Clinton Gray and Tennessee State's Ed Temple. Following the familiar script, in spite of the poverty, segregation, racism, illnesses, leg brace, and high school pregnancy, among other issues, Rudolph became the fastest woman in the world at the 1960 Olympic Games, winning three gold medals, an unprecedented achievement for an American woman in track and field. However, despite following a conventional script, and just as Oriard suggests, Rudolph's autobiography is laden with political dimensions related to race, gender, class, and disability.[25] On this point we agree with Derek Duncan, who argues that life stories like Rudolph's, written by those "outside the narratives of dominant culture[,] are, in many respects, about the resistance to prevailing ideologies of sameness."[26]

Issues of embodiment are central to Wilma Rudolph's life writing, in large part because her body was continually contrasted as "other" or marked as different from the broader, dominant society. Rudolph's recollections of her past as black, female, poor, and temporarily disabled are, at times, defined by any number of these identity markers. In one example, Rudolph remembers a teacher visiting her home to deliver a lesson because of the disability that prevented the future track great from attending school. Despondent, Rudolph recounts, "I remember she left behind these books—*See Dick Run, Watch Spot Run*—and I remember looking at the pictures of these white kids having happy times . . . then blotting the pictures in the book right out of my head" (p. 15). Rudolph's disability only added to the pain of her embodied "other" status as she confides, "I knew there was something wrong with me" because "I was supposed to be in school with the other kids" (p. 15). Bodies, including Rudolph's, are brought to the fore in autobiographical writing because, as Duncan suggests, for those "born into the wrong body, life and its writing could hardly avoid confronting corporeality as a significant and signifying fact of life."[27] Rudolph's body continually served up evidence of hierarchies of difference, which helps to explain the central place of corporeality in the text.

As a premature baby, Wilma Rudolph's cultural position as "embodied *other*" began at her birth and continued through early childhood; chronic illness and polio inform her earliest understandings of self and the limits of her corporeal reality. Rudolph's childhood revolved around her physical ailments, and at age six she realized "something was wrong" given her "crooked" leg (p. 15). Like many others, she defined herself by what she was not, saying, "I was so skinny, and I never had the strength other kids had," adding, "I was the most sickly kid in all of Clarksville" (p. 17). Two bouts with double pneumonia, scarlet fever, whooping cough, measles, chickenpox, a tonsillectomy, and an appendectomy read like a laundry list of afflictions. Rudolph confides in her autobiography, "It was like I spent the first decade of my life being sick. It wasn't until I became a teenager that I knew what it was like to be really healthy" (p. 17). In ways similar to other forms of oppression and marginalization she experienced, societal reaction to Rudolph's physical disabilities took an emotional and psychological toll on the young girl. She recalls, "I was so lonely, and I felt rejected. I would . . . close my eyes, and just drift off into a sinking feeling, going down, down, down. I cried a lot" (p. 18). In a candid accounting of the lasting insecurity she ascribes to the sometimes cruel treatment she received from others, Rudolph writes that by the time she was seven or eight years old she "lived in mortal fear of being disliked" (p. 26). To be scolded or even corrected by someone created a tremendous amount of unease within Rudolph, who took it as a personal affront.

Rudolph's description of the leg brace she wore as a child, and the reactions to it, underscore how she came to understand her body, at this young age, as a site of repression. She says, "The brace went on my leg when I was five, and I lived with *that thing* [emphasis added] for the next half-dozen years" (p. 29), taking it off when no one was looking in an effort to give literal distance between herself and the brace. Detailing the brace's restrictiveness, Rudolph remembers that it "hooked onto my leg just above the knee and went all the way down my leg and connected to my shoe" (p. 29). From Rudolph's perspective, the presence of the brace's weight, color, and feel was a continual reminder not only of her weak leg, but her flaws as a person as well. Wearing that brace, she claims, was "devastating" (p. 29). She distanced herself, when possible, from the brace and metaphorically from her own leg. In describing the medical treatment she received, Rudolph recalls doctors "forever pulling, turning, twisting, lifting *that* [emphasis added] leg" (p. 30). Her inability to walk without the aid of the brace not only affected her body but deeply influenced her identity, notions of self, and relationships with those around her.[28] After her treatments, she studied her leg for any changes, telling herself there had to be some "visible improvement" as a result of all the treatment. The leg remained "crooked" and the young Rudolph learned to "fake a no-limp walk" to keep others from knowing that no improvements were occurring (p. 31). To Rudolph, her corporeal status was the equivalent of imprisonment, impacting every aspect of her young life.

From Wilma Rudolph's point of view, her path toward a "normal" childhood and full life began the moment she could walk without the aid of a brace. In what would become an oft-quoted tale of Rudolph's larger "overcoming" disability narrative, she recalls the first time, in public, she walked without the brace. As a nine–and-a-half-year-old, she walked into church without the heavy steel support on her leg and welcomed the gaze of others upon her. That day was, according to the future track star, "one of the most important moments of my life. From that day on," she continued, "people started separating me from that brace" (p. 32). Soon after, Rudolph's mother on "one glorious day" boxed up the leg brace and returned it to the hospital. With the brace gone, Rudolph rejoiced, "I was free at last." The young girl felt reborn as a result of feeling "healthy all over my body" for the first time in her life. Indeed, Wilma Rudolph believed that her "life was beginning at last" (p. 38).

Rudolph fondly remembers junior high as one of the best times of her life as she for the first time moved through her social world with greater ease than ever before. Running, and the use of her body in movement, made Rudolph feel free. In her early track career in high school, Rudolph recalls, "[r]unning, at the time, was nothing but pure enjoyment for me" (p. 44). As she progressed through high school and experienced winning, as well as improving her techniques, she admitted, "I loved the feeling of freedom in running, the fresh air, the feeling that the only person I'm really competing against in this is me" (p. 50). Rudolph joyfully recounts her earliest lessons in the mechanics of running, of learning "how to smooth out, how to stop fighting yourself, keeping the fists loose." She credits Coach Temple's cross country workouts with helping to build her stamina and developing her ability to breathe "free and easy, naturally." Temple taught Rudolph and her teammates exercises that made her arms and legs "feel light as feathers" (pp. 69–70). She also recounted the anxiety her body felt prior to a race, sometimes resulting in vomiting, and how that tension stayed with her throughout her running career.

Her body, once the source of misery, loneliness, and limitations, became the point around which her new-found self-esteem and confidence were woven. "I ran and ran and ran every day, and I acquired this sense of determination, this sense of spirit that I would never, never give up, no matter what else happened" (pp. 69–70). For Rudolph, the transition from a child beset by illness and bodily weakness to a world-class athlete signaled movement from darkness to light, from constraint to freedom. Rudolph's young life and the disability that so informed it were cast as a problem that relentless perseverance could overcome. This narrative is not Rudolph's alone, but is also taken up by others and repeated over the next half-century forward from 1960, making it all the more important to interrogate.

Importantly, Rudolph's understanding of her identity, experiences, and her physical self, as they relate to her disability, can never be divorced from the social and cultural environment in which she lived.[29] Thus, autobiographical stories, including Rudolph's, are conceived and narrated through the cultural scripts available to her, and any author for that matter, at a particular historical moment.[30] Rudolph's autobiography, similar to those of a good many others, according to Couser, fortifies, rather than disrupts, dominant ideologies about physical impairment. He argues, "conventional rhetorics for representing disability in autobiography do tend to individualize the condition and, worse, to reinforce its stigma. Thus, although the memoir may offer a degree of access that other literary genres do not, and although it may offer a degree of control over representation that other media do not, various cultural constraints limit the counterhegemonic potential of disability memoir. Culture filters and manipulates even seemingly 'self-generated' texts."[31] Rudolph's stories are in no way immune to the larger cultural narratives about embodiment and disability, and in many ways are infused with them. In 1977, Rudolph writes physical disability as *her* [emphasis added] problem in a society that very much saw it that way, as well.

The challenges Rudolph and her family faced around her physical disability were made more complex by the realities of their class standing. Though Rudolph spends little narrative space on class specifically, the subject nonetheless informs her experiences throughout the entire text. In fact, the book's opening, which outlines her mother's and father's occupations—a domestic and a railroad porter, respectively—serves to introduce readers to the Rudolph family's working-class world. "Too proud" to accept governmental assistance, or "handouts from anybody," Rudolph's parents struggled to feed and clothe their children (p. 5). Her parents' creativity and hard work enabled the family to survive, despite the oppressiveness of being poor. Rudolph remembers her mother "going to stores and picking up old flour sacks" to makes dresses and clothing for the children (p. 14). The food Rudolph's mother occasionally brought home from her part-time employment at a white restaurant made the future track great feel "lucky" in that they were fed and clothed, unlike other African Americans in Clarksville (p. 14). Even expanding opportunities in elite world-class track did not remove the classed constraints placed upon Rudolph. At the announcement that Rudolph would represent the United States at the 1956 Games in Australia, she remembered folks' excitement in Clarksville and their desire to help defray costs to the athlete's family. Because she had few new clothes, or luggage to carry belongings she did not have, townspeople rallied, "[taking] care of everything," enabling Rudolph to make the journey "in style" (p. 85).

No embodiment issue is more clearly articulated by Rudolph in her autobiography than race and the injustices she faced as an African American. The impact of racism and its wide-ranging effects on young Wilma Rudolph are detailed in the book's first chapter and continue as a theme throughout the entire work. In the opening paragraphs Rudolph confesses two of her life's biggest and earliest disappointments, which stem initially from her favorite memories as a child. In recollections of Christmas and of the yearly Clarksville county fair, Rudolph's faith in the world around her and the things she held most dear were unsettled. Speaking to the disillusionment she felt at being told by her brother that Santa Claus did not exist, Rudolph concedes, "Santa Claus gave me hope; he gave me something to believe in when I was a very little girl" (p. 6). Life was not what she thought or hoped, and she recalls learning these difficult lessons early with Rudolph's earliest memories around race holding a central place in her autobiography. On one level, the Clarksville county fair was one of her favorite yearly events, yet the annual affair cued reminders of the racial system that marginalized and disempowered African Americans. Rudolph remembers all the "black kids" getting together to sit across the entrance to the fairgrounds, where "we'd sit there for hours and hours watching the white people go in and out, dressed in all their fineries and with their fancy horses" (p. 7). She was a young child, and it was the first time she "realized that there were a lot of white people in this world, and that they belonged to a world that was nothing at all like the world we black people lived in" (p. 7). Recognizing cultural power arrangements and racial inequality of life in the Jim Crow South, the future track star concluded, "white people treat their horses better than they treated us black people" (p. 7).

For Rudolph and other African Americans living in the Jim Crow South, race not only mattered; it meant everything. Rudolph's autobiography elaborates, sometimes in rich detail, on the myriad ways in which her blackness pervaded her life story. Rudolph, as a young child, regularly took a bus to Nashville for medical treatments on her disabled leg. The travels, shared with her mother, were continual lessons in the confines of the Jim Crow laws. Rudolph's recollections of the bus rides shed light on the stark world of boundaries demarcated by color and ingrained by convention. The trip, as remembered by Rudolph, always included "a Greyhound bus . . . the same route, and the people who were black [sitting] in the back [of the bus]" (p. 33). The "black ticket window, black waiting area, [and] black bathroom" ensured "you didn't even get near the white people who were making the same trip" (p. 33). Walking through worlds separate *and* unequal, Rudolph remarked that "[e]very once in a while, the bus would get very crowded, like around the Christmas holidays, and if there were white people who didn't have a seat, the black people were expected to give up their seats, and the black people would stand in the aisles the whole way" (p. 33). African American disenfranchisement seemed to her a way of life, normalized, and routine. So familiar and habitual were the rules and injustices of Jim Crow laws that from Rudolph's perspective, it was akin to "people eating turkeys on Thanksgiving" (p. 33).

The pigmentocracy that penetrated all aspects of life in the American South was, on some occasions, far from a simple black-and-white binary. The result created a rare instance for Rudolph in which her skin mitigated what Sidonie Smith calls the "politics of chromatism."[32] Rudolph acknowledges, "I didn't look like a little black girl at all. I had red, sandy hair, [and] a light complexion" (pp. 10–11). She continues, "[m]y brother Wesley . . . he was very black. People would see us walking together, black brother and sister, and they would say, 'Hey, little girl, what you doing walking with *him?*' My mother, you see, was very black, very dark. My father, on the other hand, had a very pale complexion. All of us kids seemed to be different colors" (pp. 10–11). This reprieve, albeit temporary for Rudolph, comes at the expense of her darker-skinned brother Wesley and does little but reinforce the notion of the black body as the abject body.

While Rudolph's recollections of racial discrimination are primarily focused on the track star's early years, experiences beyond Clarksville and athletic success did not make her immune to racial hostility in adulthood. Despite her athletic success and membership on the country's best women's track and field team, as well as on two Olympic teams (and the privilege of travel that came with these team memberships), Rudolph's ventures outside Clarksville and Tennessee continued to be marked by incidents of racism and the geographies of race. On their way to the 1956 Olympic Games in Melbourne, Australia, the American team stopped in Hawaii for the night. While walking down a Honolulu street with two other African American teammates,

Rudolph remembers a white woman gave the three athletes a "horrified look," picked up her dog, and crossed the street, with a look that asked, "What are you natives doing out in the street?" (p. 89). Rudolph laments the encounter; "I never thought I would run into racial prejudice in such a beautiful place as Hawaii, but I did, and that made me sad for the rest of the day" (p. 89). Demoralized, Rudolph concludes, [we] were members of the United States Olympic team but that fact "didn't really matter at all because we were still black, no matter what we did" (p. 89).

Rudolph's observations of others' experiences with racism as well as her own formed her ideas about who she was in an American South that subordinated African Americans as it privileged whites. However, within these experiences of exclusion and seeming powerlessness, Rudolph's autobiographical writings throw into relief many agentic or "talking back" moments responding to racial injustice.[33] Rudolph recalls the resentment she felt that her mother, like so many other black women, labored as a domestic in the homes of white Tennesseans. Rudolph recounts an early racial consciousness and "something not right" about "white folks who got all the luxury [while] we black folks got the dirty work" (p. 8). Other acts of consciousness and resistance by Rudolph and her peers were much more explicit, as she recounts:

> I remember there was this white grocery store not too far from where I lived. We would go there, and we would have to keep our mouths shut inside of the store because that was the proper . . . protocol. It was protocol: white kids could giggle and act silly, black kids had to keep their mouths shut. (p. 10)

On the way to the store, Rudolph remembers, there were taunts from white kids, "hey nigger, get outa town," which prompted physical altercations between the groups of children (p. 10).

> There was this big hill near the grocery store, and we black kids would go to the bottom of this hill on purpose, and we'd kinda be just waiting around for those kids to show up. When they did, they started up with the 'nigger, nigger, nigger' stuff again, and we'd

go after them. But we did all right in them. You know, it got to the point where we black kids used to enjoy going over to that white grocery store, and then laying low on the bottom of that hill. It was the most fun we'd have all week, the highlight. (p. 10)

Rudolph, as an adult writing her autobiography, wondered why her anger at racism and acts of resistance to it did not seem to be shared by other African Americans as a response and approach to the racial status quo. On her frequent trips for treatment on her leg as a child, Rudolph notes, "I was on that same bus from Clarksville to Nashville a couple times a week for four years, I don't know how many trips, and never once did I see a black person resist, or object, to sitting in the back" (p. 34). In explaining the reasons underlying non-responses among African Americans to racism, Rudolph comments, it just "goes to show . . . how much damage had already been done to black people in the South by that time" (p. 33).

Like many African American children living within the oppressive structures of the Jim Crow laws, Rudolph remembers even questioning her parents' responses in telling the future track great to stay silent as the appropriate retort to racist insults. According to Rudolph, her parents were always "telling us kids that we had to accept things, even though we didn't like them, that we had to accept these things because that's just the way it is. Every time one of us spoke out about something that was obviously wrong, my mother or father would say, 'Hold your tongue'" (p. 7). African American parents in the early- to mid-twentieth century in the South were forced to negotiate a solution within an impossible landscape of choices when teaching race to their children. If they or their children spoke out against racism, physical or emotional harm could result. Yet, to say nothing brought the humiliation of Jim Crow down on African Americans with its own kind of harm. "You get scars deep inside of you," Rudolph said of the racism she and others faced every day. Scars, according to the track great, "sometimes never heal" (p. 10).

Efforts by parents to instill self-respect and self-worth within their children were undercut amid the barrage of disparaging acts by whites.

Rudolph's parents like many working-class African Americans of the period instilled in their children that "proper" behavior included not talking back (especially to whites), making no public outbursts, and showing respect for all adults. African American parents believed in these values for their own sake, and thus impressed them upon their children. Moreover, it was hoped that respectable actions and conduct would undercut white notions of black inferiority.[34] Rudolph remarks, "A lot of black kids were raised that way down South, accepting things that weren't right, and their parents told them to accept these things because the parents thought they were protecting the children, protecting them from trouble or from pain" (p. 7).

As a teenager in the mid-1950s, Rudolph's talents in track began, more frequently, to take her beyond Tennessee and the racially oppressive South. With her athletic talent came opportunities and experiences that gave Rudolph a different orientation toward race and civil rights. Introduced to Jackie Robinson at the Penn Relays in Philadelphia in 1956, Rudolph writes that the baseball player complimented her athletic skills and encouraged her to keep on running. "Overwhelmed" by the interaction and the attention paid to her by Robinson, Rudolph writes that it was the "first time I had a black person I could look up to as a real hero. Jackie Robinson, after that day, was my first black hero" (p. 79). In some ways, she discounts the black role models she interacted with on a daily basis: black school teachers, her coach Clinton Gray, and college coach Ed Temple, along with Nell Jackson, the first African American woman to coach an American Olympic team (in 1956). However, Robinson was a national figure in a way that would have certainly impressed Rudolph, and her account of the introduction reveals her admiration for the barrier-breaking Robinson.

Wilma Rudolph's recollections of the Clarksville welcome-home celebration in October 1960 provide another opportunity to examine how race relations were engaged in the autobiography. The event's "social significance," according to Rudolph, extended far beyond the town's excitement at the track star's return. She "vividly" remembered all the day's events, including "the parade [which] broke the color barrier in Clarksville, and who was at the head of it but the white mayor

of town" (p. 144). The evening's tribute to the local heroine, a banquet at the armory, "was jammed with black people and white, and
that had never happened before in Clarksville" (p. 144). Clearly not, as
the color line in 1960 Clarksville, Tennessee, stretched to every corner
of commerce in the town. Thus, the idea of a thousand people, black
and white, sitting down to a meal in the same room was "socially
significant." Rudolph concluded, it "was a historic day for the town,
and certainly for me" (p. 145). As the pace of change in the racial
landscape across the South quickened in this period, Rudolph's homecoming and her remembrances of it signal the pride she felt in being
the reason for progressive social change. Interestingly, she makes no
mention of her role in demanding or even advocating for an integrated
event. This is especially curious, given Rudolph's detailed consider-
ations of racial inequality throughout the book.

Rudolph's responses to racism changed over the years, though its
emotional toll on her never ceased. In 1968, on the day civil rights
activist Martin Luther King Jr. was assassinated in Memphis, Tennessee, Rudolph was traveling home for the funeral of her favorite aunt.
She recalled the tension on the airplane and later at the bus station
in Nashville, where she and her children were waiting to board the
bus for their trip to Clarksville. A white man spit on her children and
Rudolph wrote of her response, "I saw red. I was ready to fight him on
the spot" (p. 161). The man was arrested, but the impact on Rudolph
was significant. She writes, "That topped off a very bad day . . . I think
that night was the absolute low point of my life, mentally. I became
very depressed after that and couldn't seem to snap out of it" (p. 161).
As Wilma Rudolph's autobiographical accounts make clear, her identity as an African American shaped her experiences both before and
after the track star's record-setting performance in Rome. Rudolph,
like other African American female autobiographers, did not have
the "luxury of forgetting race," and thus her narrative is profoundly
imbued by the realities of racism.[35]

Though Rudolph framed her subjectivity largely through the
prism of race, other aspects of her identity, including gender, pervade
her life story. At times, Rudolph speaks with a keen focus on the ways

in which her gendered identity informed her life course. In as many other instances, however, issues related to gender are not explicitly privileged in the narrative and must instead be read in between the lines of text. Or, as Judy Long suggests in discussing women's autobiography, we must attend to how Rudolph "writes gender" into her life story without necessarily spelling it out as such.[36] In speaking to Ann Moody's autobiography *Coming of Age in Mississippi*, author Christy Rishoi offers up an explanation of discussions of identity among African American female writers and thus of use in this context. She suggests that Moody "does not foreground gender as constitutive of identity, in part because liberal discourse allows for only one defining feature of subjectivity." As she adds, Moody's text "most often valorizes the category of race, but gender may be the central origin of the text."[37] Spelman College president Johnetta Cole, in remembering her own narratives of race and gender, admits to becoming aware of "gender issues and the complex relationship between gender and race at the end of the struggles of the sixties, partly because gender differences take a different form in the black community, partly because the race issue seemed more urgent."[38] Rudolph's narrative is similar, as cultural norms around gender are strongly woven throughout the text, though they are less centrally positioned and not as conspicuous as race. Rudolph's consciousness around her gendered identity is born out of exclusion, scorn, and difference, much in the same way she came to understand constructions of race as an African American in the Jim Crow South at midcentury.

Rudolph's entry into organized athletics as a junior high student proved to be one of her earliest recollections in which femaleness mattered. The future track great recounts, "I . . . learned some lessons about what it is like being a girl who loved sports, and about what people thought about such things" (p. 43). Indeed, for many in 1950s America, girls' and women's bodies were not thought to be equipped for or suited to the rigors of competitive sport. Characterizing these dominant narratives as "distorted," Rudolph captured the fundamental tension underlying the perspective: "You couldn't be a lady and a good athlete at the same time" (p. 43). Fears of the mannish female athlete saturated popular and medical discourses of the time, giving many cause to deny women's participation in sport. Though Rudolph had support for athletic involvement from her parents and some peers, these dominant and restrictive gender ideologies circulated in her world as well, and to them she stated, "I hated all that and I always knew, deep inside, that it was a bunch of nonsense" (p. 43). Rudolph's response poses a challenge to dominant institutional practices and ideologies. Shirley Neuman argues that bodies are "not only . . . produced or constructed by social power but also . . . potentially resistant to that power."[39] Rudolph's account provides us with a good case in point. However, the extent to which Rudolph, or any young woman, could completely disavow gender expectations is held in question as she adds, "I loved playing in the games, and I also loved being a lady after the games. I loved to dress up in pretty outfits like any other girl" (p. 44).

It is Wilma Rudolph's love of sport and detailing of the central place of competition in her life that serves to trouble traditional notions of gendered identity, and femininity in particular. Unlike her peers, Rudolph, during her early teenage years, was more "obsessed" with basketball rather than boys. As a consequence of her peers' preoccupation with boys, she claims, they "went through the motions" and never really got involved in sports because they could not "forget the roles they had to play as women or young girls" (p. 44). So while female friends worked to improve their relationships with the opposite sex, Rudolph worked at improving her skills on the basketball court. She "fell in love" (p. 41) with sports and was equally enamored with the competitive elements of the activities. Rudolph scoffed at some of her early track events in which the "play day" atmosphere of fun and frivolity usurped a more competitive environment for participants. Societal ambivalence surrounding female athleticism could not quell Rudolph's enthusiasm for sport. She remembers, "I was the first girl out there at practice and the last one to leave. I loved it so" (p. 62). As a young woman, Wilma Rudolph took herself and the sports she participated in seriously, despite the many wider cultural misgivings. Her autobiography serves as a way of understanding the body as a site of subversive practice as she challenged gender conventions around athleticism. With regard to her early sport experiences, Rudolph concludes, "[t]he other girls may not have been taking it as seriously as I was, but I was winning and they weren't" (p. 50).

Rudolph's competitiveness enabled her to participate and be successful in the highest levels of international sport. Her accomplishments were 'trailblazing,' and on at least one occasion in her autobiography Rudolph accepts credit for widening competitive track opportunities for all women in the United States during the early 1960s. As the first woman to be invited to compete in a number of prestigious previously all-male track and field invitationals, including the New York Athletic Club meet, the Millrose Games, and the *Los Angeles Times* Games, Rudolph's participation required meet organizers to include other women for her to compete against. She recalls, "I was the first, and the doors have been open ever since to women. I'm proud of that to this day. When they invited me, they always invited six or seven other girls to run against me" (p. 147).

Gender arrangements and ideologies, both within and outside the context of sport, shaped Rudolph's autobiography. Some of the experiences, as detailed by the author, are far less explicitly narrated than those outlined above, though they still speak powerfully to Rudolph's gender as well as her racial identity. The mere act of an African American woman writing her life narrative is political, and was especially so decades ago, in the sense that the lives of women of color were viewed as less appealing for, and worthy of, public consumption than (white) men's lives. Writing with a focus on gender, Long concludes that across history and its retelling, "a good woman is defined by her absence."[40] This has been especially so for African American women, whose voices, while never totally silenced, have been marginalized.[41]

Moreover, the many obstacles and experiences that Wilma Rudolph faced throughout her life and that are recounted in her story are gendered. As discussed, Rudolph was forced to negotiate the tensions surrounding femininity and athleticism, as she worked to hone her skills in track and basketball. In addition, her pregnancy, while she was a teenager in high school, added pressure for her to give up her quest to run in the Olympics and instead settle into the role of wife and mother. This was in contrast, generally, to men's entrance into public life, including sport, which is made easier given the constructions of masculinity. Men's autobiographies are no less gendered, but do not share the barriers in accessing public space found in women's stories, including Rudolph's. In this way, autobiographies "tell on" societal gender arrangements by exposing how women engage and steer through these dynamics.[42]

Wilma Rudolph's memories of her pregnancy as a high school senior total far more than a personal coming-of-age story, and instead teach us about the classed, raced, and gendered subject positions that she embodied and lived in the American South at midcentury. In the second half of the chapter entitled "Becoming a Woman," Rudolph acknowledges that by the start of her final year in high school she was "in love" with her boyfriend Robert Eldridge. Childhood sweethearts since elementary school, their relationship became "something else," as their high school years progressed (p. 108). Despite this, Rudolph was "mortified" (p. 109) when told, as part of her physical for the basketball team in her senior season, that she was pregnant. In disbelief, she comments, "I couldn't understand it. Robert and I had just started to get involved in sex, and here I was pregnant. We were both innocent about sex, didn't know about birth control or contraceptives" (p. 109). Despite a lack of knowledge about sex, Rudolph was part of a growing number of teenage girls (black and white) who were sexually active through the 1950s.[43] This change is explained, in part, by a "romantic turn" in youth and high school culture throughout the period, when an increased preoccupation with dating, romance, sex, and marriage took hold. Dating among teenagers blended seamlessly with and was fostered within any number of events and activities sponsored by high schools, from proms to sporting activities.[44] Being romantically linked conferred status on the pair among their peers. Rudolph spoke fondly of wearing Eldridge's letter jacket through the halls of Burt High noting, "we were the top couple in the school" (p. 108).

Responses to Rudolph's pregnancy among friends and family, as well as the response of the track star herself, shed light on the multiple and sometimes competing conventions surrounding teenage sexual activity and out-of-wedlock births within African American communities. The track star's fears about negative reactions to her pregnancy from parents, coaches, and friends were, for the most part, not borne out, however. Rudolph confides, "The people I loved were sticking by me, and that alone took a lot of pressure, and pain, and guilt, off my shoulders" (p. 111). Though her parents and coaches were not thrilled at the news, they, like others in the African American community during this period, were not about to cast Rudolph's transgressions as a permanent, damaging mark upon her honor.[45] In commenting on the community culture, Rudolph observes, "The black girls stayed in school pregnant, like nothing was wrong at all. There were lots of other girls in that school in the same condition that I was, and there really wasn't any stigma to it at all" (p. 112). Interestingly, Rudolph contends that the only shame she felt was not about the pregnancy per se, but the fact that the pregnancy gave some in the community the opportunity to gossip about why she was not running track her senior season of high school.

Wilma Rudolph's decision to delay marriage and enroll at Tennessee State just weeks after giving birth to her daughter, Yolanda, dislodges dominant scripts woven around gender norms and expectations of the period. Rudolph defied a more general pattern that encouraged early marriage among teens by the second half of the 1950s.[46] Well aware of the rare opportunities in front of her, Rudolph confides, "I really didn't want to become a housewife at such an early age, I knew I could still be a runner, and I wanted to be able to go to the Olympics in 1960" (p. 114). With arrangements made for the newborn to live with Rudolph's sister in St. Louis, the notion of "abandon[ing]" university enrollment and a track career was unthinkable. It "would have killed me," Rudolph concludes (p. 114). So within months of her high school graduation and with a distanced ease, Rudolph states, "I put marriage out of my head, and went off to school" (p. 114).

A scholarship awaited her there, and speaking as though the entire episode was reminiscent of a hurdle to be overcome in a track event, Rudolph notes that "all [she] had to do" in the intervening weeks after giving birth was to run on her own to prepare for the upcoming track season (p. 112). In narrating the stories about her pregnancy, Rudolph offers us insight into the embodied position she occupies as an African American woman living in the mid-twentieth-century South.

However, far more than simply the sum of her subject positions as an African American and a woman from a poor socioeconomic position, Wilma Rudolph's autobiography provides us with a valuable perspective on embodiment for someone at the intersection of multiple marginalized identities.[47] The notion of "intersectionality," first defined by legal scholar Kimberlee Crenshaw, compels us to interrogate the "multidimensionality of marginalized subjects."[48] It is near the conclusion of Rudolph's autobiography, particularly in the final two short chapters, that the author is the most explicit in detailing experiences of a life lived at the intersection of her classed, raced, and gendered identities. Tellingly, the financial and professional disappointments she had weathered in the seventeen years since Rome prompt Rudolph's recollections of her multiple identities at the margins in the second-to-last chapter, titled "Retirement." Unable to find well paying, satisfying employment, Rudolph acknowledges that she was depressed and "besieged by money problems" (p. 163). The decade that started so gloriously for Wilma Rudolph was coming to an unremarkable end by the late 1960s. After a variety of short-lived jobs around the country, Rudolph laments, "I wanted more out of life for myself and my family. Eight years had gone by since I won the three gold medals in the Olympics, and I still hadn't found fulfillment out of track that I had found in it" (p. 161). Speaking to a fundamental tension in her post-Olympic world, Rudolph concedes, "people were always expecting me to be a star; but I wasn't making the money to live like one" (p. 163). Like the accomplished female athletes before her, Rudolph was unable to capitalize on her celebrity, claiming, "I felt exploited both as a woman and as a black person, and this bothered me very much" (p. 163).

Rudolph's final chapter, and also her shortest, at only five pages, titled "Today," continues the themes of the multiple dimensions of her "embodied *other*" status. She begins the chapter with a tribute, of sorts, to three African American female Olympians largely lost to history: Alice Coachman, Mildred McDaniel, and Mae Faggs. Though she incorrectly details some of their achievements, Rudolph's point is to underscore how the politics of racism and sexism serve to explain the athletes' obscurity in memory and in the historical record. She writes, "The fact of the matter is that black women athletes are on the bottom rung of the ladder in American sports" (p. 167). In an indictment of the limited athletic opportunities available to African American women, Rudolph argues, "[m]ost of them are involved in track and field because that's the only sports [sic] still really open to them" (pp. 167–68). She continues using the third person, distancing her comments from her own first-person realities: "When their track careers are over, no matter what they've accomplished in the Olympics, there is no place for them to go. They wind up drifting back to where they began, and nobody ever hears from them again" (p. 168).[49] So, while Rudolph chose not to write this section in first person, these words speak directly to her experiences, as much as any other aforementioned African American female athlete. Despite their grand achievements in athletics, Rudolph mourns the passing of these athletes, and herself, from our collective memory.

At a loss for explanations to bring about change and greater opportunity for African American women in sport, Rudolph, like other black women in the 1970s, is clear what is *not* [emphasis added] a path to a solution. When pressed to explain her decision not to get involved in the women's liberation movement as a course of action to bring about more equitable treatment, Rudolph's response speaks to the uniqueness of African American women's lives at the intersections of multiple marginalized identities. The "women's lib movement," Rudolph begins, is "not exactly relevant to my problems" (p. 169). With regard to perspectives on employment, Rudolph notes that black women work out of necessity because the realities of racism prohibit black men from earning a wage to support a family—indeed, much as her own situation, in which she, not her husband Robert, was the sole or higher-wage-earning adult in the family. With so little available to black men, Rudolph notes, African American women worked "because they had to, not because they wanted to acquire new identities," as, she argues, was the case with white women (p. 169). She continues that the African American women with whom she has had contact "don't listen to the women's liberation rhetoric because they know that it's nothing but a bunch of white women who had certain life-styles and who want to change those life-styles. They say things like they don't want men opening doors for them anymore, and they don't want men lighting their cigarettes for them anymore. Big deal. Black women have been opening doors for a couple of centuries in this country. Black women don't quibble about things that are not important" (p. 169). Though African American women were engaged in second-wave feminist activity throughout the 1960s and 1970s, the public face of the women's liberation movement was white. The movement's direction and focus followed in that direction as well, largely serving the needs, realities, and interests of segments of the white female population.[50] This was the women's movement Rudolph saw and experienced in the decades following Rome 1960.

Rudolph's narrative comes on the heels of a number of other African American women whose voices had been pushed to the margins by the women's movement and liberation struggles for racial equality. In the first half of the 1970s, several prominent African American women wrote books, both fiction and autobiographical, which stand as points of comparison for Rudolph's life history, both in her approach and also as contextual points of reference. Toni Morrison's *The Bluest Eye* (1970) and *Sula* (1973) precede *Wilma* earlier in the decade, and both have withstood the passage of time, finding themselves on required reading lists for undergraduate students in a variety of courses. Daisy Bates, of the Little Rock Nine, and civil rights activist Anne Moody wrote their autobiographies in 1962 and 1968 (*The Long Shadow of Little Rock: A Memoir* and *Coming of Age in Mississippi*, respectively), with social activist and professor Angela Davis penning her life history in 1975.[51] In the year following the publication of *Wilma*, the Combahee River Collective published their own collection of politically minded work, which shifted the tenor and dialogue of black women's position in American culture, as well as bringing the intersection of race and gender to the forefront in the discussion of black women's identity. Rudolph's book was published only months after the Combahee River Collective, a group of black feminists, began meeting in the Northeast. The Collective published the Combahee River Collective Statement the next year. The statement has been identified as one of the "most compelling documents by black feminists"[52] and is credited with the initial use of the phrase "identity politics"—which the group defined as "a politics that grew out of our objective material experiences as Black women."[53] Though Rudolph makes no reference to the writings of those listed above, her autobiography in 1977 sits amid the increasing tide of black feminism during the period. At this point in the autobiography, as well as a couple of others, Rudolph had the opportunity to insert herself into dialogue about civil and women's rights. Her supposed insistence on an integrated welcome home parade in 1960, as well as her civil rights agitation outside a Clarksville restaurant in 1963, go unattended in *Wilma*. In the 1970s moment in which the book was written, Rudolph chose to "silence" parts of her identity/history so as to not disrupt the narrative's "end point."[54]

Wilma Rudolph, in the final few paragraphs of her autobiography, ends with a discussion about the centrality and importance of family, thus aligning herself with larger narrative patterns and themes found in women's life stories and more specifically in African American female self-writing.[55] Despite her sometimes very public life, it is the private, familial spaces that occupy the book's conclusion.[56] In the context of concluding remarks about the frustrations of underemployment and inability to capitalize on her fame, Rudolph notes that her "fulfillment today comes from my family" (p. 170). Unsure of what might lie ahead, Rudolph ends by saying, "The future? I really don't know what it holds. I've settled with my family into a nice house in a suburb of Clarksville and plan to stay there. I can tell you this, though, whatever the future holds, I'll be ready for it, for I've learned a family's a powerful thing" (p. 172).

Wilma Rudolph's embodied subject position matters and is central to the autobiographical narrative she constructs. In a provocative line of questioning, Sidonie Smith asks, "[W]hat might autobiographical writing have to do with skin?" Responding to her own inquiry, Smith adds, "[M]uch I think—as the body of the text, the body of the narrator, the body of the narrated I, the cultural body, and the body politic all merge in skins and skins of meaning."[57] Rudolph brings her lived experiences to the pages of text, and in doing so helps shed light on the nuances of the raced, classed, and gendered spaces she occupied. Our aim has been, as Smith suggests, to "look at the cultural practices that surface on the body to get at the emergence of the autobiographical subject."[58] Wilma Rudolph's autobiography is an important piece, and yet provides only a fraction of the many stories told in representing and remembering the Olympic champion. *Wilma* serves as the foundation for the 1977 television biopic, as well as a number of children's books. It is to those representations of the Olympian that we now turn.

Wilma

Biopics, Nostalgia, and Family in the 1970s

IN DECEMBER 1977 the National Broadcasting Company (NBC) aired the biographical film (or biopic) *Wilma*, detailing the first twenty years of the life of 1960 three-time Olympic gold-medalist Wilma Rudolph (played by Shirley Jo Finney).[1] Promoted as a "fact-based" drama, the film was produced by Olympic filmmaker Bud Greenspan and was part of the relatively new made-for-television movie genre, first introduced in the mid-1960s.[2] Though a number of sport biographies preceded *Wilma*, it was among the first in this category of film to feature a black woman.[3] Greenspan, speaking about the film and his depiction of Wilma Rudolph, said, "I didn't want to make a cliché out of her character. I wanted hers to be a true sports story."[4] Greenspan's "truth," according to one critic, focused "as much on Wilma's parents and coach as it [did] on Wilma."[5] Indeed the film's preoccupation with family, notably Rudolph's relationship with her father, is a (if not the) major thread around which the biopic is woven.

Part of our direction in this chapter is to try to make sense of this focus on family, especially in light of Rudolph's autobiography, on which the biopic is based. Published just months prior to the television debut of *Wilma*, Rudolph's memoir discusses family but certainly does not feature it to the same degree. We argue that Greenspan's construction of Rudolph's young life in this biopic strengthens mythical notions of family, including a reaffirmation of the institution's patriarchal center, consistent with the sport narrative. We also read this film as a product of the historical moment in which it was created, the mid- to late 1970s. Our analysis moves from the assumptive position that the biopic *Wilma*, and any cultural product for that matter, cannot and should not be examined and understood as distinct from its moment of origination. Moreover, the film looks back nearly three decades from its production date, spending a good deal of time centered on Rudolph's life in the 1950s, and in doing so offers us an opportunity to explore how history is depicted in popular film. We agree with Aaron Baker's conclusions about sport biopics and argue that *Wilma* looks "back in time through a lens of [the] present" and as a result may have more to say about the 1970s than about any mid-century moment in which the film is set.[6]

Germane to our analysis is Elsebeth Hurup's contention that film in the 1970s was "[absorbed] with the fifties" in serving as a "locus of nostalgia."[7] Nostalgia's "longing for a home that no longer exists or has never existed" plays itself out in *Wilma*, we contend, as the audience is reassured of the patriarchal nuclear family's centrality and value precisely at the historical moment in which that ideal appeared lost in a 1970s environment of change.[8] Filmmakers turned a nostalgic gaze toward the 1950s as the events of the 1970s continually threatened to erode the hopefulness and confidence embedded in the stories many Americans told themselves about their country. As Americans worked to make sense of the political, social, and economic upheavals of the 1970s, so too did filmmakers with their attempts to recapture the "mesmerizing lost reality of the Eisenhower era" on the screen.[9] Greenspan's nostalgic turn toward the past, one observer commented, enabled the producer to "push his admittedly old-fashioned ideals."[10]

Wilma, produced and aired in the 1970s, was certainly not alone in its nostalgic portrayal of an earlier time through the medium of television. Stephen Brie suggests that the television series, *The Waltons* (1972–81) served precisely this function as it provided viewers a "therapeutic flight of fancy" and "gentle escape from the trials" of the "turbulent 1970s" by gazing back at the 1930s.[11] Though there are differences, the long-running series is similar to *Wilma* in at least one fundamental way: both created in the 1970s, each evokes memories of family coherence and resilience despite the troubles faced within a clan by romanticizing a past. In each, conservative renderings of the past, presented in the text, serve to sanitize and depoliticize history. Despite the many hardships facing both the Waltons and the Rudolphs, family is presented as a self-sustaining unit, capable of meeting and overcoming challenges regardless of size or complexity.

The Waltons television series was just one of many cultural markers of the 1970s that worked to idealize a past that was either long gone or never real. Film, music, fashion, and Hollywood icons of the 1950s were swept up in a 1970s nostalgic "revival," according to a *Newsweek* article in late 1972. Writing for the magazine, Johnathan Rodgers opined that despite (or because of) being the "blandest decade ever," a "revival of those very . . . quiet years is swirling across the nation like a runaway Hula-Hoop."[12] Elvis, sock hops, and Marilyn Monroe sweatshirts, among other items and figures, characterized the uptick during the 1970s of all things midcentury. Necessitated by feelings of loss and displacement, nostalgic turns, such as these, are set amid a longing for continuity in a fragmented world. Tensions and fissures of the 1970s prompted nostalgic tendencies as a "defense mechanism" of sorts, deployed as the "accelerated rhythms of life and historical upheavals" marked the decade.[13] No social turbulence was more impactful on the construction of *Wilma* than that of the changing parameters of family life and structure, both perceived and real, over the 1970s.

For some, the nuclear family was under attack and in a state of upheaval in the 1970s as a result of broader economic, political, and social forces. The perceived decline of the American family led psychologist Urie Bronfenbrenner to conclude, in early 1977, that while it was not the first time the institution was at risk it was the worst, with the consequences "approaching the calamitous." Gone, he said, were "family picnics, long Sunday dinners, children and parents working together fixing the house, preparing meals, hiking in the woods, singing and dancing with other families or friends."[14] The family's demise in the United States was for some the result of greater numbers of women entering the paid labor force throughout the decade, the climbing divorce rate, and the women's movement, and was even connected to anxieties about the nation's perceived decline in a global context.[15] In a slight contrast to the US data, especially as it related to the demise of the black family documented in the Moynihan Report, *Good Times*, a Norman Lear produced sitcom in the 1970s, portrayed the Evans family, as an intact family living in Chicago's Cabrini Green. Still, this show devolved into a minstrel-like depiction of black family life to such a degree that cast members left the show in disgust at the portrayal of black urban life.[16]

The family was in crisis, or so it seemed, and responses to the situation informed various media constructions, including, we argue, the thematic emphasis of *Wilma*. With that said, we note that cinema's long history and consistent engagement with the sphere of family extends far beyond the 1970s. However, we counter that the particular strains perceived or real upon the American family were especially acute during the decade of the 1970s. Television's "ubiquity," according to Ella Taylor, " . . . and its intensely domestic character make it an ideal narrative form in which to observe changing ideas about family," especially so in 1970s America.[17] We believe it is important to situate *Wilma*, as a historical document, within this context, in that it offers up an explanation of the themes addressed in the film as well as those issues and tensions left out.

As family is moved to the narrative center in the film, other issues informing Rudolph's identity as a poor black girl born and raised in the Jim Crow South are obscured to the point of erasure. The ideological constraints and structural inequalities around race, gender, and class are nowhere to be seen in the film; Rudolph's early life is instead cloaked in the American mythology of individualism so characteristic of sport films, including biopics. Interestingly, Rudolph's childhood disability is given attention in the film, but only to illustrate how, with the aid of a loving family, a personal desire to overcome will prevail. Thus Rudolph, her experiences, and her story are instead framed "as adequately represented by the individual desires, goals, and emotional dramas of the main characters," according to Baker.[18] Melodrama does not permit space for history's complexity or context; Rudolph's life and her experiences are flattened, simplified, and made two-dimensional.

The film's uplifting storyline and its neglect of larger social issues and forces reflected both the general tenor of the sport film genre and Bud Greenspan's personal orientation and perspective on sport.[19]

By the time *Wilma* aired near the end of 1977, Bud Greenspan was said to be the nation's "foremost producer of sports documentaries," with the multi-part series *The Olympiad* broadcast in mid-1976 and *The Glory of Their Times* on baseball heroes of the early twentieth century televised in 1977, among others.[20] Described as a "romanticized flashback to a simpler era," *The Glory of Their Times* was a precursor of things to come in *Wilma*.[21] Thus, in many ways Bud Greenspan's *Wilma* blended well with this larger body of work that "unapologetically glorified athletes for overcoming injuries, failures, and obstacles with a straightforward storytelling style intended to strike emotional chords."[22] Indeed, for Greenspan, his "greatest kick" rested with "seeing people overcome adversity."[23] Critics of his work, including unfavorable reviews of *Wilma*, characterized the rose-colored perspective that Greenspan's films often took as "lighter fare" and even "propaganda" in their refusal to weave together anything but inspirational tales.[24] Greenspan consistently dismissed his critics by arguing that the "lyrical poetry of sports" would and should win out over the "constant drone of hyped-up sports on television."[25] Despite the sometimes critical voices of reviewers, the "cinematic comfort food" Greenspan served up seemed well suited to audiences, including the Rudolph biopic, with *Wilma* garnering forty-two percent of the primetime audience in its television debut.[26]

Our decision to include *Wilma* as part of this larger project had little to do with the film's apparent popularity with the television audience in 1977, however. Instead, part of our aim in interrogating *Wilma* is to privilege television and film as important sites of historical inquiry and knowledge. As Robert A. Rosenstone argues, "contemporary forms of expression" such as film in the twentieth century became the "chief medium for carrying the stories our culture tells itself."[27] He concludes, and we agree, that to leave these newer representations "out of the equation when we think of the meaning of the past is to condemn ourselves to ignore the way a huge segment of the population has come to understand the events and people that comprise history."[28] Indeed, for many, "Hollywood History is the only history," and for that reason the biopic and other filmic representations warrant our attention.[29]

While film may "carry the stories of our culture" to millions of people, how well that is accomplished, as well as the strength of the story, remains a topic of debate among historians, since biopics attract a fair share of attention and criticism.[30] Biopics, according to George F. Custen, are "to [social] history what Caesar's Palace is to architectural history: an enormous, engaging distortion, which after a time convinces us of its own authenticity."[31] Far from simply stretching the truth, television, Custen adds, creates myth by telling tales "suited to the reading habits of its audiences."[32] Movies, including biopics, "function as night school, a great repository of historical consciousness in these United States of Amnesia."[33] Custen quips that [people] in the United States in the second half of the twentieth century learn history by "slouching on the couch like a common vegetable watching a small box."[34] These creation stories are significant because television defines what lives are worth telling and shapes the parameters on which those lives hold, or fail to hold, value for many viewers whose historical knowledge begins and ends with television.[35]

Biopic supporters are forced to spend energy defending the genre in the face of criticism and in the context of a general disdain for and bias towards biographical film. Those championing the genre should embrace the term "biopic" despite its "pejorative odor," according to Dennis Bingham. He adds, "I believe those of us who take the genre seriously should reappropriate that tangy word 'biopic' and unfurl it in the faces of all those who have treated the genre with the smugness they accuse the biopic of possessing in volumes."[36] Choosing instead to call the category "biofilm" versus "biopic," Rosenstone, in support of film and as a counter to critics, adds that no source evidence used by historians has the corner on truth.[37] Moreover, history, for Rosenstone and others, can "never be a clear mirror of the past (as some seem to wish film to be), but must always be a proximate construction of a vanished world, a construction that contains its own fictions."[38]

Our perspective on biopics in general and on *Wilma* in particular falls between the positions argued by Custen and Rosenstone. Consequently, while we are critical of *Wilma* and its shortcomings, our intent is not to dismiss the genre in its entirety, as we are mindful of the potential importance of film to our understanding of the past. If, as Rosenstone suggests, films that have historical angles help us make meaning of the past, then *Wilma* is a good case in point. We argue this not in spite of *Wilma*'s ahistorical tendencies, but because of them.

The biopic follows a number of filmic conventions, including the oft-repeated rags-to-riches trope, which is especially characteristic of sport film and is established in the movie's first couple of minutes. By the three-minute mark of *Wilma*, viewers bear witness to the distance traveled, and the obstacles overcome, by the track star as Rudolph's triple gold medal performance on the world-wide stage is juxtaposed with the athlete's humble beginnings in rural Tennessee two decades earlier. The film opens with actual footage from the opening ceremonies at the Rome Games in 1960. An aerial shot scans the tens of thousands of fans in the stadium as a cacophonous mix of a sophisticated musical score, singing, and cheers rings out. Dozens of waving flags highlight the event's internationality. The scene rises to a crescendo as a runner enters the stadium and lights the Olympic cauldron. The excitement and electricity remain as the film cuts to the start of the women's 100 meter final eight days later. Beginning with actual Olympic footage is one way in which Olympic biopics assert their "facticity," claims Custen, and thereby can lay more solid truth claims on the footage that follows over the course of the remainder of the film.[39]

This initial scene is set in contrast to the next, as the film shifts to rural Tennessee in 1944. The cosmopolitan milieu of Rome and the Games' opening ceremony is quickly erased and replaced with images intent on highlighting the Rudolph family home, and the life from which the track star came, as slow, simple, and unsophisticated. Over the noise of a cow mooing and a handful of children playing is the crude sound of a series of single-key piano strikes. The camera pans a wooded area, highlighting a small, ramshackle cabin. Four-year-old Wilma Rudolph enters the frame, limping and frail, falling to the ground in tears. Rudolph's father and mother, working in nearby fields, quickly run to the child's aid, gathering her up in their arms and taking her into the house. Rural settings, including those featured in the film, bring their own nostalgia through a set of powerful images which mythologize the countryside and sometimes its inhabitants as founded on and committed to family, hard work, and community.[40]

Rudolph's family, from this initial scene forward, is marked as a central influence in helping her not only conquer physical disability but also set the foundation on which her future athletic success is built. In this way, *Wilma* blends well with other television biopics that have historically featured athletes whose physical disabilities are overcome in their quest toward athletic excellence.[41] Rudolph's disability and her family's response to her illness form the cornerstone of the film's first twenty-five minutes. Conversely, institutionalized and ideological patterns of disability discrimination are absent in the biopic. Instead, images and narratives of a family's determination to heal the young Rudolph occupy the film's center. In the movie's initial minutes, several of Rudolph's brothers and sisters are enlisted and receive instruction on how to best move her frail and limp leg through strengthening exercises. In a subsequent scene Rudolph's mother lectures the other children on the importance of kin, after a day in which they failed to include the young disabled girl in a basketball game. "We is all ONE family" Rudolph's mother begins, "I know you love your sister, but lovin' Wilma is not enough. You all got to treat her special . . . it ain't been easy on Wilma and you kids is all she's got." Rudolph's father, sitting in silence throughout the scolding adds, "Your mama is right. You've got to take care of your sister, special care." The scene cuts away, but not before the importance of family is restated and the patriarch is afforded, literally, the last word on the issue. Custen argues that television biopics in their work to "enshrine normalcy" situate the family as the "rock that supports all else in society; people will—and implicitly should—do anything to preserve this form."[42]

Throughout the 1970s the structure and form of the American family changed with increasing rates of divorce, children born out of wedlock, and women working outside of the home.[43] The sum of these broader cultural and social shifts prompted some observers to ask if the family would cease to exist under the weight of the tensions playing upon it. It was not simply the growing presence of more female-headed households but the absence of fathers within those spaces that stirred fear and anxiety among some during the decade. Once thought to be an issue for blacks and the poor, "families shaped by divorce and separation, single parenthood, and dual wage earner[s] were becoming more visible."[44] As the biopic aired in 1977, Bud Greenspan's nostalgic portrayal of Rudolph's family was positioned within this wider context in which the institution appeared to be in a tenuous state of flux and uncertainty. Indeed, Greenspan, in characterizing the biopic, observed, "What could be more moving and more inspirational than the story of a poor girl from a loving and large family . . ."[45]

A television production contemporary to Rudolph's biopic, *Roots*, the award-winning mini-series broadcast in early 1977, provides us with another important site to explore television constructions of family during this period. Historian Natasha Zaretsky suggests that Alex Haley's attention to "the family" in *Roots* "was a universal category that could foster a sense of connection among diverse Americans."[46] The shifting contours and tensions playing upon national identity during the decade informed constructions of the mini-series as well as explaining its overwhelming popularity. As ethno-racial groups across the United States asserted their autonomy on the heels of 1960s social movements, they challenged "melting pot" images of diversity. Interestingly, according to Zaretsky, this tendency toward cultural pluralism, versus a monolithic American populous, was well illustrated in 1976, as Bicentennial celebration planners "showcase[d] rather than downplay[ed] pluralism." The organizers urged those around the country to commemorate the occasion "within their own families and through the affirmation of kinship and blood ties."[47] Moreover, these domestic cultural shifts, combined with national and international "traumas" of the early 1970s, impacted the nation's psyche. The Vietnam War, the OPEC oil embargo, and President Richard Nixon's involvement in the Watergate scandal remained fresh in the nation's cultural memory. Subsequently, this turn toward the family resonated with many because the thought of celebrating the nation was too much of a reminder of the country's failings. Organizers instead "foreground[ed] the local, the tribal, the familial."[48] Thus, the success of *Roots*, especially among whites, was the result of its "essential conservatism; it unabashedly celebrated the family."[49] In much the same way, Greenspan says of his biopic on Rudolph, "I'm hoping the viewers see some part of their own family life and aspirations in the story of *Wilma*."[50]

Wilma follows classic lines of female biopics: familial conflict is not tangential to the movie's drama, but is integral to it, and these frictions drive the film. Importantly, these discordant moments within the Rudolph family throw into relief a range of issues, including changing gender ideologies and (whites') perceptions of black families that were dominant discourses throughout the 1970s. It is worth noting, however, that the film ends with Rudolph at age twenty, not allowing her to fulfill the classic female roles of wife and mother. Female biopics have for decades, Bingham argues, "play[ed] on tensions between a woman's public achievements and women's traditional orientation to home, marriage, and motherhood." In consequence, female biopics often find suffering (and therefore drama) in a public woman's very inability to make her decisions and discover her own destiny."[51] In *Wilma*, Rudolph struggles with others' expectations of her as a girl/woman, following the more general trend within female biopics. In addition, the drama is imagined and sustained around Rudolph's father's misgivings surrounding the young track star's budding independence, her growing intimacy with her boyfriend, and her subsequent teenage pregnancy. Rudolph's sister Tootie, early in the film, acknowledges their father's protective impulses. When asked by Coach Gray how Rudolph's parents would respond to Wilma attending an athletic summer camp with Coach Temple at Tennessee State, Tootie concedes: "I think Mama would be okay, but I don't know about

Papa. See, Skeeter's [Wilma] only fifteen and Papa don't want have happen to her what happen to me [pregnancy]."

Rudolph's father as patriarchal authority is just one of several male characters in the film who guide the young track star through life's trials. In a nearly eight minute, three-scene segment, Rudolph's college coach Ed Temple is introduced to viewers at approximately the film's twenty-six minute mark. Across the several minutes of film, Temple is center-stage, with almost no other dialogue except his own filling the screen. Indeed, no character in the film, including Wilma Rudolph's, is afforded a sequence of uninterrupted dialogue like that given to Temple in this section of the movie. Over the span of several minutes the audience is given an introduction to Temple in his multiple, as well as varied, roles on Tennessee State's campus. Whether working in the college post office, delivering a lecture as a sociology professor, or giving a "pep talk" as coach to the track squad, Temple moves through these activities with a precise, quick-witted, and commanding presence.

Temple's sage comments distinguish his place as the authority across the diverse settings in which he is represented. For example, initially Temple is in the university post office placing articles of mail into their respective slots with the help of a student assistant who comments, "Ain't got much time [to get to class] Mr. Temple." To which Temple responds, "I got plenty of time. You just worry about getting this mail out and let me worry about the time." Though standing with his back to Temple, the student's eye rolling does not even escape the coach's ability to see all. "And you can quit givin' me one of your looks," Temple quips. As the short scene ends, the exactness of Temple's routine and his control of the situation are never in question as he places the last piece of mail into a slot, saying "*now* [italics added] it's time," just at the precise moment when the school bell rings signaling a class change.

The audience's introduction to Coach Temple continues in the second of three scenes, which highlight his skills as a professor at Tennessee State. In a nearly three-and-a-half-minute soliloquy, and perhaps the movie's most puzzling scene, Temple captures the interest and attention of students as he lectures on the meaning of sociology and culture. Greenspan uses the World War II battle at Guadalcanal as a point of departure for Temple to illustrate how cultural differences between Japanese and US soldiers inform and alter reactions to provocation. Temple's lecture commences with a story of an exchange between the two warring nations' soldiers at Guadalcanal. In the middle of the night with the Japanese nearby, Temple begins, a US soldier yells out, "'Hirohito's a dirty chicken plucker!'" As more US personnel join in, Japanese troops charge out of foxholes to confront the enemy's verbal assault of their nation's leader, only to be killed by the waiting American soldiers. The Japanese, explains Temple, "love their emperor and ain't nobody can insult their emperor" even if responding, in this case, results in certain death for the soldiers. The next night, Temple continues, the Japanese attempt the same strategy on the American soldiers with shouts of "'Roosevelt's a dirty chicken plucker'" and ready themselves to shoot and kill the anticipated stampede of US troops. However, there are no charging US soldiers, much to the surprise of the Japanese. Instead, a US soldier yells back, "'you darn right Roosevelt's a dirty chicken plucker. If it wasn't for him we wouldn't be here!'" Temple concludes, "Now *that's* sociology!" Temple's lecture example is as interesting as it is baffling. Like other examples in *Wilma*, the Guadalcanal story can be read as having more to say about the political climate of the 1970s than the midcentury time in which it is set. In the immediate post-Nixon era of the mid- to late 1970s, the public's cynicism about US political leadership, including the Office of the President, was at its zenith. The nation's trust and confidence in elected officials was shaken to the core on the heels of the Watergate scandal, leaving in its wake a palpable feeling of betrayal among many in the United States toward those in the nation's highest office.[52] Ultimately, Greenspan's lengthy attention to acquainting viewers with Temple offers us little toward understanding the context of 1950s America and importantly the tensions and issues playing upon Wilma Rudolph. But while we do not learn much about the period, we do learn a great deal about Ed Temple, and the scene helps to establish the coach as an authority.

While Ed Temple is privileged as the primary character in these protracted scenes, he and Rudolph's father are not the only male figures who occupy the film's center. The track star's high school coach, Clinton Gray, as well as her boyfriend, Robert, are central to the film. It is Rudolph's relationships with each of these men that form the foundation on which this film is built. Rudolph's athleticism and her many achievements in that arena are an afterthought in the biopic; male characters' emotions and motivations are principal. For example, Rudolph's growing autonomy stirred unease for her father, and that became one of the biopic's major storylines. When asked by Coach Temple if Rudolph, who was still in high school, could attend Tennessee State's summer camp in track, the young athlete's father first makes reference to his daughter's sickly childhood: "my little girl had lots of bad times when she was growin'. Don't want no more bad times." For him, "bad times" no longer meant the pain of a childhood leg infirmity, but rather an issue integrally connected to Rudolph's maturation in young womanhood. Rudolph's father continues, "Her [Rudolph's] sister Tootie did all this runnin' and schoolin' before her. All she got was bad. Tootie's a mama and the child ain't got no papa. You know what I'm sayin?" To which Coach Temple is quick to respond, "Yes sir, I do. Mr. Rudolph, I got rules and they rules like for my own child. Your little girl break any of my rules I'll send her home faster than you can shake a stick." The scene ends as Rudolph's father agrees, permitting his daughter to attend Temple's camp, but not before restating, "this one [Wilma] ain't gonna have no more bad times. You know what I'm saying?" As the two patriarchs negotiate the boundaries and conditions of young Rudolph's life, she is voiceless throughout and, as in numerous other scenes in the film, is not even present over the course of the exchange between her father and future coach.

We see Rudolph's relationship with Robert deepen over the course of the film and her father's anxieties grow as a result. Just after the young couple leaves on a date, Rudolph's father asks her mother suspiciously, "They keepin' company?" To which Rudolph's mother replies, "Lord have mercy. If Skeeter and Robert goin' together means they's

keepin' company, they's keepin' company. What you thinkin' about
Ed? Well now, nothin' going to stop Skeeter from goin' to college."
Rudolph's mother's lenient perspective on her daughter's growing
intimacy with Robert is set in contrast to the track star's hyper-vigi-
lant and cautious father, who views the relationship with skepticism.

The active presence of African American men, and in particular
Rudolph's father as the ultimate patriarchal authority on this point
and others, in the young athlete's life and within the context of her
family and community, is significant, given misgivings throughout
the 1970s about the perceived failings of "the black family."[53] While
family arrangements changed for all families, regardless of race and
ethnicity, over the 1970s, none seemed more threatening to white
society as those within black families. Skyrocketing unemployment
rates among black men and relatively high divorce rates nurtured stereotypes of black men as lazy, immoral, and violent. The 1970s hit
Good Times reinforced these images of black men with several male
characters, including the father, being unemployed, and JJ, the son,
being presented as lazy and unmotivated.[54] Unable to take his rightful place as head-of-household, the black man was believed unable
to fulfill his familial and societal obligations, resulting in the ruin of
the institution of the family. In this view, black women shouldered
their share of blame as well. Described as controlling matriarchs, black
women were said to have far too much power within the home.[55] Black
families, it seemed in this worldview, were far removed from the white
nuclear family ideal. With structural and ideological barriers around
race left unattended, black men and women were instead cast as social
deviants unable or unwilling to create and sustain environments in
which the patriarchal nuclear family existed and flourished. With that
said, Greenspan's attention to Rudolph's pregnancy might be said to
spur racist stereotypes of black families that permeated the 1970s.
However, we assert that the positioning of men in the biopic as central
to family functioning and in control undermine this reading. Far from
absent, the black men in Wilma Rudolph's life are very much present,
reaffirming patriarchal conventions and the institution's authority and
rightful place in the process.

Rudolph's father's fears are realized and the track star does get pregnant while still in high school. Rudolph's pregnancy prompts several exchanges in which tensions are marked by competing perspectives on marriage and motherhood as well as female ambition. Soon after it is known that Rudolph is pregnant, Coach Temple and her father debate and struggle over the athlete's future in a terse exchange. Angry at his daughter's pregnancy, Rudolph's father informs Coach Temple that his daughter will remain at home to care for her child, rather than accept the athletic scholarship offered by Tennessee State University. Temple makes his desires clear as well: "When all of this business is over I still want Wilma to come to the college." To which Rudolph's father responds, "she ain't goin' to no college . . . the child gonna be a mama. She gonna take care of her child like her mama."

Single parent families and teenage pregnancy, issues said to be threatening America's families in the 1970s, also seemed on the verge of imperiling the Rudolphs'. However, Greenspan reassures viewers that the child's father, Robert, is eager to take on his parental obligations as head-of-household. Robert claims he would marry Rudolph immediately but adds, "all Skeeter want to do is go to the Rome Olympics." Well within the bounds of the classic female biopic, *Wilma* plays on the conflicts that appear to inevitably rise out of and parallel women's ambition. Robert again makes his position clear by asking Rudolph, "What's wrong with getting married?" To which Rudolph replies, "Robert, you know I love you, right? But if we get married now, everything is lost, school, the Olympics. I know I don't ever want to lose you." The biopic's drama is powered by Rudolph's angst in having to reconcile the competing pressures of personal ambition and obligation to family. As society in the 1970s struggled with the shift in women's roles, specifically the growing number of women's achievements in education and careers, so too did Greenspan's construction of Rudolph's life.[56]

Wilma Rudolph's actions are consistently scrutinized by the men in the film, as her conduct is debated, evaluated, and judged by her father, coaches, and boyfriend. Their voices, and not Rudolph's, fill the frame. One particular exchange between Coach Gray and Robert is illustrative of the tenor of the discourse surrounding Rudolph. Coach Gray asks Robert what might be at the core of the recent tensions and subsequent arguments between the young couple. To which Robert responds:

> Well when she come back from the Olympics [Australia] two years ago with a medal I thought she'd act up some then. All the other girls acting up and being jealous, whispering behind her back, laughing and gigglin' you know. Saying funny things. First time they talk about how big she was, call her funny lookin' and coach's pet. Makin' fun of us goin' together. Saying Skeeter goin' with me 'cause now that she's an Olympic star she got to go out with a hot-shot basketball and football captain.

Robert's narrative, in addition to being paternalistic, centrally positions him as a main feature in Rudolph's life. In addition, it implies that Rudolph's achievements in winning an Olympic medal at the 1956 Games earned her the privilege of coming back to Clarksville, Tennessee, to date Robert Eldridge. The film's construction of Rudolph as dependent on male figures in her life and the authoritative space they hold is exemplified as this same scene continues. Coach Gray asks Robert if he and Rudolph ever discuss her father, who is in ailing health. "We talk about her papa all the time," Robert responds, adding "She tell me all the time when Papa go I got to look after her all the time. I tell her Papa ain't goin' nowhere and she gets a little teary eyed and tells me she knows Papa got to go sometime and how glad she is and lucky she is to have me to look after her." In this way *Wilma* joins with many other productions in the visual genre by fostering the notion, according to Karen Hollinger, that "women should grant men primary importance in their lives because they are the only ones upon whom women can [and should] rely."[57]

The tensions between Rudolph and her father are settled in one of the movie's final scenes where the track star makes it clear that individual aspirations and public glory are rendered meaningless unless family bonds remain strong.

I know you're angry Papa, but there's somethin' I gotta tell you.
Robert and me, we should have waited, but we didn't know nothin'.
Now I'm goin' to have a baby and I still don't know nothin', but I
want to learn things. I want to learn things in college and I want to
go to the Olympic Games. But most of all I want the baby to have
what I had. Coach Gray, he taught me how to play basketball—and
that was good. Coach Temple, he taught me how to run track—and
that was good. But you and Mama—you and Mama's my home.
You is everything I really love. I can do without the basketball and
I can do without the track but I can't do without you and Mama.
I only remember a couple of things in my life, Papa. I remember
sittin' on your lap and you talkin' to me when I was sick. And I
remember you gave me my first pair of real shoes. And I remember
all the times we used to sit at the dinner table eatin' and talkin'—
that's what I remember, Papa. And that's what I want my baby to
have. You and Mama, 'cause that's the best I could give her. That's
what I want, Papa.

Rudolph's devotion and commitment to her family is paramount,
eclipsing individual ambition and achievement, and her superior athleticism is barely an afterthought in this scene and throughout the
film. Instead, we are reminded that the family worthy of our attention, according to Leslie Fishbein, "never forget[s] its roots nor its
obligations to its patriarch."[58]

What is striking about the film is not simply men's presence and
principal place in reconstructing Wilma Rudolph's life, but the near
exclusion of women and relationships between and among them.
Rudolph's relationship with her mother, for example, is given far less
attention and energy in the film than those between the track star
and her father, coaches, and boyfriend. The rare scene in which only
Rudolph and her mother are present is far less an exchange between
the two and much more an address from the older woman to her
daughter. Rudolph's mother, in an effort to explain her husband's dis-
pleasure over his daughter's pregnancy and resolve the familial tension over the issue, reminds the young track star of the patriarch's

love for his family and the real reason for his anger. "Wilma," her mother confides, "he ain't angry cause you're gonna be a mama, he's angry at Coach Gray, Coach Temple, and Robert 'cause they all done take you away from him." Rudolph's mother concludes, "All these years, child, your papa been fussin' over you. I just think it's time you did a little fussin' over him." Bingham notes that narrative exchanges such as these blend seamlessly with the "time-honored female biopic tradition" where the telefilm "is as much about a man" as it is the woman for whom the movie is named.[59] The scene ends as mother and daughter hug amid their tears and without the young Rudolph uttering a word. There is little room in this film for a bond to form between mother and daughter, since Rudolph's relationship with her father dominates many of the narrative spaces, even those scenes when he is not present.

In much the same way, connections between Rudolph and other girls or women never materialize in the biopic. When relationships between and among women are brought to the fore in *Wilma* they are just as likely to be characterized as being contentious as harmonious. Women's friendships in film (and, we contend, in *Wilma*) are, according to Hollinger, "plagued by jealousy, envy, and competition for men, and they teach women to beware of and fear one another."[60] For example, as highlighted previously in one of the conversations between Coach Gray and Robert, Rudolph's anxiety is said to be the result of catty behavior directed at the track star from her girlfriends and teammates. Robert claims, "all the other girls [are] acting up and being jealous, whispering behind her back." The focus on tensions between women serves to erase and trivialize bonds between females as it "relieves men of any responsibility for women's problems."[61]

In another of the film's sequences we are again reminded of the tensions among women whose relationships are distinguished by insecurity, distrust, and resentfulness, as well as the distance dividing female characters. At a daylong "visitors' day" respite from summer camp workouts at Tennessee State in the summer 1955, Coach Gray, Robert, Tootie, and her young child join Rudolph for a picnic lunch. The two men and Rudolph's sister are introduced to Martha Hudson, another high school student invited to attend Temple's summer work-outs. Rudolph describes Hudson as her "best friend" and someone with whom she runs relays. Hudson's appearance marks only one of three brief episodes in the film when Rudolph is seen engaging in any way with another female athlete. Interestingly, Rudolph and Hudson never speak directly to each other in this scene, and actually only once throughout the entire film do they have a narrative exchange, albeit a very brief one. Their friendship emerges magically and viewers never see the relationship between the two young women grow. This should not surprise us; as Mary Celeste Kearney notes, "what appears to be threatening about films that privilege girls' relationships with one another . . . is not female bonding per se but the marginalization or absence of males and heterosexuality."[62]

Coach Gray's wise counsel marks the next segment of the "Visitor's Day" scene as he offers Rudolph more than strategic coaching tips. Gray asks Hudson how Rudolph is performing at camp.

MARTHA HUDSON: Skeeter don't like beatin' anybody that's older. She could have won lots of races.

COACH GRAY: And Temple say in the beginning you want to go home because you can't beat nobody.

WILMA RUDOLPH: That's before I knew I could beat 'em. Once you know in your heart you can win, it don't matter that you win.

Rudolph's response prompts Gray to give the prodigy some of his "philosophy," which presumes a certain level of suspicion about relationships between and among girls. "If you know you can win, and the other girls know you can win, then you better win," notes Rudolph's high school coach. "Because if you don't," he adds, "the other girls gonna think you playin' with them." The fragility of female bonds is shored up through the efforts of one of Rudolph's male mentors (Gray), as he enlightens the track star on the best way to negotiate relationships with her teammates.

The scene continues, as does the attention paid to jealousy as the perceived cornerstone of female relationships. Coach Gray's "philosophy" continues, "[Y]ou're all runnin' for Coach Temple, you're a team. If you win, Martha wins. If Martha wins, you win. That's why Coach Temple has you all training together. It's the same as with the basketball team. Some nights you don't score your 20 points, so Sara Curtis scores 20 and we win anyway." Gray's lecture provokes an exchange between Rudolph and Robert that explicitly emphasizes female relationships bound by mistrust and insecurity.

> WILMA RUDOLPH: Sara Curtis ain't never gonna score no 20 points!
>
> ROBERT ELDRIDGE: Skeeter (Wilma) don't like no Sara Curtis.
>
> WILMA RUDOLPH: Sara Curtis keep givin' you those eyes . . . can't score nothin' with no two black eyes.
>
> ROBERT ELDRIDGE: Well Skeeter let me be the first to give you the information. Sara Curtis already has two black eyes.

In Greenspan's *Wilma*, women's presence and their voices, including Rudolph's, are negligible. When girls and women are in the frame and given dialogue, the narratives either focus on the needs and emotions of men or the deficiencies of female bonds. Relationally, male characters maintain a hegemonic position around a narrative center in the film, which, ironically, is about a woman.

Bud Greenspan's mythical sense of family and his preoccupation with it in *Wilma* not only privileges male authority but also "nourishes the belief that problems can be solved in small decentralized units."[63] Indeed, issues and conflicts begin and end within the bounds of family in the biopic, erasing broader structural and cultural forces at work in assembling the contours of Wilma Rudolph's life and experiences. Made-for-TV movie families during this period, including the Rudolphs, are represented as though they were "hermetically sealed from the community [and] wider social institutions that surround [them]," essentially vacuum-packed in their isolation.[64] For example, the biopic's near total omission of any discussion of race or racism makes invisible and de-historicizes the realities and injustices faced by the Rudolphs as a black family living in the mid-twentieth-century American South.[65]

The film's scant attention to racism is relegated to a single three-minute scene in which Wilma Rudolph is not even present. Instead, Coach Temple delivers a monologue (the second half of an eight-minute-long, three-scene introduction of the character) to a group of young women, presumably Tennessee State Tigerbelles, on the importance of longer distance running. "You're going to run cross country for one reason and one reason only," Temple informs them, "because colored kids ain't supposed to run cross country because colored kids is only supposed to run sprints. Now this team here at Tennessee State is gonna upset that popular theory. You realize you gonna be pioneers? That you gonna prove to the entire world that colored kids can run more than 100 yards." Racism is trivialized in the film by naming it a "popular theory," while it is simultaneously tightly contained in scope and in substance. In Greenspan's worldview the profound impact of racism on the lives of Rudolph and her teammates is reduced to not being able to run events longer than one hundred yards in track. Temple's character in the film conflates the limitations on distance running for women with racism rather than sexism. In reality, at the time, there were no Olympic events for women longer than two hundred yards.[66]

In addition, in situating Coach Temple as *the* champion of race and equality the biopic bolsters a view of African American history in which individual rather than collective action is the lead function in spurring social change.[67] In doing so, *Wilma* shares common ground with other television docudramas, whereas Eric Foner suggests that the "personal is political" slogan of the 1960s is reconfigured in the 1970s so that the "political is unfailingly personal."[68] Even within an otherwise hyperbolically positive review of the film, Diane Mermigas of the Arlington Heights, Illinois, *Daily Review* concedes, "the drama doesn't dodge but does subdue the race issue that may have existed while Wilma was growing up. . . ."[69] Attention to the structural inequalities and cultural ideologies that play upon raced identities complicate the regularly told tale of self-determination in sport film. Thus, so as not to disrupt "utopian" narratives, these broader social forces are ignored in sport film, including in Greenspan's production of *Wilma*.[70]

Though there is evidence that the film was popular among the viewing public in December 1977, reviews of the film were mixed. The critical commentaries of *Wilma* provide us with a bit of insight concerning how the film and its dominant messages were read by viewers at its moment of creation. Greenspan's romanticized construction of Rudolph's life and the past itself as a made-for-television production underscored the medium's "determination to be inspirational" yet "distressingly sticky" at the same time, quipped a reviewer for the *New York Times*. The review highlights Greenspan's attention to Rudolph's pregnancy and unmarried status as the script had the "young woman worrying if her disciplinarian father could be persuaded to forgive her." According to the reviewer, the "inevitable reconciliation was milked" for all that it could muster.[71]

Significantly, the *New York Times* review was quick to point out the incongruities between Greenspan's version of the truth and Rudolph's autobiographical retelling of her life. "But Miss Rudolph's published autobiography indicates that, while her father was against Wilma's ever seeing her boyfriend again, he was otherwise fairly reasonable from the start." Instead, in Greenspan's retelling, Rudolph's father is portrayed as the rightfully uncompromising patriarch whose duty it was to protect his daughter. The *Times* notes that other important details of Rudolph's life were left out of the script so that the television plot could neatly wind its way to the "twin dramatic goals of family reunion and Olympic success." For example, the review called attention to the autobiography, in which Rudolph feared that her sister wanted to take custody of her child while the track star was in college and training for the Rome Games. That "complication," according to the *Times*, was conveniently ignored in *Wilma*, as were all the other "less inspirational aspects of Wilma's subsequent development," including "her charges of being ripped off by various promoters and agencies, or her disdain for most white women's liberation movements." Airing those issues would do little to promote Greenspan's idealized tale of Rudolph's life. *Wilma*, the review concluded, was reduced to "strained baby food."[72]

Writing more generally about docudramas' flaws, Mark Harris includes *Wilma* in his 1978 review of the genre. Society pays a "heavy price for TV's distorted portraits" of the famous and infamous within docudrama, according to Harris. For that author, docudramas in their attempt to take us into the past "neither dramatize nor [document] history." We are instead "seeing ourselves, watching our own fantasies of life." Wilma Rudolph, like so many others featured in the relatively new visual class, is "purified beyond belief," Harris concludes. Similar to the *New York Times* review, Harris is critical of the docudrama's inability to *be critical*. Docudramas must also be marketable commodities, and as such must treat the individuals highlighted as "nice," especially if those individuals are still alive. He concludes, "Wilma's tender father, her ever-loving family, her all-wise coaches are all so appealing that I began to yearn for a little natural human irritation."[73]

Perhaps the film's least favorable review was offered by the *Christian Science Monitor*. The paper offered up as critical a condemnation of Greenspan as of the film itself. The biopic "isn't going to win any prizes for speed . . . or subtlety," the review began. Greenspan's production, according to the publication, is hopelessly "handicapped by a simplistic, ponderous script" though it is "blessed with a superb group of actors who almost manage to make it a winner." Its criticisms of Greenspan and his production continued, stating that the "labored storyline, obvious dialogue, and overextended drama" make the story in "desperate need of a better coach (make that director and writer) to pace it properly." Interestingly, the reviewer was moved by the portrayal of familial bonds, but not in the way intended by Greenspan. The *Monitor* remarked, "Wilma's dependency on her father is carried just a bit too far for a healthy relationship." Additionally, as debates and tensions raged in 1970s society concerning out-of-wedlock births, especially among black women, the review called into question the "uneven morality of some of the characters [as] an unwed pregnancy and continuing unmarried status seemingly is acceptable as long as the end result is winning gold medals." The review even took issue with the film's ending, which did not quite satisfy the reviewer, who believed a more suitable finish to the story would have highlighted Rudolph's eventual marriage to the baby's father. "And although the film chooses to end with Wilma's Olympic victory and poignant plan to return to her dad, who is home minding her illegitimate baby, the facts of her life indicated that she eventually married the father of the child," the *Monitor* continued. "*Wilma* was written, directed, and produced by Bud Greenspan," the review concludes. "Luckily, he didn't act in it as well."[74]

The film concludes at a point fairly close to where it began, with Rudolph's nuclear family, specifically her father, center stage. In the final scene Rudolph calls her family from Rome soon after her three-gold-medal performance. Her father is on the porch with Rudolph's small child and is called in to speak with his daughter. Their exchange is brief, and in it Rudolph's father repeatedly asks "when you comin' home?" To which the track star responds, "I miss you and Mama, I want to come home." Rudolph's "I love you Papa" ends the film's narrative and her father returns to the porch with his granddaughter in his arms. In the tradition of classic biopics, according to Kegan Doyle, *Wilma* remains "safe, ideologically speaking," through to its conclusion.[75] Throughout Greenspan's film, Wilma Rudolph is rendered an "object in a story of which she is ostensibly the subject."[76] True to the conventions of classic female biopics, the female protagonist is relatively voiceless as decisions about her present and future are made for her. Moreover, Rudolph's public achievements in athletics are devalued and insignificant in relation to the film's larger story of the private: the familial bonds that connect the track star and her father. Finally, the film remains detached from broader social tensions as it continually works to reassure us of home and the family's stable presence in the lives of those living in 1970s America.

6

Against All Odds

Reading Rudolph over Four Decades
of Children's Literature

> *"Wilma Rudolph's short life was a triumph over pain, pov-*
> *erty, and racism. She became a winner by never quitting."*
> —Corinne J. Naden and Rose Blue, *Wilma Rudolph*[1]

AGENCY AND ITS RELATIONSHIP to achievement form the cornerstone of this passage by Corrine J. Naden and Rose Blue, which
appears near the conclusion of their 2004 biography about Wilma
Rudolph. This book on Rudolph, part of the African American Biographies series, and the others in the series were written to tell "inspiring stories" about "well-known African Americans who overcame
tremendous odds, such as racism and poverty, and went on to leave
their lasting marks in the world."[2] Far from an anomaly, the narrative
and the perspectives it represents are a dominant theme spread over
the books about the track great that were written for young readers
from 1975 to 2011. In many ways, the Wilma Rudolph books' preoccupation with agency, including the example above, blends seamlessly
with time-honored patterns in juvenile literature, and specifically in
biographies for children. Rags-to-riches stories are the featured narratives across the genre, and Rudolph's history as a poor, black, and
disabled girl who eventually wins several Olympic medals may help
to explain the fair number of books that have been written and continue to be penned about the athlete.[3] Writing over thirty years ago,
Jon Stott offered that biographies of sport heroes were imbued with

155

American Dream ideology and "Cinderella-type" storylines, creating mythical representations of the athletes. The fabrication process is assisted, Stott adds, by obscuring certain aspects of the athletes' lives, while other details are overemphasized.[4] Indeed, biographies written for children about sport heroes and other figures intended, as William Zinsser notes, to only "bring the good news."[5]

More recently, some scholars have argued that there has been a subtle change afoot in biographical work written for young readers, with the result that the didactic, mythic, and romanticized stories to which Stott alluded have been dislodged slightly.[6] In their place are more nuanced stories than those previously written, in which the complexities of the individual's life are introduced to the reader. Subjects' experiences, once only presented as finite episodes, most often ending in triumph and cleanly captured by the writer, follow a far less simple narrative arch in recent years. This change is driven, in part, according to Beverly Klatt, because "youthful readers have come to expect formerly taboo topics in their books."[7] Thus the "whitewashed realities" of the "stiff, unreal characters" presented in biographies written for children have been altered, albeit slightly, in recent years.[8]

Totalizing narratives of achievement and progress are troubled in more contemporary work by a text's content, as well as the style and aesthetic features of the book itself. For example, earlier books' near-total reliance on the written word created page after page of a monochromatic visual image for the reader. Thus, as Gale Eaton suggests, what was implied within that structure was that a "successful life, like a good story, was a unified whole," with little or no narrative interruptions or deviations. Conversely, more recent biographies for young readers, the author suggests, present a "colorful smorgasbord of anecdotes, quotations, and boxed sidelights," which impact how individual readers approach a book and the meanings they take from it.[9] The fragmented page of varied fonts, colors, etc. stands to encourage children to think of and "read" the biographical characters' lives as less monolithic and less a neat, unified whole as implied in previous work.

We read the total of twenty-one books written about Wilma Rudolph over the past three and a half decades bearing in mind the larger trends in biographies for children described above. The books under review comprise what we believe to be all of the biographies for children written, to date, about the track great. All but three of the twenty-one books under review were published after Rudolph's death in 1994, with the vast majority written since 2000. We acknowledge and seek to more fully interrogate the ways in which the collection on Rudolph departs from more historical, conventional tales of individuals and their achievements in biographical texts. There is, in fact, a small amount of evidence to suggest that the direction of recent Rudolph biographies is to situate the track star more critically in relation to dynamics of racism, classism, sexism, etc. that so mattered to her life story. Ultimately, however, we argue that little has changed, since the aspects of Rudolph's life that gain traction are those that support dominant understandings of achievement in the face of impediments. Little can get in the way of Rudolph's path to success, except the athlete herself, because agency, as imagined in these books, always trumps constraint. As Lee Engfer's 2006 book on Rudolph makes clear, "she will always be remembered for her determination and her ability to overcome obstacles."[10] The books that comprise this collection make sure that our remembrances of Rudolph for the most part stay this course. Rudolph's story as told in these books does little to challenge or subvert cultural power arrangements that created and sustained the obstacles against which the athlete "overcame."

Of the various forms of representation, books written for children about Wilma Rudolph are the most popular, and thus especially critical to our analysis in *(Re)Presenting Wilma Rudolph*. Interestingly, in contrast, despite numerous books for children, there remains no adult biography on Rudolph. Given the sheer volume of children's books, it stands to reason that some young readers come to "know" Wilma Rudolph through this genre, thus underscoring the texts' importance that much more. Moreover, biographies written for children more generally, and Rudolph's collection specifically, are significant, given their "unique mixture of education, entertainment, persuasion, and pleasure."[11] We agree that the genre serves an important cultural function, as juvenile biographies act as "powerful vehicles for the circulation of public values and public memory."[12] In this chapter, we examine representations of Rudolph as she is depicted in stories for young readers, with particular attention to the "overcoming" narratives that so saturate the texts. We address the continued interest in her story for children and focus on several themes in the books, namely race, gender, poverty, and disability, in that they, to a greater or lesser degree, become the foundation on which Rudolph's success is measured. In casting these aspects of her identity as obstacles over which Rudolph successfully triumphed, the books serve to advance mythical notions of social progress and the individual agent's role in that process. In doing so, the children's books represented in this collection reinforce meritocratic ideas at the expense of more comprehensive understandings of how inequality, at a structural and ideological level, limited Rudolph's opportunities and outcomes over the course of her entire life.

Despite the healthy number of children's book titles about Wilma Rudolph, they remain, on balance, inadequately sourced, which may help to explain the intensely repetitive features of the books across the decades. The authors' continuing reliance on Wilma Rudolph's autobiography, written in 1977, clearly has its hold on the many books under review. Whatever demarcation can be made between legend and biography is blurred when authors tend to look toward a narrow range of sources, and especially so in texts aimed at children.[13] *Wilma: The Story of Wilma Rudolph* establishes the framework for many of the books, with a good share of the total number relying heavily on direct quotes, while others follow the autobiographical storyline very closely.[14] Others take a slightly different, though no less objectionable, tack, relying exclusively or heavily on previously published books written for children about Wilma Rudolph.[15] Thus the books' direction, orientation, scope, and reach are severely restricted to the breadth of a single book written decades before. Few of these authors venture much beyond the autobiography and far fewer, still, consider any number of primary source documents available about Rudolph and her experiences.

The realities of Wilma Rudolph's young life provide incredibly fertile ground on which to draft a story for children about dominant understandings of agency, autonomy, and perseverance. Within the texts, Rudolph's life course, though thrown some obstacles, is ultimately seen as being under the total command of the track star herself. Constraints around race, gender, class, and physical ability are entertained in some of the narratives, though only to be minimized or dismissed by a chapter or book's end. Anne Donegan Johnson's 1996 *The Value of Overcoming Adversity: The Story of Wilma Rudolph* provides one of the most striking examples in which individuals are portrayed as "engines of action."[16] Biographical agents, as described in this series, are able to create change in their lives and the lives of others in a seeming vacuum, free of broader social forces. Johnson's text is part of the Value Tales series of books, which incorporate objects, insects, and animals as companions to the main subjects who act as their "conscience" in many ways.[17] In Rudolph's value tale, she is befriended by a mosquito, named "Skeeter," who, for the remainder of the story sticks with her and defines adversity for the young girl with a brace, provides her with motivational talks, and helps push her to realize greatness. This exchange between Rudolph and "Skeeter" underscores agency's place:

> One day, Skeeter asked Wilma, "What do you think is your greatest achievement?"
>
> Wilma said, "My three gold medals, I guess."
>
> Skeeter shook his head. "Your triumph is your life. Look at all the obstacles that you've overcome. Why don't you tell your story? Maybe you can inspire others to overcome adversity, too."[18]

One of the collection's more original delivery methods is an audio book entitled *Chris and Amy Meet Wilma Rudolph, Olympic Gold Medalist: A "Movies in My Mind" Adventure.* Unfortunately, despite the unique way Rudolph's story is told, there is little else about the tale that could be considered pioneering. One of the six stated values of the series is the central character's ability to "triumph over adversity."[19] The books feature a young duo, Chris and Amy, whose time travels take them on adventures in which messages around self-determination, as the pathway to success, are paramount. In "meeting"

Wilma Rudolph, the young pair hear that the track great is a "true hero," who "showed the world that with courage, hard work, and determination, anything is possible and *nothing* should ever get in the way of our dreams."[20]

Though the examples listed above are some of the more explicit in their dominant message of an individual agent's ability to overcome barriers, that theme appears and is the most common motif throughout all of the books under review in this chapter. The result is a series of books in which the broader historical, political, and social conditions that gave rise to and sustained Wilma Rudolph's marginalized reality are obscured. To speak of Wilma Rudolph's life only as a story of inspiration negates the potential for identifying and changing power structures that persist in disenfranchising and silencing folks along lines of class, race, gender, and physical ability.

The "overcoming" theme is established early across the many books written about Rudolph. The stories often begin at the beginning of her life and include the fact that she was a premature baby born into poverty. Near the start of many of the books are narratives informing readers of Rudolph's fragile start to life. Rudolph, according to Amy Ruth, born prematurely and underweight, was "not expected to live." Rudolph's parents "prayed for their tiny daughter's survival" and "[m]iraculously, baby Wilma began to thrive."[21] Lee Engfer's very colorful 2006 graphic novel begins with the red and bolded chapter heading "THE SICKLY KID" with an accompanying image of Rudolph's anxious-looking parents in an exchange with the doctor. Baby Rudolph screams in her mother's arms, "Oh, Dr. Coleman, do you think she'll make it?" Rudolph's mother asks. To which the doctor, seeming to foretell the future, responds, "I'll do the best I can. She looks like a fighter."[22] Rudolph's sick and weak start to life serves to frame her future achievements on the track as even more unbelievable. Residents in her hometown did not believe the "sickly baby would live," let alone grow up to "become the fastest woman runner in the world," as Mary Dodson Wade narrates in her 2009 book.[23] Rudolph's story of triumph over the many obstacles set in her path begins with her premature birth, but certainly does not end there.

The books are quick to detail Rudolph's childhood in poverty, using that reality as another way to mark the distance she traveled in her struggle and conquest over life's hindrances. To be sure, poverty seems, according to Stott, a "necessary starting point" in the context of sport biographies written for children.[24] Stott's observations about poverty's essential place in books for children are confirmed across many of the texts about Rudolph. Moreover, the books about Rudolph remark on the role of her family in the face of adversity, and their orientation toward work more specifically. Despite the fact that Rudolph's parents both worked, Wayne Coffey conceded, "making ends meet wasn't easy."[25] Interestingly, Maria Jose Botelho notes that class as an element of books for children is often reduced to a "cultural tag-along," or even "overlooked" behind themes of race and gender, believed to be more central to telling a life story about an African American woman.[26] Such is not the case over the span of children's books about Rudolph, since the family's poverty is brought to the fore to further throw into relief the against-all-odds plot. Discussions around class standing give authors an avenue to comment on and affirm family as resilient and resourceful in struggling with and against poverty. A family's deep commitment to and for each other hold the narrative center, thereby continuing to uncouple class from power relations.[27] Johnson's Value Tales Series book on Rudolph is a good case in point, as poverty is not only a primary piece to the narrative, but is romanticized. For example, in the book, several bright-eyed and smiling children gather around her parents as Rudolph's father holds an infant, while her mother mends the family's clothes. The Rudolphs, according to the book, "were hard-working people who refused to accept welfare." Implied, of course, in Johnson's writing is that those who accept welfare have no work ethic. With what is presumed to be an outhouse visible beyond the image of the happy family, the narration continues, "Their crowded home had no indoor bathroom. Mrs. Rudolph sewed the children's clothes from old flour sacks. Although the family was poor, there was always plenty of love to go around."[28]

Wilma Rudolph's disability as a youngster is perhaps the most prominent feature brought into focus over each of the children's books, even eclipsing attention paid to the future Olympian's premature birth and early life in poverty. Rudolph's childhood disability, though omnipresent over the range of texts, is the least conceptualized of her multiple identities. Disability is not presented as a social construction but is, instead, portrayed as far removed from the larger social structures and relations of power in which it is embedded. Derived largely from Rudolph's autobiography, the stories of her childhood illnesses and health issues, like the "born prematurely into poverty" tales, change very little over the span of the books under review in this chapter and the three-and-a-half decades in which the texts were published. In many ways, Kathleen Krull's 1996 book, for children aged six to nine, titled *Wilma Unlimited: How Wilma Rudolph Became the World's Fastest Woman*, is consistent with the other books in characterizing an aspect of Rudolph's disability. In this instance, Krull details the moment when Rudolph, entering a Sunday church service, removed her leg brace for the first time.

> She hung back while people filled the old building. Standing alone, the sound of hymns coloring the air, she unbuckled her heavy brace. . . . Whispers rippled throughout the gathering. Wilma Rudolph was *walking*. Her large family, her family's friends, everyone from school—each person stared wide-eyed. The singing never stopped, it seemed to burst right through the wall and into the trees. Finally, Wilma reached a seat in the front and began singing too, her smile triumphant.[29]

Krull's version, with its crescendo-like trajectory, and others found throughout many of the children's books, track very closely to Rudolph's autobiographical retelling of this event. Krull's text is accompanied by lively and colorful art, creating visually pleasing and engaging pages upon which the miraculous happens. Rudolph seems reborn as her ability to walk, now without the aid of braces, removes her from a dark and shackled past toward the light and freedom of a new life. This narrative arc, originating from Rudolph's autobiography, pervades the stories retold about her disability in patterned form well over a dozen times since the athlete's death in 1994.

Figure 6.1. Wilma Rudolph removing her leg brace. Illustration from *WILMA UNLIMITED: How Wilma Rudolph Became the World's Fastest Woman* by Kathleen Krull, illustrated by David Diaz. Illustration copyright 1996 by David Diaz. Reprinted by permission of Harcourt Children's Books, an imprint of Houghton Mifflin Harcourt Publishing Company. All rights reserved.

Descriptions of Rudolph's ailments, characterized through the children's books, repeat oft-told disability tropes grounded in stereotypes, as well as narrow and hierarchical conceptualizations of physical difference. Books written for children about Wilma Rudolph remain mired in a past with an emphasis on demonizing the individual and the impairment, rather than a society that constructs and sustains inequalities, negative attitudes, and misrepresentations toward those with disabilities. As prominent disability-studies scholar Rosemarie Garland-Thomson argued recently, "Disability is becoming a civil rights issue rather than simply a medical problem." Moreover, she adds that "[d]isability studies challenges our collective representation of disability, exposing it as an exclusionary and oppressive system rather than the natural and appropriate order of things."[30] As scholars and advocates over the past two or three decades are moving us away from a view that stigmatizes someone with a disability as "abnormal," "deviant," or "less-than," the authors of many of the texts written about Wilma Rudolph do not engage in this same progressive trend. Instead, Rudolph's disability is framed simply as another hurdle to be overcome in the track star's life. Her ability to walk without a brace and eventually to become the world's greatest female runner signals Rudolph's "defeat" of disability, and another marker of her determination and will to overcome all barriers toward success. In this way, Rudolph's story blends seamlessly with larger achievement "against the odds" narratives. Inspirational scenarios such as those in children's books about Rudolph's disability feature individual agency, but do little to expose and interrogate the myriad constraints shaping the athlete's life and experiences.

Two primary elements are central to our analysis around disability within the books under examination. First is the way normalcy is constructed and sustained through narratives of Rudolph's disability. This interpretive angle enables us to focus more keenly on the construction of normalcy versus the construction of disability. In doing so we hope to engage a perspective rarely taken in children's books about Wilma Rudolph; "that the 'problem' is not with the person with disabilities," but rather, the issue lies "in the way that normalcy is constructed to create the 'problem' of the disabled person."[31] Second, we explore how disability is de-politicized in the texts and marked as distinct from any social context.

The notion that disabled bodies trouble the normal and thus must be managed and separated from the larger community is a historically deep-rooted phenomenon and one that persists to the present. Said to "contaminate" bodies deemed "normal," those with disabilities remain threats to the populous more generally.[32] Rosemarie Garland-Thomson notes that disabled bodies are viewed as "corporeal departures from dominant expectations," and as a result, the disabled "never go unpunished." Moreover, she adds, bodies are managed, in the sense that "conformities are almost always rewarded."[33] The benchmarks of normalcy work not only to marginalize, invalidate, and silence some bodies, but also to confirm the bounds of the natural and thus "the good body" for others.[34] Rudolph's body is constructed not only as different, but judged as "less-than," and thus far removed from notions of "normal," in a reoccurring pattern across many of the books.

The texts about the track star written for children suggest and assign value to normalcy, and in doing so, remove Rudolph's "crippled" body from consideration. It was difficult for Rudolph "to feel like a normal kid," one author concluded.[35] Other authors stressed the valiant efforts by Rudolph to hide what was seen as a flawed gait. The young Rudolph "fought hard not to limp. She tried to never give in to her weak muscles . . . and she got good at not limping."[36] In highlighting the ways that Rudolph "desperately tried to be normal," this narrative clip does little but shame individuals for their disabilities, as it reconfirms the centrality of able-bodiedness and definitions of normality.[37] The passages reinscribe what Robert McRuer calls "compulsory able-bodiedness," which is formed on the assumptive position that able-bodied identity is the standard to which we, including Rudolph, should all aspire.[38] Other books in the collection applaud Rudolph's courageous efforts to attain normalcy, but concede that "being disabled caused most of her attempts to fail."[39] As an adolescent, Rudolph regained her ability to walk without her brace, becoming, as one author claimed, just "like other children," and thus comfortably, as Paul Darke suggests, within the bounds of normalcy.[40] In total, the books, rather than problematizing homogeneity, take another tack, one that presents physical difference as a failing and something to be corrected. Furthermore, in denying corporeal difference as "a continuum of normative physiology," the normal/abnormal binary is cemented for readers of these texts with Rudolph's disabled body and those of others beyond the bounds of normalcy.[41]

Technologies, in this case Rudolph's leg brace, employed to enable movement and freedom are instead viewed as a burden and an inhibitor to her wholeness, as well as a major contributing factor in further marking the future track star as abnormal.[42] The language used in various books to describe Rudolph's leg brace draws upon larger discourses of confinement, limitation, and abnormality in relation to disability. Rudolph, along with various members of her family, worked tirelessly "to free her leg from the prison of that steel brace," one of the text's author's claims.[43] Rudolph's brace "went from her knee to her ankle" another account observed, "she couldn't take it off until she went to bed at night, and she always had to wear brown oxfords for the brace to fasten to."[44] The brace Rudolph wore to foster mobility was characterized by the dominant, able-bodied society as doing exactly the opposite, as it confined and marked her with its weight, cumbersomeness, and ugliness.[45] According to many of the books, Rudolph's brace distanced her from all she was not: "normal."

When Rudolph was able to walk without the brace, it was "retired from service" and her mother presented her with the "best gift" imaginable, a "pair of shiny, and normal, black leather shoes."[46] Rudolph and her mother "wrapped the hated brace in a box and mailed it back to the hospital. As soon as Wilma sent that box away, she knew her life was beginning all over again."[47] Framed in this way, Rudolph's freedom, and by proxy, life's fullest pleasures, go to those who do not "suffer" from disability. The brace, as a symbol and reminder of Rudolph's disability, is removed, and so does not impinge upon the path to normalcy and a life worth living.

Beyond narrative, Rudolph's leg brace is featured among several of the images in the children's books written about her, even appearing on one of the covers.[48] In another representation, Rudolph is seated, with her head in her hands (brace in view), passively watching other children play basketball. The brace, it seems from this illustration, prevents her from being included in games with her peers, confirming the perspective that ableist ideas about movement prevent Rudolph's inclusion. In one depiction, a pair of leg braces hangs on a wall with the caption, "Wilma had to wear a leg brace such as these when she was growing up. She could not run or play games because of the brace."[49] In Johnson's 1996 book Rudolph stands, her head and shoulders stooped, with a forlorn gaze towards other children who are laughing at her because of the leg brace, which is in clear view.[50] Attention drawn to the brace in the ways stated above points to the brace as the central component hindering Rudolph and her involvement in and enjoyment of games and of life. Rudolph's "problem" as portrayed in the children's books under review stems from her braces, rather than from the "ill-conceived attitudes that attend people with disabilities."[51]

As a whole, the children's books about Wilma Rudolph depoliticize disability, rendering the issue a private and individual affair. In doing so, they present disability as a personal tragedy with its focus on Rudolph and her impairment, as opposed to as a narrative of the literal and figurative barriers and public attitudes that disable her. Even as civil rights issues have become more extensively documented across children's literature in recent years, the same cannot be said for the genre's treatment of disability.[52] Unfortunately, this series of books about Rudolph and her disability remain consistent with the larger pattern of misrepresentation and exclusion. It is disability's common reference point as a story constructed in a larger narrative that inevitably creates ableist discourses. As Davis argues, a person *becomes* disabled, thus generating a sequence of narrative events or a story. He adds, in "narrativizing an impairment, one tends to sentimentalize it," linking it to "individualism and the drama of the individual story."[53] Our attention is then fixed on single characters and their impairments. Through the narrative, these single actors, including Wilma Rudolph, become the story's heroes or villains, muting our sensitivity to disability and to those cultural arrangements of power to which it is connected.

Wilma Rudolph's story is devoid of any political and social context, and is filled instead with stereotypes and misrepresentations of disability. Most striking of the accounts is the repeated tale of Rudolph as lonely and pitifully unhappy. Rudolph's disability, portrayed as a burden, lent itself to the darkness she was said to be going to inhabit over life's course. As one author reported, "The news spread around Clarksville: Wilma, the lively girl, would never walk again," adding that "what hurt [Rudolph] most was [that] the local school didn't let her attend because she couldn't walk. Tearful and lonely, she watched her brothers and sisters run off to school each day, leaving her behind."[54] Other narratives reiterated Rudolph's emotions as a child unable to join with other youngsters, "feeling alone and rejected, Wilma cried a lot. . . ."[55] She, according to another text, "desperately wanted to be part of family life."[56] The implication is that her illness kept Rudolph from her own family, steering her further down a path to misery. Indeed, in these accounts and others scattered throughout the books, Rudolph's detachment from school, peers, and childhood recreational activities dominates the narratives. Disability is depicted both as an "isolated and individual affair" with "storytellers artificially extract[ing] the experience of disability from its necessary social contexts."[57]

Writing about the trends among scholars and activists over the past three decades, Tom Shakespeare notes the challenges posed both to the individualistic perspective and to an over-medicalized orientation toward disability.[58] Unfortunately, these patterns to which he writes are not evident in the books about Rudolph, as the texts maintain regressive views of disability. Ato Quayson reminds us that from the perspective of disability as an individual or personal tragedy, the narrative's focus tends toward a view which positions responsibility for accommodating the impairment directly on the individuals or their families.[59] In taking an individualistic perspective, the books position Rudolph and her family as the central agents in confronting and combating illness, as the texts simultaneously underscore the important role medicine plays in the process of recovery and cure. Focused attention on the "problem" centers a solution within the individual and her family; thus, the structural and public components of disability are obscured. For example, Amy Ruth's book opens with attention on the individual (by contrast to the societal) clearly in view. Rudolph, Ruth begins, "sat on her bed, her skinny legs stretched out in front of her. . . . [A]n older brother massaged her crooked right leg."[60] Similarly, Mary Dodson Wade's 2009 account localizes disability as it confirms the good that comes from it. She writes, "All of her family's help paid off," when Rudolph soon "took off her brace and walked."[61]

When Rudolph and her family are not at the center of the frame, medicine and its unproblematized role in relation to disability are. Those with a disability are "placed under an obligation to want to get well," as their physical reality is continually conceived as a biological liability with medical involvement its only aid.[62] David Mitchell and Sharon Snyder maintain that "[d]isabilities are exclusively narrated as a debilitating phenomenon in need of medical intervention and correction."[63] This "medical model" conceptualization of disability features medicine and, importantly, its fix of the "problem." For Rudolph, medical intervention is constructed and presented as a "legitimate [source] of help."[64] The texts highlight the work doctors, nurses, and family members performed on Rudolph's leg as they twisted, lifted, massaged, exercised, and soaked the youngster's limb. For her part, Rudolph "focused on doing everything possible to get better."[65] Medical intervention, seen as an obligation, informs dominant narratives in which a subject's total attention is and should be directed toward using science to rid oneself of a disability. Across the texts, individualized and over-medicalized narratives are routine, and as a result, Rudolph's experiences are reduced to her impairment, and it remains the focus of those around her to remedy the impairment.

Narratives about Rudolph's own resolve to strengthen and eventually "fix" her leg are featured, and underscore individual agency's dominant position in these texts. In Johnson's text the starkness of this orientation is clear when Rudolph is instructed, "if you want to get better, you have to fight your illness. You have to overcome adversity. . . . Don't waste time feeling sorry for yourself, just try harder!"[66] Rudolph's personal attributes, including her will and determination to defeat illness, are detailed and written into the narrative center, thus dislodging any discussion of disability's larger political and social realities from the page. Rudolph's "true grit" enabled her to transform "disabilities into remarkable abilities that set her apart from others," according to another author.[67] Rudolph "kept up her courage" in her struggle with illness, an author shared.[68] In another account, Rudolph's remarkableness is underscored by the writer's observation that "Wilma's mother used to marvel at the quiet courage and unusual determination of her little girl," with a "[r]emarkably positive attitude."[69] This perspective persists through to the most recent children's books about Rudolph and builds on well-worn representations of the "supercrip" who rises above and moves beyond disability.[70] In a book written in 2011, Jennifer Joline Anderson claims that Rudolph had "beaten all the odds" as she "battled deadly illnesses and won." And now, the author continues, "through sheer determination, she had amazed the doctors by learning to walk again."[71] Rudolph's disability is made into a temporary obstacle along her path, mainly because she had enough spunk "to [shed] her handicap" in order to be successful, in what is treated as a competition where "winning" means walking without the aid of a brace.[72]

How children and adults "hear" and understand the tales within the Wilma Rudolph series of texts is beyond the scope of this work. However, we highlight Anne Finger's memoir about her experiences with polio in the 1950s and her remembrances of Wilma Rudolph's story as an interesting bit of evidence on this point. Finger recounts, "I hated hearing about Wilma Rudolph," whose "tagline," she recalls, was, "A Negro girl from the South who overcame a childhood bout with polio . . . to win" Olympic gold medals. Hearing this frequently repeated story, Finger remembers, "I felt a sense of shame. If she could do it, why couldn't I?" Interestingly, Finger goes on to question the story as a legend, wondering if it was "repeated so often that it took on a life of its own."[73]

It is precisely Finger's reactions to the story told to her about Rudolph's life and disability that trouble us about the narratives in the children's books about the track star. Finger's words as well as those of Garland-Thomson remind us of the criticalness of disability's representation to readers and other observers. According to Garland-Thomson, "the way we imagine disability through images and narratives determines the shape of the material world, the distribution of resources, our relationships with one another, and our sense of ourselves."[74] In relying heavily, and at times exclusively, on Rudolph's autobiography written in the 1970s, the texts flatten all complexity surrounding disability, failing to engage with or trouble dominant ideas about normalcy, difference, and cultural power. Each book in the collection is, using Paul Darke's phrase, a "normality drama" in which the "problem" is that of the individual or of medicine and only to be tolerated until it can be overcome.[75] Societal influences on and participation in the continuance of disability as a social oppression are obscured with disability reduced to a tragedy or triumph story. In the children's books about Wilma Rudolph we ask: a "triumph" for whom?

Moreover, the books' inability to link Rudolph's experiences to broader historical and social relationships of power around poverty and disability are consistent with the ways in which gender issues are engaged (or not engaged) across the collection. Unlike poverty and disability, however, gender tensions, as they played out in Rudolph's life and athletic experiences, are more absent than present in the texts, where silences in the narrative hold sway. The sexism Rudolph faced— the systematic ways girls were prevented from or limited in participating in competitive sports—is infrequently acknowledged and rarely contextualized in these books.[76] When gender inequalities around women and sport are addressed, they are likely to be presented as a relic of a long-gone past. Narrative phrasing such as "in those days" or "there was some prejudice at the time against girls getting seriously involved in sports" anchors inequality around gender to a historical social ill.[77] Generalized statements about women's place in sport, which are to some degree accurate, nonetheless misrepresent the contemporary state of fairness in athletics. For example, in distancing the past from the present, Anderson remarks that in the post-Title IX era there is a "wide range of opportunities for young women."[78] Relative to before the passage of Title IX in 1972, indeed there are more opportunities for females to involve themselves in athletics; but arguably, gender inequality persists. Unfortunately, these nuances are lost across the entire collection of books about Rudolph.

Beyond very terse, simplified statements, a majority of the books fail to even mention sexism, let alone examine its dynamics in relation to sport in broader 1950s and 1960s America. For example, Coffey explains that girls "were not very serious about sports" during the 1950s, and that Rudolph didn't share the prevailing attitude that sports were only for boys.[79] Similarly, Jo Harper retells a story from Rudolph's autobiography in which she was confronted with people's attitudes about girls and sports. Told by a friend of her mother's that sports are un-ladylike, Rudolph refrains from saying anything, and then thinks to herself, "*I love sports, but I'm a lady . . . Nobody likes pretty clothes and dressing up more than I do. And just look how I managed not to answer back to Mother's friends. That was very lady-like.*"[80] Tom Streissguth, in a sidebar on the six-player game entitled "Ladylike Basketball," writes, "[m]any people of that era thought that girls shouldn't be playing boys' games, so these rules made the game as ladylike as possible."[81] These cursory observations about gender, physicality, and sport do little to provide readers with any sense of the cultural constraints Rudolph faced as a female whose passions included athletics. Anne Schraff acknowledges that while "there was some prejudice at the time against girls getting seriously involved in sports," little could stop Rudolph, who "ignored the prejudices and went all out in sports."[82] Such narrative framing remains consistent with a grander thematic emphasis on Rudolph's agency in this and the other books for children we are examining.

The texts overwhelmingly fail to historicize Wilma Rudolph's accomplishments on the track, and those of her Tigerbelle teammates, in relation to female involvement in competitive sport in the United States. Historical change is characterized by many of the books' authors as achieved through the actions of a single individual, and instantaneous. Rudolph's efforts serve as the fulcrum for social change in Alice Flanagan's text: as the author comments, "track and field had always been considered a 'man's sport' and was limited to males. But Wilma's dominance in the sport helped to change all that."[83] Indeed, the collection, for the most part, neglects broader social movements for gender equality in the United States, both in and outside of sport.[84] Biography's aim, to highlight an individual life, can silence the place and position groups, societal institutions, and socially sanctioned norms and beliefs occupy in historical change and continuity: so seems to be the case in children's books about Rudolph.[85] The dominant message across many of the texts about Rudolph is that individual acts reign supreme over collective will to bring about societal transformation. Important to note, as well, is the absence of a discussion or even an acknowledgment of Tennessee State's preeminent position in women's track-and-field competition, beginning in the early 1950s and lasting through the early 1970s. Maureen Smith's text is the only book to recognize the significant role the historically black Tennessee State played in producing the decades-long elite women's track program.[86] As a consequence, Rudolph competes as a solo female, with teammates and competitors rarely mentioned by name and team accomplishments silenced. Thus, Rudolph's "hero[ine] in a vacuum" status actually mutes rather than amplifies her accomplishments as it misdirects readers' understanding of social change.[87]

When Rudolph's gendered identity is discussed in the books, the tendency is towards conventional understandings of femininity and athleticism. Heteronormativity, for instance, pervades the books in discussions of boyfriends and marriage, as well as in physical descriptions offered of Rudolph. The collection's first book, written in 1975, is rooted in heteronormativity: Rudolph's relationship with "Bob" Eldridge is central to the story, reifying dominant ideas about women and femininity. Jacobs's treatment of Rudolph is noteworthy in part because her three part series, titled "Women Who Win," all focused on female athletes.[88] A reader might expect a series coming on the heels of the women's movement, focusing on female athletes, and published in 1975 to present a different level of consciousness in regard to gender and sexism. Such, unfortunately, is not the case. Jacobs's heteronormative account of Rudolph's life focuses on her relationship with her eventual husband, Robert Eldridge, who throughout the book is referred to as "Bob Eldridge."

Jacobs positions Bob Eldridge throughout the book as an individual who plays a meaningful role throughout Rudolph's life, sometimes even de-centering the track star from the narrative's focus. After Rudolph's Olympic triumphs, Jacobs recounts, "[a]ll the Rudolphs celebrated. Bob Eldridge made sure that everyone in Clarksville knew of Wilma's win, he broadcast the news all over town."[89] The Olympian's accomplishments seem as much about her boyfriend and future husband. Jacobs writes that when Rudolph graduated from high school, "She walked proudly beside Bob Eldridge—grinning at him and feeling strange in her cap with its floppy tassel. Her high school years were over. Now she'd start a grown-up life away from home. Wilma was glad that Bob Eldridge would be a familiar part of that life."[90] Jacobs elevates Eldridge to Rudolph's level in the story, making her story as much about his success as her own by noting his own athletic exploits, including his All-American status in basketball. Despite the many financial and emotional hardships endured by the couple, Jacobs instead chooses to portray a "happily ever after" tale. After graduation the two married and "planned an active future together—Bob went to work as an engineer, and Wilma taught junior high school," Jacobs narrates. The book's final pages continue this thematic push with photographs of the happy couple and Jacobs's concluding remarks that Rudolph had indeed "found a quieter glory in her work, her husband, and her children."[91] Streissguth tells a similar story of Rudolph's wedding, again reinforcing the female athlete's heterosexuality. The event, Streissguth recounts, was held in a "big open field, decorated with an altar and hundreds of blue flowers." He concludes, "Soon afterward, Wilma learned she was expecting another baby."[92]

Jacobs and Streissguth represent the heteronormative pattern that runs through many of the books. The narratives mark Rudolph's looks as they reinscribe heterosexuality. Tom Biracree's focus does both, commenting after a picture of Rudolph with her children and husband that with Rudolph's "good looks and tall, graceful stature, she even modeled occasionally."[93] Others followed similar narrative lines, with Rudolph's physical appearance at the fore. According to Ruth, as Rudolph moved toward adolescence she was "blossoming into a beautiful young woman with sparkling eyes and a warm friendly smile."[94] In allaying fears that readers might have about Rudolph's femininity, the author continued, quick to explain the track's star's choice of hairstyle. Rudolph, according to Ruth, "kept her brown hair cropped short in a style that was easy to manage and conducive to athletics."[95] Discussions about clothes, hair, and make-up have long been threads woven into biographies about women written for children, and Rudolph's stories told to young readers do not deviate from these larger patterns.[96] The specter of the "mannish" athlete persists to the most contemporary of Rudolph's biographies; as one author noted, "she [Rudolph] proved that a woman could be feminine and graceful and still burn up the track."[97]

Wilma Rudolph's physical appearance and body become the points around which the demonstration of gendered normalcy is reinscribed. One photo in particular illustrates this, and in doing so, the way female athletes have long struggled with the objectification of their bodies.[98] Jacobs includes a full-page image of Rudolph from the rear, with the athlete's buttocks and legs the only parts of her body visible, her head and torso bent forward at a ninety-degree angle. Rudolph, according to the author, was "bending over in a position runners often use to relax their leg muscles, when a photographer took this shot of her long and lovely legs—legs thought hopelessly crippled by polio sixteen years before."[99] Twenty-five years later, Flanagan includes a similar photo of Rudolph stretching with her scissored legs spread in the air as three male photographers hover just feet from the athlete, with cameras at the ready.[100]

As discussed, the books engage Rudolph's gendered identity and the realities of her life as a female athlete in selective ways. Rudolph's teenage pregnancy and the treatment it receives in the books is a good case in point. To their credit, several of the chapter books do introduce Rudolph's pregnancy while a high school student. In doing so they join the nascent trend in biographies written for children to introduce issues once thought of as off-limits.[101] Those books that do include details of the athlete's pregnancy, however, tread lightly and in most instances treat the "unexpected complication" as just that.[102] The cursory attention paid to the pregnancy in a handful of the books is focused on the supportive familial response Rudolph received upon news that she was carrying her first child. In a rare admission of the challenges faced by Rudolph as a woman, Ruth acknowledges the stresses faced by the athlete as a newlywed and new mother.[103] Biracree offers readers a historical-context snapshot in trying to explain the culture surrounding Rudolph. Three decades ago, the author notes, "there were very few references to sex on television or on the radio and very little discussion of the subject in popular magazines or newspapers."[104] Anderson's sidebar "Teen Pregnancy in the 1950s" rounds out these exceptions to the more general rule of either ignoring the birth of Rudolph's first child or focusing narrow attention on individual responses to the "problem."[105] Rudolph's pregnancy, when addressed, is positioned narrowly, divorced from the complexities of the wider historical moment.

The silence in these books around sexism and the limited opportunities girls and women enjoyed in sport during the 1950s and 1960s, and some would argue today, reminds us of the staying power of sport as a masculine domain. Conceived as "natural" for boys and men, sport spaces remain the assumed province of males in our society. The lack of adequate reflection on the impact of sexism in this collection of books about one of the greatest female athletes of the twentieth century signals how tacit assumptions about gender and sport persist. While Rudolph's story is inspirational, the accounts of her life as an African American female offer very little to empower girls to be physically active and view their accomplishments as equal to their male counterparts. The books' inability to bring gender tensions and inequality out of obscurity reinforces our culture's continuing inability to understand male centrality in sport as a social construction.

The theme covered in these biographies that appears to have the most transgressive potential is race, because it is the only aspect of Rudolph's life story connected, in any meaningful way, to broader structures of power and inequality. Unlike gender, issues related to race are much more thoroughly examined in the books; relatively lengthy details about segregation, racial inequality, and the civil rights movement occupy a number of the texts. The discussions about race move the books away, albeit slightly, from their moored position in which Rudolph is de-contextualized from her surroundings. In providing a bit of historical context around racial issues and tensions, the books transition the telling of Rudolph's experiences from what VanderHaagen calls "history of a life" to "history through a life."[106] The protagonists take on a bit more historical significance in the latter, rather than the former, approach to writing.

Our analysis of the ways in which racial issues are addressed in the collection is very much informed by Herbert Kohl's provocative essay on biographies written for children and centered on Rosa Parks. In calling for "radical children's literature," Kohl asks, in broad terms, that we begin to create children's books that engage in, rather than running from, identifying and interrogating social problems, including those around race. These books might then lend themselves more easily to a celebration of collective resistance among marginalized groups, as opposed to continually re-affirming the status quo and individuality. In examining the books about Wilma Rudolph, we weigh these general approaches to reading race in children's literature, as well as some of Kohl's more specific strategies. Even as we concede attempts by some of the books to contextualize Rudolph's experiences with racial issues and tensions, we conclude that the collection is anything but radical, as defined and outlined by Kohl.[107]

To the collection's credit, structural racism, specifically segregation, is addressed, to varying degrees, in many of the books. For some of the texts, Rudolph's medical treatment as a youngster at Meharry Medical Center in Nashville offered up an early opportunity to introduce the practice of racial segregation and inequality. For example, in explaining the availability of medical care for young Rudolph, Engfer notes, "Wilma's parents could not go to the hospital because it allowed white patients only. In Clarksville, Tennessee, there was no hospital for 'colored' people." The author adds that, as African Americans, Rudolph and her mother were forced to "sit at the back of the bus," when the two made the weekly hour-long bus trips to Nashville for medical treatment. The author states, a full bus meant that African Americans were "expected to give up their seats to white riders."[108] That detail is a rare occurrence across the collection in which an author acknowledges that the flip side of black disenfranchisement is white privilege. Others allude to the racism Rudolph faced on the trips to Nashville with her mother, though they minimize its harshness and cruelty. For example, Johnson notes that "[o]ther hospitals were closer, but Meharry Medical Center was the nearest one that accepted black people as patients."[109] The author adds, "Wilma *liked* [authors' italics] the trips . . . because they gave her a chance to see the world beyond her *cozy* [authors' italics] home."[110] Johnson's description is a romanticized version of Rudolph's autobiography, in which the track great discusses the journeys across the Jim Crow South as more an ordeal than pleasurable adventure. Similarly, Flanagan explains that Rudolph needed to go to Meharry Hospital in Nashville, a medical facility "for black people founded by two black doctors." To the author, it seems the only "painful" part of the experience for Rudolph was the treatment on her leg. Far from a stark reminder of racism and injustice, "the long bus ride," as described by Flanagan, "gave Wilma a chance to get out of Clarksville. It opened up a new world for her—one full of possibilities."[111] Of course, despite the previous passage's suggestion, racism's boundaries were not confined to Clarksville.

Discussions around segregation, related to Rudolph's trips to Nashville as well as other places, often frame the practice as unfair rather than racist on both a structural and an ideological level. In doing so, the narratives fail in communicating the severity of racial injustice on African Americans and the subsequent privilege afforded whites by whites. For example, Coffey includes a brief section titled "Living with Racism," and in the glossary at the end of the book defines segregation as "When people of different races are not allowed to live and go to school together."[112] Similarly, Sherrow explains that "laws in the South treated black people unfairly," and as a result, Rudolph's family, like other black families, faced prejudice. In continuing to detail Jim Crow, the author notes, "white doctors took care of white people, and black doctors took care of black people."[113] Though children may be able to better understand the notion of "unfairness" when the observation is stated in this way, the statement nonetheless does not speak to the system's power inequities or the fact that whites gain advantage from perpetuating the racial status quo.

While the threads of Wilma Rudolph's relationship to segregation are sometimes wound very tightly, they are as often detached from discussions about the realities of racial apartheid in the American

South at midcentury. For example, Flanagan notes, "Blacks could not buy things on credit and were denied opportunities for jobs and education." Importantly linking these broader patterns of discrimination to Rudolph's world, the author continues, "white people had so many modern conveniences in their homes, and yet they hired people like her mother to clean their houses and serve them breakfast in bed." However, on the page opposite this narrative stands a photo of a white police office next to a sign, "Waiting Room for White Only. By Order Police Dept"; and a caption that reads, "When Rudolph was growing up, African-Americans and Caucasians *seemed* [emphasis added] to live in two different worlds."[114] This photo and caption stand out as noteworthy, in part, because we are left wondering how this stock photo blends with Rudolph's experiences in Tennessee; the author makes no link for the reader. Moreover, the caption's ambivalent wording obscures Jim Crow's viciousness as tentative.

In still a number of other books, Rudolph's experiences are distanced from attempts to critically explore segregation and racism. Maria Jose Botelho and Masha Kabakow Rudman conclude that biographical narratives distance the famous people from their surroundings, becoming "larger than life" in the process. In addition, the individuals and the lives they led are "rendered separate or isolated from the collective currents of participation."[115] We agree with the authors, that this should not be used as an excuse to divorce the biographical character from the wider social and political context. Tom Biracree's book serves as another example in which racism is acknowledged, with photographs helping to illustrate what segregation looked like. In this book, published in 1988 as part of the Black American series, details of Rudolph's experiences as an African American woman are lost in relation to the wider social problem of racism. Biracree includes several photos in his book that highlight desegregation, such as a 1958 photo of Tom Hawkins, African American basketball player at Notre Dame. Also included is a photo of the Little Rock Nine cohort of African American students attempting to enter Central High School in 1957.[116] As in the Flanagan book, what is missing in Biracree's text is an association between the stock photos and Rudolph or her hometown of Clarksville. Like other books in the collection, he does little to place Rudolph within this discriminatory practice. Thus, the explanatory potential and power of understanding racial oppression by highlighting links between Rudolph and broader systems of exclusion are severed.

The "nothing is impossible" formula that stretches across biographies for children and those about Wilma Rudolph extends to a perspective on racism that reduces it to a personal problem to be conquered.[117] In detailing the range of barriers that Rudolph was forced to navigate, Naden and Blue note, "poor health was not the only obstacle to Wilma's success. She also had to overcome segregation."[118] From this point of view, the onus for change is on Rudolph and not on the oppressive systems of inequality that surrounded her, nor on the white establishment that perpetuated the structure. Readers' focus and attention is centered on the individual action in response to a social problem, rather than on the issue. In commenting on Rudolph's fortitude, Amy Ruth concludes of the track star, "She vowed to break out of the poverty and servitude that had plagued her family for generations."[119] Rudolph and her success, as constructed in these narratives, become evidence in support of mythology around the power of individualism to create positive progress in her life and those of others. Rudolph was, according to Ruth, "proof there was life beyond prejudice and poverty."[120] These happily-ever-after narratives affirm Rudolph's resilience, but do little to alter the dynamics of prejudice and poverty.

The focus on individualism is a theme carried in a variety of ways throughout the texts, and includes details about Wilma Rudolph's single, brief meeting as a teenager with Jackie Robinson, documented in over half of the books. The same "overcoming" narratives that populate Rudolph's experiences are fundamental to the authors' descriptions of why Robinson is deserving of admiration. Like Rudolph, Robinson "fought a tremendous battle against racial bigotry and won," according to Biracree.[121] Described as an "inspiration to blacks," Robinson "suffered insults, rough play, and even deaths threats" in his journey to integrate major league baseball in the 1940s.[122] Robinson's presence in biographies for young readers about Rudolph underscores the universality of an American success story grounded in self-reliance.[123] Johnson, in meritocratic language, writes, "Wilma whispered to the mosquito, 'Maybe someday I'll be a hero like him.' The mosquito buzzed, 'I bet you will—if you try hard enough!'"[124] It was important for some authors to instruct readers not only *what* Robinson did, but *how* he did it. Robinson's "natural talent" and "easy going personality" helped him win fans, in spite of the racism, according to Naden and Blue.[125] The baseball great earned the nation's respect when he "overcame bigoted taunts and insults with grace and style."[126] Because Robinson was celebrated as a symbol of racial progress and integration, the inclusion of Robinson and his links to Rudolph reinforces the ethos of individualism as the path to success in the face of racism. Robinson's successful story of integrating major league baseball serves as a model for Rudolph, whose own stories serve as a model to others, including the young readers.[127]

As might be imagined, in this collection of literature the place of resistance to the racial power structure is minimal, and when featured is likely to rest with single agents versus collective opposition. Interestingly, Harper's story of Rudolph is the only one to describe the athlete's resistive responses to racism as a child, though the narrative is not without its problems. Harper's book, part of a series on famous Americans, creates imagined scenes, including one in a chapter titled "How Do You Fight Society?"[128] In it, the author partially fictionalizes an interaction discussed in Rudolph's autobiography, between a group of African American children, of which Rudolph was a part, and a group of white children. A confrontation outside of a Clarksville grocery story between the young people is said to illustrate how Rudolph "personally met prejudice at a young age." On this occasion the white children yelled things at Rudolph and other black children, like "Hey, nigger, get out of town!"; "Look out, darky!"; "Enie, meanie, miny, moe, grab that nigger by the toe!"; "Spook, spook, spook!"; "Teacher, teacher, don't hit me, hit that nigger behind that tree. . . ." Though the fights could be "nasty," the author shared, "Wilma got satisfaction out of them."[129] What are young readers to make of this story, which is certainly one of the most difficult and hurtful stories around racism in the books? Harper's use of "nigger" in the story is especially concerning, largely because there is no effort to discuss the harmful effects of the word, and it stands as the starkest example of overt racism in the books about Rudolph. Harper uses this story to end her chapter, with the next chapter addressing Rudolph's entry into organized sport, reinforcing a perspective that racism is temporary and eradicating it comes with the turn of the page to a new chapter. Segregation, as told by Harper and a number of others, is a barrier for Rudolph to overcome as an individual, and that helps increase the inspirational aspect of her accomplishments.

Wilma Rudolph's resistance, as an adult, to racial discrimination, and her participation in the civil rights movement, are barely footnotes across the books in this collection. Indeed, held at the margins are the ways in which Rudolph's individual and collective actions were aimed at unsettling rather than reinforcing status quo politics and paradigms. Though the struggle for civil rights heated up throughout the 1950s, with boycotts, sit-ins, school desegregations, and other demonstrations, we see very little evidence of that in the books, even when Rudolph injects herself into the resistance. In an insert entitled "Racism and Segregation in the Deep South," Amy Ruth details institutional and ideological aspects of racism and collective resistance to oppression. Forthright in its testament to the horrors of racial injustice, it is equally honest in situating the communal responses among African Americans and their allies. In the tensions before and following the passage of the 1964 Civil Rights Act, Ruth acknowledges, "[t]housands of ordinary citizens . . . lost their lives in the struggle to end racism and segregation in the United States."[130] The bold narrative is an anomaly amid the larger collection of books, with very few considering black acts of resistance to racism.

Scarcely present on the pages of text are Rudolph's acts of resistance to racial discrimination, including her insistence on an integrated homecoming parade and the athlete's involvement in efforts to integrate Shoney's restaurant in Clarksville in 1963. When covered in the books, these two issues rarely prompt broader discussions about and connections to civil rights agitation. A few of the books narrate the homecoming celebration's integrated composition, but only three acknowledge Rudolph's involvement in making this happen, though others are quick to highlight the seemingly happy ending as "Wilma brought Clarksville together."[131] The Shoney's protest is presented in similar fashion; it sits awkwardly within the four books in which it appears.[132] For example, in Biracree's book there is no accompanying narrative to the photo and caption of the incident. In Anderson's text the discussion is literally relegated to the margins, being included in a sidebar entitled "Protesting Segregation." Ruth's book provides the stock photo of Rudolph trying to open a locked restaurant door, accompanied by a single sentence of narrative on the subject. Maureen Smith's book provides one sentence on the incident. The attempts by Rudolph and a number of other African Americans to integrate the Clarksville Shoney's Restaurant in 1963, like other forms of resistance, are barely represented in the texts. In choosing not to include Rudolph's acts of resistance, and those of others, the books fail to tell the important story of "collective decision-making, willed risk, and coordinated action," as Kohl suggests. In making this choice, the books about Wilma Rudolph elect, instead, to follow conventional storytelling paths for young readers that privilege mythical notions of social change while silencing the presence and strength of communal resistance.[133]

In a recent *Good Morning America* segment, Kathleen Krull's book about Wilma Rudolph drew the attention of Juju Chang, one of the program's hosts, and consequently a national television audience. Rudolph's tale, as offered by Chang, was part of a week-long series, entitled "Be Inspired!," in which each of the program's handful of anchors and hosts detailed an individual who stirred them. Chang led the segment: "It's been an incredible week of inspirations that we've shared," she began. Chang, whose young son, Jared, brought the book to her attention, was clearly taken with Rudolph's story and chose it as her point of inspiration to communicate with her co-hosts and the national audience. Children's books, Chang conceded, can be "incredibly mind-numbing," but, she added, not Krull's story of Rudolph, which can be a *"lasting* source of inspiration." Chang said of the book and of Rudolph, "I didn't know of the extent of her inspirational life, and I want you to meet the amazing Olympic champion who was my inspiration . . ."[134] Clearly, Chang found Rudolph's story *inspirational*, as have countless others, through the tales told in the twenty-one children's books written about the track great. The books written about Rudolph, like so many other biographical texts written for children, are composed with the intent to "leave readers with lumps in their throats."[135] They do just that: the books continually reconstruct and strengthen dominant values of agency and individualism, especially as they relate to cultural and social constraints. Indeed, depicting achievement in children's books, including in those about Wilma Rudolph, encourages young readers to "make a difference," but rarely incites them to "challenge the rules of the world they inherit."[136]

7

On the Margins of Memory

The Politics of Remembering and Forgetting
Wilma Rudolph through Material Culture

WILMA RUDOLPH has been commemorated in a variety of spaces, including a US postage stamp, a statue, a road race, a state historical marker, a residential center, an indoor track, street names, and a stretch of highway.[1] In this chapter, we seek to interrogate the processes of memorializing Rudolph and the subsequent ways in which she has been both remembered and forgotten, through a closer study of several memorial sites. We examine the process of memorialization, and also the final "product": specifically, several markers within her hometown of Clarksville, Tennessee; the postage stamp; and sites of memory on the Tennessee State campus. Clarksville, host to Rudolph's integrated parade, once again emerges as a "character" in Rudolph's narrative and in the racial stories the city told about itself and its citizens as they honored their native daughter.

After coming home to Clarksville with three gold medals, Rudolph struggled to capitalize on her track and field success. Limited opportunities for women in the sport eventually forced Rudolph to retire from track and field and return to her hometown, where she found employment as a teacher at her former elementary school. She continued to find various jobs for short stretches of time. However, she was usually hired because of her athletic accomplishments and not necessarily for her job skills, which often left Rudolph ill-prepared for these positions. Despite employment challenges, athletic-related accolades continued, however, as she won a number of prestigious awards and was inducted into several Halls of Fame for her triple gold medal performance.[2] While both Clarksville and Tennessee State were quick to remember her every Olympiad, such efforts were well after her track and field career were finished, with many coming after her death in 1994.

In Clarksville, Rudolph is commemorated in a variety of ways, including a statue, a state historical marker, and a stretch of Highway 79. Her gravestone is also a site of memorialization, and will be included in this chapter. Each remembrance of the former track great illustrates how politicized and contentious the process of memorialization can be. For example, Rudolph's statue initially prompted great debate as to where it should be located, eventually finding a place on Clarksville's Riverfront Walk, only to be moved in October 2012 to the new Wilma Rudolph Event Center at Liberty Park. Being outside of the town's core, Rudolph's statue holds a peripheral position relative to the numerous other memorials and statues occupying Clarksville's center. The city's most famous daughter is marginalized, literally and symbolically, in relation to Clarksville's history—past, present, and future. Place matters, even in death: Rudolph is buried in Foston Memorial Gardens, a small cemetery for African Americans in Clarksville. Similarly, we examine the placement of the historical marker and the location of the highway named for her, as well as the segregated cemetery, sometimes in juxtaposition with other markers and statues. These spaces and tributes, we argue, are imbued with power illuminating gendered and racialized constructions of cultural landscapes.

Richard Schein, in writing about cultural landscapes, reminds us that cities and spaces are racially coded, and following Toni Morrison, posits that "*all* American landscapes can be seen through a lens of race, *all* American landscapes are racialized."[3] Dolores Hayden suggests that "public space can nurture a subtle and profound sense of what it means to be an American and act as a storehouse for social memory and identity. This power of place, this power of ordinary urban landscapes to encompass a shared history and a shared civic identity remains untapped for most ethnic history and for most women's history."[4] Murray Phillips, Mark O'Neill, and Gary Osmond echo Hayden, contending, "[T]he way that athletes from marginalized groups have been recalled in public monuments is a rich vein for investigation. As with much traditional history, monuments inside and outside of sport have predominantly celebrated 'heroic [white] manhood.'. . . . These artifacts communicate not just one version of the past, but multiple narratives that are seen, interpreted, and used by individuals and groups in myriad ways."[5] This chapter examines the multiple ways Rudolph is remembered through various elements of material culture. More specifically, our aim is to explore how public monuments honoring Rudolph in Clarksville explicitly celebrate an African American female in an urban landscape largely void of such representation. We contend that the process of commemoration marginalizes Rudolph, in both symbolic and structural ways, as much as it pays homage to the athlete.

Whether by a statue or a postage stamp, the process of remembering Wilma Rudolph is as much about forgetting as it is about recall. This dichotomy is a provocative one, especially as it exposes the racialized cultural landscape of Rudolph's hometown of Clarksville, a place central to the process of memorializing the track star. Andrew Butterfield, in writing about various ways that individuals are remembered and commemorated, sees monuments as "the products of primary human needs; and they serve these needs in a way that nothing else can serve them. People build monuments not because they do not know what else to do, but because there are wounds so deep that only monuments will serve to honor them."[6] We consider the Rudolph memorial sites as they relate to Clarksville's wounds, many inflicted primarily as a result of the city's history of segregation, and its struggles to come to terms with the civil rights movement and efforts to integrate. In this chapter, we assess and interrogate the numerous efforts to memorialize Rudolph using material culture. While we include the postage stamp and the various remembrances of Rudolph at Tennessee State, our primary focus centers on Clarksville and four memorials for Rudolph: the re-naming of Highway 79 in her honor, the statue of Rudolph by Howard A. Brown, her gravestone in Foston Memorial Gardens, and the state historical marker erected beside the re-named Wilma Rudolph Boulevard.

These various sites of memory and commemoration serve as physical reminders of Rudolph's origins in Clarksville, and pay tribute to the athlete while also celebrating the city. We contend that these assorted representations of Rudolph serve multiple, though sometimes competing, purposes, rooted in honor and celebration. Examined as a collection, they indicate the growing importance of physical statuary and objects in the continued construction of narratives related to Rudolph and her achievements. Taken as a whole, the sites of memory included here illustrate not only the power of public monuments to communicate a history, but the particular political and cultural meanings attached to those monuments. Commemorations to Rudolph, largely since her death, write and re-write historical narratives, and as a result, are struggled and fought over by antagonists who are well aware of the power entrenched in stamps, statues, and street signs.

Tennessee State Remembers Rudolph

Like many colleges and universities across the country, Tennessee State has remembered important contributors to their campus history with names on buildings and other facilities, as well as on physical statuary. It comes as no surprise, then, that Tennessee State, Rudolph's alma mater, has led with its own efforts to commemorate their most famous Olympian.[7] Similar to other sites of memory, Tennessee State's tributes to Rudolph tell us as much about the institution doing the remembering as they tell about the track great. Eager to remember Rudolph as an important figure in their past, the university has sprinkled structural reminders around the campus. The school's indoor track is named for the track great, and a dormitory on the edge of campus is also named for her. Like other "factual" claims associated with Rudolph's past, the sign out front incorrectly recalls her winning four gold medals rather than three.[8] The "modern six story structure," approved by the Tennessee State Regents, features suite-style rooms, a cafeteria, beauty salon, and lounges: the new home to 420 women. At the unveiling ceremony, Coach Temple spoke, telling the audience, "The center is certainly named after a classy young lady.

It's a great tribute. Wilma would have been awfully happy that such a magnificent structure was named in her honor."[9] Additional areas of campus bear reminders of the school's Olympic past. Tigerbelle Drive, for example, is situated on the edge of campus, and a major thorough-fare running adjacent to campus is named Ed Temple Boulevard. Near the track facilities, an "artistic" sculpture honors the school's multiple Olympians.

Perhaps nowhere else on the historically black college campus are there more memories of Rudolph than the Tennessee State University Library. It includes a number of exhibitions showcasing the Tiger-belles, with several cases devoted to the Olympian. These showcases are numerous and contain newspaper and magazine clippings, pho-tographs, and other items such as relay batons. There are two rooms on the second floor devoted to storing the memorabilia collected by Coach Ed Temple, encased with walls of glass panes allowing a pass-erby to look into them but restricting access. In addition, the Ten-nessee State University Archives, also located in the library, contain materials related to Rudolph and the Tigerbelles.

The University and its archives are central institutions whose self-appointed charge it has been to memorialize Wilma Rudolph. Its abil-ity to remember Rudolph is hindered, however, by the realities of a historical legacy of second-class status afforded historically black col-leges and universities in the United States. Remembering Rudolph's past is made a bit more difficult in this space, where materials have not been indexed and catalogued. Files and other materials related to Rudolph and her Tigerbelle teammates are not consistently labeled, while others are in no particular order. Some items in the archives were the handiwork of Ed Temple's wife, Charlie, who pasted articles into scrapbooks, though often without dates and names of newspa-pers. The status of the artifacts associated with Rudolph in the Ten-nessee State University Library underscores a consequence of chronic underfunding of historically black schools. This, in turn, throws into sharp relief the politics of materiality and how angles of power play upon remembering.[10]

Wilma Rudolph as a Postcard Stamp

Receiving one of the nation's "highest tributes,"[11] Rudolph was honored with a United States postage stamp on July 14, 2004. After a lengthy selection process by the Citizens' Stamp Advisory Committee, Rudolph was issued as the fifth stamp in the Distinguished American series, joining US Army four-star General Joseph Stilwell (2000), Florida Democrat Claude Pepper (2000), Arkansas Senator Hattie W. Caraway (2001), and novelist Edna Ferber (2002).[12] Rudolph's twenty-three cent stamp, which at the time would have covered the cost of mailing a postcard or the second ounce of first-class letters, was designed by Richard Sheaff. Illustrated by Canadian scratchboard artist, Mark Summers, Rudolph's likeness, a headshot, presents her as the twenty-year-old athlete at the 1960 Olympic Games. The US Postal Service does consider the artwork on stamps to be just that—artwork, with the USPS sponsoring exhibits that display and discuss stamps as pieces of art. The USPS contends that "capturing the essence of a subject at stamp size is something only a select group of artists has mastered."[13] Peter Emmerich, whose art appears on the Art of Disney stamps, claims, "For an illustrator working in the US, what could be more exciting than creating the art for a postage stamp? I think even a *New Yorker* cover would be in second place. For stamps, your artwork is reproduced in an edition of millions, and then sent all over the world."[14] Moreover, the USPS, in making the stamps and their subjects accessible to the public, creates mini-biographies of their subjects to indicate that they are "stamp worthy." David Failor, the executive director of Stamp Services for the postal service, speaking to the significance of being honored with a stamp, said, "When you look at the stamp program, it's really a reflection of America, who we are, the people that made us great, the events that made us great, the things that reflect our culture and diversity."[15]

Rudolph's USPS biography, provided in the release of the stamp, is familiar, and reiterates points in the athlete's life that are highlighted in so many other formats. In the press release notifying the public, Rudolph is identified as having her left leg "crippled by polio," which caused her to wear a leg brace until she was twelve years old. Rudolph, according to the release, won three gold medals at the 1960 Rome Olympic Games on a sprained ankle and retired at the "height of her success" in 1962. "Respected for her perseverance and grace," Rudolph won a number of awards for her athletic accomplishments. The short biography ends with Rudolph's 1994 death.[16] Similarly, in their review of the stamp, the *Journal of Sport Philately* focused on her childhood illnesses, life in the segregated South, and her athletic accomplishments. The publication heralded the Rudolph stamp and noted that it was for her a "fitting honor [to be] the first Olympian commemorated on a US definitive stamp," one that replaced the twenty-three cent George Washington stamp. As a definitive stamp, Rudolph's "visage will appear frequently on mail."[17]

Rudolph's stamp was unveiled in Sacramento, California, as part of the 2004 US Track and Field Olympic Trials, which allowed for a midfield ceremony celebrating the athlete and her stamp. In attendance were former teammates and other American Olympians, including several Tennessee State Tigerbelles, Jackie Joyner-Kersee, Bob Beamon, and Billy Mills.[18] At the Sacramento first-day-of-issue dedication, US Postal Service vice president Henry Pankey proclaimed his delight in honoring Rudolph's accomplishments with the new stamp, pleased that Rudolph's "unforgettable smile" would "grace a new postage stamp," and he included his summation of her story, telling the crowd, "Wilma Rudolph was simply amazing. She overcame a number of debilitating illnesses to become one of this nation's greatest athletes. She taught us, among other things, not to allow our circumstances to hinder our potential to succeed."[19] Pankey's remarks made clear the cultural significance of Rudolph's image on a postage stamp, telling the audience that the Postal Service understands "the power our stamps have in helping to celebrate special people—like Wilma Rudolph—who have helped to define our world." Rudolph's compelling biography was alluded to again when Pankey ended, "In this small way, we have created a lasting tribute to her perseverance and accomplishments."[20] There was also a second release of the stamp hosted in Clarksville, Rudolph's hometown, an event held the day after Sacramento's release, with a ceremony at the St. Bethlehem post office and another ceremony in front of Rudolph's statue on Riverside Drive.[21] The city was disappointed that the first day of issue was not happening in Clarksville, noting that the event was good public relations for the Olympic trials, but dismissive of Rudolph's hometown. The editors of the *Leaf-Chronicle* claimed that "the stamp will not only bring more attention to Rudolph but it will shine the spotlight favorably on Clarksville as well."[22] St. Bethlehem postal manager John Padgett was confused by the decision to have Sacramento host the first-day-of-issue ceremony, reminding the public that Clarksville was the only American city to have a post office on Wilma Rudolph Boulevard.[23] This exchange represents a small, yet important, illustration of the contested nature of commemoration and remembering.

In her statements to the US House of Representatives two days after the dedication of Rudolph's stamp, Tennessee representative Marsha Blackburn acknowledged Clarksville mayor Don Trotter and Clarksville postmaster Wayne Scott for putting Rudolph forward for the long awaited honor. Blackburn saw the stamp as a "fitting reminder of her accomplishments" and predicted Clarksville residents would purchase the stamp honoring their former resident.[24] Reverend Jimmy Terry of Clarksville stated, "I just think it's way past due, but I'm excited that America is honoring her achievements on a national and international level." He hoped the stamp would help support the efforts to have Rudolph honored with a historic marker.[25]

The stamp did indeed draw attention locally and across the globe since its release in 1994; the small artwork has been included in various postal exhibitions, highlighting Rudolph's inclusion in "Women and Stamps" as well as "African Americans and Stamps."[26] Other countries honored Rudolph with stamps prior to the United States; these include Mongolia (along with Jesse Owens, in 1969), Liberia in conjunction with the 1984 Summer Games, Grenada in 1996, and Australia, in a series of six different images.[27]

Gary Osmond provides one of the most comprehensive arguments for the academic examination of postage stamps, and his work supports our premise that Rudolph on a postage stamp is a significant and symbolic honor. According to Osmond, stamps "lack the sweep and emotion of films, the depth and authenticity of books, the permanence and immediacy of statues . . . [and] appear to be at best 'modest monuments' of little long-term consequence as historical evidence."[28] Despite these shortcomings, Osmond asserts that stamps merit serious consideration, signifying "government documents" that simultaneously serve utilitarian and commemorative functions. Stamps are sources of "symbolic messages," according to Osmond, and "as histories in miniature they offer selective readings of the past."[29]

Not all Americans, however, were impressed with Rudolph supporters' particular readings of the past in the honor bestowed on the Olympian. On the white supremacist website "Stormfront," a discussion thread included posts that suggested drawing nooses around Rudolph's image. In addition, it was also offered that putting a stamp of a Klansman on a horse adjacent to Rudolph's image would create the appearance of the athlete running for her life. Another post recalled returning the Rudolph stamps to the post office to exchange them for stamps of George Washington, someone the writer felt deserved a stamp. Another post included a link to what they perceived to be Rudolph's "sob story."[30] These perspectives illustrate the notion that our beliefs about the past and those who occupied it can be multivocal and contentious.

Wilma Rudolph Boulevard

As we suggested at the beginning of the chapter, Rudolph's hometown of Clarksville has memorialized its heroine by renaming a stretch of highway, installing a roadside marker, creating and installing a statue, and raising funds to erect her gravestone. We turn our attention for the remainder of the chapter to these sites of memory and the various ways each underscores the politics of remembering and memorializing the former Olympic champion. On May 7, 1992, the Clarksville City Council voted to approve the renaming of a stretch of US Highway 79, also known as Guthrie Highway, for Wilma Rudolph. Only a month earlier, the city council had rejected the proposal by a nine-to-three vote. In what has been described as a "hotly contested political issue," the reversal by the city council came as a result of an amendment which provided business owners along the highway prior to January 1994 with time to change their stationary and other printed materials.[31] The compromise, offered by the Trane Company, Sears, and other large businesses along the highway, led Councilman Mark Holleman to comment, "We need to portray a positive image and create harmony and good will. It already has the honorary designation and we need to go ahead and make it permanent: we need to go ahead and name it."[32] Holleman's statement illustrates the city leaders' desire to frame the town as a racially harmonious place to live, a theme echoed throughout the process of the renaming of Guthrie Highway as much as other Rudolph sites.

The months leading up to the eventual compromise were a time of renewed soul-searching for Clarksville residents, business owners, and politicians, with the initial efforts to honor Rudolph renewing dialogues around the city's racial past. Efforts to honor Rudolph had begun years earlier. In April 1986, Representative Stan Darnell proposed a resolution later approved by the Tennessee General Assembly to rename US 79 North for Wilma Rudolph. On May 14, 1986, the general assembly approved the name change as honorary rather than official, resulting in what Representative Peggy Steed Knight claimed was the erection of a "little dinky sign," which Knight saw as an insult to Rudolph and her accomplishments.[33] Knight's 1992 legislative efforts, which she admitted were thirty years too late, were proposals to officially rename US 79 North as Wilma Rudolph Boulevard and to post signs at the exits of the city proclaiming it as the hometown of Rudolph.

Needing a two-thirds approval of Clarksville's city council, the resolutions were met with opposition. Initially, the resistance to the name change was explained as the actual process of the name change rather than the honoring of Rudolph, as expressed by Representative Tommy Head, who reported, "The people in that area don't support it . . . I haven't had the first person who lives on that road or who has a business there to tell me they support it. They are not concerned about who it's named after—just changing the name."[34] Knight disagreed with Head's assessment, claiming that the opposition was rooted in gender and racial discrimination, a claim supported by Reverend Jerry Jenkins, president of Clarksville's NAACP, who lamented, "It takes some of the joy away when you have to fight to get things done." Jenkins went further, suggesting that if a white man from Clarksville had won three gold medals, "his reception would have been quite different. At the base of what everybody says, it is racial."[35]

The news coverage of the issue prompted Clarksville resident Vic Williams to write a letter to the editor of the local *Leaf-Chronicle*, saying the proposal was "inane" and "destitute of merit." Mr. Williams suggested there were dozens of other Clarksville natives worthy of such an honor, and attempts to be apolitical in his explanation. "Whether you are white, black, or somewhere in between, I see no honor, nor claim to fame, nor a benefit to mankind, just because you might be able to outrun a jackrabbit," quipped the Clarksvillian. He continued, "With no discredit to Ms. Rudolph, if her ability to run is a major claim to fame for Clarksville, then, in my opinion, Clarksville is in trouble." Williams even suggested that former State Representative Stan Darnell, who was the originator of the resolution years earlier, lost his re-election bid as a result of his efforts to rename the thoroughfare.[36] Despite Williams's opposition, the very next day, Knight's bill to erect signs honoring Rudolph at the exits for Clarksville was passed in the State Senate by a vote of thirty-two to zero.[37] Perhaps in a response to Williams, but at the least, reflective of their desire to reframe the discussion around their city's image, the *Leaf-Chronicle* authored an editorial, "Recognizing Hero," only days after Williams's letter appeared in their pages. The editorial reminds Clarksville residents of Rudolph's inspiring life story of "overcoming childhood polio to become a premiere track star," and claims that only a "select number of communities can boast of being the hometown of a gold medal Olympian." Stating that Rudolph's "spirit shines on in Clarksville," the newspaper's editors stated the "signs would just provide a way of telling those folks traveling along the interstate that Clarksville and Tennessee are proud of their native daughter and all that she has accomplished."[38]

In the week that followed, the newspaper published a number of letters to the editor responding to the controversy, largely in support of Rudolph and the city's embrace of the Olympian. Naomi Sample, lamenting the poor behavior so often highlighted in the news, saw Rudolph as an inspiration, and chided her neighbors for their opposition; "We need someone who fights when it's easier to quit. Wilma Rudolph is such a person. When faced with the possibility of never walking, she walked; and having walked, she ran; and having run, she excelled. She brought pride and honor to our nation, to our state, and to our town. Don't belittle it and don't diminish it." Sample continued in a vein that acknowledged the opposition of local businesses; "It makes one wonder just what sort of people are running the businesses along Wilma Rudolph Boulevard that none want that stretch of highway named for her. Oh yes, Clarksville, you are working very hard toward beautification, and you are doing a good job. What a shame that there is still ugliness within."[39] Similarly, Randall Madison wondered if the businesses would actually lose more money by offending Clarksville's African American residents who would discontinue shopping as a result of the resistance, and echoed previous statements made by Reverend Jenkins, suggesting there would be no controversy if the honor was a tribute to a white male from Clarksville. Madison concluded that it was time for Clarksville residents to "come together for the good of our city and community."[40] Margie Caso wrote that she was "appalled" at Vic Williams's letter to the editor and thought the city "should feel proud and honored to pay tribute to a Clarksville native, who excelled so well in her field."[41] Montgomery county commissioner Houston Wade supported the suggestion of another reader to name the street Rudolph grew up on, rather than a main highway, for the athlete. After all, according to Wade, Rudolph "is not an Oprah Winfrey or Bill Cosby."[42]

The vote to rename US 79 North, known locally as Guthrie Highway, was set for April 2. Councilman Alvin Oldham, responsible for bringing the vote to the council, reportedly had signatures from sixty-five businesses and five hundred residents along the corridor to be renamed. It was reported before the vote that Tennessee Department of Transportation Commissioner Jim Evans had told Mayor Don Trotter that the city was responsible for passing the ordinance to rename the highway, a move already approved by the state legislature.[43] At the April 2nd council meeting, in a "slap in the face to the black community," the Clarksville city council rejected the proposal to rename Guthrie Highway for Rudolph by a decisive nine 'no' votes to three 'yes' votes, with Oldham, W. L. Burnett, and Sam Johnson representing the members in favor of the name change. The nine council members voting 'no' explained that the costs to business owners to change their letterhead and stationary would simply be too costly to justify a name change. Oldham was disappointed and noted the city had named other streets for individuals without voting and claimed, "[t]here has not been this kind of problem in other cities." Likewise, Burnett pointed out the number of African Americans who attended the council meeting, proclaiming, "[t]his is the first time in my 20 years on the council that I've seen this many blacks. That should tell you how important this is to them. Not only blacks, but there are whites who feel that this should be done. I think that for too long, maybe the black community has been shortchanged. And if we vote this down, I feel sure we will send a message throughout this community which will not be good."[44]

The message was heard throughout Clarksville, with more letters to the editor expressing disappointment, embarrassment, and charges of racism toward the southern city. Byron Lawrence saw the rejection as an insult to all Clarksville residents and thought the decision explained why Rudolph no longer lived in her hometown. He noted the number of other Clarksville residents honored with street names, none of which were world champions like Rudolph, and urged all Clarksville residents regardless of their race to support the renaming efforts. Lawrence closed his letter wondering, "What kind of message are the officials of Clarksville sending we people of color, when they refuse to honor Ms. Rudolph with a street bearing her name. But we have in our community a Gallows Hollow pumping station. Gallows Hollow speaks for itself."[45]

High school student Dawn Wilson was inspired by Rudolph, and was "ashamed of the treatment this city has extended toward Ms.

Rudolph." Wilson suggested if Rudolph was "a white, male baseball player, we would have streets, schools, and parks named after her." Wilson then gave her fellow Clarksville residents a history lesson on their hometown hero:

> Our town's recognition of this inspiring Olympian is long overdue. Clarksville can never make up for the years of shabby, backhanded treatment toward their native daughter, but naming a road or a school in her honor would be a start. In the August 1989 edition of National Geographic, Ms. Rudolph related her story of how after she returned from the Olympics, Clarksville tried to have a parade for her. She refused to attend the parade on the basis that it would be segregated. Maybe it is time to have that parade now; but, of course, from the recent attitudes of some of our citizens, I gather that Clarksville has not advanced much since 1960. To the city of Clarksville: step into the '90s.[46]

Magnolia Elliot was not surprised by the council's decision, but did think they made the wrong decision. Elliot recalled being at the parade for Rudolph after her gold-medal performances and overhearing another resident claim, "Well, it took a black woman to put Clarksville on the map," and chided her city for not moving in the direction of other cities who had named streets for prominent African Americans, listing Cleveland, Ohio, naming a street for Martin Luther King Jr., and Louisville, Kentucky, honoring Muhammad Ali.[47] Carolyn Cowan was straightforward in charging the council with racism. Cowan wrote to the newspaper, saying, "Pardon me, Clarksville, but your racism is showing. Not only your racism, but your sexism as well. I'm referring to the people who opposed the re-naming of Guthrie Highway to honor Wilma Rudolph Boulevard." Like other letter writers, she believed that if the individual had been white and male, there would be no controversy. The excuse of ordering new stationery was an indication to Cowan that the merchants did not "value the patronage of the black community," which according to Cowan, was a significant percentage of the city's population. She ended her letter with a statement connecting the council's decision to the reputation of the city. "It is unfortunate," writes Cowan, "that the opposition has given another opportunity for more bad publicity across the state for Clarksville."[48] Wayne Stanley echoed Cowan's sentiments about the place of Rudolph's identity and the discussion with his letter. "First off," he begins, "the lady has two strikes against her. One she's black and the other being female. If a William Rudolph, white male, had won four Olympic medals, this town would be Rudolphville not Clarksville. To use the excuse of people having to spend extra money on stationery is absurd as no extra money would have to be spent."[49]

The *Leaf-Chronicle* recognized the chasm in the city as a result of the vote, and published a second editorial in less than two weeks addressing the name change. Noting the numerous honors Clarksville had already bestowed on their hometown hero, including the city's first integrated events in 1960 welcoming Rudolph home with a parade and banquet, and the naming of a pavilion at Fairgrounds Park, the newspaper suggested finding another landmark in the city to name for the Olympian or maybe a new school or the next major highway in the city. The editorial closed, "Ms. Rudolph accomplished something in the field of athletics that only a select few can lay claim to. She did it after suffering a terrible disease and during an era when blacks and women did not have nearly as many opportunities as they do today. Her success, then, should be an inspiration to all of us— black and white, male and female—on how perseverance can triumph over adversity. If naming something in her honor will help to remind us of that important lesson, then City Council should by all means do so."[50]

Several days later, the debate continued with the Rudolph Boulevard Group considering a "selective buying" campaign aimed at businesses along Guthrie Highway. The group was scheduled to meet in three weeks "to assess progress toward the name change and move to the next stage of action of the campaign as dictated by current events," specifically the upcoming city council vote on May 7. In the same edition, reader Wayne Stanley, in his second letter to the editor in a week, argued the same points; Rudolph's race and gender were working against her in the name change debate.[51] Over a week later, three letters to the editor appeared in the newspaper, with two arguing in support of the name change. J. D. Corbett noted that Clarksville was home to Bruce Jenner Drive, Mark Spitz Drive, and Jim Thorpe Drive, yet none of these men hailed from Clarksville. He also noted the absence of any streets named for African American Olympians, male or female, and closed his letter asking, "What will it take for African-American Olympic champions to be honored in Clarksville?" Clarice Ciardy-White felt the 9–3 vote against the name change was "blatant racism," and was "ashamed and disappointed" in her hometown. Reader Vic Williams, however, celebrated the integrity of the nine votes against the name change, arguing that Rudolph should have never been considered, "when so many notable Clarksvillians here, [for] too long, lacked recognition of their achievements, personal sacrifice, perseverance against hopeless odds, and their bravery and unselfish commitment to preserve our freedoms and way of life." In Williams's view, military heroes were more worthy than "the ability to run a 100 yards a few fractions of a second faster than someone else on a particular day."[52]

At the moment Clarksville was engaging in debate over the boulevard, nationwide attention turned to the Los Angeles riots (sparked by the acquittal of the four white police officers in the beating of Rodney King). The events in Southern California were clearly on the minds of Clarksville residents. Though geographically far from Clarksville, the issue had impact nonetheless, reminding Clarksville residents of racial injustices and possible responses to such disparities.[53] On the front page of the May 1 edition of the *Leaf-Chronicle*, an article, "No Local Rallies Over L.A. Riots," detailed the beating of a Clarksville teen at the hands of a "gang of black males," but made no connection between the riots in Los Angeles. However, "supporters" of the Committee to Promote Wilma Rudolph Boulevard said the "police brutality decision should raise the consciousness of black Americans regarding the lack of progress in race relations."[54] In that same edition, and only a week before the City Council's May 7 vote, in reaction to the Council's original vote, Clarksville citizen Ora L. Corbett made her position clear. In a letter to the editor, Corbett opined that

Rudolph should be "a number one candidate for hometown honors," noting that Rudolph had often called Clarksville home.[55]

In its second vote on the issue in as many months, the Clarksville City Council voted nine to three to rename Guthrie Highway for Wilma Rudolph on May 7, 1992. Not devoid of controversy, an amendment stipulating that the official name change be delayed for two years appeased those with continuing reservations. The time delay compromise ultimately led to the proposal's passage.[56] At least one reader was paying attention to the changed minds of council voters. Reader Vic Williams, in his third letter to the editor on the subject, suggested Councilman Charles Patterson resign his seat. One reason provided by Williams was Patterson's "apparent caving in to the demands of the Negro community with what I deem to be a political cowardice on May 7 when he voted in favor" of the Rudolph name change, when he had originally voted against it.[57] Still, despite the agreed upon delay until 1994, discussions were already underway as how best to make the transition with the highway signs. A few days later, the *Leaf-Chronicle*, in an editorial, "Good Resolution," applauded the decision of the city council to name the highway for Rudolph. The editors acknowledged the debate that surrounded the naming of the highway, including the perceived racism felt by many black Clarksvillians. The editors suggested that "Clarksville doesn't need the type of widespread, adverse publicity that it had started to receive as a result of the controversy." In closing the editorial, the newspaper stated, "And now, Clarksville can finally put this issue behind it and work on other, weightier matters that affect those who live in this community."[58] Perhaps not a surprise, the local press was unable or unwilling to see a debate over a street name as symbolic of broader racial issues and tensions. The newspapers did not mention the Los Angeles riots, or whether they believed the Council felt any pressure to reverse their decision, instead celebrating the city's vote and ability to move forward.

As the time drew near for businesses to shift to the new Rudolph designation, the city government's ambivalence remained in evidence. Clarksville city attorney David Haines suggested it was at the discretion of each business to identify its address as Wilma Rudolph

Boulevard and that the city had little control of the matter, noting, "[T]he resolution simply changed the road's designation."[59] Haines noted that one resulting problem might be a delay in postal service. Mark Baggett, the owner of St. Bethlehem Pawn Shop, was not opposed to the change, but suggested that people who were "just needed something else to gripe about." He asked, "What's in a name change?"[60]

Derek Alderman noted similar resistance from business owners to the renaming of Ninth Street in Chattanooga, Tennessee to become one of 730 places in the United States with roads named in honor of Martin Luther King Jr.[61] Real estate developer T. A. Lupton argued that he would have difficulty in renting office space along the proposed road; stating that the street was not related to King, was no longer a "solid black street," and "no longer a residential street or rundown business street," but had become a "top class business street that (could) play a great part in the future of Chattanooga."[62] Alderman identifies several hundred American cites with streets named for the slain civil rights leader and views street naming to be "the latest chapter in a long line of African American struggles for social justice."[63] Alderman concludes that the streets named for King commemorate the civil rights movement, but more importantly, address the "unfinished nature of King's dream of racial equality and social justice."[64] In this way, the debate surrounding the renaming of the highway for Rudolph echoes similar debates and arguments. Interesting connections, between the athlete and the civil rights leader, reflect the symbolism shared surrounding their names on street signs and the workings of power in the process.

The location of the Boulevard itself is also rich with symbolism and imbued with the legacies of racism in the American South. The stretch of Highway 79 named for Rudolph is located in St. Bethlehem, once a small town outside Clarksville. But with the infusion of the Trane Company, Sears, and other businesses, St. Bethlehem has developed into an industrial park, blurring the boundaries of the expanding city of Clarksville.[65] Rudolph was born in St. Bethlehem in 1940, when Clarksville was segregated. During her childhood, Rudolph's family moved from the rural St. Bethlehem to the city of Clarksville, where her mother worked as a domestic and her father as a porter, and she attended segregated schools. Naming the stretch of road for Rudolph outside the city boundaries is one example of "social geography," which is "shaped by both white prejudice and social bonds within a black culture."[66] Maoz Azaryahu suggests that street naming is "laden with political meaning and represents a certain theory of the world that is associated with and supportive of the hegemonic social-political order."[67] Street names, according to Alderman, serve to legitimize "a selective vision of the past, making historical representations appear to be the natural order of things."[68] At the same time, street names can also symbolize "a shift in the racialized balance of power between blacks and whites as well as racial progress within communities."[69] This does not, however, appear to be the case for Clarksville in relation to Rudolph Boulevard.

Rudolph Boulevard both serves as a space/location for the athlete to remain outside the heart of Clarksville, and simultaneously affirms the former Olympian's identity as part of the community. Clarksville claims Wilma Rudolph as a symbol of individual success and as someone able to overcome poverty and segregation. Yet, racism's legacies endure and are evidenced in the very locations designated to "honor" Rudolph. Poverty and racial segregation relegated Rudolph's family home to the outskirts of town, distanced from Clarksville's civic and economic core. Efforts to pay homage to Rudolph rest on the same geographies of race that removed her family, and other African Americans, from the city's center decades earlier. In death, Wilma Rudolph remains distanced from the town that continually seeks to claim her as its most famous daughter. David Sibley, in writing about spatial and moral boundaries, discusses imaginary geographies, where minorities are located "elsewhere," which is often a "spatial periphery," such as the edge of a city, "distant from the locales of the dominant majority."[70]

Over Rudolph's lifetime, Clarksville did integrate, and African Americans became active and engaged citizens at most levels of local politics. The politics of remembering, so evident in Clarksville, are shared in other places as well. Other southern heritage sites have skill-fully promoted their sites while leaving out significant racial storylines. Samuel Dennis, in his analysis of Hampton Plantation State Historic Site in South Carolina, found no reminders of the slave labor that had been integral to the functioning of the plantation. Consistent with other heritage sites, the location was developed to tell visitors the story of the white inhabitants of the land at the expense of the labor of the slave families.[71] According to W. Fitzhugh Brundage, "the tourist South became a stage on which southerners presented the South both as they wanted to see it and as they imagined tourists wanted to expe-rience it."[72] By 1994, when the new street signs were posted along Highway 79, the remnants of the segregated Clarksville of Rudolph's coming of age in the 1960s had been virtually "erased." The impor-tance of place/site naming was certainly not lost on Rudolph, who upon seeing her name on a street sign, commented, "I've seen my name in a lot of different places, but it doesn't have the same meaning as this."[73]

Rudolph's Gravestone

Soon after Rudolph's death in November 1994, the Wilma Rudolph Memorial Committee was formed. Tasked with raising funds to place a headstone at Rudolph's grave, the committee did so the follow-ing year.[74] Rudolph's headstone is quite elaborate, both in compari-son with the surrounding markers and as an individual piece of art.[75] The gravestone's front features an image of Rudolph. Etched into the stone, the artistic rendering has Rudolph's chin resting in her hands as she gazes straight ahead. With earrings clearly apparent and hair styled, the mature depiction is in contrast to the youthful sketch of the athlete on the postage stamp. In death she is imagined as an adult aging gracefully.

Olympic imagery is central to the grave marker: the Games' torch and five rings, along with a depiction of Rudolph's three gold medals, are on the gravestone. Below this, to the right, on the front side, but on a separate stone not level with her name and image, is an image of a gas-burning lamp on a book. Under Rudolph's image is her name

Figure 7.1. Wilma Rudolph's gravestone in Clarksville, Tennessee. Reprinted with permission of Maureen M. Smith.

in capital letters, WILMA GLODEAN RUDOLPH, with her date of birth and date of death underneath: JUNE 23, 1940–NOV 12, 1994. Below that, in smaller capital letters, CITIUS—ALTIUS—FORTIUS (the Olympics motto). On the base, almost mirroring these three words, in capital letters, are their English translations: FASTER—HIGHER—STRONGER. On the top of her gravestone, which is not horizontal, there is text reading down and across, in capital letters, and centered. The text details her participation in the 1956 and 1960 Olympic Games, as well her three gold medals in 1960. It also notes several of her awards and hall-of-fame memberships.[76] The inscription on the marker reads like a vita whose "facts" are impossible to change or forget, since they are permanently marked in stone. Rudolph's headstone is larger than most of the gravestones in the cemetery, including those of her parents, with her mother's headstone adjacent, and her father's small headstone some distance away under a tree on the edge of the cemetery. The cemetery marks a space of African American geography segregated from white Clarksville.

Cemeteries are "powerful cultural spaces . . . sites of public and private memorial representations" of the past, according to Mike Huggins. Gravestones, in his view, act as "material objects, reflecting and assigning significance to beliefs that can be opened up for analysis," serving as "spaces for public display." On the subject of athletes, Huggins contends that when a gravestone assigns "special significance to an individual's sporting rather than family role, [it is] suggestive of the meanings ascribed to contemporary sport, articulating and resonating with sporting identities. [Gravestones] become active texts, heavily laden with cultural value, providing yet another social construction of a star's sporting 'identity.'"[77] Indeed, woven throughout Wilma Rudolph's gravesite memorial is her identity as an athlete.

Beyond Rudolph's gravestone, the cemetery more generally acts as a site of memory, providing an important space in understanding racial geographies of the American South.[78] African American cemeteries and burial grounds represent historic markers of racial segregation. Foston Memorial Gardens is operated by Foston Funeral Homes, a business created by Herman W. Foston and C. A. Dowdy in 1938. According to Foston's website, the business served other critical functions in the black community in addition to their funeral services. During segregation, Foston's served as a "form of community agency: providing food [and] clothing, locating housing, making personal loans, and assisting many local school children." By necessity, Foston's functioned as more than a funeral home, by also providing transportation to medical facilities that served African Americans.[79] Karla F. C. Holloway's work details the meaningful roles black funeral homes such as Foston's served in their communities. Holloway explores the history of black funeral homes and their development as a business in black communities across the United States, as well as "the last rites of color-coded lifestyles."[80] Writing about ceremonies connected to death in African American communities in the early twentieth century, H. W. Odum suggested, "It is a great consolation to the Negro to know that he will be buried with proper ceremonies and his grave properly marked." Given the marginalization and silencing African Americans endured in a racist society, this assurance of being counted at the end of a life cannot be overstated.[81] Roberta Hughes Wright and Wilbur B. Hughes explain that the importance of burial societies is rooted "in the belief that the soul of an African American would eventually return to the mother continent—but only if the body was given a proper burial and respectful send-off."[82]

Rudolph's burial in this black space is reflective of these traditions in African American communities. Buried in Foston Memorial Gardens with her mother and father, she occupies the segregated space, Clarksville's black cemetery, signifying a practice rooted in racial discrimination. According to Huggins, "Gravestones, tangible and visible, and the graveyards in which they are situated are equally rich with markers of class, habitus, gender and celebrity. Cemeteries were potentially 'hierarchical landscapes' providing the middle classes with opportunities to display their power and authority through choice of cemetery as well as through large-scale monuments."[83] Such middle-class spaces, for blacks, could very well be in segregated cemeteries. That Rudolph was initially buried without a headstone, celebrated a year after her death only when an appropriate marker could be afforded, is part of this hierarchical landscape. The community efforts to erect a headstone remind us of the important role cemeteries serve as a "key site for remembrance."[84]

Running on Water: A Statue of Wilma Rudolph

The same committee that raised funds to construct and erect the athlete's gravestone then turned its attention to honoring the hometown hero and hired a local artist to construct a statue of Rudolph. This was not the first statue-like representation of Rudolph. In 1986, artist Roy Tamboli created a bust that was placed in the art gallery of the First Bank of Tennessee in Memphis.[85] Two years later, Howard A. Brown constructed his own bust of Rudolph, which went on display at the Clarksville-Montgomery County Historical Museum.[86] Brown was selected as the artist for the statue project, and called it the "highlight" of his career. The statue of Rudolph was funded by donations from over fifty-four hundred individuals and twenty corporate sponsors.[87] The statue depicts a life-size Rudolph as she looked so many times crossing the finish line, head back, arms pumping. Brown's artistry is evident in his presentation of Rudolph not as a refined, clean representation of the athlete, but rather as a piece of art: her body is a collection of smudges, Brown's handiwork on display.

The Rudolph statue was unveiled in Clarksville's McGregor Park in July, to coincide with the 1996 Atlanta Olympic Games, though the statue was only on display for one day before returning to the workspace for another eighteen months. At the unveiling, Clarksville mayor Don Trotter proclaimed, "This marks another finish line in the history of Wilma Rudolph. This statue represents the spirit of Wilma Rudolph that is in all of us," reminding his fellow citizens that the act of commemorating the former athlete was also an act of community for Clarksville.[88] Michael Schudson identifies this connection with statues as "resonance," and states that the "extent to which the reputation of a figure resonates with the public determines . . . the cultural influence of that historical representation and the population that will have its identity defined by this commemoration."[89] Trotter's comments were echoed in an editorial published the day of the statue's dedication. The editorial's writer saw the statue as a means of celebrating and preserving the memory of Rudolph, since "Clarksvillians hear the name 'Wilma Rudolph' so frequently that it tends to lose some of its power." The editorial recalled that

> [w]hen Wilma returned to Clarksville from the 1960 Olympics, our city—and country—were divided by race and hatred. . . . [W]e are now a community that can come together to celebrate a local's accomplishments, regardless of race or sex. Clarksville continues to grow, progressing into a preeminent southern city. Many tourists come to our town to visit the varied attractions we have to offer. Now, as they (tourists) drive down one of Clarksville's main thoroughfares, they will see our symbol of hope, achievement, and unity . . . Wilma crosses the finish line to come home to Clarksville—Gateway to the New South.[90]

Figure 7.2. Statue of Wilma Rudolph at the Wilma Rudolph Event Center in Clarksville, Tennessee. Reprinted with permission of Gena R. Shire-Sgarlata.

The statue of Rudolph is used to confirm a perspective that the city's, and even the region's, history of racial tension is, in fact, past. The South and Clarksville urge us to consider this a new day in terms of race relations, and Wilma Rudolph's image helps to lay the foundation on which this orientation is envisioned and sustained.

Three years later, "Gateway to the New South" became the city's new slogan and could be seen on street signs and tourist brochures promoting the new southern city that had a statue of an African American female, which validated the progress the city had made and distanced them from the "old South." Clarksville's efforts to remember Rudolph came during a time period when other southern cities were reexamining their histories within the civil rights movement. For example, in 1992, Birmingham redesigned previously segregated

Kelly Ingram Park as "A Place for Revolution and Reconciliation," according to Owen J. Dwyer, "to commemorate the protests that led to the desegregation of the city."[91] From civil rights monuments to slave plantations, southern cities devised new ways to attract visitors and retell their histories. The city of Clarksville published, in the mid-2000s, a pamphlet identifying prominent Rudolph sites in the area, reaffirming the multiple roles the athlete played, even in death, to serve her hometown. The pamphlet includes a map, indicating her burial site, the statue, and the historic marker, all on the edges of the city claiming her and promoting itself as "Gateway to the New South." Butterfield suggests that a monument is "one of the means by which an aggregate of individuals transforms itself into a community that feels bound together by a common moral experience and a common historical framework. It is proof that that past is real, and that the past is still present. A monument is where the mythical and historical memory of a person or an event comes to earth and, by adopting material form, lives on."[92] Rudolph's former coach, Ed Temple, commented that the tribute was "almost 40 years too late," concluding that the honor should "have happened many years ago."[93]

Once completed, the committee hoped "to display the statue in a prominent place, such as the new wing of the Clarksville-Montgomery County Museum," where it was to remain until 2003.[94] In March 2001, there was some debate about the possibility of relocating the statue on the Riverwalk, but Rudolph's sister, Charlene, was concerned it would be vandalized and wanted to "make sure it's in a safe place where it still can be shared with everyone." Phil Kemmerly, District Commission chairman, explained that "[t]he family was concerned with placing it down there . . . so therefore we suspended that movement and the family decided they would prefer to have it in a more secure setting." The Rev. Jimmy Terry, who spearheaded the fundraising efforts, said he had never been in support of the statue being along the riverfront, and argued that it should remain at the museum. Museum director Ned Crouch was pleased, noting that the staff and visitors alike enjoyed the statue, and considered it a "great piece of art," by a respected local artist.[95]

Still, despite the agreement among Rudolph's family members, Reverend Terry, and the museum, a decision was made in 2003 to relocate the statue to McGregor Park along the riverfront. The statue again was touted as a symbol of the city, "proud to be the home of Wilma Rudolph." The monument to the Olympic champion would help share that pride with "all who visit Clarksville."[96] One reporter's headline read, "Wilma Rudolph Statue Reclaims Rightful Place." A former classmate of Rudolph's noted that Riverside Drive was one of the "most attractive parts of the city," and voiced the hope that "the city will keep on improving it so more people will want to come down here and see her." Rudolph's cousin brushed aside any fear of vandalism, saying "I don't think they would have brought her out here if they were still worried (about vandalism). She needs to be out where people can see her. She put Clarksville on the map."[97] Reverend Terry was satisfied with the statue finally finding a "permanent resting place" that would be open to visitors at all times. Mayor Trotter considered the riverfront to be a "much more prominent and fitting place for the statue," and while recognizing that the statue didn't belong to the city, they were happy to have it on city grounds. Gene Washer, a member of the Rudolph Memorial Committee, liked the riverfront location and found it a "fitting tribute."[98]

The placement of Wilma Rudolph's statue on the riverfront was only permanent until its next move. Indeed, the statue seems to have covered as much ground as the Olympian traversed in her athletic career on the track, and the riverfront location was not the statue's last resting spot. In October 2012, the statue was relocated to its most prominent location, at the entrance of the new Wilma Rudolph Event Center at Liberty Park. The 150-acre park includes a dog park, a fishing marina, walking trails, and the new event center. The event center replaced the tornado-damaged Wilma Rudolph Pavilion located at Clarksville's Fairgrounds Park, and provides indoor/outdoor meeting space for weddings, meetings, dinners, and other Clarksville events. In addition to the statue, the event center named for Rudolph is adorned on the building's façade with silhouettes of Rudolph running, and with various Rudolph quotes etched into the sidewalk

Figure 7.3. The newly opened Wilma Rudolph Event Center in Clarksville, Tennessee. Reprinted with permission of Gena R. Shire-Sgarlata.

approaching the center's entrance. These quotes, selected by the land-scape architect Bruce Lunde for their inspiration, use Rudolph's own words to continue the construction and re-construction of her narra-tive. For example, the first quote reads, in all capital letters, "I HAD A SERIES OF CHILDHOOD ILLNESSES; SCARLET FEVER, PNEUMONIA, POLIO. I WALKED WITH BRACES UNTIL I WAS AT LEAST NINE YEARS OLD."[99] In this way Rudolph's own words, highlighted as they are, reify particular scripts about the track star. The event center is located well above the water, making the statue's new location safe and secure from any rising waters. At the statue's former riverfront site, the fencing and base remain, reminding residents that something once stood in the space.

Who and how we remember the past and its players is politi-cized and racialized, and a statue's placement becomes the hinge on which impassioned debates occur. Places have value. Johnathan Leib, for example, detailed the conflict over the location and placement of a statue of Arthur Ashe in his hometown, Richmond, Virginia. Citizens, both black and white, opposed the athlete's statue being set on the city's famous Monument Avenue with statues of Confederate "heroes." Did Ashe's statue belong in a black neighborhood? Did he deserve to be among the Confederate "heroes"? If a statue of Ashe celebrated him as a hero, did one have to acknowledge and recognize the Confederate statues also as "heroes"?[100] There was no such fight for Wilma Rudolph; her statue was always on the edges of the city, as opposed to the city's public square or main street, where numerous memorials to others reside. Standing in front of the city hall, and erected in 2002, is a statue of John Montgomery, who "claimed" Clarksville when he was on a hunting expedition. In 1999, a tornado damaged much of downtown Clarksville, and in the renovations of the area surrounding the courthouse, the city erected a number of statues, including Nora Witzel, a "pioneer of early 20th century small town photography," dedicated in 2007. The photographer stands with camera in hand, while the figure of a small dog looks up at her. Near Witzel in the city center sits a statue, erected in 2003, of an unidentified man sitting on a park bench reading the headlines from the *Leaf-Chronicle* the day after the destructive tornado.[101] A state historic marker stands on the downtown site of the former home of Confederate soldier Horace L. Lurton, whose residence was destroyed in the 1999 tornado. Along the street adjacent to the city hall, a number of memorials commemorate Clarksville's past, including fallen soldiers from several of the nation's wars, from World War I to Vietnam. The Daughters of the American Revolution, the city's first courthouse, and citizens killed by Indians in the late seventeen hundreds are each honored with a memorial. Brundage, in his examination of southern culture and historical memory, suggests that the "civic landscape of the South looks the way it does because of both persistent inequality etched and erected in public spaces and dogged efforts to revise the terrain."[102] An assemblage of people (and one animal) occupy Clarksville's core, lending credence to Brundage's claims.

Despite its place on the margins of town for most of its existence, the statue of Rudolph was quite progressive at the time (and remains so), as few females in the United States are honored with statues. As subjects of memorials, female athletes, and specifically female athletes of color, are even fewer in number. Martha Norkunas notes that the number of monuments to women has not increased over the years, but the categories have shifted. Once cast as "passive victims of disaster or servants to the community," some prominent women are now portrayed as pioneers and workers. In male-dominated occupations, such as inventors, sports figures, and adventurers, women are recognized as "honorary men."[103] Of the almost seventy thousand sites listed in the National Register, approximately 360, or less than four percent of all monuments, pay tribute to women.[104] Norkunas sees the cultural landscape as a "sea of maleness," with men's images in evidence on buildings, roadways, squares, trees, waterways, and monuments, "inscribing the landscape with masculinity." This reality underscores monuments' position in cementing "male dominance of public space [where] valor is defined as a male province, as is history."[105] This scarcity of women on the cultural landscape serves as a powerful reminder of what and who is worth commemorating in our public space. Norkunas contends that commemorative spaces in cities "serve as symbols of the relationship between power, space, and gender."[106] Sites of memory that centralize men and maleness "describe nothing at all but rather simply *are* the way the world is."[107]

When Rudolph received her statuary honor, she was among very few African American women to have statues in public places; and even in 2014, Rudolph remains only one of a select group, whose growth has been slow. Her fellow athlete, Wimbledon champion Althea Gibson, was honored with a statue in 2012 in Newark, New Jersey, adjacent to a tennis complex named in her honor.[108] That same year, civil rights leader Fannie Lou Hamer was immortalized in bronze in Ruleville, Mississippi, and in February 2013, Rosa Parks was remembered with a life-size statue in Washington's Capitol, in Statuary Hall.[109] Two other African American women have previously been commemorated with permanent objects: Harriet Tubman in Harlem and Baltimore, and Sojourner Truth in Florence, Massachusetts.[110] Given the dearth of statues of women, and especially African American women (even in 2014), the efforts of Clarksville's citizens to remember her in such a way was somewhat ahead of its time.

For years Rudolph's statue stood alone on the riverfront, far removed from the other Clarksville public sites and monuments. The three-foot-high fence that surrounded it provided protection from vandals, but it simultaneously inhibited visitor access and obstructed sight lines.[111] Because the statue's base was so high, and the identifying marker on the statue lies on top of the figure, one must either be tall enough to see over the edge or stand on the rail to read the text. One of the features museum visitors had enjoyed about the "piece of art" was that "it's sculptural, it's tactile, it's fluid in movement."[112] The riverfront location limited audience interaction to be visual, rather than visual and textual, adding an additional layer of distance between the statue and the viewer.

On yet another level, we find the statue's placement by the waterway richly symbolic, given the paradoxical relationship between African Americans and rivers during slavery and beyond. Historically, rivers were a site of both liberation and bondage for African Americans. Rivers and other waterways served as a potential pathway to freedom as slaves moved northward via the "underground railroad." Water was also one of several ways slaves were "sold down the river" into the Deep South, in an effort to provide the labor upon which the cotton industry fueled northern demand for the product.[113] The statue's place on the waterfront for nearly a decade on one hand symbolized power and agency. Yet the figure remained vulnerable as it sat at the water's edge. This was no more clearly in evidence than when, in May 2010, the geographic area in and around Clarksville received over thirteen inches of rain in just two days. The Cumberland River overflowed its banks as a result of the torrential rain, overtaking objects in its path, including Wilma Rudolph's statue. The former track great's figure appeared to be running on water as floodwaters covered the statue's base up to the athlete's ankles. Thus, Rudolph's status was elevated to the level of miraculous; much in the same way, collective memories of the athlete rest upon the iconization of her.

The State Historical Marker

A few weeks after the return of Rudolph's statue to the Riverwalk in 2003, Rudolph was honored with a state historical marker at the intersection of Old Trenton Road and Wilma Rudolph Boulevard by the Tennessee Historic Commission. The decision to place the $1,500 marker at that intersection was explained as "appropriate" because Rudolph had grown up on Trenton Road.[114] Pulling on similar tropes of agency, the marker refers to the "native of Clarksville" as one who "overcame illness, poverty, and segregation."[115] It notes her attendance at Burt High School and Tennessee A&I, without explicitly recognizing Burt High School as a segregated high school even after the Brown vs. Board of Education ruling, or Tennessee State as the state's only public historically black college. Brundage suggests that "to acknowledge the black past" raises "knotty questions about the legacies of slavery as well as current race relations," which challenge the region's identity.[116] This public forgetting, then, is fundamental to the act of collective memory. Though Rudolph was a member of numerous halls of fame, the marker mentions only her induction into the National Women's Hall of Fame, omitting her membership in the Black Athletes Hall of Fame, her NAACP Award, and her other numerous achievements. At the dedication, Bobby Petties, Rudolph's cousin, considered it one of the proudest days in the family's life: "By having the marker here so people can see it from now on, even if they don't know who she is, they can find her inspiration here. Everybody is patterned after somebody. If she could do it in the 1950s and 1960s, they should have no problems in the 2000s."[117] Perhaps the "it" to which he refers is the belief that Rudolph overcame poverty and segregation a half-century ago, so those in the present day have few excuses deterring their path to success.[118] Of interest, of course, is that class issues and racism for Rudolph did not cease with three gold medals; they persisted through to the end of her life.

Figure 7.4. Wilma Rudolph's State of Tennessee Historic Marker, located on Wilma Rudolph Boulevard on the outskirts of Clarksville, Tennessee. Reprinted with permission of Maureen M. Smith.

The location, as noted in the discussion of the naming of Wilma Rudolph Boulevard, returns us to the question of the cultural landscape of Clarksville. The marker is located outside the city of Clarksville, on the edges of the city, "the spatial periphery."[119] It is a busy intersection without sidewalks, limiting the foot traffic and opportunities for people to happen upon the marker, which details her accomplishments, including her Clarksville roots. On the day we located the marker we were aided by a map and two sets of eyes scanning the roads' edges, finally locating the sign against the backdrop of a temporary firework stand and a dirt parking lot.[120]

While it is difficult to fully assess the impact of street names and historical markers relative to their being noticed, years after the Rudolph Boulevard street sign and historical marker were erected, at least one Clarksville resident opined on the location and honor. Ann Pryor, in her letter to the editor for the *Leaf-Chronicle*, wondered why Wilma Rudolph Boulevard was not kept clean. She continued by making a connection between the lack of upkeep and the honor of having a space named for an individual.

> It was a grand day when it was named after one of Clarksville's respected citizens, so why isn't the grass mowed all the way up the boulevard instead of certain areas? When visitors get off the interstate to this exit, it's an eyesore, because we have a wonderful display of restaurants and businesses along the boulevard, but there's a lot of maintenance that needs to be done to preserve this area. Come on now, please show a little more respect to Wilma by maintaining this area 100 percent, and please stop letting the grass grow taller than me.[121]

Conclusion

Ed Temple, speaking at Wilma Rudolph Day in 1984, challenged Clarksville, reminding the city that Rudolph had put "Clarksville on the map." He wondered what Clarksville had to say for Rudolph and expressed his hope that eventually the city would do "something fitting" for her, such as "naming a street or section of interstate highway after her."[122] Erika Doss suggests that "shame about the nation's transgressions is generally absent in terms of how most Americans think about themselves and the nation."[123] But Temple's pointed comments, when considered in the context of decades of neglect, point out the muddied motives of the southern city. Pride, most certainly, with some vestiges of shame and reparations, is at work with the multiple remembrances of Rudolph in her hometown. Rudolph herself said, "You can do a million things in this world, and go a million places, but it doesn't mean anything unless you're accepted at home."[124] Clarksville is, after all, a central character in Rudolph's stories. Rudolph lived to see Wilma Rudolph Boulevard, but not Howard A. Brown's statue of her or the state historical marker. In remembering Rudolph in the days following her death, Coach Temple remarked on the meaning of commemoration, prodding the campus to erect something in her name. "She's had boulevards named after her, the indoor track at Tennessee State is named after her, but I think a big bronze statue of Wilma on the campus—somewhere everybody can see—, with a list of her accomplishments, is fitting. . . . Tennessee State needs to utilize this and do something big, really big that everyone can see. I think that speaks for itself. Seeing, I think, is the best."[125] Temple's comment speaks to the significance, meaning, and symbolism of statues and other physical objects.[126] Butterfield tells us, "[T]he monument cannot be understood without looking at its dynamic, immaterial dimension—at the acts of remembrance for which it is used."[127]

Upon Rudolph's death, Clarksville, too, considered the multiple ways they remembered their most famous citizen and how those honors reflected on their city. The local press outlines Clarksville's role in making memories of Wilma Rudolph. "Here in Clarksville," the *Leaf-Chronicle* begins, "there's a pavilion at Fairgrounds Park named in her honor, and people who drive on US 79 North are traveling on Wilma Rudolph Boulevard. Those are outward recognitions for a hometown woman who made it big. We Clarksvillians also will carry within us the memory of the little girl with a leg brace who went on to dazzle the world, and we can point with pride that she was one of us."[128]

Patricia Vertinsky, Sherry McKay, and Stephen Petrina suggest paradoxically that "[n]ot every memorial helps people to remember things, or ensure that future generations will remember things as precisely as the present one does. It is as if once we assign monumental form to memory we have to some degree divested ourselves of the obligation to remember."[129] Much like the 1960 integrated parade, Clarksville's first, albeit temporary, memorial to Rudolph, contemporary and more permanent monuments of Rudolph are another "story space" used to tell similar stories about Rudolph. We see Rudolph and the dominant narratives of her life as illustrative of Nathan's concept of "a story told is a story retold."[130] It is our contention in this examination of the multiple ways Wilma Rudolph has been memorialized that cultural landscapes, such as Clarksville, are worthy sites of interrogating both social and place memory as integral to the writing of history.

Conclusion

To Tell the Truth

IN THE WEEKS AND MONTHS following Rudolph's gold medal winning performance in Rome she was celebrated and feted in a number of ways, including parades, dinners, and appearances on *The Ed Sullivan Show*, as well as the December 5, 1960, episode of the CBS game show, *To Tell the Truth*.[1] Rudolph, it seemed, was everywhere and it was within many of these spaces that aspects of track great's past were initially deployed, emphasized, minimized, manipulated, and distorted, creating the stories that would come to define and redefine the athlete for decades. We find Rudolph's 1960 appearance on *To Tell the Truth* especially compelling, and thus choose to highlight it here for a couple of reasons. On one level a close reading of the episode throws into relief how distortions and inaccuracies were cemented within a tale producers and consumers were eager to embrace. Moreover, the title of the show, *To Tell the Truth* is a layered moniker with its own embedded ironies at work, given the many truth claims that surface in the stories we create and tell about the track great.

The popular game show's format revolved around a celebrity panel asking questions of three contestants in order to determine which contestant was the "real" individual and which two were the imposters. Hosted by Bud Collyer, the episode's celebrity panel was made up of Don Ameche, first timer and substitute Johnny Carson, Betty White, and Kitty Carlisle.[2] The show begins with the three contestants standing in silhouette as the narrator proclaims, "One of these young ladies won three gold medals in the 1960 Olympic Games." The silhouette and the uncertainty that it evokes is removed, but the "real" Olympic champion remains obscured, as in sequence a light shines into the faces of the contestants.[3] One by one each of the women declares, "My name is Wilma Rudolph." With the "real" track star's identity still shrouded, Collyer, as the host, begins the game by reading Rudolph's affidavit card.

> I, Wilma Rudolph, as a child was unable to walk. This past summer in Italy I won three Olympic gold medals for running. I am the only American woman in the history of the Olympic Games to be a triple gold medal winner. Signed, Wilma Rudolph.

This affidavit is important, in our view, because it, in a seemingly formal way, makes claims to the "real" Wilma Rudolph. In addition, it popularizes a narrative of Rudolph that focuses on her early child-hood disability, while it presents her as the *only* American woman to have achieved the triple gold medal accomplishment. Thus, the contours of her story take shape as selective elements are highlighted and inaccuracies are declared as fact. In the process of the reading of the affidavit by Collyer, these claims are assigned to Rudolph, even as she remains voiceless.

After a series of innocuous questions by the celebrity panelists, such as "Did you go into Rome at all?," "How many years have you been running?," and so forth, it was time for the votes to determine the "real" Wilma Rudolph. Johnny Carson disqualified himself given the fact that he knew the "real" Rudolph, and the other panelists seem not to have been aided by the question-and-answer sequence. Don Ameche's "pure guess" correctly identified contestant number three as the "real" Rudolph. Similarly, Betty White's vote was "strictly on a hunch," though she too was able to accurately name the Olympic gold-medalist.

The contestants' physicality gave Kitty Carlisle all she needed to know in identifying the "real" Wilma Rudolph. Carlisle, who considered the Olympic achievement "an absolutely miraculous feat," also noted that each of the contestants had "marvelous legs." She elaborated in detailing her decision: "I voted for number one based on the legs," Carlisle rationalized. "Number three [Wilma Rudolph] has rather lovely but slender legs and number two and one had sturdier legs and number one looks like a champion to me." The contestants' verbal responses seemed to provide little assistance to Carlisle, who instead only needed a visual inspection of the trio's lower limbs to distinguish imposters from the authentic Rudolph. These backhanded compliments underscore the physical, exotic, and unknown, and are made starker as they stand in contrast to Carlisle's coiffed, pearled appearance.

The track star rises from her seat in response to Collyer's, "will the 'real' Wilma Rudolph please stand up," yet from this point forward she is seen but not heard. Though the "real" Rudolph is finally confirmed, there is little attention directed toward her except Collyer's pronouncement that "we're mighty proud to have you with us tonight." Interestingly, contestants one and two are provided the opportunity to speak for and identify themselves as Julia Robinson, social group worker for the New York Housing Authority, and Fran Bennett, a telephone operator for Hayes Registry. Rudolph, on the other hand, is silent, as others speak for and about her in the clip. The process is a telling one, in which aspects of Rudolph's story are highlighted/hidden with broader agendas in mind. Indeed, in *To Tell The Truth*, whose truth is being told, and by whom?

In Wilma Rudolph's autobiography the track star lamented the perspective taken in an elementary school "Negro" history course she had completed, saying, "it was geared to providing us with black heroes, not telling us the facts of life. The object of it all was to give us black kids somebody to be proud of, not to tell us that we were still oppressed."[4] Though on one level, Rudolph understood the motivations of parents and school officials to "protect" young African Americans from the harsh realities of racism, she also remained frustrated by the paternalism. "There's no excuse," she concluded, for the fact that elementary school children did not "[know] a thing about slavery."[5] Ironically, the approach, which Rudolph so disliked, in the "black heroes" tales she learned as a child became the prominent chord upon which her own life story was played for school children and others across the track star's life, upon her death, and thereafter.

By the age of twenty, Wilma Rudolph was a four-time Olympic medal winner; thus, her story of athletic achievement was, arguably, one worth retelling. Unfortunately, the narratives of Rudolph's past are confined to a limited range of accounts, and took on what Daniel A. Nathan calls "narrative physics."[6] The stories themselves gain momentum, creating energy that prompts them to be continually told and retold. The interpretative accounts of Rudolph's life, told to us through television, film, newspaper chronicles, a statue, a postage stamp, obituaries, autobiography, or children's books, can be understood as various "story spaces" according to Alun Munslow.[7] For Munslow, these "spaces" clearly draw upon elements of a "once real world" but their creation is always in relation to the authorial perspectives of the producer.

Our aim in reading across an array of popular narratives was to expose the stories created and told about Wilma Rudolph over the past several decades. Drawing upon foundational tenets of the cultural turn in sport history, we were interested in the meanings associated with various representations and remembrances of the former track great. We "read" parades, movies, books written for children, and statues, among other items, as important texts surrounding Wilma Rudolph in which ideologies about race, achievement, gender, and nationhood were transmitted. Far from ideologically free, our collective memories of Rudolph, as told to us through these various sites, are "partial, always owned, always vested with special interests."[8]

Thus, as we have argued, Rudolph's rags-to-riches triumph, as told by many observers over the course of a half-century, is one that blends seamlessly with dominant values of self-determination and agency. This tale of Rudolph's life is one that circulates most freely, and has done so in varying degrees since 1960. In this preferred reading, issues around race, class, gender, and physical ability are constructed merely as hurdles which the track star cleared in a race to notoriety and success. Social inequality is positioned as a relic of the past, put more securely to rest each time Rudolph's story is retold. For the most part, this primary thread of the track star's past seems irrepressible; time does little to challenge or change the meanings we bestow on Rudolph and her legacy. Rudolph's story and the athlete herself are frozen in a 1960 moment because to extend the story is to expose the layers of racism/sexism she faced throughout her life and into adulthood. Such a perspective, if repeated with frequency, would challenge the master narratives of agency and achievement. Moreover, the oft-told, narrow range of stories about Rudolph, repeated and transmitted via children's books, film, the press, statues, and landmarks, tell us far more about the moment of creation and the creator than about the track great.

However, "story spaces," including those about Rudolph, are far from monolithic and static. The cultural meanings that swirled around the Olympic medalist were never fixed, and have, at times, been struggled over by those interested in historicizing Rudolph's past. As example, elements within the black press have, as we have demonstrated, long been a point around which dominant representations of Rudolph and her past are contested. Moreover, the track great's own words and actions formed acts of resistance, often in tension with the more expansive and entrenched tales circulating around Rudolph. Finally, the relatively recent exchanges between and among various factions in Clarksville over the placement of the athlete's statue and the street named in her honor reveal the dynamic and multiple meanings attached to Rudolph.

In early twenty-first-century America the distortions and even myths surrounding Rudolph continue to hold center stage, but they do so as they have always done, set amid a wider range of "story spaces" created and received by those for whom Rudolph's achievements signified something else. Writing recently, African American scholars Nikky Finney and Melissa Harris-Perry have invoked remembrances of black female athletes.[9] They do so not because racism and sexism are elements of a long-ago past, as dominant narratives of Rudolph would have us believe, but precisely because those realities remain. Used as a strategy against racial and gender inequality, stories that inspire are told to young African American girls by their mothers to instill both pride and hope, according to Harris-Perry. Thus, tales about Harriet Tubman, Rosa Parks, Venus and Serena Williams, Althea Gibson, and we add Wilma Rudolph, centrally position black women and their achievements. This is not to displace or deny ongoing inequalities. Instead, these stories and the inspirational elements pulled from them serve as weapons against continuing racial and gender injustice.

Remembrances of African American athleticism, including that of Wilma Rudolph, feature prominently in the work of award-winning poet Nikky Finney. In an explanation of the poem "Shaker: Wilma Rudolph Appears While Riding the Althea Gibson Highway Home," Finney writes:

> Wilma Rudolph and Althea Gibson were huge heroes of mine growing up. Huge. I loved tennis and I loved Track & Field. I always wondered if I would ever write a poem that might equal the beauty and power of an Althea Gibson forehand or a Wilma Rudolph lean into the tape. I was home several years ago, driving to my parent's house one night and discovered that one of the old highways had been renamed the Althea Gibson highway. This is what led me to the other thoughts I had on that road driving two land highways home.[10]

The poem was written as part of a larger collection, *Head Off and Split*, which earned Finney the National Book Award for poetry in 2011. Saying of the influences upon the book, Finney concedes, "I am incredibly drawn to history; the history that has been told by the lion hunter but not the lion."[11] Like those who authored the many dominant representations of Rudolph, Finney and Harris-Perry *needed* to construct and conceptualize particular remembrances of the track great and other African American female athletes. However, their reasons for doing so and the meanings they associated with the athletes share little in common with the dominant narratives about Rudolph and the specific motivations for telling those stories. Harris-Perry and Finney enact memories of Rudolph and other athletes more locally, more privately, that speak directly to the realities of their lives as African American women. Such a process disrupts the "memories-created-from-above"[12] paradigm, and though no less selective it exposes the wide range of meanings conferred upon the past and historical actors within it, including Wilma Rudolph.[13]

Over the course of writing this book, we occasionally allowed ourselves to engage in conversations that attempted to understand Rudolph's decisions related to certain events. For example, why didn't she write about her involvement in integrating Shoney's in her 1977 autobiography? Or discuss in some detail her trip to Africa? Did she not see these as pivotal moments in her life (in the ways that we admittedly do)? We often lamented her early death and the loss of her voice and opportunity to "re-write" her story. Mindful, of course, that her second autobiography, like the first, would be a re-construction of past events pulled from her memory, we nonetheless pondered how/why the stories might have looked and sounded had she lived into the twenty-first century. Maybe Rudolph would share more details, explain her decisions, and reveal more of the barriers she faced even after her athletic successes. A more nuanced picture of Rudolph as an adult might have appeared, no longer frozen in time as a twenty-year-old triple gold-medal winner. How would the changes enjoyed by female athletes in recent years have changed the celebration of Rudolph, had she lived past her fifty-four years?

While there is much we cannot know, what is certain is the fact that remembrances of Rudolph will continue to be invoked into the future, for a variety of reasons, by individuals and groups. We were reminded of the unending persistence of this process as we completed the final revisions on *(Re)Presenting Wilma Rudolph* in June 2014. The anniversary of Rudolph's birthday was marked by the website "A Mighty Girl" with a post on their Facebook page.[14] The site celebrated Rudolph's birthday with a photo of the track great running, an inspirational quote, a brief description of Rudolph ("A model of determination and resiliency, Rudolph contracted polio as a young child and wore leg braces for years. . . ."), and linked to further readings on the athlete. Interest in the post was high as it received numerous comments from observers. One follower, for example, urged Angelina Jolie to make a movie on THIS Olympian. Another wrote, "Wow—polio, scarlet fever, whooping cough, and measles, then Olympian. No excused [sic] people!!!" One respondent posted, "NO government programs either, back then she did it and it was her victories," which resulted in another follower posting that there had, in fact, been government programs, but that Rudolph was still "amazing."[15] Others posted their thanks for Rudolph's inspiration, with a few moms noting that their elementary-age children had reads books on Rudolph in schools. Clearly, the distance of over a half-century since she blazed around the track at the Rome Olympics has not lessened agency's central place in stories we tell ourselves about Rudolph.

Memories of Wilma Rudolph will continue to be created and circulated within public consciousness as the twenty-first century advances. No doubt as well, the finite, mythic representations and remembrances of Rudolph will persist in iconizing the track great into the future. Memory, as Jeffrey Olick reminds us, is not a "vessel of truth, but a crucible of meaning," and the remembrances of Rudolph, in featuring certain tales over others, offer us far more insight about ourselves, as well as the moment and origin of creation than the Olympic champion.[16] Additionally, the various "story spaces" we earnestly re-circulate about Rudolph obscure the layered complexities of the track great's life, ultimately undercutting the full richness and power of the tale being told.[17] Celebrity panelist Betty White explained her decision to choose the "real" Rudolph from the impostors on *To Tell The Truth*. Rudolph, according to White, muddied truth, "really trying not to be who she really is." As with the remembrances upon which representations of Rudolph have been and continue to be constructed, we ask if it is even possible for "the real Wilma Rudolph [to] please stand up?"

Notes

Bibliography

Index

Notes

Introduction

1. "Scorecard: Fast Train from Clarksville," *Sports Illustrated*, November 21, 1994, 13.

2. Ira Berkow, "Sports of the Times: Forever the Regal Champion," *New York Times*, November 13, 1994.

3. Mike Cronin, "Reflections on the Cultural Paradigm," *Sporting Traditions* 27 (2010): 6. *(Re)Presenting Wilma Rudolph* is positively influenced by the work of several scholars in sport history. These include Catriona Parratt, "Wasn't It Ironic? The Haxey Hood and the Great War," in *Deconstructing Sport History: A Postmodern Analysis*, ed. Murray G. Phillips (Albany: State University of New York Press, 2006), 131–46; Susan Birrell, "Approaching Mt. Everest: On Intertextuality and the Past as Narrative," *Journal of Sport History* 34 (2007): 1–22; Daniel A. Nathan, *Saying It's So: A Cultural History of the Black Sox Scandal* (Urbana: University of Illinois Press, 2003); Jaime Schultz, *Qualifying Times: Points of Change in US Women's Sport* (Champaign: University of Illinois Press, 2014); Douglas Booth, *The Field: Truth and Fiction in Sport History* (London: Routledge, 2005); Gary Osmond, "Photographs, Materiality and Sport History: Peter Norman and the 1968 Mexico City Black Power Salute," *Journal of Sport History* 37, no. 1 (2010): 119–37; and Murray G. Phillips, ed., *Deconstructing Sport History: A Postmodern Analysis* (Albany: State University of New York, 2006).

4. Jaime Schultz, "Leaning into the Turn: Towards a New Cultural Sport History," *Sporting Traditions* 27, no. 2 (2010): 50.

5. Ibid., 55.

6. Nathan, *Saying It's So*, 8.

7. Maurice Halbwachs, *On Collective Memory*, ed. and trans. Lewis A. Coser (Chicago: The University of Chicago Press, 1992), 26.

8. Astrid Erll, "Cultural Memory Studies: An Introduction," in *A Companion to Cultural Memory Studies*, ed. Astrid Erll and Ansgar Nünning (Berlin: Walter De Gruyter, 2008), 5.

9. Jill A. Edy, *Troubled Pasts: News and the Collective Memory of Social Unrest* (Philadelphia: Temple University Press, 2006), 2.

10. Wulf Kansteiner, "Meaning in Memory: A Methodological Critique of Collective Memory Studies," *History and Theory* 41, no. 2 (2002): 189.

11. Jan Assmann, *Moses the Egyptian: The Memory of Egypt in Western Monotheism* (Cambridge, MA: Harvard University Press, 1997), 9.

12. Jeffrey K. Olick, Vered Vinitzky-Seroussi, and Daniel Levy, "Introduction," in *The Collective Memory Reader*, ed. Jeffrey K. Olick, Vered Vinitzky-Seroussi, and Daniel Levy (New York: Oxford, 2011), 17.

13. Kansteiner, "Meaning in Memory," 195.

14. Bridget Fowler, *The Obituary as Collective Memory* (New York: Routledge, 2007), 8.

15. Ibid., 10. For more on Nora's "lieux de memories," see Pierre Nora, *Realms of Memory: Rethinking the French Past*, trans. Arthur Goldhammer, 3 vols. (New York: Columbia University Press, 1996–98), 1:1.

16. Janice Hume, *Obituaries in American Culture* (Jackson: University Press of Mississippi, 2000), 15.

17. Andreas Huyssen, *Twilight Memories: Marking Time in a Culture of Amnesia* (New York: Routledge, 1995), 3.

18. Edy, *Troubled Pasts*, 2.

19. Hume, *Obituaries in American Culture*, 16.

20. Fowler, *The Obituary as Collective Memory*, 7.

21. Philip Hersh, "Her Life's a Sprint, Legacy Long Running, Track Legend Wilma Rudolph Dies; Inspiration Spanned Generations," *Chicago Tribune*, November 13, 1994, Sports, 3.

22. Hume, *Obituaries in American Culture*, 12.

23. Fowler, *The Obituary as Collective Memory*, 11.

24. We surveyed a number of American newspapers from metropolitan areas, in addition to newspapers from Rudolph's hometown of Clarksville and her home state of Tennessee. We also looked at several African American newspapers that were in publication at the time of her death. Our survey included the following: Joe Edwards, "Olympic Legend Wilma Rudolph Dies, Clarksville Native Succumbs to Brain Cancer at Age 54," *Leaf-Chronicle*, November 13, 1994, A1; "Olympic Legend Wilma Rudolph Dies, Accomplishments Will Never Be Forgotten," *Leaf-Chronicle*, November 13, 1994, A1, A16; Bert Rosenthal, "Rudolph Beat the Odds, Clarksville Native Was an Inspiration," *Leaf-Chronicle*, November 13, 1994, B1, B3; Frank Litsky, "Wilma Rudolph, Star of the 1960 Olympics, Dies at 54," *New York Times*, November 13, 1994; Ira Berkow, "Sports of the Times: Forever the Regal Champion," *New York Times*, November 13, 1994; sidebar, Atlanta *Journal-Constitution*, November 13, 1994, A1; Althelia Knight, "Olympic Track Star Wilma

Rudolph Dies," *Washington Post*, November 13, 1994, D5; "Clipboard," *Washington Post*, November 13, 1994, D1; "Inside," *Washington Post*, November 13, 1994, 1; Philip Hersh, "Her Life's a Sprint . . . ," *Chicago Tribune*, November 13, 1994, Sports, 3; "Top of the Wire," New Orleans *Times-Picayune*, November 13, 1994, C1; Frank Litsky, "Wilma Rudolph, Regal Hero of Olympic Track, Dies at 54," *Louisville Courier-Journal*, November 13, 1994, A1, A16; Bert Rosenthal, "Wilma Rudolph: 'Born to Run,' Three-Time Olympic Gold Medal Winner Was an Inspiration to Young People around the World," *Atlanta Journal-Constitution*, November 13, 1994, A3 (this Rosenthal article also appeared in the *Boston Globe*, with credit to AP (the Associated Press), and in the *Detroit Free Press*, with credit to Rosenthal); and Mark Gray, "Sports of the World: Rudolph Fought Her Way across the Final Finish Line," *Atlanta Daily World*, November 17–18, 1994, 6. Other articles that were published in the days following her death, though not necessarily considered obituaries, include: "Funeral Plans Change for Legend," *Leaf-Chronicle*, November 15, 1994, A1, A3; "Remembering Her for How She Lived, Clarksvillians Mourn Death of Hometown Olympian," *Leaf-Chronicle*, November 15, 1994, A4; Chip Cirillo, "Rudolph Put City On Map," *Leaf-Chronicle*, November 15, 1994, B1, B4; "Rudolph Memorial Scheduled," *Leaf-Chronicle*, November 16, 1994, A1; Darwin Campbell, "City Says Goodbye to One of Its Greats," *Leaf-Chronicle*, November 18, 1994, A1, A8; Darwin Campbell, "Hometown Recognition Was Slow in Coming," *Leaf-Chronicle*, November 18, 1994, A8; Darwin Campbell, "Olympian Bid Last Farewell, Thousands Remember Runner as Inspiration," *Leaf-Chronicle*, November 19, 1994, A1, A15; Richelle Thompson, "Friends Recall Legacy of Hometown Track Star," *Leaf-Chronicle*, November 19, 1994, A1, A15; Dwight Lewis, "Wilma Rudolph Graced Our Lives and Left Too Soon," Nashville *Tennessean*, November 20, 1994, 12–13; Bernadette Burden, "Wilma Rudolph: 'Born to Run,' Star's Fellow Athletes Say She Was a Champ On and Off the Track," *Atlanta Journal-Constitution*, November 13, 1994, A3; Terence Moore, "Rudolph Leaves Immortal Legacy of Hope for Physically Disabled," *Atlanta Journal-Constitution*, November 13, 1994, E3.

25. Fowler, *The Obituary as Collective Memory*, 156.

26. "Wilma Rudolph, Champion, Inspiration," *Tennessean*, November 13, 1994, 17.

27. Fowler, *The Obituary as Collective Memory*, 225.

28. Milton C. Sernett, *Harriet Tubman: Myth, Memory, and History* (Durham, NC: Duke University Press, 2007), 315.

29. Roseann M. Manduziuk and Suzanne Pullon Fitch, "The Rhetorical Construction of Sojourner Truth," *Southern Communication Journal* 66 (2001): 135.

30. Mark Gray, "Sports of the World: Rudolph Fought Her Way," 6.

31. Hume, *Obituaries in American Culture*, 19.

32. Frank Litsky, "Wilma Rudolph, Star of the 1960 Olympics, Dies at 54," *New York Times*, November 13, 1994. The initial error was corrected on November 25, 1994; the second error was not corrected.

33. Aleida Assmann, "Canon and Archive," in *A Companion to Cultural Memory Studies*, ed. Astrid Erll and Ansgar Nünning (Berlin: Walter De Gruyter, 2008), 97.

34. Ethelda Bleibtrey is the first American woman to win three gold medals in one Olympic Games. She accomplished this at the 1920 Olympic Games in Antwerp, in swimming events (the 100-meter freestyle, the 300-meter freestyle, and as the anchor leg of the 400-meter relay). Bleibtrey was inducted into the International Swimming Hall of Fame in 1967. See http://www.ishof.org/Honorees /67/67ebleibtrey.html, accessed December 24, 2012. For more on Bleibtrey, see Mark Dyreson, "Icons of Liberty or Objects of Desire? American Women Olympians and the Politics of Consumption," *Journal of Contemporary History* 38 (2003): 435–60. Also see "Elthelda Bleibtrey Resigns from W.S.A.," *New York Times*, October 20, 1921, 24; "Elthelda Bleibtrey, 76, Won 3 Medals for Swimming in 1920 Olympic Games," *New York Times*, May 9, 1978, 42; and "Olympic Star to Be Wed, Elthelda Bleibtrey, Swimmer, Will Marry Sportsman Cowboy," *New York Times*, September 8, 1940, 4.

35. Madison won three gold medals at the 1932 Olympic Games in Los Angeles. Though overshadowed at the Games by her American teammate Babe Didrikson, Madison was celebrated with a parade in her hometown of Seattle. Madison surrendered her amateur status to appear in films, and in 1936 suggested that the United States should boycott the Olympic Games in Nazi Germany. She struggled financially throughout her adult life and died at the early age of fifty-six after suffering from cancer and diabetes. For more on Madison's swimming career and post-swimming life, see "Coast Star Leaves for US Swim Meet," *New York Times*, July 9, 1931, 21; Arthur J. Daley, "Miss Madison Captures National 220-Yard Free Style Swimming Championship," *New York Times*, April 19, 1931, 144; L. De B. Handley, "Players of the Game: Miss Helene Madison—Record-Breaker Extraordinary," *New York Times*, December 1, 1930, 29; "Helene Madison Enters Film," *New York Times*, September 12, 1932, 13; "Helene Madison Married," *New York Times*, March 7, 1937, 86; "Helene Madison, Olympic Swimmer," *New York Times*, November 27, 1970, 42; Casey McNerthney, "Remember When: A Seattle Gold Medalist of Another Era," *Seattle P-I* (the online version of the Seattle *Post-Intelligencer*), August 12, 2008, http://blog.seattlepi.com/thebigblog/2008/08/12/remember-when-a-seattle-gold-medalist-of-another-era/, accessed August 1, 2011; "Miss Madison Helps Set Swim Relay Record; Her Team to Compete in Title Tests Here," *New York Times*, March 12, 1931, 33; "Miss Madison Likely to Default Titles," *New York Times*, July 8, 1931, 37; "Miss Madison, Olympic Star, Will Retire from Swimming," *New York*

Times, August 10, 1932, 19; "Miss Madison Sets Another Swim Mark," *New York Times*, April 8, 1931, 27; "New York Women Retain Swim Title," *New York Times*, March 18, 1930, 28; "Miss Madison Will Compete in Distance Swims on Coast," *New York Times*, April 25, 1930, 30; "Miss Madison Wins Indoor Swim Title," *New York Times*, May 1, 1932, 123; "Mrs. Sayville Springs Upset over Miss Madison," *New York Times*, July 25, 1932, 21; "Stars to Swim at Rye," *New York Times*, July 3, 1932, 73; "Title Swim Tests Will Start Today," *New York Times*, April 28, 1932, 25; and "Two More World Swim Marks Are Lowered by Miss Madison," *New York Times*, July 14, 1930, 28.

36. A short biography of von Saltza and her swimming accomplishments appears on the website of the International Swimming Hall of Fame, into which she was inducted in 1966: http://www.ishof.org/Honorees/66/66cvonsaltza.html, accessed May 10, 2013. Also see chapter 2 of this book.

37. Florence Griffith-Joyner was the next African American female to win three Olympic gold medals in track and field in 1988. Griffith-Joyner won the same three events as Rudolph: the 100-meter, the 200-meter, and the 4x100-meter relay. "Flo Jo," as she was known, was celebrated for both her athletic prowess and her physical attractiveness, again similarly to Rudolph.

38. Barry Schwartz, "Collective Forgetting and the Symbolic Power of Oneness: The Strange Apotheosis of Rosa Parks," *Social Psychology Quarterly* 72 (2009): 125.

39. Ibid., 132.

40. Ibid.

41. Rosenthal, "Wilma Rudolph: 'Born to Run,'" A3. This article is also in the *Boston Globe* (with credit to AP) and the *Detroit Free Press* (with credit to Rosenthal) (see n. 24).

42. Catherine Clinton, *Harriet Tubman: The Road to Freedom* (New York: Little, Brown and Company, 2004), Preface.

43. Until 1968, when it was renamed by the state legislature, this campus was formally Tennessee Agricultural and Industrial (A&I) University. However, it has more commonly been referred to as Tennessee State. Consistent with the usage of the times, and by Rudolph in her book, we will use Tennessee State in the remainder of this book.

44. Alon Confino, "Collective Memory and Cultural History: Problems of Method," *The American Historical Review* 102 (1997): 1393.

1. "Wilma's Home Town Win"?

1. Neal Bowers, *Out of the South: Poems* (Baton Rouge: Louisiana State University Press, 2002), 42–43.

2. "More Than 1,100 to Attend Banquet," *Leaf-Chronicle*, October 3, 1960, 7.

3. Aram Goudsouzian, "Wilma Rudolph: Running for Freedom," in *Tennessee Women: Their Lives and Times*, vol. 1, ed. Sarah Wilkerson Freeman and Beverly Green Bond (Athens: University of Georgia Press, 2009), 317.

4. "Clarksville Set to Honor Wilma," *Tennessean*, September 13, 1960, 17.

5. "Wilma Hopes to Justify Faith of Those Who Believe in Her," *Leaf-Chronicle*, October 5, 1960, 1.

6. "Wilma Rudolph Banquet to Be Staged October 4," *Leaf-Chronicle*, September 21, 1960, 1; "More Than 1100 to Attend Banquet," *Leaf-Chronicle*, October 3, 1960, 7.

7. "'Wilma-Ralph Day' A-Coming! Tennessee to Spread Red Carpet for Olympic Aces," *Norfolk (VA) Journal & Guide*, September 10, 1960, 1; Robert M. Lipsyte, "Wilma Rudolph Pauses Briefly for Medal, Visit, and Plaudits," *New York Times*, September 27, 1960, 46.

8. See, for example, "Wilma to Be Honored," *Leaf-Chronicle*, September 12, 1960, 1; "All Clarksville Set for Wilma," *Tennessean*, September 22, 1960, 26; "Mayor Greets A&I Stars," *Tennessean*, September 27, 1960, 18; "Wilma Rudolph Expected Back in States Sept. 26," *Leaf-Chronicle*, September 21, 1960, 6; "'Wilma-Ralph-Day' A-Coming!" *Norfolk Journal & Guide*, 1.

9. For a good overview of the legal challenges to racial injustice see Michael J. Klarman, *From Jim Crow to Civil Rights: The Supreme Court and the Struggle for Racial Equality* (New York: Oxford University Press, 2004).

10. On public opinion among southern whites during the civil rights era, see Taeku Lee, *Mobilizing Public Opinion: Black Insurgency and Racial Attitudes in the Civil Rights Era* (Chicago: University of Chicago Press, 2002), 161–68.

11. Highlighting Clay's and McDaniel's homecoming festivities is not meant to imply that other African American athletes from the South did not also suffer the injustices of segregation upon their return home. For example, on tensions related to Alice Coachman's 1948 homecoming to Albany, Georgia, following her gold medal victory, see Jennifer H. Lansbury, "Alice Coachman: Quiet Champion of the 1940s," in *Out of the Shadows: A Biographical History of African American Athletes*, ed. David K. Wiggins (Fayetteville: University of Arkansas, 2006), 159.

12. Fox, "Atlanta Olympian Showed Russians," *Atlanta Constitution*, December 11, 1956, 18. Also see Fox, "Olympic Titlist McDaniel Latest of Atlanta Champs," *Atlanta Constitution*, December 21, 1956, 21.

13. Noble Dixon, "He Acclaims Another of State's Champions," *Atlanta Constitution*, December 7, 1956, 4.

14. "Miss McDaniel Brings Honor to Nation," *Atlanta Constitution*, December 12, 1956, 8.

15. Marion E. Jackson, "Sports of the World," *Atlanta Daily World*, December 20, 1956, 7.

16. Marion E. Jackson, "Sports of the World," *Atlanta Daily World*, December 21, 1956, 7. Jackson's use of the word "tan" was common practice in the Black press to refer to people of color.

17. Scott E. Buchanan, *Some of the People Who Ate My Barbeque Didn't Vote for Me: The Life of Georgia Governor Marvin Griffin* (Nashville, TN: Vanderbilt University Press, 2011), 252.

18. Jackson, *Atlanta Daily World*, December 21, 1956, 7.

19. Douglas Nunn, "Cassius Clay Praised; Pummeled, and Cheered at Airport, in Motorcade, and at Central High," *Louisville Courier-Journal*, September 10, 1960, 1.

20. "A Louisville Hero in Ancient Rome," *Louisville Courier-Journal*, September 8, 1960, section 1, 9.

21. Nunn, "Cassius Clay Praised . . . ," *Courier-Journal*, September 10, 1960, 12.

22. Muhammad Ali, with Herbert Muhammad and Richard Dunham, *The Greatest: My Own Story* (New York: Random House, 1975), 60. For his recollections on the summer preceding the Games and his return home, see pages 58–61. In this chapter we refer to Cassius Clay, now known as Muhammad Ali, as "Clay" when we are referring to the athlete in 1960. We refer to him as "Ali" when speaking of the boxer in the present time period.

23. Nunn, "Cassius Clay Praised . . . ," *Courier-Journal*, September 10, 1960, 1, 12.

24. For more on the Louisville Group's sponsorship of Ali, see Michael Ezra, *Muhammad Ali: The Making of an Icon* (Philadelphia: Temple University Press, 2009); Ezra addresses the Louisville Group's treatment of Ali, their influence on Ali, their financial investment in Ali, and their power over Ali. Also see David Remnick, *King of the World: Muhammad Ali and the Rise of an American Hero* (New York: Random House, 1998), 108–11.

25. Ezra, *Muhammad Ali*, 12.

26. Remnick, *King of the World*, 106. Remnick also tells the story of Clay, only a few weeks after his welcome-home parade, being driven around Louisville in the backseat of a pink Cadillac with fellow gold medalist Wilma Rudolph.

27. Muhammad Ali with Hana Yasmeen Ali, *The Soul of a Butterfly: Reflections on Life's Journey* (New York: Simon & Schuster, 2004), 39. This is similar to the mythic story of Ali throwing his medal into the Louisville River after one of these encounters. For example, see Remnick, *King of the World*, 90–91. Remnick recounts a press conference during which Ali disputes his own published accounts of the mythic "medal in the river" story.

28. Sallie A. Marston, "Public Rituals and Community Power: St. Patrick's Day Parades in Lowell, Massachusetts, 1841–1874," *Political Geography Quarterly* 8, no. 3 (1989): 261.

29. Kathleen O'Reilly and Michael E. Crutcher, "Parallel Politics: The Spatial Power of New Orleans's Labor Day Parades," *Social and Cultural Geography* 7, no. 2 (2006): 248. New York City's Canyon of Heroes stands as one of the few examples of a city's efforts to provide a physical reminder of the parades that have occurred along its streets, with granite markers along the parade route honoring the celebrants. For more on these markers, as well as on tickertape parades in New York, including a podcast on the history of parades along Broadway, go to www.downtownny.com (accessed December 24, 2012).

30. Michael Woods, "Performing Power: Local Politics and the Taunton Pageant of 1928," *Journal of Historical Geography* 25, no. 1 (1999): 58.

31. Joshua Hagen, "Parades, Public Space, and Propaganda: The Nazi Culture Parades in Munich," *Geografiska Annaler: Series B, Human Geography* 90, no. 4 (2008): 350.

32. Lily Kong and Brenda S. A. Yeoh, "The Construction of National Identity through the Production of Ritual and Spectacle: An Analysis of National Day Parades in Singapore," *Political Geography* 16, no. 3 (1997): 227.

33. Ibid., 220.

34. R. D. Sack, quoted in Hagen, "Parades, Public Space, and Propaganda," 350.

35. Kong and Yeoh, "The Construction of National Identity through the Production of Ritual and Spectacle," 222.

36. "Wilma's Home Town Win," *LIFE,* 17 October 1960, 110–12, 114.

37. Nathan, *Saying It's So*, 12.

38. We cite this in capital letters when the newspaper or source does so.

39. James C. Cobb, *Away Down South: A History of Southern Identity* (New York: Oxford University Press, 2005), 212–13.

40. Patricia Levy, *Iconic Events: Media, Politics, and Power in Retelling History* (Lanham, MD: Lexington Books, 2007), 3.

41. W. Fitzhugh Brundage, "Introduction: No Deed but Memory," in *Where These Memories Grow: History, Memory, and Southern Identity,* ed. W. Fitzhugh Brundage (Chapel Hill: University of North Carolina Press, 2000), 4.

42. Maurice Halbwachs, *On Collective Memory,* ed. and trans. Lewis A. Coser (Chicago: The University of Chicago, 1992), 25.

43. Tom Siler, "Clarksville Girl Little Known in Native State," *Leaf-Chronicle,* September 2, 1960, 1. It is worth noting that Rudolph's talents as both a basketball player and also a track and field athlete at Burt High School were reported in the *Leaf-Chronicle* beginning in 1956, though this reporting tended to be local. See for example: "Burt in State Tonight," *Leaf-Chronicle,* March 15, 1956, 6; "Burt Girls Qualify for State Track," April 23, 1956, 6.

44. Bobby L. Lovett, *The Civil Rights Movement in Tennessee: A Narrative History* (Knoxville: University of Tennessee Press, 2005), 128.

45. James G. Stahlman, "Two Olympic Champions," *Nashville Banner*, September 3, 1960, 4. For a short description on the political leanings of the Nashville papers during the period, see Gene Roberts and Hank Klibanoff, *The Race Beat: The Press, the Civil Rights Struggle and the Awakening of a Nation* (New York: Alfred A. Knopf, 2007), 227.

46. "A Life of Foot Deformity Once Faced Swift Wilma," *Tennessean*, September 6, 1960, 1.

47. Iwona Irwin-Zarecka, *Frames of Remembrance: The Dynamics of Collective Memory* (Piscataway, NJ: Transaction, 1994), 119.

48. Wilma Rudolph with Martin Ralbovsky, *Wilma: The Story of Wilma Rudolph* (New York: Signet, 1977), 29–39. In securing the rights to reprint excerpts from Rudolph's book, we agreed to initially cite the work as "From *Wilma: The Story of Wilma Rudolph* by Wilma Rudolph and Bud Greenspan, copyright © 1977 by Bud Greenspan. Used by permission of Dutton Signet, a division of Penguin Group (USA) LLC"; for all subsequent references to this book, we will cite it as "Rudolph, *Wilma*."

49. Michael Shirley and George E. Sims, "Introduction," in *Making a New South: Race, Leadership, and Community after the Civil War*, ed. Paul A. Cimbala and Barton C. Shaw (Gainesville: University Press of Florida, 2007), 3–4.

50. "Big Welcome Awaiting Wilma in Clarksville," *Nashville Banner*, September 13, 1960, 19.

51. "An Honor Well Deserved," *Leaf-Chronicle*, September 13, 1960, 4.

52. Stephen V. Ash, "A Community at War; Montgomery County 1861–1865," *Tennessee Historical Quarterly* 36 (1977): 208–21; Thomas H. Winn, "Liquor, Race and Politics: Clarksville during the Progressive Period," *Tennessee Historical Quarterly* 49 (1980): 207–17.

53. US Bureau of the Census, *US Census of Population: 1960. Vol. 1, Characteristics of the Population, Part 44, Tennessee* (Washington, DC: US Government Printing Office, 1963), 44–11.

54. Lovett, *The Civil Rights Movement in Tennessee*, 30.

55. US Bureau of the Census, *US Census of Population: 1960. Vol. 1*, 44–146.

56. For example, see Bill Morris, "HEW Says Cobb School Single Integration Flaw," *Leaf-Chronicle*, April 26, 1973, 1, 14; Marcia Steagall, "Black Residents Criticize Board's Handling of Issues," *Leaf-Chronicle*, April 25, 1973, 1, 12; Marcia Steagall, "Desegregation Plan Passes," *Leaf-Chronicle*, April 11, 1973, 1.

57. US Bureau of the Census. *US Census of Population: 1960*, 44–175.

58. Ibid., 44–252.

59. "A Fine, Unselfish Deed," *Leaf-Chronicle*, February 15, 1962, 4.

60. "Stand Up!" *Nashville Globe*, March 25, 1960, 4.

61. Ernest L. Woods, "What Is the Public?," *Leaf-Chronicle*, December 27, 1960, 4.

62. Mrs. S. Johns, "She Wonders," *Leaf-Chronicle*, December 8, 1960, 4.

63. Ibid., 4.

64. "The Thinking Negro Veterans of Clarksville and Montgomery County," *Leaf-Chronicle*, November 1, 1960, 4.

65. William H. Rogers, "An Answer," *Leaf-Chronicle*, November 4, 1960, 4.

66. Harry Bolser, "Tennessee Comet: Ankles Weak after Polio Run Strong in Olympics," *Louisville Courier-Journal*, September 11, 1960, section 1, 10.

67. A. B. Snellings, "Sends Congratulations," *Leaf-Chronicle*, September 14, 1960, 4.

68. "Nation-Wide Publicity; Plans Completed for Wilma Rudolph Day," *Leaf-Chronicle*, September 28, 1960, 1, 5.

69. "'Segregated Life Will All but Kill Me,' Olympic Girl Champ Dreads Coming Home," *New York Amsterdam News*, September 10, 1960, 1.

70. Cobb, *Away Down South*, 1.

71. "America Gets Set to Honor Wilma," *Tennessean*, September 25, 1960, 8F.

72. "Wilma Rudolph Honored," *Leaf-Chronicle*, October 4, 1960, 4.

73. W. W. Barksdale, "PROCLAMATION," *Leaf-Chronicle*, October 4, 1960, 7.

74. Brundage, "Introduction," 5.

75. "A Program Well Planned," *Leaf-Chronicle*, October 6, 1960, 4.

76. Ibid., 4.

77. "Wilma's Home Town Win," *LIFE*, October 17, 1960, 110–112, 114.

78. "Wilma Hopes to Justify Faith of Those Who Believe in Her," *Leaf-Chronicle*, October 5, 1960, 1; "A Program Well Planned," *Leaf-Chronicle*, October 6, 1960, 4. Rudolph also remembered this story and valued it; see Rudolph, *Wilma*, 144–45.

79. Sylvia M. Jacobs, "James Emman Kwegyir Aggrey: An African Intellectual in the United States," *Journal of Negro History* 81 (1996): 47–61; Daniel Boamah-Wiafe, "Dr. James Emman Kwegyir Aggrey of Achimota: Preacher, Scholar, Teacher, and Gentleman," in *Black Lives: Essays in African American Biography*, ed. James L. Conyers Jr. (New York: M. E. Sharpe, 1999), 182–96.

80. Renee C. Romano, "Narratives of Redemption: The Birmingham Church Bombing Trials and the Construction of Civil Rights Memory," in *The Civil Rights Movement in American Memory*, ed. Renee C. Romano and Leigh Raiford (Athens: University of Georgia, 2006), 108.

81. It is argued that the "watershed" moment of black resistance to racial oppression in the American South happened with the Greensboro, North Carolina, sit-ins in February 1960. See William H. Chafe, *Civilities and Civil Rights: Greensboro, North Carolina and the Black Struggle for Freedom* (New York: Oxford University Press, 1981), 71.

82. Horace Talley, "Why Not Burt," *Leaf-Chronicle*, September 27, 1960, 4.

83. "Rudolph Reunites Hometown Just as She Did During Her Life," *Frederick Post*, November 19, 1994, B5.

84. Cameron Collins, "Wilma Rudolph Marker Unveiled," *Leaf-Chronicle*, July 4, 2003, 1C.

85. Matt Rennels, "Wilma Rudolph Remembered Far Beyond Olympic Victories," *Leaf-Chronicle*, February 15, 2007, 1B.

86. David Maraniss, *Rome 1960: The Olympics That Changed the World* (New York: Simon & Schuster, 2009), 420.

87. Brian Lanker, *I Dream a World: Portraits of Black Women Who Changed America* (New York: Stewart, Tabori, and Chang, 1989), 140–41.

88. Cobb, *Away Down South*, 263. On late twentieth-century migration patterns among African Americans from North to South, see William W. Falk, Larry L. Hunt, and Matthew O. Hunt, "Return Migrations of African-Americans to the South: Reclaiming a Land of Promise, Going Home, or Both?," *Rural Sociology* 69, no. 4 (2004): 490–509.

89. Cobb, *Away Down South*, 262.

90. Peter Applebome, "A Sweetness Tempers South's Bitter Past," *New York Times*, July 31, 1994, 1, 20.

91. W. Fitzhugh Brundage, *The Southern Past: A Clash of Race and Memory* (Cambridge, MA: Belknap Press of Harvard University, 2005), 5–6.

2. "She Isn't Colored, She Is Gold"

1. Jerry Footlick, "Wilma Reserves Hurrying for the Cinders Only," *Tennessean*, September 6, 1960, 24.

2. Stuart Hall, ed., *Representation: Cultural Representations and Signifying Practices* (London: Sage Publications, 1997), 234.

3. We chose to order this chapter by speaking separately to each of the athletes, rather than presenting an intermingled analysis. In this way our hope is to make more clear how each woman's identity was dependent on the others, and formed not on a binary but rather in a mediated construction among the three athletes.

4. Susan Cahn, *Coming on Strong: Gender and Sexuality in Twentieth-Century Women's Sport* (New York: Free Press, 1994), 111.

5. Arthur Daley, "Sports of the Times: A Vindication of Sorts," *New York Times*, September 23, 1956, 198.

6. See, for example, Cahn, *Coming on Strong*, 117; Rita Liberti, "'We Were Ladies, We Just Played Basketball like Boys': African American Womanhood and Competitive Basketball at Bennett College, 1928–1942," *Journal of Sport History* 26, no. 3 (1999): 575–76. For an examination of more nuanced treatments of African American educational leaders' understanding of and commitment to black female athleticism, see Martha H. Verbrugge, *Active Bodies: A History of Women's*

Physical Education in Twentieth-Century America (New York: Oxford University Press, 2012), 124–50.

7. See, for example, K. Sue Jewell, *From Mammy to Miss America and Beyond: Cultural Images and the Shaping of US Social Policy* (London: Routledge, 1993), 35–46.

8. "Olympic Quintessence," *LIFE*, September 19, 1960, 11.

9. See, for example, "Norton Runs Out of Passing Zone," *New York Times*, September 9, 1960, 20; "Wilma Rudolph Sets 2 Records," *New York Times*, April 17, 1960, S7; "Scorecard," *Sports Illustrated*, February 13, 1961, 8; Lafayette Smith, "The Girls in the Olympics," *Today's Health*, October 1964, 28–31.

10. Cahn, *Coming on Strong*, 111.

11. "Girl on the Run," *Newsweek*, February 6, 1961, 54.

12. "Scorecard," *Sports Illustrated*, February 13, 1961, 8.

13. Brian Glanville, "The Amazons," *Mademoiselle*, May 1965, 167.

14. Marguerite H. Rippy, "Commodity, Tragedy, Desire: Female Sexuality and Blackness in the Iconography of Dorothy Dandridge," in *Classic Hollywood, Classic Whiteness*, ed. Daniel Bernardi (Minneapolis: University of Minnesota Press, 2001), 179. Lena Horne and Diahann Carroll are two other African American actresses of the period whose careers underscore the politics of representation along gender and racial lines. On the tensions surrounding these and other actresses see Charlene B. Regester, *African American Actresses: The Struggle for Visibility* (Bloomington: Indiana University Press, 2010).

15. Donald Bogle, *Toms, Coons, Mulattos, and Bucks: An Interpretive History of Blacks in American Films*, 4th ed. (New York: Continuum, 2001), 166.

16. Regester, *African American Women Actresses*, 287.

17. Ibid., 328.

18. Bogle, *Toms, Coons, Mulattos, Mammies, and Bucks*, 375.

19. John Peyser, quoted in Bogle, *Toms, Coons, Mulattos, Mammies, and Bucks*, 478.

20. Jim Murray, "A Big Night for Wilma," *Sports Illustrated*, January 30, 1961, 48.

21. World Speed Queen," *New York Times*, September 9, 1960, 20.

22. Tex Maule, "Whirling Success for the US," *Sports Illustrated*, July 30, 1962, 18. Maule uses Rudolph's new, though short lived, married name.

23. *Mademoiselle*, January 1961, 85.

24. Barbara Heilman, "Like Nothing Else in Tennessee," *Sports Illustrated*, November 14, 1960, 48.

25. "Scorecard," *Sports Illustrated*, February 13, 1961, 8; "Double Sprint Champion Hurries Only on Track," *New York Times*, September 6, 1960, 44.

26. Heilman, "Like Nothing Else in Tennessee," *Sports Illustrated*, November 14, 1960, 48.

27. L. I. Brockenbury, "Wilma Captivates Sports Arena Throng," *Los Angeles Sentinal,* January 26, 1961, B9.

28. Harley Tinkham, "Spike Aces Vie Tonight at Arena," *Los Angeles Mirror,* 21 January 1961, 1.

29. James Murray, "A Big Night for Wilma," *Sports Illustrated,* January 30, 1961, 48.

30. Sid Ziff, "The Inside Track: Coliseum and Arena Scalpers Need Curbing," *Los Angeles Mirror,* January 20, 1961, part 3, 1.

31. Murray, "A Big Night for Wilma," 49.

32. Jeane Hoffman, "Speedy Wilma Rudolph Not Interested in Racing Men," *Los Angeles Times,* January 16, 1961, section C, 1.

33. Sid Ziff, "Wilma Has Men Scared," *Los Angeles Mirror,* January 17, 1961, part 4, 1.

34. Harley Tinkham, "Won't Run against Men, Insists Wilma Rudolph," *Los Angeles Mirror,* January 19, 1961, part 4, 1.

35. Hoffman, "Speedy Wilma Rudolph Not Interested in Racing Men," section C, p. 1; Tinkham, "Won't Run against Men," part 4, 1.

36. "Wilma Gets a Free Ride," *Los Angeles Mirror,* January 20, 1961, part 3, 5.

37. "Out in Front," *Los Angeles Times,* January 20, 1961, section C, 3.

38. Sid Ziff, "The Inside Track: Wilma Proves They're Not All 'Muscle Molls,'" *Los Angeles Mirror,* January 23, 1961, part 5, 1.

39. Ziff, "The Inside Track," part 5, 1; Hoffman, "Speedy Wilma Rudolph Not Interested in Racing Men," section C, 1.

40. Jessie Mae Brown, "Your Social Chronicler," *Los Angeles Sentinel,* January 26, 1961, 2B.

41. Brad Pye Jr., "Prying Pye: America's Finest," *Los Angeles Sentinel,* January 19, 1961, 8B.

42. L. I. Brockenbury, "Tying the Score: Wilma Becomes a Lady," *Los Angeles Sentinel,* January 26, 1961, B9.

43. Ibid., B9.

44. "Storming the Citadel," *Time,* February 10, 1961, 57.

45. "Millrose Track Chief Predicts Meet Records Here on Friday," *New York Times,* February 1, 1961, 44.

46. "Storming the Citadel," *Time,* 57.

47. Ibid.

48. "Olympic Wedding," *Atlanta Constitution,* August 24, 1960, 30; "Two Married Couples Separated at Olympics," *Louisville Courier-Journal,* August 18, 1960, section 2, 4; "A-Second Olympic Romance," *San Francisco Chronicle,* September 4, 1960, 23.

49. "Wilma, Ray Tell Secret: 'In Love,'" *San Francisco Chronicle*, September 3, 1960, section 1, 1.

50. "Tragic Slip by Norton Hits Wilma," *Tennessean*, September 9, 1960, 36.

51. Will Grimsley, "Norton Fouls on Exchange, Is Olympic Goat," *Southern Illinoisan*, September 9, 1960, 11.

52. Les Matthews, "Sports Whirl," *New York Amsterdam News*, February 11, 1961, 23.

53. Ramona J. Bell, "Competing Identities: Representations of the Black Female Sporting Body from 1960 to the Present" (PhD diss., Bowling Green State University, 2008), 62.

54. Maxine Leeds Craig, *Ain't I a Beauty Queen? Black Women, Beauty, and the Politics of Race* (New York: Oxford, 2002), 35.

55. Karen W. Tice, "Queens of Academe: Campus Pageantry and Student Life," *Feminist Studies* 31, no. 2 (2005): 256.

56. Rudolph, *Wilma Rudolph*, 138–39.

57. Craig, *Ain't I a Beauty Queen*, 27.

58. Ibid., 37.

59. Ed Temple with B'Lou Carter, *Only the Pure in Heart Survive* (Nashville, TN: Broadman, 1980), 50–51.

60. Pete Waldmeir, "Press Box," *Detroit News*, October 9, 1962, 1D.

61. This is a very interesting contrast with Rudolph, since at the time, both women were mothers: however, Rudolph's motherhood is never mentioned.

62. For example, see "Women's Title Track Meet to Be Held at Shaker Heights," *Amateur Athlete*, August 1957, 15; Roxanne Andersen, "They Knew We Were There!" *Amateur Athlete*, January 1957, 11; "Brown, Rudolph Show Why They Are Top US Olympic Hopes," *Pittsburgh Courier*, July 23, 1960, 26; "Rafer Johnson Leads Olympic Parade," *Los Angeles Sentinel*, August 25, 1960, 7.

63. Beginning in 1956, Brown made the *New York Times* headlines as Mrs. Brown when she won the Olympic trials with two meet-record performances. It was common practice for married female athletes to be identified as "Mrs. ____."

64. We borrow this concept of Brown serving as the "colored 'foil'" to Rudolph's nonwhiteness from Tiffany Gilbert, "American Iconoclast: 'Carmen Jones' and the Revolutionary Divadom of Dorothy Dandridge," *Women's Studies Quarterly* 33, no. 3/4 (Fall–Winter, 2005): 244. Gilbert discusses Pearl Bailey as playing the colored foil to Dorothy Dandridge in the film *Carmen Jones*.

65. Sid Ziff, "The Inside Track: Russ Laughs at Earlene," *Los Angeles Mirror*, September 3, 1960, 7.

66. William Barry Furlong, "Venus Wasn't a Shot-Putter," *New York Times Magazine*, August 28, 1960, 14.

67. Glanville, "The Amazons," 167.

68. "Fred Russell in Rome," *Nashville Banner*, September 1, 1960, B46. This comparison with Didrikson was not meant as a compliment.

69. Glanville, "The Amazons," 167.

70. Andrea Shaw, "The Other Side of the Looking Glass: The Marginalization of Fatness and Blackness in the Construction of Gender Identity," *Social Semiotics* 15 (August 2005): 151.

71. Huston Horn, "Girls on the Go-Go-Go," *Sports Illustrated,* July 25, 1960, 14.

72. "They Said It," *Sports Illustrated*, August 17, 1964, 10.

73. Ziff, "Something's Wrong—Earlene," *Los Angeles Mirror*, September 6, 1960, part 3, 1.

74. "Brundage to Stay in Olympic Post?," *Atlanta Constitution*, August 19, 1960, 36.

75. Earl S. Clanton III, "Negro Trains US Women's Olympic Squad," *Cleveland (OH) Call & Post*, August 13, 1960, 1D; Earl S. Clanton III, "Fifteen Tan Girls Are Set for Rome," *Pittsburgh Courier*, August 13, 1960, 26.

76. Celes King III, "Track Troops Go Full Blast Today," *Los Angeles Sentinel*, September 1, 1960, B7.

77. Celes King III, "It's Over but Memories Linger On," *Los Angeles Sentinel*, September 15, 1960, B7.

78. Celes King III, "LA Spikers Romp in Rome Olympics," *Los Angeles Sentinel*, September 8, 1960, 1A.

79. Peter N. Stearns, *Fat History: Bodies and Beauty in the Modern West* (New York: New York University Press, 2002), 91–92.

80. Diane Roberts, *The Myth of Aunt Jemima: Representations of Race and Region* (New York: Routledge, 1994), 5.

81. Ibid., 5–6.

82. M. M. Manring, *Slave in a Box: The Strange Career of Aunt Jemima* (Charlottesville: University Press of Virginia, 1998), 24.

83. Roberts, *The Myth of Aunt Jemima*, 1.

84. Ibid.

85. Ibid., 150.

86. Ibid., 163.

87. Horn, "Girls on the Go-Go-Go," *Sports Illustrated*, 14.

88. Jewell, *From Mammy to Miss America and Beyond*, 40.

89. Glanville, "The Amazons," 167.

90. Roberts, *The Myth of Aunt Jemima*, 1.

91. Doris Witt, *Black Hunger: Food and the Politics of US Identity* (New York: Oxford University Press, 1999), 22.

92. Andrea Shaw, "The Other Side of the Looking Glass," 146.

93. "For the Record," *Sports Illustrated*, July 6, 1959, 7.

94. "Pat on the Back," *Sports Illustrated*, September 16, 1956, 84.

95. A short biography of von Saltza and her swimming accomplishments appears on the website of International Swimming Hall of Fame, to which she was inducted in 1966: http://www.ishof.org/Honorees/66/66cvonsaltza.html Accessed May 10, 2013.

96. *Amateur Athlete* provided regular coverage of women's swimming in the 1950s and 1960s. However, very little academic work has looked at pre-Title IX swimming. See Cahn, *Coming on Strong*, 129–30.

97. Earl Ruby, "Ruby's Report: US Girl Sets Record," *Louisville Courier-Journal*, August 17, 1960, section 2, 5.

98. "16-Year-Old Blond Hope," *LIFE*, May 30, 1960, 80A.

99. Marina Warner, *From the Beast to the Blonde: On Fairy Tales and Their Tellers* (New York: Farrar, Straus and Giroux, 1994), 364.

100. Richard Dyer, *WHITE* (New York: Routledge, 1997), 4.

101. Warner, *From the Beast to the Blonde*, 363.

102. "Table of Contents," *LIFE*, August 22, 1960, 2.

103. Furlong, "Venus Wasn't a Shot-Putter, SM14.

104. Cahn, *Coming on Strong*, 110–39.

105. "Next Week," *Sports Illustrated*, July 14, 1958, 3.

106. "Despite All, a Delightful Show," *Sports Illustrated*, September 14, 1959, 22.

107. "16-Year-Old Blond Hope," *LIFE*, May 30, 1960, 80A.

108. George Walsh, "The Old Champion (Age 17) Bows Out," *Sports Illustrated*, August 21, 1961, 8.

109. Horn, "Girls on the Go-Go-Go," 14.

110. "16-Year-Old Blond Hope," 82.

111. Glanville, "The Amazons," 167.

112. Earl Ruby, "Ruby's Report: Too Much Leg Art," *Louisville Courier-Journal*, September 7, 1960, 6.

113. Glanville, "The Amazons," 167.

3. Running with the Story

1. Raymond Johnson, "One Man's Opinion: Wilma Making Lasting Mark in Spine-Tingling Sprints," *Tennessean*, September 5, 1960, 5.

2. Stephen Wagg and David L. Andrews, eds., *East Plays West: Sport and the Cold War* (New York: Routledge, 2007), 2.

3. W. Scott Lucas, "Beyond Diplomacy: Propaganda and the History of the Cold War," in *Cold War Propaganda in the 1950s*, ed. Gary D. Rawnsley (New York: St. Martin's, 1999), 17.

4. "Men—Medals—Marxism," *Newsweek*, August 9, 1960, 79.

5. Wagg and Andrews, *East Plays West*, 3.

6. Penny M. von Eschen, *Satchmo Blows up the World: Jazz Ambassadors Play the Cold War* (Cambridge: Harvard University Press, 2004), 4.

7. Mary L. Dudziak, *Cold War Civil Rights: Race and the Image of American Democracy* (Princeton, NJ: Princeton University Press, 2000), 8.

8. Melinda M. Schwenk, "'Negro Stars' and the USIA's Portrait of Democracy," *Race, Gender and Class* 4, no. 4 (2001): 116. USIA refers to the United States Information Agency.

9. Damion Thomas, "Let the Games Begin: Sport, US Race Relations and Cold War Politics," *The International Journal of the History of Sport* 24, no. 2 (2007): 157–71.

10. The Soviet Union's first appearance in the Olympic Games is in 1952 at the summer Games in Helsinki, Finland. Four years later, the USSR competed in the 1956 Winter Games in Cortina d'Ampezzo and the summer Games in Melbourne, Australia. For more on the early development of Soviet Olympic sport, see "The USSR and Olympism," *Olympic Review* 84 (October 1974): 530–57; and James Riordan, *Sport in Soviet Society: Development of Sport and Physical Education in Russia and the USSR* (Cambridge: Cambridge University Press, 1977). For background information on pre–World War II Soviet sport, see Barbara J. Keys, *Globalizing Sport: National Rivalry and International Community in the 1930s* (Cambridge: Harvard University Press, 2006).

11. Jenifer Parks, "Verbal Gymnastics," in *East Plays West*, ed. Wagg and Andrews, 27.

12. Ban Wang, as cited in Wagg and Andrews, *East Plays West*, 3; see B. Wang, "The Cold War, Imperial Aesthetics, and Area Studies," *Social Text* 20, no. 3 (2002): 45–65.

13. Wagg and Andrews, *East Plays West*, 4.

14. "World Is Watching, Coach Says in Pep Talk to American Team," *New York Times*, July 28, 1958, 17.

15. Joseph M. Turrini, "'It Was Communism versus the Free World': The USA-USSR Dual Track Meet Series and the Development of Track and Field in the United States, 1958–1985," *Journal of Sport History* 28, no. 3 (2001): 429. Also see "Events and Discoveries: Moscow's Invitation," *Sports Illustrated*, April 22, 1957, 24; and Pincus Sober, "U.S. Track and Field Teams Compete in Moscow, Warsaw, Budapest, Athens!" *Amateur Athlete*, September 1958, 5–6.

16. Turrini, "'It Was Communism versus the Free World,'" 430. Also see Tex Maule, "Those Darlin' Djerachle," *Sports Illustrated*, July 28, 1959, 22–23; "World Is Watching, Coach Says in Pep Talk to American Team," *New York Times*, July 28, 1958, 17; Max Frankel, "Soviets Defeat US Track Team," *New York Times*, July 29, 1958, 1, 27; Dick Drake, "Athletes View Europe Trip," *Track and Field News*,

September 1963, 11; James Riordan, "The USSR and the Olympic Games," *Stadion* 6 (1980): 291–313; "Moscow's Hero," *Time*, August 11, 1958, 52; and "The Summit for Rafer," *LIFE*, August 11, 1958, 91.

17. Cahn, *Coming on Strong*, 130.

18. "U.S. Girls Wake Up!" *Amateur Athlete*, December 1946, 10; Roxy Atkins Andersen, "Why European Superiority," *Amateur Athlete*, December 1951, 10.

19. "Powers Calls for 'Co-ed' Meets," *Amateur Athlete*, July 1953, 26. The United States had only recently begun competing in other international competitions, such as the Pan-Am Games, between Olympiads. "4 Tigerbelles Represent U.S.A. at Pan-Am Games," *The Meter* (Tennessee State University), February 1955, 5. The Pan-Am Games were held in Mexico City. The four Tigerbelles were Isabelle Daniels, Mae Faggs, Margaret Davis, and Patricia Monsanto (discus thrower). Monsanto was the first African American female to represent the United States in any of the throwing events.

20. Cahn, *Coming on Strong*, 131. The Soviet Union did quite well in their first Olympics appearance in 1952, finishing second to the United States in the overall medal count, with twenty-two gold medals, thirty silver, and nineteen bronze, for seventy-one total medals. In Cortina d'Ampezzo, at their first Winter Games, the Soviets won the overall medal count with sixteen medals (seven golds, three silver, and six bronze). At the 1956 Summer Games in Melbourne, the Soviets won the overall medal count with ninety-eight medals (thirty-seven gold, twenty-nine silver, and thirty-two bronze); the United States finished with seventy-four medals, including thirty-two gold. Their 1956 team had 233 male athletes and 39 female athletes.

21. Turrini, "'It Was Communism versus the Free World,'" 433.

22. John V. Grombach, "The Cold War in International Athletics," *American Mercury*, June 1960, 40.

23. "Reds Hope to Rule Sports Too: 12 Million Athletes in Training to Beat the West," *US News & World Report*, August 20, 1954, 35–37. Also see "If Russia Wins Olympic Games—Red Athletes Will Become Bigger Weapon in 'Cold War,'" *US News & World Report*, February 10, 1956, 35–36, 38–39; "Are Reds World's Best Athletes? It Depends on What Sport You're Talking About," *US News & World Report*, December 14, 1956, 71–73.

24. Cahn, *Coming on Strong*, 130.

25. "Powers Calls for "Co-ed" Meets," *Amateur Athlete*, July 1953, 26.

26. Dr. Charles A. Bucher, "Are We Losing the Olympic Ideal?," *Sports Illustrated*, August 8, 1955, 52–58.

27. Cahn, *Coming on Strong*, 132.

28. Ibid., 131.

29. "Tennessee State Tigerbelles Victorious in National Championship," *The Meter*, January 1959, VII (5), 5. Fifth straight indoor AAU team title. Also see

Alfrances Lyman, "Tigerbelles Win Twelve First Places during the Summer," *The Meter*, September 1959, VII (6), 5.

30. "TSU Tigerbelles," *The Meter*, November 1958, VII (2), 5.

31. "Fastest Women in the World," *Ebony*, June 1955, 27.

32. Ibid.

33. Mary Snow, "Can the Soviet Girls Be Stopped," *Sports Illustrated*, August 27, 1956, 6–11.

34. Wendell A. Parris, "The American Negro in the Sixteenth Olympiad," *Negro History Bulletin*, May 1957, 179–80. Parris also noted that American males singlehandedly beat their Soviet opponents in track and field, winning fifteen gold medals to the Russians' three, with African American males playing a significant role in the US victories.

35. "TSU Tigerbelles," *The Meter*, November 1958, VII (2), 5.

36. Turrini, "'It Was Communism versus the Free World,'" 432; Hank Soloman, "It Happened in Philly," *Amateur Athlete*, August 1959, 6–12; Dick Bank, "U.S. Women Make History," *Track and Field News*, October 1958, 12; Bert Nelson, "Of People and Things," *Track and Field News*, September 1959, 7.

37. Tom Siler, "Wilma Sprang from Depths of Poverty to Gold Medal" *Atlanta Constitution*, September 3, 1960, 10.

38. Braven Dyer, "Europe Catching Up with U.S.," *Los Angeles Times*, September 11, 1960, H2.

39. Fred Russell, "Rudolph Jewel of Consistency in Heat Races: Always a Winner," *Nashville Banner*, September 6, 1960, 14.

40. "No Sour Grapes," *Appleton (WI) Post-Crescent*, September 15, 1960, 10.

41. Robert E. Lee, "Nixon Urges End of Dispute, More Power Project Action," *Long Beach (CA) Independent*, September 14, 1960, 1.

42. See, for example, "Olympic Champ Meets Nixon," *Corpus Christi (TX) Times*, October 10, 1960, 12.

43. "TOP RUNNERS," *Oneonta (NY) Star*, October 11, 1960, 1.

44. Dean Gordon B. Hancock, "Between the Lines: Ten-Tenths versus Nine-Tenths," *Atlanta Daily World*, September 30, 1960, 4.

45. David K. Wiggins and Patrick B. Miller, *The Unlevel Playing Field: Documentary History of the African American Experience in Sport* (Champaign: University of Illinois Press, 2003), 206.

46. Frances Walters, "Hail Olympic Winners," *Baltimore Afro-American*, September 24, 1960, 4.

47. Wiggins and Miller, *The Unlevel Playing Field*, 206.

48. "TSU Tracksters Win Seven Gold Medals at the Olympics," *The Meter*, October 1960, 2.

49. Marion E. Jackson, "Sports of the World," *Atlanta Daily World*, October 2, 1956, 6.

50. Bill Brower, "1960 Olympic Closeups," *Atlanta Daily World*, September 15, 1960, 6.

51. Bill Nunn Jr., "Tan Stars Spark US in Wins over Russia," *Pittsburgh Courier*, July 25, 1959, 25.

52. Christian G. Appy, ed., *Cold War Constructions: The Political Culture of US Imperialism, 1945–1956* (Amherst: University of Massachusetts, 2000), 2.

53. Bill Nunn Jr., "Negroes Enable USA to Save Face in Track," *Pittsburgh Courier*, August 1, 1959, 27.

54. Wendell Smith, "Brotherhood Prevails among N.C. Athletes," *Pittsburgh Courier*, July 14, 1956, 27.

55. Marion Jackson, *Atlanta Daily World*, July 25, 1958, 5.

56. A. S. "Doc" Young, "How Negro Colleges Tumbled Sports Barriers," *Negro Digest*, November 1962, 36.

57. *Wilma Rudolph: Olympic Champion* (film). (1961). US Information Agency. (Available from Archives II, Record Group 306.5247).

58. Nicholas J. Cull, *The Cold War and the United States Information Agency: American Propaganda and Public Diplomacy, 1945–1989* (Cambridge, UK: Cambridge University Press, 2008), 1.

59. Walter L. Hixson, *Parting the Curtain: Propaganda, Culture, and the Cold War, 1945–1961* (New York: St. Martin's, 1998), 121.

60. Ibid., 125.

61. Lucas, "Beyond Diplomacy," 17.

62. Schwenk, "'Negro Stars,'" 130.

63. Ibid., 122.

64. de Hoog, quoted in Schwenk, "'Negro Stars,'" 127.

65. Hixson, *Parting the Curtain*, 130.

66. Dudziak, *Cold War Civil Rights*, 51.

67. Schwenk, "'Negro Stars,'" 128.

68. Hixson, *Parting the Curtain*, 136.

69. For an interesting piece on the relationship between theme songs/music and 1950s and 1960s television shows, see Joni M. Butcher, "The Bardic Utterance in Situation Comedy Theme Songs, 1960–2000" (PhD diss., Louisiana State University and Agriculture and Mechanical College, 2003).

70. Hixson, *Parting the Curtain*, 87.

71. President Dwight D. Eisenhower quoted in William Inboden, *Religion and American Foreign Policy, 1945–1960: The Soul of Containment* (Oxford: Cambridge University Press, 2008), 20. On the relationship between Americanism, Cold War

rhetoric, and religion during this period, see Stephen J. Whitfield, *The Culture of the Cold War* (Baltimore: Johns Hopkins University Press, 1996).

72. Maureen M. Smith, *Wilma Rudolph: A Biography* (Westport, CT: Greenwood, 2006), 82–83. This observation is based on an exchange between the authors and a former teammate of Rudolph's at a fiftieth anniversary celebration of the Rome Olympics, hosted by the American Academy in Rome, October 2010.

73. "Wilma Finds Key to City Doesn't Work," *Pittsburgh Courier*, June 8, 1963, 3.

74. These goodwill trips were in addition to a campaign that included the USIA video series, as well as a series of US government-produced pamphlets.

75. Lucas, "Beyond Diplomacy," 37.

76. For example, see Cahn, *Coming on Strong*; Damion L. Thomas, *Globetrotting: African American Athletes and Cold War Politics* (Urbana: University of Illinois Press, 2012); and the Wagg and Andrews collection, *East Plays West*.

77. Thomas, "Let the Games Begin," 163; also see Thomas, *Globetrotting*.

78. Richard Stites, "Heaven and Hell: Soviet Propaganda Constructs the World," in *Cold War Propaganda in the 1950s*, ed. Gary D. Rawnsley (New York: St. Martin's, 1999), 92.

79. Dudziak, *Cold War Civil Rights*, 56.

80. Von Eschen, *Satchmo Blows Up the World*, 255.

81. Maureen M. Smith, "Bill Russell: Pioneer and Champion of the Sixties," in *Out of the Shadows: A Biographical History of African American Athletes*, ed. David K. Wiggins (Fayetteville: University of Arkansas Press, 2006), 230–31; also see Bill Russell with Taylor Branch, *Second Wind: The Memoirs of an Opinionated Man* (New York: Random House, 1979), 88.

82. Russell with Branch, *Second Wind*, 88.

83. Gilbert Rogin, "We Were Grown Men Playing a Child's Game," *Sports Illustrated*, November 18, 1963, 82.

84. "Biceps and Choirs: Senate Group Backs Them to Promote US Abroad," *New York Times*, July 18, 1956, 54.

85. New African nations: The first year listed is the year of independence. The second year listed is the year the nation's National Olympic Committee was granted membership in the International Olympic Committee. Each NOC may have formed years prior to membership: Algeria (1962/1964), Benin (1960/1962), Burkina Faso (1960/1972), Burundi (1962/1993), Cameroon (1960–61/1963), Central African Republic (1960/1965), Chad (1960/1964), Congo (1960/1964), Côte d'Ivoire [Ivory Coast] (1960/1963), Democratic Republic of the Congo (1960/1968), Gabon (1960/1968), Ghana (1957/1952), Guinea 1958/1965), Kenya (1963/1955), Madagascar (1960/1964), Malawi (1964/1968), Mali (1960/1963), Mauritania

(1960/1979), Morocco (1956/1959), Niger (1960/1964), Rwanda (1962/1984), Senegal (1960/1963), Sierra Leone (1961/1964), Somalia (1960/1972), Sudan (1956/1959, Tanzania (1961/1968), Togo (1960/1965), Tunisia (1956/1957), Uganda (1962/1956), Zambia (1964/1964).

86. For one example of how Africa was viewed in terms of sport development, see Reggie Alexander, in a May 29, 1961, letter to IOC secretary Otto Mayer: "The new Africa, in its process of 'growing up' is inclined to throw off connections with the old world. It is all a part of the psychological process of being seen as independent. Properly handled this process can be turned to advantage by showing Africa that it really is an equal 'member of the family.'" Alexander thought one way to indicate the IOC's support and inclusion of Africa was to host a meeting on the continent; Alexander to Mayer, 29 May 1961, IOC Archives, Lausanne, Switzerland, folder: Reginald S. Alexander, Biographie/Correspondance 1960–1969. For the Soviet perspective on Africa, see K. Andrianov, "Correspondance: A Letter of URSS to the Mr. Avery Brundage," *Bulletin du Comité International Olympique*, No. 72, November 1960, 71–72. Andrianov was central to the development of the International Aid Commission, formed in the months after the 1963 Friendship Games. See Minutes of the Conference of the Executive Board of the International Olympic Committee, Lausanne, Switzerland, June 5, 1963, 3. For more on the formation of this aid committee, see Minutes of the 58th Session of the IOC, Athens, Greece, June 19–21, 1961, 6–7, IOC Archives. Andrianov's file in the IOC Archives is full of letters written in English to IOC president Avery Brundage and future president Juan Antonio Samaranch. Among the many ideas Andrianov shares are those related to the development of the aid commission, specific to the assistance of African nations.

87. Mary Jo Festle, *Playing Nice: Politics and Apologies in Women's Sports* (New York: Columbia University Press, 1996), 201.

88. Festle, *Playing Nice*, 201–02.

89. Michael D. Davis, *Black American Women in Olympic Track and Field* (Jefferson, NC: McFarland, 1992), 58–59.

90. Terry Valos Gitersos, "The Sporting Scramble for Africa: GANEFO, the IOC, and the 1965 African Games," *Sport in Society* 14 (2011): 651. Only a few months before the Friendship Games, IOC president Avery Brundage told members of the executive board that it was up to the IOC to follow the "evolution" of new African countries "very closely." Brundage wanted the organization to "avoid granting recognition to committees representing very small countries which only possess a very vague notion of sport matters and of what olympism [sic] stands for." See Minutes of the Conference of the Executive Board of the International Olympic Committee, Lausanne, Switzerland, February 4, 1963, 3, IOC Archives, Lausanne, Switzerland. The first IOC patronage of a major sporting event in Africa came with the First African Games, hosted in Brazzaville, Congo, in 1965; see Minutes of the Meeting of the

Executive Board, Lausanne, Switzerland, April 11, 13, 1965, 3, IOC Archives. These Games were considered the "successor of 'Le Jeux de l'Amitie.'" There was some debate about the use of the name "African Games" if not every country was invited. See Minutes of the Meeting of the Executive Board of the IOC, Tokyo, Japan, October 16, 1964, 2, IOC Archives. Also see Minutes of the Meeting of the Executive Board of the IOC, Lausanne, Switzerland, June 26–27, 1964, 1–3; IOC Archives.

91. "Friendship Games," *Dakar Matin*, April 11, 1963, special issue, 7.

92. "'Black Gazelle' Expected in Dakar This Morning," *Dakar Matin*, April 13, 1963, 1.

93. "Wilma Rudolph Meets the President," *Dakar Matin*, April 22, 1963, 1.

94. "Wilma Due Tomorrow," *Daily Graphic*, April 25, 1963, 15.

95. "Wilma Rudolph Is Here," *Daily Graphic*, April 29, 1963, 15; "Wilma Off to Mali," *Daily Graphic*, May 1, 1963, 1. The first African Games were in 1961. The IOC sent a survey to African nations in 1962 and then hosted the Friendship Games in Dakar, Senegal, in 1963. Twenty-four countries attended. By 1963, most African nations were already opposed to South Africa's apartheid policies and practices. These countries threatened to boycott the 1964 Games as a result of South Africa's inclusion.

96. The *New York Times* had several very brief mentions of Rudolph's travels in Africa; see "Wilma Rudolph Off to Senegal," *New York Times*, April 13, 1963, 33; "Senegal in Salute to Wilma Rudolph," *New York Times*, April 14, 1963, 168; "Wilma Rudolph to Tour Ghana," *New York Times*, April 24, 1963, 55; "Wilma Rudolph in Upper Volta," *New York Times*, May 6, 1963, 40.

97. Michael Davis, *Black American Women*, 127–28.

98. Ibid., 127.

99. Ibid.

100. "The Ace Athletes," *Daily Graphic*, April 30, 1963, 1.

101. "Wilma: I Have Enjoyed Stay," *Daily Graphic*, May 2, 1963, 11.

102. "Our Athletes Praised," *Daily Graphic*, April 30, 1963, 10.

103. "Wilma: I Have Enjoyed Stay," *Daily Graphic*, May 2, 1963, 11.

104. In the three months following Birmingham, another seventy-five southern cities were the sites of over 700 protests and demonstrations, which resulted in over 10,000 arrests. For more on this time period and the civil rights movement, see Taylor Branch, *Parting the Waters: America in the King Years, 1954–1963* (New York: Touchstone Books, 1988); Adam Fairclough, *Better Day Coming: Blacks and Equality, 1890–2000* (New York: Viking, 2001); and Harvard Sitkoff, *The Struggle for Black Equality, 1954–1992* (New York: Hill and Wang, 1993).

105. In early June, President Kennedy met with civil rights leaders at the White House. On June 11, Alabama governor George Wallace confronted two African American students who had enrolled at the University of Alabama, finally stepping aside to allow their entry. The next day, civil rights leader Medgar Evers was

assassinated outside his home. On August 28, 1963, over 200,000 Americans marched on Washington with King. For more on this time period, see Fairclough, *Better Day Coming*, 249–93.

106. As cited in Marion E. Jackson, "Sports of the World," *Atlanta Daily World*, May 1, 1963, 5.

107. W. K. Stratton, *Floyd Patterson: The Fighting Life of Boxing's Invisible Champion* (Boston: Houghton Mifflin, 2012), 159–62.

108. Jackie Robinson, "Southern Nightmare Stirs 'Back Our Brothers' Action," *Chicago Defender*, week of May 25–31, 1963, n.p.

109. Jackie Robinson, "Strange Words from Hitler Racist Victim Jesse Owens," *Chicago Defender*, week of June 1–7, 1963, n.p.

110. Charles J. Livingston, "Ralph Metcalf, Jesse Owens Row over Jackie Robinson, Top Personalities at Odds over Handling of Birmingham Issue," *Atlanta Daily World*, May 23, 1963, 5. Patterson's thoughts related to his trip and his motivations for his participation are expressed in an interview with WSB-TV out of Atlanta, Georgia. To view this short clip, see "WSB-TV newsfilm clip of former heavyweight boxing champion Floyd Patterson speaking to a reporter about the civil rights movement in Birmingham, Alabama, 9 May 1963," Civil Rights Digital Library, Clip 35383, Athens, GA: Digital Library of Georgia and Walter J. Brown Media Archives and Peabody Awards Collection, University of Georgia Libraries, 2007, http://dlg.galileo.usg.edu/crdl/id:ugabma_wsbn_35383. Limited coverage of the two athletes' trip was included in the *New York Times*; see Claude Sitton, "Birmingham Talks Reach an Accord on Ending Crisis," *New York Times*, May 10, 1963, 1, 14; Claude Sitton, "Rioting Negroes Routed by Police at Birmingham," *New York Times*, May 8, 1963, 1, 28; "Integration Funds Asked," *New York Times*, May 7, 1963, 33; Richard J. H. Johnston, "NAACP Urges Mass Picketing," *New York Times*, May 8, 1963, 28; "Rights Pact Halts Alabama Strife," *New York Times*, May 12, 1963, 164; "Robinson and Patterson Exhort Birmingham Crowd," *New York Times*, May 14, 27; "2 Negro Athletes Plan a Community," *New York Times*, May 10, 1963, 14.

111. Charles J. Livingston, "Ralph Metcalf, Jesse Owens Row over Jackie Robinson," 5.

112. Charles J. Livingston, "Living with Sports," as quoted in Marion E. Jackson, "Sports of the World," *Atlanta Daily World*, June 2, 1963, 5.

113. Jackie Robinson, "Strange Words from Hitler Racist Victim Jesse Owens," n.p.

114. Charles J. Livingston, "Ralph Metcalf, Jesse Owens Row over Jackie Robinson," 5.

115. "Athlete in Protest," *New York Times*, May 30, 1963, 32; "Wilma Finds Key to City Doesn't Work," *Pittsburgh Courier*, June 8, 1963, 3; Marion E. Jackson, "Sports of the World," *Atlanta Daily World*, June 4, 1963, 5.

116. *Pittsburgh Courier*, June 8, 1963, 3.

117. Jackson, "Sports of the World," June 4, 1963, 5.

118. From a Taxpayer, "Letters to the Editor," *Leaf-Chronicle*, May 22, 1963, 4.

119. Ronald Meuschell, "Letters to the Editor," *Leaf-Chronicle*, May 22, 1963, 4.

120. Mrs. Wyatt, "Letters to the Editor," *Leaf-Chronicle*, May 27, 1963, 4.

121. "Wilma Plans to Get Job in Cl'ville," *Leaf-Chronicle*, May 28, 1963, 6.

122. "Negroes Denied Service at Shoney's," *Leaf-Chronicle*, May 29, 1963, 1.

123. "Negroes Try Integration Here Again," *Leaf-Chronicle*, May 30, 1963, 1, 10.

124. "Six Shots Fired into Clyde Foust's Home," *Leaf-Chronicle*, May 31, 1963, 1.

125. Ibid., 9.

126. "Truce Reported in Racial Dispute with Shoney's," *Leaf-Chronicle*, May 31, 1963, 1.

127. "Group Favors Desegregation of Restaurants," *Leaf-Chronicle*, June 3, 1963, p. 1.

128. "Public Facilities in City Open to All by Council Vote," *Leaf-Chronicle*, June 7, 1963, 1.

129. T. W. Mayhew, "Letter to The Editor," *Leaf-Chronicle*, June 10, 1963, 4.

130. Von Eschen, *Satchmo Blows Up the World*, 24.

131. According to Rudolph's earliest interviews in preparing for her 1990 deposition in *Haynes v. Shoney's*, Rudolph wrongly recalled the Shoney's incident occurring soon after the Olympic Games. So it is unclear just how directly her African experience influenced her decision to participate in the civil rights action. Still, her 1990 interview was close to thirty years after the event, making her timing somewhat understandable. Complicating matters, Sam Lacy wrongly placed the episode on the day after her 1960 parade in Clarksville. If she was denied service in 1960, we did not find evidence. Moreover, Lacy includes the 1963 photo of Rudolph opening the Shoney's door, directly linking his 1960 snub to the photo. See Lacy, "Seven Olympics and Counting Reporter to Black America," *Olympics 1988*, 30–33; located in *Haynes et al. v. Shoney's, Inc.* Papers, 1959–1997, Box 147, Folder 27, Wilma Rudolph, Claude Pepper Library, Florida State University, Tallahassee, Florida. Despite her inclusion in Lacy's article, she is minimally addressed, accounting for two sentences, and is seen in one quarter-page sized photo.

132. "Winsome Wilma—Ambassador American," *The Meter*, December 1960, 2.

133. Mal Whitfield, "'Let's Boycott the Olympics': Olympic Champ Asks Negro Athletes to Act," *Ebony*, March 1964, 95–96, 98–100. Also see Marion Jackson, "Sports of the World," *Atlanta Daily World*, April 13, 1963, 5.

134. For more on the various protests of African American athletes in the civil rights movement, see Adolph H. Grundman, "The Image of Intercollegiate Sports

and the Civil Rights Movement: A Historian's View," *Sport in Higher Education*, 339–45; Donald Spivey, "The Black Athlete in Big-Time Intercollegiate Sports, 1941–1968," *Phylon* 44, no. 2 (1983): 116–25; David K. Wiggins, "'The Year of Awakening': Black Athletes, Racial Unrest and the Civil Rights Movement of 1968," *The International Journal of the History of Sport* 9, no. 2 (1992): 188–208; David K. Wiggins, "Prized Performers, but Frequently Overlooked Students: The Involvement of Black Athletes in Intercollegiate Sports on Predominantly White University Campuses, 1968–1972," *Research Quarterly for Exercise and Sport* 62, no. 2 (1991): 164–77.

135. Anita Verschoth, "Slight Change of Pace for Wilma," *Sports Illustrated*, September 7, 1964, E6.

136. Ibid., E7.

137. Ibid., E6.

138. Ibid., E8.

139. Steve Watkins, *The Black O: Racism and Redemption in an American Corporate Empire* (Athens: University of Georgia Press, 1997), 112. For a complete read of Rudolph's deposition, including notes taken in early versions, see *Haynes v. Shoney's Inc.* Papers, Box 147, Folder 27, Wilma Rudolph. Also included in Rudolph's folder are several articles from the *Leaf-Chronicle* that document the 1963 event, the 1988 article by Sam Lacy, as well as correspondence to Rudolph from the law offices of Thomas Warren, Tallahassee, Florida.

140. Verschoth, "Slight Change of Pace," E7.

141. Jonathan Scott Holloway, *Jim Crow Wisdom: Memory and Identity in Black America since 1940* (Chapel Hill: University of North Carolina Press, 2013), 39.

4. Examining the Autobiographical Self

1. Rudolph, *Wilma*, 5.

2. Sidonie Smith and Julia Watson, *Reading Autobiography: A Guide for Interpreting Life Narratives* (Minneapolis: University of Minnesota Press, 2010), 50.

3. James W. Pipkin, *Sporting Lives: Metaphor and Myth in American Sports Autobiographies* (Columbia: University of Missouri Press, 2008), 59.

4. G. T. Couser, *Signifying Bodies: Disability in Contemporary Life Writing* (Ann Arbor: University of Michigan, 2009), 47.

5. Kristi Siegel, *Women's Autobiographies, Culture, Feminism* (New York: Peter Lang, 1999), 6.

6. Mary M. Gergen and Kenneth J. Gergen, "Narratives of the Gendered Body in Popular Autobiography," in *The Narrative Study of Lives*, vol. 1, ed. Ruthellen Josselson and Amia Lieblich (Newbury Park, CA: Sage Publications, 1993), 193.

7. Andrew C. Sparkes, "Bodies, Narratives, Selves, and Autobiography: The Example of Lance Armstrong," *Journal of Sport and Social Issues* 28, no. 4 (2004): 398.

8. Rosi Braidotti quoted in Derek Duncan, "Corporeal Histories: The Auto-biographical Bodies of Luisa Passerini," *Modern Language Review* 93, no. 2 (1998): 372.

9. Babe Didrikson Zaharias as told to Harry Paxton, *This Life I've Led: My Auto-biography* (New York: A. S. Barnes, 1955); Althea Gibson as told to Ed Fitzgerald, *I Always Wanted to Be Somebody* (New York: HarperCollins, 1958); Lynda Huey, *A Running Start: An Athlete, a Woman* (New York: Quadrangle/New York Times Book Co., 1976).

10. See, for example, Jackie Joyner-Kersee with Sonja Steptoe, *A Kind of Grace: The Autobiography of the World's Greatest Female Athlete* (New York: Grand Central, 1997); Jennie Finch and Ann Killion, *Throw like A Girl: How to Dream Big and Believe in Yourself* (New York: Triumph Books, 2011); Gabrielle Reece and Karen Karbo, *Big Girl in the Middle* (New York: Three Rivers, 1998).

11. Gary Osmond, "Shimmering Waters: Swimming, Autobiography and Social Memory," *Sporting Traditions* 20, no. 1 (2003): 64.

12. Jennifer Jensen Wallach, *Closer to Truth Than Any Fact: Memoir, Memory, and Jim Crow* (Athens: University of Georgia Press, 2008), 4.

13. Michael Oriard, "Autobiographies," in *African-Americans in Sport*, vol. 1, ed. David K. Wiggins (Armonk, NY: M. E. Sharpe, 2004), 17.

14. Gunnthórunn Gudmundsdóttir, *Borderlines: Autobiography and Fiction in Postmodern Life Writing* (Amsterdam: Rodopi, 2003), 53.

15. Pipkin, *Sporting Lives*, 5.

16. John Paul Eakin, *Living Autobiographically: How We Create Identity in Narrative* (Ithaca, NY: Cornell University Press 2008), 22.

17. Gudmundsdóttir, *Borderlines*, 54.

18. Sidonie Smith and Julia Watson, *Reading Autobiography*, 15.

19. Ibid.

20. Pipkin, *Sporting Lives*, 2–3.

21. Oriard, "Autobiographies," 16.

22. Ibid. By 1977, a good number of African American male athletes had already penned their life stories (sometimes more than once), helping to establish the patterns Oriard describes. For example, see Henry Aaron with Furman Bisher, *Aaron, R. F.* (Cleveland: World, 1969); Ali with Durham, *The Greatest* (1975); Arthur Ashe with Frank Deford, *Portrait in Motion* (Boston: Houghton Mifflin, 1975); Jim Brown with Myron Cope, *Off My Chest* (Garden City, NY: Doubleday, 1964); Bob Gibson, *From Ghetto to Glory* (Englewood Cliffs, NJ: Prentice Hall, 1968); Joe Louis, Chester L. Washington, and Haskell Cohen, *My Life Story, by Joe Louis* (New York: Duell, Sloan and Pearce, 1947); Jesse Owens with Paul Niemark, *Blackthink: My Life as Black Man and White Man* (New York: Morrow, 1970); Floyd Patterson with Milton Gross, *Victory over Myself* (New York: Random House, 1962); Frank Robinson and

Al Silverman, *My Life in Baseball* (New York: Doubleday, 1968); Jackie Robinson, *Baseball Has Done It* (Philadelphia: Lippincott, 1964); Jackie Robinson with Alfred Duckett, *Breakthrough to the Big Leagues* (New York: Harper & Row, 1965); Jackie Robinson with Alfred Duckett, *I Never Had It Made* (New York: Putnam, 1972); and Bill Russell with William McSweeney, *Go Up for Glory* (New York: Coward-McCann, 1966). In the years following Rudolph's book, African American men continued to tell their stories. For example, see Hank Aaron with Lonnie Wheeler, *I Had a Hammer: The Hank Aaron Story* (New York: HarperCollins, 1991); Arthur Ashe with Neil Amdur, *Off the Court* (New York: New American Library, 1981); Arthur Ashe and Arnold Rampersad, *Days of Grace: A Memoir* (New York: Alfred A. Knopf, 1993); Jim Brown and Steve Delsohn, *Out of Bounds* (New York: Zebra Books, Kensington, 1989); Joe Louis with Edna and Art Rust, *Joe Louis: My Life* (New York: Harcourt Brace Jovanovich, 1978); and Bill Russell with Taylor Branch, *Second Wind* (1979).

23. Bryan Curtis, in Sidonie Smith and Julia Watson, *Reading Autobiography*, 272.

24. Autobiographical writing by African Americans is a means of asserting, according to Butterfield (p. 3), "their right to live and grow. It is a bid for freedom, a beak of hope cracking the shell of slavery and exploitation. It is also an attempt to communicate to the white world what whites have done to them." See Stephen Butterfield, *Black Autobiography in America* (Amherst: University of Massachusetts Press, 1974). For more on African American autobiography, see Shari Benstock, ed., *Feminist Issues in Literary Scholarship* (Bloomington: Indiana University Press, 1987); Henry Louis Gates Jr., ed., *Bearing Witness: Selections from African-American Autobiography in the Twentieth Century* (New York: Pantheon Books, 1991); James Craig Holte, *The Ethnic I: A Sourcebook for Ethnic-American Autobiography* (New York: Greenwood, 1988).

25. Oriard, "Autobiographies," 370.

26. Duncan, "Corporeal Histories," 370.

27. Ibid.

28. G. T. Couser, "Autopathography: Women, Illness, and Lifewriting," in *On the Literary Nonfiction of Nancy Mairs: A Critical Anthology*, ed. Merri Lisa Johnson and Susannah B. Mintz (New York: Palgrave MacMillan, 2011), 138.

29. Barbara Satina and Francine Hultgren, "The Absent Body of Girls Made Visible: Embodiment as the Focus in Education," *Studies in Philosophy and Education* 20 (2001): 522.

30. Sidonie Smith and Julia Watson, ed., *Women, Autobiography, Theory: A Reader* (Madison: University of Wisconsin Press, 1998), 23.

31. Couser, *Signifying Bodies*, 47.

32. Sidonie Smith, "Identity's Body," in *Autobiography and Postmodernism*, ed. Kathleen Ashley, Leigh Gilmore, and Gerald Peters (Amherst: University of Massachusetts Press, 1994), 283.

33. Sidonie Smith, *Subjectivity, Identity, and the Body: Women's Autobiographical Practices in the Twentieth Century* (Bloomington: Indiana University Press, 1993), 20.

34. Jennifer Ritterhouse, *Growing Up Jim Crow: How Black and White Southern Children Learned Race* (Chapel Hill: University of North Carolina Press, 2006), 83, 90–94.

35. Christy Rishoi, *From Girl to Woman: American Women's Coming-of-Age Narratives* (Albany: State University of New York Press, 2003), 92.

36. Judy Long, *Telling Women's Lives: Subject/Narrator/Reader/Text* (New York: New York University Press, 1999), 9.

37. Rishoi, *From Girl to Woman*, 94; Ann Moody, *Coming of Age in Mississippi* (New York: Dial, 1962).

38. See Mary Catherine Bateson, *Composing a Life* (New York: Penguin, 1989), 45.

39. Shirley Neuman, "Autobiography, Bodies, Manhood," in *Women, Autobiography, Theory: A Reader*, ed. Sidonie Smith and Julia Watson (Madison: University of Wisconsin Press, 1998), 416.

40. Long, *Telling Women's Lives*, 27.

41. Johnnie Stover, *Rhetoric and Resistance in Black Women's Autobiography* (Gainesville: University Press of Florida, 2003), 20–38. In addition to the differences between the autobiographical writings of women and men, there is a difference between the autobiographical writings of African American women and white women. For more on these racial differences see Elizabeth Fox-Genovese, "To Write My Self: The Autobiographies of Afro-American Women," in *Feminist Issues in Literary Scholarship*, ed. Shari Benstock (Bloomington: Indiana University Press, 1987), 161–80; Nellie Y. McKay, "Race, Gender, and Cultural Context in Zora Neale Hurston's *Dust Tracks on a Road*," in *Life/Lines: Theorizing Women's Autobiography*, ed. Bella Brodzki and Celeste Schenck (Ithaca, NY: Cornell University Press, 1988), 175–88; Toni Morrison, as cited in Carolyn G. Heilbrun, *Writing a Woman's Life* (New York: Ballantine Books, 1988), 61.

42. Long, *Telling Women's Lives*, 9.

43. Sandra L. Hofferth, Joan R. Kahn, and Wendy Baldwin, "Premarital Sexual Activity among US Teenage Women over the Past Three Decades," *Family Planning Perspectives* 19, no. 2 (1987): 49.

44. Cahn, *Coming on Strong*, 212.

45. Ibid., 117.

46. Ibid., 260.

47. Jennifer C. Nash, "Re-thinking Intersectionality," *Feminist Review* 89 (June 2008): 1–15.

48. Kimberlee Crenshaw, *Demarginalizing the Intersection of Race and Sex: A Black Feminist Critique of Antidiscrimination Doctrine, Feminist Theory, and Anti-racist Politics* (Chicago: University of Chicago Legal Forum, 1989), 139.

49. Philippe Lejeune, Annette Tomarken, and Edward Tomarken, "Autobiography in Third Person," *New Literary History* 9, no. 1 (1977): 39.

50. Rosalyn Baxandall, "Re-Visioning the Women's Liberation Movement's Narrative: Early Second Wave African American Feminists," *Feminist Studies* 27, no. 1 (2001): 225–45.

51. Daisy Bates, *The Long Shadow of Little Rock: A Memoir* (New York: David McKay Company, 1962); Angela Davis, *Angela Davis: Autobiography* (New York: Hutchinson, 1975); Ann Moody, *Coming of Age in Mississippi* (New York: Dial, 1968); Toni Morrison, *The Bluest Eye* (New York: Holt, Rinehart and Winston, 1970); Toni Morrison, *Sula* (New York: Knopf, 1973).

52. Harriet Sigerman, *The Columbia Documentary History of American Women since 1941* (New York: Columbia University Press, 2003), 316.

53. Duchess Harris, "From the Kennedy Commission to the Combahee Collective: Black Feminist Organizing, 1960–1980," in *Sisters in the Struggle: African American Women in the Civil Rights–Black Power Movement,* ed. Bettye Collier-Thomas and V. P. Franklin (New York: New York University Press, 2001), 300.

54. Gabriela Spector-Mersel, "Mechanisms of Selection in Claiming Narrative Identities: A Model for Interpreting Narratives," *Qualitative Inquiry* 17, no. 2 (2011): 174.

55. Stover, *Rhetoric and Resistance,* 180; Long, *Telling Women's Lives,* 49.

56. Mary Jean Green, "Structures of Liberation: Female Experience and the Autobiographical Form in Quebec," in *Life/Lines: Theorizing Women's Autobiography,* ed. Bella Brodzki and Celeste Schenck (Ithaca, NY: Cornell University Press, 1988), 190.

57. Smith, "Identity's Body," 267.

58. Ibid., 270.

5. *Wilma*

1. Ending the film when Rudolph is only twenty years old is a pattern that appears in most of the children's books written about Rudolph (see chapter six of this book). Throughout this chapter, we reference the film; see *Wilma* (DVD), directed by Bud Greenspan (1977; New York, NY: S'more entertainment, 2006). *Wilma* was written, directed, and produced by Bud Greenspan. Originally created as 35mm movie for television, the film has been reproduced in various formats, such

as VHS and DVD. All rights to the film are owned by Cappy Productions, Inc. Any quoted materials from the film were taken from the authors' transcription of the film, and permission was obtained from Cappy Productions to quote directly from the film.

2. *Wilma, Rushville, Indiana Republican,* December 19, 1977, 8. On the origination and development of movies made for television, see Douglas Gomery, "Television, Hollywood, and the Development of Movies Made-for-Television," in *Regarding Television: Critical Approaches—An Anthology,* ed. E. Ann Kaplan (Fredericksburg, MD: University of America Press, 1983), 120; George F. Custen, "The Mechanical Life in the Age of Human Reproduction: American Biopics, 1961–1980," *Biography* 23 (2000): 131.

3. Prior to *Wilma,* two other movies featured a black woman as the protagonist: including *Lady Sings the Blues* (1972; theatrical release), about the life of Billie Holiday, and *The Autobiography of Miss Jane Pittman* (1974; made for television), which is based on Ernest Gaines's novel. On these and other made-for-television movies in the 1970s with black women as central characters, see Donald Bogle, *Primetime Blues: African Americans on Network Television* (New York: Farrar, Straus, and Giroux, 2001), 233–50. Other television films on athletes include *Babe* (1975), about Babe Didrikson, *Brian's Song* (1971), about the Chicago Bears' Brian Piccolo, and *Something for Joey* (1977), about 1973 Heisman Trophy winner John Cappelletti.

4. Bud Greenspan, quoted in Diane Mermigas, "*Wilma* Unique Sports Drama," *Daily Herald* (Arlington Heights, IL), December 19, 1977, 5.

5. Mermigas, "*Wilma* Unique Sports Drama," 5.

6. Aaron Baker, *Contesting Identities: Sports in American Film* (Urbana: University of Illinois Press, 2003), 7.

7. Elsebeth Hurup, "Bridge over Troubled Water: Nostalgia for the Fifties in Movies of the Seventies and Eighties," in *Cracking the Ike Age: Aspects of Fifties America,* ed. Dale Carter (Denmark: Aarhus University Press, 1992), 56.

8. Svetlana Boym, *The Future of Nostalgia* (New York: Basic Books, 2001), xiii.

9. Fredric Jameson, *Postmodernism, or, The Cultural Logic of Late Capitalism* (Durham: Duke University Press, 1991), 19. An example of this type of film is *American Graffiti.*

10. Gary Deeb, "Beauty, Not Money, Most Important in Athletics," *News-Dispatch* (Jeannette and Irwin, PA), January 21, 1978, 7.

11. Stephen Brie, "The Land of the Lost Content: Living in the Past with *The Waltons,*" *Americana: The Journal of American Popular Culture (1900–present)* 28 (2008): 4.

12. Johnathan Rodgers, "Back to the '50s," *Newsweek,* October 16, 1972, 76.

13. Boym, *The Future of Nostalgia,* xiv.

14. Urie Bronfenbrenner, "The Calamitous Decline of the American Family," *Washington Post*, January 2, 1977, C1, C3.

15. Stephanie Coontz, *The Way We Never Were: American Families and the Nostalgia Trap* (New York: Basic Books, 1992), 162–79; Natasha Zaretsky, *No Direction Home: The American Family and the Fear of National Decline* (Chapel Hill: University of North Carolina Press, 2007), 9–23.

16. *Good Times* premiered in 1974 and was a spin-off of another Lear production, *Maude*. At the time, the show was considered a breakthrough, because it represented urban poverty and depicted a black family with two parents. See Bogle, *Primetime Blues*, 197–207. For more on *Good Times* and representations of blacks on television in the 1970s, see Herman Gray, "The Politics of Representation in Network Television," in *Channeling Blackness: Studies on Television and Race in America*, ed. Darnell M. Hunt (New York: Oxford University Press, 2005), 155–74; Darnell M. Hunt, "Black Content, White Control," in *Channeling Blackness*, 267–302.

17. Ella G. Taylor, *Prime-Time Families: Television Culture in Postwar America* (Berkeley: University of California Press, 1989), 1.

18. Baker, *Contesting Identities*, 8.

19. This is consistent with the sport narrative, as well as Greenspan's approach to presenting sport to the American audience.

20. Deeb, "Beauty, Not Money, Most Important in Athletics," 7.

21. Ibid.

22. Richard Sandomir, "Bud Greenspan, 84, Dies; Filmed Olympics in Glory," *New York Times*, December 26, 2010, D7.

23. Deeb, "Beauty, Not Money, Most Important in Athletics," 7.

24. T. Rees Shapiro, "Emmy Award-Winning Olympic Documentarian," *Washington Post*, December, 27, 2010, 4.

25. Sandomir, "Bud Greenspan, 84, Dies; Filmed Olympics in Glory," D7.

26. Shapiro, "Emmy Award-Winning Olympic Documentarian," 4; on Wilma's share of the television audience, see Deeb, "Beauty, Not Money, Most Important in Athletics," 7.

27. Robert A. Rosenstone, *History on Film/Film on History* (Harlow: UK: Pearson Longman, 2006), 3.

28. Ibid., 4.

29. Mark C. Carnes, *Past Imperfect: History According to the Movies* (New York: Henry Holt and Company, 1995), 9.

30. Rosenstone, *History on Film/Film on History*, 3.

31. George F. Custen, *Bio/Pics: How Hollywood Constructed Public History* (New Brunswick, NJ: Rutgers University Press, 1992), 7.

32. Ibid., 219.

33. Carnes, *Past Imperfect*, 9.

34. Custen, "The Mechanical Life in the Age of Human Reproduction," 131.

35. Ibid., 155.

36. Dennis Bingham, *Whose Lives Are They Anyway: The Biopic as Contemporary Film Genre* (New Brunswick, NJ: Rutgers University Press, 2010), 13.

37. Robert Rosenstone, "In Praise of the Biopic," in *Lights, Camera, History: Portraying the Past in Film*, ed. Richard Francaviglia and Jerry Rodnitzky (College Station: Texas A&M University Press, 2007), 11–29. For a thoughtful discussion on the importance of the biopic as a point of historical inquiry, see Murray G. Phillips and Gary Osmond, "Filmic Sports History: Dawn Fraser, Swimming and Australian National Identity," *The International Journal of the History of Sport* 26 (2009): 2126–42.

38. Robert A. Rosenstone, "Reel History with Missing Reels?," *Perspectives on History* (online) 37 (1999), accessed June 30, 2011.

39. George F. Custen, "Making History," in *The Historical Film: History and Memory in Media*, ed. Marcia Landy (New Brunswick: Rutgers University Press, 2001), 76.

40. Nathan, *Saying It's So*, 177; Troy D. Paino, "Hoosiers in a Different Light: Forces of Change v. the Power of Nostalgia," *Journal of Sport History* 28 (2001): 63–64; Brie, "The Land of the Lost Content," 6–7.

41. Custen, *Bio/Pics*, 224; Custen cites HBO's *The Terry Fox Story* (1981).

42. Ibid., 224, 226.

43. These trends were predicted in the controversial Moynihan Report issued in 1965. See Daniel Patrick Moynihan, *The Negro Family: The Case for National Action* (Washington, DC: Office of Policy Planning and Research, US Department of Labor, 1965).

44. Zaretsky, *No Direction Home*, 11. On the changing gender arrangements in 1970s society see Beth Bailey, "She 'Can Bring Home the Bacon': Negotiating Gender in the 1970s," in *America in the 70s*, ed. Beth Bailey and David Farber (Lawrence: University Press of Kansas, 2004), 107–28; Zaretsky, *No Direction Home*, 9–17; Coontz, *The Way We Never Were*, 162–69.

45. Bud Greenspan, quoted in Diane Mermigas, "Olympic Medalist Wilma Rudolph Delighted with Television Production," *Daily Herald* (Arlington Heights, IL), December 19, 1977, 5. For a good discussion on the cinematic representations of family, see Carl Boggs and Tom Pollard, "Postmodern Cinema and the Demise of the Family," *Journal of American Culture* 26 (2003): 445–53.

46. Zaretsky, *No Direction Home*, 156.

47. Ibid., 154.

48. Ibid., 148.

49. Leslie Fishbein, "*Roots*: Docudrama and the Interpretation of History," in *Why Docudrama? Fact-Fiction on Film and Television*, ed. Alan Rosenthal (Carbondale: Southern Illinois University Press, 1999), 290.

50. Greenspan, quoted in Mermigas, "Olympic Medalist Wilma Rudolph Delighted with Television Production," 5.

51. Bingham, *Whose Lives Are They Anyway?*, 213.

52. Zaretsky, *No Direction Home*, 1.

53. James T. Patterson, *Freedom Is Not Enough: The Moynihan Report and America's Struggle over Black Family Live—From LBJ to Obama* (New York: Basic Books, 2010), 129–44.

54. When John Amos, the actor who portrayed James Evans (father) decided to leave *Good Times*, he lamented "it might mean the show would revert to the matriarchal thing—the fatherless Black family. TV is the most powerful medium we have, and there just are not enough Black male images—which I think James Evans is—on TV;" see Bogle, *Primetime Blues*, 204. Esther Rolle, who portrayed the mother, Florida Evans, also left the show after being frustrated by the presentation of black male characters in the show. For more on Rolle's resistance, see Christine Acham, *Revolution Televised: Prime Time and the Struggle for Black Power* (Minneapolis: University of Minnesota Press, 2004). Chapter seven is titled "Black Women and Power in *Julia* and *Good Times*."

55. Zaretsky, *No Direction Home*, 8; also see Jewell, *From Mammy to Miss America and Beyond*.

56. Bruce J. Schulman, *The Seventies: The Great Shift in American Culture, Society, and Politics* (New York: The Free Press, 2001), 159–76. Although the women's liberation movement was active during this time period, Greenspan seems to have missed it, as least as reflected in his film.

57. Karen Hollinger, *In the Company of Women: Contemporary Female Friendship Films* (Minneapolis: University of Minnesota Press, 1998), 207.

58. Fishbein, "*Roots*," 282.

59. Bingham, *Whose Lives Are They Anyway?*, 230.

60. Hollinger, *In the Company of Women*, 207.

61. Ibid.

62. Mary Celeste Kearney, "Girlfriends and Girl Power: Female Adolescence in Contemporary US Cinema," in *Sugar, Spice, and Everything Nice: The Cinemas of Girlhood*, ed. Frances Gateward and Murray Pomerance (Detroit: Wayne State University Press, 2002), 131.

63. Fishbein, "*Roots*," 290.

64. Ella G. Taylor and Andrea S. Walsh, "'And Next Week—Child Abuse': Family Issues in Contemporary TV Movies," in *Culture and Communication:*

Methodology, Behavior, Artifacts, and Institutions, ed. Sari Thomas (Norwood, NJ: Ablex, 1987), 173.

65. This is a film made by a white man for a white audience. For more on the influence and control of white producers/directors on black content, see Gray, "The Politics of Representation in Network Television," 155–74; Hunt, "Black Content, White Control," 267–302; and Stephen Vider, "Sanford versus Steinberg: Black Sitcoms, Jewish Writers, and the 1970s Ethnic Revival," in *Transition* 105 (2011): 21–29.

66. The 800-meter run was re-introduced at the 1960 Olympic Games, after a thirty-two year absence; the 400-meter run was not offered. The 220-yard, 440-yard, and 880-yard were offered at the AAU outdoor nationals in 1958, and the 200-meter and 800-meter were offered at the 1958 dual meet between the US and USSR. See Louise Mead Tricard, *American Women's Track and Field: A History, 1895–1980* (Jefferson, NC: McFarland, 1996), 373–415. On distance running and his training of the Tigerbelles, Temple said, "In the morning we would all come out and work on distance. At that time, we were running about two miles. You've got to realize that in the fifties they weren't thinking about long distance running." See Tricard, *American Women's Track and Field*, 426.

67. Kegan Doyle, "Muhammad Goes to Hollywood: Michael Mann's Ali as Biopic," *Journal of Popular Culture* 39 (2006): 384–85.

68. Eric Foner, "The Televised Past," *Nation*, June 16, 1979, 724.

69. Mermigas, "*Wilma* Unique Sports Drama," 5.

70. Baker, *Contesting Identities*, 223.

71. John J. O'Connor, "TV: Holidays," *New York Times*, December 20, 1977, 53. This is another reminder that the film ends when Rudolph is only twenty years old, relatively young for the subject of a biopic.

72. Ibid.

73. Mark Harris, "Docudramas Unmasked," *Chicago Tribune*, March 8, 1978, section 3, B12.

74. Arthur Unger, "Wilma Rudolph—Runner's Saga," *Christian Science Monitor*, December 16, 1977, 22.

75. Doyle, "Muhammad Goes to Hollywood," 386.

76. Bingham, *Whose Lives Are They Anyway?*, 233.

6. Against All Odds

1. Corinne J. Naden and Rose Blue, *Wilma Rudolph* (Chicago: Raintree, 2004), 59. Naden and Blue's sixty-three page biography on Rudolph is part of series of biographies that "tell the inspiring stories of musicians, writers, actors, educators, sports heroes, and leaders whose determination and talent continue to set examples today. Readers will be fascinated to learn about the lives of well-known African Americans

who overcame tremendous odds, such as racism and poverty, and who went on to leave their lasting marks in the world."

2. Ibid.; this phrase comes from the back cover of the book.

3. We include twenty-one titles in this analysis: Jennifer Joline Anderson, *Wilma Rudolph: Track and Field Inspiration* (Mankato, MN: ABDO, 2011); Terre Lintner, *Wilma Rudolph: A True Winner* (New York: Macmillan/McGraw Hill, 2010); Stephanie Macceca, *Wilma Rudolph: Against All Odds* (Huntington Beach, CA: Teacher Created Materials, 2010); Mary Dodson Wade, *Wilma Rudolph: Amazing Olympic Athlete* (Berkeley Heights, NJ: Enslow, 2009); Eric Braun, *Wilma Rudolph* (Mankato, MN: Capstone, 2006); Lee Engfer, *Wilma Rudolph: Olympic Track Star* (Mankato, MN: Capstone, 2006); Maureen M. Smith, *Wilma Rudolph* (2006); Tom Streissguth, *Wilma Rudolph* (Minneapolis, MN: Twenty-First Century Books, 2006); Jo Harper, *Wilma Rudolph: Olympic Runner* (New York: Aladdin Paperbacks, 2004); Naden and Blue, *Wilma Rudolph* (2004); Anne Schraff, *Wilma Rudolph: The Greatest Woman Sprinter in History* (Berkeley Heights, NJ: Enslow, 2004); David Conrad, *Stick to It! The Story of Wilma Rudolph* (Minneapolis, MN: Compass Point Books, 2003); Mark Cooper and Carl Johnson, *Chris and Amy Meet Wilma Rudolph, Olympic Gold Medalist: A "Movies in My Mind" Adventure* (Imagination Development Group, 2002), compact disc; Alice K. Flanagan, *Wilma Rudolph: Athlete and Educator* (Chicago: Ferguson, 2000); Amy Ruth, *Wilma Rudolph* (Minneapolis, MN: Lerner, 2000); Victoria Sherrow, *Wilma Rudolph* (Minneapolis, MN: Carolrhoda Books, 2000); Ann Donegan Johnson, *The Value of Overcoming Adversity: The Story of Wilma Rudolph* (La Jolla, CA: Value Communications, 1996); Kathleen Krull, *Wilma Unlimited: How Wilma Rudolph Became the World's Fastest Woman* (San Diego, CA: Voyager Books/Harcourt, 1996); Wayne Coffey, *Wilma Rudolph* (Woodbridge, CT: Blackbirch Press, 1993); Tom Biracree, *Wilma Rudolph: Champion Athlete* (New York: Chelsea House, 1988); and Linda Jacobs, *Wilma Rudolph: Run For Glory* (St. Paul, MN: EMC, 1975). The prescribed audiences for the collection of books varies, with some books identified as being for young readers and others for youthful readers. Many of the books identify a grade level or age range as their readership target. Many of the books for young readers in grades four and above are structured as chapter books, and we focus our attention largely on this group of books. Maureen Smith's 2006 book was part of a series for high school readers, and as such, was able to address several topics that some of the "young reader" books did not (such as Rudolph's pregnancy). For that series, Smith was contacted by the publisher and asked to submit a manuscript on Rudolph. The parameters provided were related to word length and the deadline, with little input from the publisher as to the content. Samples of other books in the series were provided. At the conclusion of that process, Smith recognized the need for an additional work on Rudolph that was not

intended to engage young readers, but rather, a book rooted in academic research and written for an adult readership.

4. Jon C. Stott, "Biographies of Sports Heroes and the American Dream," *Children's Literature in Education* 10, no. 4 (1979): 174.

5. William Zinsser, *Extraordinary Lives: The Art and Craft of American Biography* (New York: American Heritage, 1986), 18.

6. Gale Eaton, *Well-Dressed Role Models: The Portrayal of Women in Biographies for Children* (Oxford: Scarecrow Press, 2006), 3–5; Sara Christine VanderHaagen, "So You Will Always Remember: Creating Public Memories and Inventing Agents in Biographical Texts for Children (PhD diss., Northwestern University, 2010), 79. There is far from a consensus on this trend; see, for example, Marc Aronson, "Selective Memory," *School Library Journal* 54, no. 3 (March 2008): 34.

7. Beverly Klatt, "Abraham Lincoln: Deified Martyr, Flesh and Blood Hero, and a Man with Warts," *Children's Literature in Education* 23, no. 3 (1992): 128.

8. Christine Duthie, "'It's Just Plain Real!' Introducing Young Children to Biography and Autobiography," *New Advocate* 11, no. 3 (1998): 222.

9. Eaton, *Well-Dressed Role Models,* 18.

10. Engfer, *Wilma Rudolph,* 27. Engfer's 31-page book is part of a series titled "Graphic Biographies." Other individuals presented in this series include Benjamin Franklin, Helen Keller, Elizabeth Cady Stanton, Matthew Henson, Cesar Chavez, and Patrick Henry. The only other athlete this series (by 2006) is Jackie Robinson.

11. VanderHaagen, "So You Will Always Remember," 31.

12. Ibid.

13. Judith V. Lechner, "Accuracy in Biographies for Children," *New Advocate* 10, no. 3 (1997): 232–33.

14. Engfer's book, for example, even highlights narrative clips that are taken directly from Rudolph's 1977 autobiography.

15. See, for example, Ruth's book, published in 2000.

16. VanderHaagen, "So You Will Always Remember," 168.

17. Johnson's sixty-three-page book is one of forty-one books in the Value Tales series. Each book matches an individual with a value. Other individuals in this series (and their respective values) include the Wright Brothers (the value of patience), Abraham Lincoln (the value of respect), Ralph Bunche (the value of responsibility), Marie Curie (the value of learning), Sacagawea (the value of adventure), Jim Henson (the value of imagination), and Mother Theresa (the value of humility). In addition to Rudolph, four other athletes are included in the series: Arthur Ashe (the value of dignity), Terry Fox (the value of facing a challenge), Jackie Robinson (the value of courage), and Maurice Richard (the value of tenacity). All of the books in the series are authored by Ann Donegan Johnson or Spencer Johnson, MD. In the Ashe biography, published in 1994, the tennis player does not have a sidekick similar

to Rudolph's "Skeeter." The book does discuss his segregated childhood and his involvement in the fight to end apartheid in South Africa, as well as his death from AIDS. In the biography of Jackie Robinson, published in 1977, the baseball star is given a ragball by his mother. The ragball becomes an animated friend, "Rags," when Robison hits it with his baseball bat—and serves the same motivational role as "Skeeter," traveling with Robinson during his stint in the Army as well as his major league baseball career.

18. Ann Donegan Johnson, *The Value of Overcoming Adversity*, 60.

19. The "Movies in My Mind" website, About Us, http://www.moviesinmy mind.com/about.html, accessed 10 May 2013.

20. This is taken from the narration of *Chris and Amy Meet Wilma Rudolph*.

21. Ruth, *Wilma Rudolph*, 8. Ruth's book is 112 pages. Other biographies in the A&E *Biography* series include John Glenn, Louisa May Alcott, Princess Diana, and Nelson Mandela. Other athletes covered in the series include Jesse Owens, Arthur Ashe, Bruce Lee, and Jesse Ventura.

22. Engfer, *Wilma Rudolph*, 4.

23. Mary Dodson Wade, *Wilma Rudolph*, 5.

24. Stott, "Biographies of Sports Heroes and the American Dream," 178.

25. Coffey, *Wilma Rudolph*, 10.

26. Maria Jose Botelho, "Reading Class: Disrupting Power in Children's Literature" (PhD diss., University of Massachusetts, Amherst, 2004), 24.

27. Botelho, "Reading Class," 25.

28. Ann Donegan Johnson, *The Value of Overcoming Adversity*, 8.

29. Krull, *Wilma Unlimited*. Krull's thirty-seven page book, not part of a series, won a number of recognitions: the ABA's Pick of the Lists, the ALA Notable Children's Books, the Parents' Choice Award, the *Booklist* Editors' Choice, the *Bulletin* Blue Ribbon Book award, the *School Library Journal* Best Book of the Year, the Jane Addams Book Award, and listing as one of the New York Public Library's 100 Titles for Reading and Sharing (see the back cover of Krull's book for this list).

30. Rosemarie Garland-Thomson, "Disability and Representation," *PMLA* 120, no. 2 (2005): 523.

31. Lennard J. Davis, *Enforcing Normalcy: Disability, Deafness, and the Body* (Brooklyn: Verso Books, 1995), 23–24; Also see Angharad Beckett, Nick Ellison, Sam Barrett, and Sonali Shah, "'Away with the Fairies?': Disability within Primary-age Children's Literature," *Disability and Society* 25, no. 3 (May 2010): 373–86.

32. Anne Finger, *Elegy for a Disease: A Personal and Cultural History of Polio* (New York: St. Martin's, 2006), 9.

33. Rosemarie Garland-Thomson, *Extraordinary Bodies: Figuring Disability in American Culture and Literature* (New York: Columbia University Press, 1997), 7.

34. Ibid.

35. Linda Jacobs, *Wilma Rudolph*, 22. The use of outdated terms like Jacobs's use of "cripple" to characterize young Rudolph fortunately does not persist across the publication dates, though the tragedy-view of disability does. Coffey, *Wilma Rudolph*, 11.

36. Harper, *Wilma Rudolph*, 14–15. Harper's 184 pages, aimed at readers ages 8–12, is part of the "Childhood of Famous Americans" series (by 2004, there were fifty-nine books in the series). A sampling of those included in this series: Susan B. Anthony, Neil Armstrong, Crispus Attucks, Buffalo Bill, Harry Houdini, Andrew Jackson, Mahalia Jackson, John Muir, Annie Oakley, Rosa Parks, Ronald Reagan, Betsy Ross, Harriet Tubman, and George Washington. Other athletes included in the series are Roberto Clemente, Joe DiMaggio, Lou Gehrig, Jackie Robinson, Knute Rockne, Babe Ruth, and Jim Thorpe.

37. Flanagan, *Wilma Rudolph*, 12. Flanagan's 124-page book on Rudolph made it the tenth biography to be included in the "Ferguson Career Biographies" series. Others featured in the series are Maya Angelou, Leonard Bernstein, Shirley Temple Black, George Bush, Bill Gates, John Glenn, Martin Luther King Jr., Charles Lindbergh, and Sandra Day O'Connor.

38. Robert McRuer, *Crip Theory: Cultural Signs of Queerness and Disability* (New York: NYU Press, 2006), 8–9. On more positive portrayals of the characters and their relationship to disability in children's books, see Jeanne Willis and Tony Ross, *Susan Laughs* (New York: Henry Holt and Company, 2000); and Lola M. Schaefer, *Some Kids Use Wheelchairs* (North Mankato, MN: Pebble Books, 2008).

39. Flanagan, *Wilma Rudolph*, 12.

40. Biracree, *Wilma Rudolph*, 41; Paul Anthony Darke, "The Changing Face of Representations of Disability in the Media," in *Disabling Barriers—Enabling Environments*, ed. John Swain, Sally French, Colin Barnes, and Carol Thomas (London: Sage, 2004), 103.

41. David T. Mitchell and Sharon L. Snyder, "Introduction: Disability Students and the Double Bind of Representation," in *The Body and Physical Difference: Discourses of Disability*, ed. David T. Mitchell and Sharon L. Snyder (Ann Arbor: University of Michigan, 1997), 3.

42. Ellen Rubin and Emily Strauss Watson, "Disability Bias in Children's Literature," *The Lion and the Unicorn* 11, no. 1 (1987): 62.

43. Biracree, *Wilma Rudolph*, 39. Biracree's 169-page biography was one of seventeen biographies in the Melrose Square Black American Series. Other athletes presented in the series were Jackie Robinson, Althea Gibson, and Jesse Owens. Other black Americans in the series were Ella Fitzgerald, Nat Turner, Paul Robeson, Louis Armstrong, Scott Joplin, Matthew Henson, Malcolm X, Chester Himes, Sojourner Truth, Billie Holiday, Richard Wright, James Baldwin, and Marcus Garvey.

44. Harper, *Wilma Rudolph*, 2–3.

45. See, for example, Coffey, *Wilma Rudolph*, 13. The brace was "unattractive and heavy"; Schraff, *Wilma Rudolph*, 19. Rudolph, according to the author, was determined to get rid of the "cumbersome leg brace"; Streissguth, *Wilma Rudolph*, 14. "Despite the brace, she played outside every day with friends and schoolmates."

46. Streissguth, *Wilma Rudolph*, 15. Streissguth's 104-page biography was one of eighteen titles in the "Sports Heroes and Legends" Series. Rudolph and Michele Kwan were the only female athletes included in the series. Other athletes presented in the series were Alex Rodriguez, Barry Bonds, Dale Earnhardt Jr., Derek Jeter, Hank Aaron, Ichiro Suzuki, Jesse Owens, Joe DiMaggio, Lance Armstrong, Lou Gehrig, Mickey Mantle, Muhammad Ali, Roberto Clemente, Sandy Koufax, Tiger Woods, and Tim Duncan.

47. Krull, *Wilma Unlimited*.

48. Harper, *Wilma Rudolph*, cover. There are three collaged images of Rudolph on the book's cover. In the foreground is a young Rudolph holding a basketball, with a brace on her leg. In the background are two images. The first is a young Rudolph, seated with her leg brace on, looking out a window watching other children play. Interestingly, both of those images are in color. The third image, in black and white, is of Rudolph as an adult running down a track in a "USA" uniform with the Olympic rings behind her.

49. Naden and Blue, *Wilma Rudolph*, 14.

50. Ann Donegan Johnson, *The Value of Overcoming Adversity*, 18.

51. Ato Quayson, *Aesthetic Nervousness: Disability and the Crisis of Representation* (New York: Columbia University Press, 2007), 2.

52. Emiliano L. Ayala, "'Poor Little Things' and 'Brave Little Souls': The Portrayal of Individuals with Disabilities in Children's Literature," *Literary Research and Instruction* 39, no. 1 (1999): 103–17.

53. Lennard J. Davis, *Enforcing Normalcy*, 3–4.

54. Krull, *Wilma Unlimited*.

55. Flanagan, *Wilma Rudolph*, 19.

56. Ruth, *Wilma Rudolph*, 18–19.

57. David T. Mitchell and Sharon L. Snyder, *Narrative Prosthesis: Disability and the Dependencies of Discourse* (Ann Arbor: University of Michigan Press, 2000), 19; see also Tom Shakespeare, "Cultural Representation of Disabled People: Dustbins for Disavowal?," *Disability and Society* 9, no. 3 (1994): 284.

58. Tom Shakespeare, "The Social Model of Disability," in *The Disability Studies Reader*, 2nd ed., ed. Lennard J. Davis (New York: Routledge, 2006), 197.

59. Quayson, *Aesthetic Nervousness*, 2.

60. Ruth, *Wilma Rudolph*, 7.

61. Wade, *Wilma Rudolph*, 6.

62. Mitchell and Snyder, *The Body and Physical Difference*, 2.

63. Ibid., 1.

64. Alan Gartner and Tom Joe, "Introduction," in *Images of the Disabled, Disabling Images*, ed. Alan Gartner and Tom Joe (New York: Praeger, 1987), 4.

65. Coffey, *Wilma Rudolph*, 13.

66. Johnson, *The Value of Overcoming Adversity*, 20.

67. Flanagan, *Wilma Rudolph*, 12–13.

68. Jacobs, *Wilma Rudolph*, 11.

69. Coffey, *Wilma Rudolph*, 13.

70. Jack A. Nelson, "The Invisible Cultural Group: Images of Disability," in *Images that Injure: Pictorial Images in the Media, Second Edition*, ed. Paul Martin Lester and Susan Dente Ross (Westport, CT: Greenwood, 2003), 177; Beckett et al., "'Away with the Fairies?,'" 376; G. T. Couser, "Conflicting Paradigms: The Rhetorics of Disability Memoir," in *Embodied Rhetorics: Disability in Language and Culture*, ed. James C. Wilson and Cynthia Lewiecki (Carbondale: Southern Illinois University Press, 2001), 80.

71. Anderson, *Wilma Rudolph*, 22.

72. Biracree, *Wilma Rudolph*, 41.

73. Finger, *Elegy for a Disease*, 125–26.

74. Garland-Thomson, "Disability and Representation," 523.

75. Paul Darke, "Cinematic Representations of Disability," in *The Disability Reader: Social Science Perspectives*, ed. Tom Shakespeare (New York: Continuum, 1998), 190.

76. The silencing around gender and sexism is especially interesting as reflected in two biographies which list Billie Luisi-Potts, executive director of the National Women's Hall of Fame, as a consultant (Braun, *Wilma Rudolph*; Engfer, *Wilma Rudolph*), leading one to believe that gender might be the focus of each. Neither specifically focuses on gender or sexism; however, Braun (p. 15) and Engfer (p. 19) both wrongly identify Rudolph as the first American woman to win three gold medals at the Olympic Games. Engfer (p. 27) does suggest in his concluding pages that Rudolph's "success paved the way for other black women athletes."

77. Anderson, *Wilma Rudolph*, 25; Schraff, *Wilma Rudolph*, 22.

78. Anderson, *Wilma Rudolph*, 26.

79. Coffey, *Wilma Rudolph*, 19.

80. Harper, *Wilma Rudolph*, 39–40. Statements are italicized by Harper because italicizing indicates that Rudolph is thinking/talking to herself. According to the inside front cover of the book, "History is fleshed out with fictionalized details, and conversations have been added to make the stories come alive to today's reader, but every reasonable effort has been made to make the stories consistent with the events, ethics, and character of their subjects."

81. Streissguth, *Wilma Rudolph*, 20.

82. Schraff, *Wilma Rudolph*, 22.

83. Flanagan, *Wilma Rudolph*, 75–76.

84. Ruth, *Wilma Rudolph*, 50–51, and Anderson, *Wilma Rudolph*, 26, serve as the exceptions to the pattern. Smith, *Wilma Rudolph*, 8–9, 31–32, 49–50, and 105–6, offers the only detailed examination, in the entire collection of books, of Rudolph's accomplishments in relation to gendered and racialized constructions of female athleticism during the period.

85. Gary Fertig, "Using Biography to Help Young Learners Understand the Causes of Historical Continuity and Change," *Social Studies* 99, no. 4 (2008): 147.

86. Smith, *Wilma Rudolph*, 48.

87. Roger D. Launius, "Heroes in a Vacuum: The Apollo Astronaut as Cultural Icon," *Florida Historical Quarterly* 87, no. 2 (fall 2008): 174.

88. Linda Jacobs published three books titled *Women Who Win*, with each covering four female athletes. The first book included Janet Lynn ("Sunshine on Ice"), Olga Korbut ("Tears and Triumphs"), Shane Gould ("Olympic Swimmer"), and Chris Evert ("Tennis Pro"). The second book, in addition to Rudolph, included Laura Baugh ("Golf's Golden Girl"), Evonne Goolagong ("Smiles and Smashes"), and Cathy Rigby ("On the Beam"). The four athletes in the third book were Mary Decker ("Speed Records and Spaghetti"), Joan Moore Rice ("The Olympic Dream"), Annemarie Proell ("Queen of the Mountain"), and Rosemary Casals ("The Rebel Rosebud").

89. Jacobs, *Wilma Rudolph*, 27. Interestingly, Rudolph's autobiography counters this attention paid to Eldridge, though through part of the athlete's story, he does occupy a central place in the text.

90. Ibid., 28–29.

91. Ibid., 33.

92. Streissguth, *Wilma Rudolph*, 87.

93. Biracree, *Wilma Rudolph*, 100.

94. Ruth, *Wilma Rudolph*, 26.

95. Ibid.

96. Eaton, *Well-Dressed Role Models*, 216–17.

97. Anderson, *Wilma Rudolph*, 94. Anderson's biography is part of the Legendary Athletes Series, which totals eight books: Muhammad Ali, Arthur Ashe, Roberto Clemente, Magic Johnson, Billie Jean King, Jesse Owens, and Babe Didrikson.

98. The ways female athletes are depicted in the sport media is a prolific area of study (including, in part, analysis of photographs and language used to describe and write about female athletes). For examples of some of the earlier works on this topic, see Mary Jo Kane, "Media Coverage of the Female Athlete before, during and after Title IX: *Sports Illustrated* revisited," *Journal of Sport Management* 2,

no. 2 (1988): 87–99; and Mary Jo Kane and Janet B. Parks, "Mass Media Images as a Reflection of Historical Social Change: The Portrayal of Female Athletes before, during and after Title IX," in *Psychology and Sociology of Sport: Current Selected Research*, vol. 2, ed. Lee Vander Velden and James H. Humphrey (New York: AMS, 1990): 133–50.

99. Jacobs, *Wilma Rudolph*, 12.

100. Flanagan, *Wilma Rudolph*, 58.

101. Eaton, *Well-Dressed Role Models*, 247. Rudolph's teenage pregnancy is referenced in the books by Anderson, Flanagan, Harper, Ruth, Schraff, Smith, and Streissguth.

102. Flanagan, *Wilma Rudolph*, 53.

103. Ruth, *Wilma Rudolph*, 88–89.

104. Biracree, *Wilma Rudolph*, 71.

105. Anderson, *Wilma Rudolph*, 60; Biracree, *Wilma Rudolph*, 71.

106. VanderHaagen, "So You Will Always Remember," 176.

107. Herbert Kohl, *Should We Burn Babar? Essays on Children's Literature and the Power of Stories* (New York: New Press, 1995), 66–68.

108. Engfer, *Wilma Rudolph*, 7.

109. Ann Donegan Johnson, *The Value of Overcoming Adversity*, 12.

110. Ibid., 13.

111. Flanagan, *Wilma Rudolph*, 18–19.

112. Coffey, *Wilma Rudolph*, 10–11, 60.

113. Sherrow, *Wilma Rudolph*, 11. Sherrow's forty-eight-page biography is one of the twenty-seven "On My Own" biography titles, which include three other athletes: Babe Didrikson Zaharias, Jesse Owens, and Jackie Robinson.

114. Flanagan, *Wilma Rudolph*, 14–15.

115. Maria Jose Botelho and Masha Kabakow Rudman, *Critical Multicultural Analysis of Children's Literature: Mirrors, Windows, and Doors* (New York: Routledge, 2009), 211.

116. Biracree, *Wilma Rudolph*, 43–44.

117. Elizabeth Segel, "In Biography for Young Readers, Nothing Is Impossible," *The Lion and the Unicorn* 4, no. 1 (1980), 12.

118. Naden and Blue, *Wilma Rudolph*, 5.

119. Ruth, *Wilma Rudolph*, 13.

120. Ibid., 98.

121. Biracree, *Wilma Rudolph*, 53.

122. Ruth, *Wilma Rudolph*, 40–41.

123. VanderHaagen, "So You Will Always Remember," 174.

124. Ann Donegan Johnson, *The Value of Overcoming Adversity*, 29.

125. Naden and Blue, *Wilma Rudolph*, 23.

126. Schraff, *Wilma Rudolph*, 31. Schraff's biography is one of forty-six books in the African-American Biography series. Only two other athletes are presented the series: Jackie Robinson and Jesse Owens.

127. The inclusion of Jackie Robinson in many of the series is no surprise. The barrier-breaking athlete continues to serve as an inspiring historical lesson for young readers, much in the same way Rudolph's story does.

128. Harper, *Wilma Rudolph*, 28–33.

129. Ibid., 32–33.

130. Ruth, *Wilma Rudolph*, 11.

131. Schraff, *Wilma Rudolph*, 58.

132. Biracree, *Wilma Rudolph*, 95; Anderson, *Wilma Rudolph*, 88; Ruth, *Wilma Rudolph*, 86, 88; Smith, *Wilma Rudolph*, 73.

133. Kohl, *Should We Burn Babar?*, 44–47.

134. Juju Chang, "Juju's Inspiration: Runner Wilma Rudolph, *Good Morning America*, aired May 20, 2010, video clip, accessed March 5, 2013, http://abcnews.go .com/GMA/Inspirations/video/jujus-inspiration-runner-wilma-rudolph-10698456.

135. Wendy Saul, "Living Proof: Children's Biographies of Marie Curie," in *How Much Truth Do We Tell the Children? The Politics of Children's Literature*, ed. Betty Bacon (Minneapolis, MN: MEP Publications, 1988), 227.

136. Eaton, *Well-Dressed Role Models*, 4.

7. On the Margins of Memory

1. For a discussion of the various types of material remembrance sites related to athletes, see John Bale, *Sports Geography*, 2nd ed. (London: Routledge, 2003).

2. These awards and inductions include Black Athletes Hall of Fame (1973), National Track and Field Hall of Fame (1974), International Sports Hall of Fame (1980), Women's Sports Foundation Hall of Fame (1980), US Olympic Hall of Fame (1983, Humanitarian of the Year Award of the Special Olympics (1985), National Collegiate Athletic Association's Silver Anniversary Award (1987), Jackie Robinson Image Award of the National Association for the Advancement of Colored People (1989), and National Sports Award (1993). See Wayne Wilson, "Wilma Rudolph: The Making of an Olympic Icon," in *Out of the Shadows: A Biographical History of African American Athletes*, ed. David K. Wiggins (Fayetteville: University of Arkansas Press, 2006), 221.

3. Richard H. Schein, "Race and Landscape in the United States," in *Landscape and Race in the United States*, ed. Richard H. Schein (New York: Routledge, 2006), 4. Schein cites Morrison, *Playing in the Dark* (Cambridge, MA: Harvard University Press, 1990), 4–8.

4. As cited in Martha K. Norkunas, *Monuments and Memory: History and Representation in Lowell, Massachusetts* (Washington, DC: Smithsonian Institution

Scholarly Press, 2002), 100; see Dolores Hayden, *The Power of Place: Urban Landscape as Public History* (Cambridge, MA: MIT Press, 1995)

5. Murray G. Phillips, Mark E. O'Neill, and Gary Osmond, "Broadening Horizons in Sport History: Films, Photographs, and Monuments," *Journal of Sport History* 34, no. 2 (2007): 286–87.

6. Andrew Butterfield, Monuments and Memories, *New Republic*, February 3, 2003, 27–32. http://www.newrepublic.com/article/monuments-and-memories.

7. Interestingly, the Tennessee State University bookstore sells no clothing or merchandise that capitalizes on its most famous female athletes, with Tigerbelle gear noticeably absent.

8. This error in reporting the number of gold medals won was noted on our trip to Clarksville and Nashville in June 2007. The error remained as recently as April 2014.

9. "Wilma Rudolph Center to Be Named in Star's Honor," *Jackson Advocate*, TSU Special Collections, August 1995, 3–9. Also see "Residence Center Named for Wilma Rudolph," *Tennessee State University ACCENT*, August 1995, 1–2.

10. See for example, J. D. Anderson, *The Education of Blacks in the South, 1860–1935* (Chapel Hill: University of North Carolina Press, 1988); Bobby L. Lovett, *America's Historically Black Colleges and Universities: A Narrative History from the Nineteenth Century into the Twenty-First Century* (Macon, GA: Mercer University Press, 2011).

11. Information accessed from http://www.pnc3.us/pnc3.org/booklets/data/2004/rudolph-v.htm. A link on this page leads the reader to Stamp News Release Number: 04–041.

12. According to Alyson Kuhn, "A Philatelic Field Trip: Smithsonian National Postal Museum," *Step inside Design Magazine*, May/June 2007, suggestions for stamp subjects submitted to the committee exceed 50,000 annually. Article available at http://www.pointeradvertising.com/creative_brief/08_07_main_art.html. Kuhn quotes David Failor, the USPS's executive director of Stamp Services, "The committee narrows these down to an average of twenty-five subjects annually. Any subject ultimately chosen must have broad national appeal." Rudolph's stamp value varies from the other four in the Distinguished Americans Series; Stilwell's stamp value is ten cents, Edna Ferber's stamp value is eighty-three cents, Caraway's stamp value is seventy-six cents, Pepper's stamp value is thirty-three cents. Paul Robeson was honored with a stamp just a few months after Rudolph, becoming the twenty-seventh stamp in the Black Heritage Series.

13. Ibid.

14. Ibid.

15. Chantel Escoto, "Wilma Rudolph to Be Featured," *Leaf-Chronicle*, November 24, 2003, A1.

16. Stamp News Release Number: 04–041. Accessed at http://www.pnc3.us /pnc3.org/booklets/data/2004/rudolph-pr.htm.

17. "The 'Definitive' Wilma Rudolph," *Journal of Sport Philately* (Spring 2005) 43, no. 3: 24–25.

18. "The 'Definitive' Wilma Rudolph," 24. Rudolph's stamp was issued in three formats (sheets of twenty and two types of booklets), which also contributed to the expectation that "even more collectible varieties will appear over time" (see p. 24).

19. "Legendary Wilma Rudolph Honored with Postage Stamp," *OVC Sports Forum Community*, July 15, 2004, accessed at http://ovcsports.yuku.com/topic /1431

20. "Wilma Rudolph Runs Again on Definitive US Stamp during Olympic Team Trials in Sacramento," *PR Newswire*, July 14, 2004, accessed at http://www .prnewswire.com/news-releases/wilma-rudolph-runs-again-on-definitive-us-stamp -during-olympic-team-trials-in-sacramento-71276517.html.

21. "Stamp Honors Great Woman," *Leaf-Chronicle*, July 14, 2004, B1.

22. Ibid.

23. Chantal Escoto, "Wilma Rudolph Stamp to Debut July 14," *Leaf-Chronicle*, June 24, 2004, A1, A3.

24. Marsha Blackburn, "Honoring the Wilma Rudolph Stamp," July 16, 2004, Available on the Project Vote Smart website, http://votesmart.org/public-statement/50649/honoring-the-wilma-rudolph-stamp#.UVjRZhjn_Dc. Also see "Stamp Honors Great Woman," *Leaf-Chronicle*, July 14, 2002, B1.

25. Chantel Escoto, "Wilma Rudolph to Be Featured," *Leaf-Chronicle*, November 24, 2003, A1. Also see William Lyles III, "Rudolph Honored with US Postage Stamp," *Urban Journal*, week of June 30, 2004.

26. Women on Stamps: Part 2, created by Lauren Golden and Christine Mereand; Arago: Exhibits, Smithsonian National Postal Museum. Three other female athletes were included in the exhibit: tennis player Hazel Wrightman, Olympic track and field athlete Babe Didrikson, and Olympic swimmer Helene Madison. For visuals of the exhibit, including images of the stamps, see "Arago: Exhibits," http:// arago.si.edu/index.asp?con=4&cmd=2&eid=298&slide=title.

27. These international stamps are all available on eBay for purchase. For the Mongolia stamp, see *Philately Newsletter*, no. 19, April 1969, 247.

28. Gary Osmond, "'Modest Monuments'? Postage Stamps, Duke Kahanamoku and Hierarchies of Social Memory," *Journal of Pacific History* 43, no.3 (2008): 313. "Modest monuments" is a phrase coined in John Bale, *Roger Bannister and the Four-Minute Mile: Sports Myth and Sport History* (London: Taylor & Francis, 2004), 132.

29. Osmond, "'Modest Monuments'?," 313–14.

30. Stormfront.org. http://www.stormfront.org/forum/t251902-2/. These posts run from December 2004 to November 2005, and were most recently accessed on January 2, 2013.

31. The second vote also came just days after the Los Angeles Riots, April 29–May 4, 1992. One article implies that Clarksville did not want similar rioting if the vote was rejected. See "No Local Rallies over L.A. Verdict," *Leaf-Chronicle*, May 1, 1992, 1A.

32. Terry Hollahan, "Council OKs Boulevard Designation," *Leaf-Chronicle*, May 8, 1992, A1, A2.

33. Bettina Tilson, "Residents Debate Renaming Road for Rudolph," *Leaf-Chronicle*, March 14, 1992, A1, A2.

34. Ibid. Tommy Head should have been no stranger to the act of honoring individuals involved in athletics. His sister, Pat Head Summitt, was the head coach of the women's basketball team at the University of Tennessee from 1974 until 2012.

35. Ibid.

36. Letters, *Leaf-Chronicle*, March 19, 1992, A4.

37. Bettina Tilson, "'Rudolph' Bill Heads to Tennessee House," *Leaf-Chronicle*, March 20, 1992, A1, A11.

38. "Recognizing Hero," Editorial, *Leaf-Chronicle*, March 22, 1992, A4.

39. Naomi Sample, Letters: "Why Name Controversy?," *Leaf-Chronicle*, March 22, 1992, A5.

40. Randall K. Madison, Letters: "Why Not Change Name?," *Leaf-Chronicle*, March 24, 1992, A4.

41. Margie (Carter) Caso, Letters: "Paying Tribute to Rudolph," *Leaf-Chronicle*, March 25, 1992, A4.

42. Houston Wade, Montgomery County commissioner, Letters: "A Good Way to Honor Rudolph," *Leaf-Chronicle*, March 29, 1992, A5. Wade is responding to a suggestion made in a previous letter to the editor from Janie Robinson (no date for this letter). We find the letter writer's comment about the celebrity status, and perhaps acceptability to a largely white television audience, to be an interesting insight for this time period (when both Winfrey and Cosby were enjoying a celebrity among Americans because they articulated values closely linked to white America).

43. Terry Hollahan, "City Council to Determine Travel Policy," *Leaf-Chronicle*, March 31, 1992, A1, A2; Terry Hollahan, "Rudolph Boulevard Name Change in the Hands of the City Council," *Leaf-Chronicle*, April 1, 1992, A11.

44. Terry Hollahan, "City Council Votes down Rudolph Blvd. Proposal," *Leaf-Chronicle*, April 3, 1992, A1, A5.

45. Byron Lawrence, Letters: "Rudolph Deserves Honor," *Leaf-Chronicle*, April 7, 1992, A4. Gallows Hollow is a neighborhood in Clarksville, located on the site of the city's former gallows, this according to Tim Pulley, Clarksville-Montgomery County Public Library, email correspondence with Rita Liberti, February 20, 2013.

46. Dawn Wilson, Letters: "Story Has Been Inspiration," *Leaf-Chronicle*, April 7, 1992, A4.

47. Magnolia Elliot, Letters: "Council Made Right Decision," *Leaf-Chronicle*, April 7, 1992, A4. In the April 8, 1992, edition, the paper recognized that the title of the letter should have read "Council Made Wrong Decision."

48. Carolyn P. Cowan, Letters: "Excuses Are Not Ringing True," *Leaf-Chronicle*, April 8, 1992, A4.

49. Wayne Stanley, Letters: "No Good Reason Not to Change," *Leaf-Chronicle*, April 12, 1992, A4.

50. "*Leaf-Chronicle* Editorial: Honoring Rudolph," April 8, 1992, *Leaf-Chronicle*, A4.

51. Wayne Stanley: "No Good Reason Not to Change," April 12, 1992, *Leaf-Chronicle*, A5.

52. Letters, "What Were the Real Reasons?," J. D. Corbett; "Ashamed of City's Actions," Clarice Ciardy-White; "Honor Community Heroes," Vic Williams, *Leaf-Chronicle*, April 23, 1992, A4.

53. The Los Angeles riots occurred between April 29 and May 4, 1992, after four white police officers were acquitted in the beating of African American Rodney King. There were fifty-three deaths, with over two thousand individuals injured, millions of dollars of damages to businesses in Los Angeles, and over ten thousand arrests. For more on the Los Angeles riots, see Robert Gooding-Williams, ed., *Reading Rodney King: Reading Urban Uprising* (New York: Routledge, 1993).

54. "No Local Rallies over L.A. Verdict," *Leaf-Chronicle*, May 1, 1992, A1.

55. Letters, "Hometown Should Honor Her," *Leaf-Chronicle*, May 1, 1992, A4.

56. Terry Hollahan, "City OKs Boulevard Designation," *Leaf-Chronicle*, May 8, 1992, A1.

57. See Letters, "Patterson Should Resign Seat," *Leaf-Chronicle*, May 17, 1992, A5.

58. Editorial, "Good Resolution," *Leaf-Chronicle*, May 12, 1992, A4.

59. Jimmy Settle, "Changing Signs, Changing Minds," *Leaf-Chronicle*, December 26, 1993, C1.

60. Ibid., C4.

61. Derek H. Alderman, "Street Names as Memorial Arenas: The Reputational Politics of Commemorating Martin Luther King Jr. in a Georgia County," in *The Civil Rights Movement in American Memory*, ed. Renee C. Romano and Leigh Raiford (Athens: University of Georgia Press, 2006), 67.

62. Derek H. Alderman, "Naming Streets for Martin Luther King Jr.: No Easy Road," in *Landscape and Race in the United States*, ed. Richard H. Schein (New York: Routledge, 2006), 214.

63. Alderman, "Naming Streets for Martin Luther King Jr.," 222.

64. Ibid., 232. Also see Derek H. Alderman, "A Street Fit for a King: Naming Places and Commemoration in the American South," *Professional Geographer* 52 (2000): 672–84; Derek H. Alderman, "Street Names and the Scaling of Memory: The Politics of Commemorating Martin Luther King Jr. within the African-American Community," *Area* 35 (2003): 163–73; Derek H. Alderman, "Street Names as Memorial Arenas: The Reputational Politics of Commemorating Martin Luther King Jr. in a Georgia County," *Historical Geography* 30 (2002): 99–120; and Owen Dwyer and Derek H. Alderman, *Civil Rights Memorials and the Geography of Memory* (Chicago: Center for American Places at Columbia College Chicago, 2008).

65. The Trane Company established itself in Clarksville in 1958. Trane expanded in 1960, doubling the size of the plant, and expanded twice more in the 1960s, involving the construction of a new plant. See "History of Clarksville Chamber," http://clarksvillechamber.com/about/history-clarksville-chamber/.

66. David Sibley, *Geographies of Exclusion: Society and difference in the West* (London: Routledge, 1995), 46.

67. Maoz Azaryahu, "German Reunification and the Politics of Street Names: The Case of East Berlin," *Political Geography* 16 (1997): 480.

68. Alderman, "Naming Streets for Martin Luther King Jr.," 221.

69. Ibid.

70. Sibley, *Geographies of Exclusion*, 9.

71. Samuel F. Dennis, "Seeing Hampton Plantation: Race and Gender in a South Carolina Heritage Landscape," in *Landscape and Race in the United States*, ed. Richard H. Schein (New York: Routledge, 2006), 78–80.

72. Brundage, *The Southern Past*, 184.

73. Tricard, *American Women's Track and Field*, 419.

74. Diane Tsimekles, "Legacy Lives On," *Leaf-Chronicle*, June 22, 1995, A1, A2. Members of the Wilma Rudolph Memorial Committee: A list of the committee members is included at the end of the article: F. Gene Washer, publisher of the *Leaf-Chronicle*; Joe White, assistant to Sal Rinella (president of APSU); Robert Thompson, Montgomery County executive; T. G. White, retired Northwest High School principal; Wendell Gilbert, APSU Vice President of development; George Halford, Economic Development Council president; Larry Meriweather, owner of Foston's Funeral Home; Don Trotter, mayor of Clarksville; Doug Ray, editor of the *Leaf-Chronicle*; Don Conner, associate publisher of the *Leaf-Chronicle*; Charles Hand, owner of Ideal Distributing Co. and Ramada Inn-Riverview; Flora Richbourg, retired principal of Byrns Darden Elementary School; Dr. Lindel H. Brookes,

dentist; Sharon G. Fields, coordinator for the Exceptional Family Member Program at Fort Campbell; Faye Smalley, businesswoman; Walton Smith Jr., Clarksville Area Chamber of Commerce president.

75. This is similar to tennis player Arthur Ashe's gravestone in the historically black cemetery Woodland in Richmond, Virginia. See Karla F. C. Holloway, *Passed On: African American Mourning Stories* (Durham, NC: Duke University Press, 2003), 201.

76. The full text reads: 1956/OLYMPIC BRONZE/MEDAL-AUSTRALIA/ 1960/THREE/OLYMPIC/GOLD MEDALS/ITALY/1961/JAMES E./SUL-LIVAN AWARD/1961/BABE DIDRIKSON/ZAHARIAS TROPHY/1961/ ASSOCIATED PRESS/FEMALE ATHLETE/OF THE YEAR/1973/BLACK/ ATHLETES/HALL OF FAME/1974/NATIONAL TRACK/AND FIELD// HALL OF FAME/1983/UNITED STATES/OLYMPIC HALL/OF FAME/ AWARDED/NAACP/IMAGE AWARD.

77. Mike Huggins, "Gone but Not Forgotten: Sporting Heroes, Heritage and Graveyard Commemoration," *Rethinking History: The Journal of Theory and Practice* (December 2012): 490, 482. For a similar analysis of a different group remembered in artwork on their graveyard markers, see Richard E. Meyer, "Images of Logging on Contemporary Pacific Northwest Gravemarkers," in *Cemeteries and Gravemarkers: Voices of American Culture*, ed. Richard E. Meyer (Logan: Utah State University Press, 1989), 61–85. Meyer is instructive in the ways gravestones as artwork have changed since the late nineteenth century, when the art was particularly interesting.

78. Darlene O'Dell, *Sites of Southern Memory: The Autobiographies of Katharine Du Pre Lumpkin, Lillian Smith, and Pauli Murray* (Charlottesville: University Press of Virginia, 2001), 1.

79. Website of Foston's Funeral Home. http://www.fostonfuneralhome.com /fh/aboutus/history.cfm?&fh_id=11374. Foston's Funeral Home remained central to the Clarksville African American community into the 1960s. According to notes taken for Rudolph's deposition in a 1990 lawsuit against Shoney's restaurant, Louise Foston helped in the organization of the African Americans, including Rudolph, in trying to integrate the restaurant. See notes dated April 14, 1990, in the folder of Wilma Rudolph; *Haynes et al. v. Shoney's Inc.*, Papers, Box 147, Folder 27. For more on the history of black funeral businesses, see Karla Holloway's chapter, "'Who's Got the Body?': The Business of Burial," in Holloway, *Passed On*, 15–56.

80. Holloway, *Passed On*, 27.

81. H. W. Odum, *Social and Mental Traits of the Negro* (1910), as cited in Roberta Hughes Wright and Wilber B. Hughes III, *Lay Down Body: Living History in African American Cemeteries* (Detroit: Visible Ink Press, 1996), 268.

82. Wright and Hughes, *Lay Down Body*, 268. Wright and Hughes, in their ethnography of African American cemeteries, include several pages on Tennessee,

although Clarksville is not included in their work. For more on Tennessee's black cemeteries, see 133–44. Included in their analysis is the burial site of author Alex Haley, officially The Alex Haley State Historic Site and Museum, the first state-owned historic site in western Tennessee and the first honoring an African American in Tennessee.

83. Huggins, "Gone but Not Forgotten," 487.

84. Ibid., 490.

85. "People and Places," *Daily Globe* (Ironwood, MI), September 3, 1986, 11. Roy Tamboli, the artist, remembers that Rudolph attended the unveiling of the bust and that she liked his work. He maintains that it was his idea to create the bust of Rudolph for the First Tennessee Heritage collection, which sought to honor great Tennesseans. The bust, in 2008, was in a Memphis bank. Email correspondence between Roy Tamboli and Maureen Smith, April 28–29, 2008.

86. "Gold Medalist Immortalized in Bronze," Photo, *Leaf-Chronicle*, July 2, 1988, A1.

87. Marc Ira Hooks, "Olympic Athlete Honored," *Leaf-Chronicle*, July 19, 1996, A1, A6. The statue's cost was $80,000, of which half had been raised by February 1996. See "Statue to Honor Olympic Runner Halfway There," *Syracuse (NY) Post-Standard*, February 28, 1996, D2. Located next to the Rudolph statue, on the base of the overpass, are plaques that include the names of donors to the project.

88. Marc Ira Hooks, "Olympic Athlete Honored," *Leaf-Chronicle*, July 19, 1996, A1.

89. This is Alderman's reading of Schudson's writings on "resonance." See Alderman, "Street Names as Memorial Arenas," 83.

90. "Rudolph Memorial Unites Community," *Leaf-Chronicle*, July 18, 1996. TSU Special Collections. This is deliberate work that considers the tourist inter-pretation of the town. For example, see Greg Ramshaw and Sean Gammon, "More Than Just Nostalgia? Exploring the Heritage/Sport Tourism Nexus," *Journal of Sport Tourism* 10, no. 4 (2005): 229–41.

91. Owen J. Dwyer, "Interpreting the Civil Rights Movement: Contradiction, Confirmation, and the Cultural Landscape," in *The Civil Rights Movement in American Memory*, ed. Renee C. Romano and Leigh Raiford (Athens: The University of Georgia Press, 2006), 8.

92. Andrew Butterfield, "Monuments and Memories," 27–32.

93. Hooks, "Olympic Athlete Honored," A6.

94. Marc Ira Hooks, "Rudolph Statue Dedication Set," *Leaf-Chronicle*, July 7, 1996. TSU Special Collections.

95. Mardee Roberts, "Wilma Rudolph Statue Won't Go to Riverfront," *Leaf-Chronicle*, March 27, 2001, A1. For more on the vandalism of statues, specifically

statues of African American athletes, see Victoria J. Gallagher and Margaret R. LaWare, "Sparring with Public Memory: The Rhetorical Embodiment of Race, Power, and Conflict in the *Monument to Joe Louis*," in *Places of Public Memory: The Rhetoric of Museums and Memorials*, ed. Greg Dickinson, Carole Blair, and Brian L. Ott (Tuscaloosa: University of Alabama Press, 2010), 87–112. Synthia Sydnor addresses the inclusion of a fence around the Michael Jordan statue at the United Center in Chicago (more to keep visitors from touching it, rather than to prevent vandalism); see Synthia Sydnor, "Sport, Celebrity and Liminality," in *Getting into the Game: Anthropological Perspectives on Sport*, ed. Noel Dyck (New York: Berg, 2000), 235. Olympic gold medal sprinter Tommie Smith worries about vandalism of the statue of himself and his teammate John Carlos at San Jose State University in his book: Tommie Smith with David Steele, *Silent Gesture: The Autobiography of Tommie Smith* (Philadelphia: Temple University Press, 2007), 239.

96. Alane Megna, "Statue Moved to New Home," *Leaf-Chronicle*, June 23, 2003, A4.

97. Jill Noelle Cecil, "Wilma Rudolph Statue Reclaims Rightful Place," *Leaf-Chronicle*, June 24, 2003, B1.

98. Chantal Escoto, "City Will Relocate Statue to Riverfront," *Leaf-Chronicle*, June 19, 2003, B1.

99. Brian Eason, "Clarksville's Wilma Rudolph Statue May Be Moving Again," March 11, 2010, *Leaf-Chronicle*. Also see Lester Black, "Liberty Park and Wilma Rudolph Pavilion Open," October 24, 2012, *Leaf-Chronicle*, A1; Brian Eason, "Construction under Way on 'Breathtaking' Facility," April 18, 2011, *Leaf-Chronicle*, A1; Brian Eason, "Rudolph Pavilion Plans Are Unveiled in Clarksville," March 18, 2010, *Leaf-Chronicle*; Allison Smith, "Renovated Liberty Park Opens Friday in Clarksville," May 15, 2012, *Leaf-Chronicle*. Other quotes from Rudolph include: "THE FEELING OF ACCOMPLISHMENT WELLED UP INSIDE OF ME, THREE OLYMPIC GOLD MEDALS. THAT WAS SOMETHING NOBODY COULD EVER TAKE AWAY FROM ME . . ."; "I'M IN MY PRIME, THERE'S NO GOAL TOO FAR, NO MOUNTAIN TOO HIGH"; "I BELIEVE IN ME MORE THAN ANYTHING IN THIS WORLD"; "I DON'T KNOW WHY I RUN SO FAST, I JUST RUN"; "I LOVED THE FEELING OF FREEDOM IN RUNNING, THE FRESH AIR, THE FEELING THAT THE ONLY PERSON I'M COMPETING WITH IS ME"; and "BY THE TIME I WAS 12 I WAS CHALLENGING EVERY BOY IN OUR NEIGHBORHOOD AT RUNNING, JUMPING, EVERYTHING."

100. Jonathan Leib, "The Witting Autobiography of Richmond, Virginia: Arthur Ashe, the Civil War, and Monument Avenue's Racialized Landscape," in *Landscape and Race in the United States*, ed. Richard H. Schein (New York: Routledge, 2006), 187–211. Also see Jaime Schultz, "Contesting the Master Narrative:

The Arthur Ashe Statue and Monument Avenue in Richmond, Virginia," *International Journal of the History of Sport* 28, nos. 8–9 (2011): 1235–51.

101. Taken directly from the plaque adjacent to the statue of Witzel titled "Nora." These observations related to locations of public monuments were noted on our trip to Clarksville in June 2007.

102. Brundage, *The Southern Past*, 7.

103. Norkunas, *Monuments and Memory*, 92.

104. Ibid., 94. These numbers come from a 1998 study and reflect the US data.

105. Ibid., 95.

106. Ibid., 99.

107. Carolyn Kay Steedman, *Landscape for a Good Woman*, as cited in Norkunas, *Monuments and Memory*, 100.

108. Gibson's statue was erected on March 28, 2012, at Essex County Branch Brook Park. Sculpted by Oregon artist Jay Warren, the statue depicts Gibson with her tennis racket, lunging for a ball. New Jersey governor Chris Christie and tennis great Billie Jean King were on hand at the unveiling ceremony. For more see, Maureen Smith, "America's Sport Statues: Myths, Memories, and Meanings: A Case Study of Three Recent Statues," paper presented at A Mirror of Our Culture, Sport and Society conference, St. Norbert College, De Pere, WI, 2012. Also see "Bronze Statue of Civil Rights Pioneer Althea Gibson Dedicated in Essex County," *Independent Press*, March 28, 2012, http://www.nj.com/independentpress/index.ssf/2012/03/bronze_statue_of_civil_rights.html; Eunice Lee, "Statue of First Black Woman to Win Wimbledon Unveiled in Newark Park," *Star-Ledger*, March 29, 2012, http://www.nj.com/news/index.ssf/2012/03/statue_of_first_black_woman_to.html; Paul Milo, "Althea Gibson Statue Unveiled," *Maplewood Patch*, March 30, 2012, http://maplewood.patch.com/articles/althea-gibson-statue-unveiled-91cb01d8.

109. For more on the Hamer statue, see the website www.fannielouhamer.info .hamer_statue.html. In addition to information on the statue, including donors, the website includes curriculum, a list of the members of the Hamer Legacy Committee, and photos of the statue and the surrounding Fannie Lou Hamer Memorial Garden. Parks is the first woman to be honored with a life-size statue in the Capitol. Sojourner Truth is remembered with a bust. See Ashley Southall, "Statue of Rosa Parks Is Unveiled at Capitol," *New York Times*, February 27, 2013, A18. Southall notes that Parks's statue is within sight of a statue of Jefferson Davis, president of the Confederacy during the Civil War.

110. For more on Tubman and the ways she has been remembered, see Sernett, *Harriet Tubman: Myth, Memory, and History*; specific to monuments of Tubman, see pages 244–46. For more on Tubman's statue in Harlem, see Timothy Williams, "Why Is Harriet Tubman Facing South?," *New York Times*, November 13, 2008, available at http://cityroom.blogs.nytimes.com/2008/11/13/why-is-harriet

-tubman-facing-south/. The online responses to the author's question are particularly revealing and provide a small glimpse into how the public reads statues. For an interesting local perspective, the blog "Manhattan Unlocked: The Unbelievably Rich and Inordinate History of Manhattan" addresses the Tubman statue and includes photos; see http://manhattanunlocked.blogspot.com/2010/11/harriet-tubman-statue -not-your-typical.html. For more on the Sojourner Truth statue, visit the website Sojourner Truth Memorial, http://sojournertruthmemorial.org. The website includes photos of the statue and a walking map tour, as well as information on Truth.

111. See Sydnor, "Sport, Celebrity and Liminality," 235.

112. Roberts, "Wilma Rudolph Statue Won't Go to Riverfront," A1.

113. Thomas C. Buchanan, *Black Life on the Mississippi: Slaves, Free Blacks, and the Western Steamboat World* (Chapel Hill: University of North Carolina, 2004), 5.

114. "Marker to Honor Wilma Rudolph," *Tennessean*, March 20, 2003, TSU Special Collections. Also see Cameron Collins, "Wilma Rudolph Marker Unveiled," *Leaf-Chronicle*, July 4, 2003, C1; Stacy Smith Segovia, "City to Honor Rudolph," *Leaf-Chronicle*, July 2, 2003, D1.

115. We made these observations on our trip to Clarksville in June 2007.

116. Brundage, *The Southern Past*, 185.

117. Collins, "Wilma Rudolph Marker Unveiled," C1.

118. Rudolph found employment often in positions that were "segregated" in nature, from teaching at the Cobb Elementary to working as part of Operation CHAMP in urban American cities. She also faced financial difficulties throughout her adult life, including filing for bankruptcy.

119. This a phrase borrowing from the concepts and examples shared in Sibley, *Geographies of Exclusion*.

120. Authors' trip to Clarksville, June 2007.

121. Letters, *Leaf-Chronicle*, September 4, 2006, A4. Letter from Ann Pryor.

122. Sharon Forster, "City Honors Rudolph's Achievements," *Leaf-Chronicle*, September 2, 1984, A1, A2.

123. Erika Doss, *Memorial Mania: Public Feeling in America* (Chicago: The University of Chicago Press, 2010), 256. Doss's fifth chapter focuses on the role of shame in the construction of statues, specifically Duluth's Lynching Memorial (although she includes a number of other sites that remember shameful events).

124. Forster, "City Honors Rudolph's Achievements," A1, A2.

125. Ralph Cruze, "Coach Edward Temple Remembers Wilma Rudolph's Last Lap," *The Meter*, November 17, 1994, 1, 3.

126. Stride and his colleagues speak to the role statues play in modern society. See Chris Stride, Ffion E. Thomas, John P. Wilson, and Josh Pahigian, "Modeling Stadium Statue Subject Choice in US Baseball and English Soccer," *Journal of Quantitative Analysis in Sports* 8, no. 1 (2012): 1–37.

127. Andrew Butterfield, "Monuments and Memories," 27–32.

128. "Remembering Her for How She Lived," *Leaf-Chronicle*, November 1994. TSU Special Collections.

129. Patricia Vertinsky, Sherry McKay, and Stephen Petrina, "No Body/ies in the Gym," in *Disciplining Bodies in the Gymnasium: Memory, Monument and Modernism*, ed. Patricia Vertinsky and Sherry McKay (London and New York: Routledge, 2004), 171.

130. "A story told is a story retold" is borrowed from Nathan's conclusion, *Saying It's So*, 217. Nathan, in writing about why the Black Sox scandal is so often told, concludes, "an untold story tends to stay untold, whereas an often told story tends to be repeated."

Conclusion

1. Rudolph appeared on "The Ed Sullivan Show" on October 2, 1960, along with New York Yankees baseball players Roger Maris, Elston Howard, Whitey Ford, and Moose Skowron. Guest stars on Sullivan's show that episode, which re-aired on July 16, 1961, included Bob Newhart, the McGuire sisters, Danny Thomas, Mickey Rooney, and Earl Grant.

2. This was episode 44, season 4. Subsequent references in this chapter to Rudolph's appearance on the show should be attributed to this particular episode. The other contestants on the show in episode 44 were Alan B. Christie and Matt Kaminsky. http://www.youtube.com/watch?v=zSdSa2O48zg (accessed on 7/10/10).

3. Shawan M. Worsley, *Audience, Agency, and Identity in Black Popular Culture* (New York: Routledge, 2010), 49.

4. Rudolph, *Wilma*, 27.

5. Ibid., 28.

6. Nathan, *Saying It's So*, 217.

7. Alun Munslow, *Narrative and History* (New York: Palgrave Macmillan, 2007), 6.

8. Birrell, "Approaching Mt. Everest," 4.

9. Nikky Finney, "Shaker: Wilma Rudolph Appears While Riding the Althea Gibson Highway Home," *Head Off and Split: Poems* (Chicago: TriQuarterly, 2011), 48–49; Melissa V. Harris-Perry, *Sister Citizen: Shame, Stereotypes, and Black Women in America* (New Haven, CT: Yale University Press, 2011), 101–02.

10. Nikky Finney, email message to Rita Liberti, May 4, 2012.

11. Nikky Finney, interview with Cat Richardson. "Winner Interview: Nikky Finney." http://nikkyfinney.net/documents/winner_interview.pdf, accessed June 15 2013.

12. Confino, "Collective Memory and Cultural History," 1394.

13. In assessing the legacy of Harriet Tubman, and trying to reconcile the iconic Tubman with the factual Tubman, Sernett offers a conclusion that is helpful in reading Rudolph:

> The power of Tubman as icon today derives essentially from the public's perception of her as an American hero. In spite of the differences of constructing an accurate history of her life, our individual and collective memories of her resonate so strongly because Harriet Tubman's life story causes us to reflect on both the good and the bad in the larger American story. . . . As long as some Americans believe that they suffer injustice, however defined, they will find Tubman a useful symbol of their struggle to achieve parity with those enjoying the full benefits of economic and political citizenship. Their Tubman may be more fiction than fact. . . . To those who view the findings of the recent historical scholarship on Tubman disquieting, as if demythologizing the symbol robs it of its power to comfort or inspire, I say: "Look again!" The Harriet Tubman who emerges from the pages of the new biographical research still deserves an honored place in the chronicle of the Story of America. (See Sernett, *Harriet Tubman*, 317–18.)

This is similar to the most recent scholarly examination of civil rights icon Rosa Parks. In her introduction, Jeanne Theoharis eloquently explains her efforts to "deconstruct the popular narrative" of Parks (Jeanne Theoharis, *The Rebellious Life of Mrs. Rosa Parks* [Boston: Beacon, 2013], xvi).

14. According to their Facebook page, "A Mighty Girl" is the "world's largest collection of books, toys, and movies for parents, teachers, and others dedicated to raising smart, confident, and courageous girls." As of July 5, 2014, the page has over 514,000 likes (followers who receive daily postings from A Mighty Girl). A Mighty Girl's Facebook page, accessed July 5, 2014, http://www.facebook.com /amightygirl.

15. As of July 5, 2014, the "A Mighty Girl" post on Rudolph's June 23 birthday had over 3,900 likes, 1,600 shares, and 41 comments.

16. Jeffrey K. Olick, *The Politics of Regret: On Collective Memory and Historical Responsibility* (New York: Routledge, 2007), 97.

17. One recent effort to give Rudolph a more complex treatment came in 1999, when ESPN compiled a list of the "Top 100 Athletes of the 20th Century." Rudolph came in on their list at number forty-one. For more, see M. B. Roberts, "Rudolph Ran and World Went Wild," ESPN.com, http://espn.go.com /sportscentury/features/00016446.html; Larry Schwartz, "Her Roman conquest," ESPN.com, http://espn.go.com/sportscentury/features/00016446.html.

ESPN produced short biographical videos for each athlete and aired these episodes at the close of the century. The episode examining Rudolph included some of her financial problems later in life. Unfortunately, this video is virtually inaccessible to the public. The only copy available to the public is located at New York's Museum of Television and Radio.

Bibliography

Aaron, Henry, with Furman Bisher, *Aaron, R. F.* Cleveland: World, 1969.

Aaron, Henry, with Lonnie Wheeler. *I Had a Hammer: The Hank Aaron Story.* New York: HarperCollins Publishers, 1991.

Acham, Christine. *Revolution Televised: Prime Time and the Struggle for Black Power.* Minneapolis: University of Minnesota Press, 2004.

Alderman, Derek H. "Naming Streets for Martin Luther King Jr.: No Easy Road." In *Landscape and Race in the United States*, edited by Richard Schein, 215–38. New York: Routledge, 2006.

———. "A Street Fit for a King: Naming Places and Commemoration in the American South." *Professional Geographer* 52 (2000): 672–84.

———. "Street Names and the Scaling of Memory: The Politics of Commemorating Martin Luther King Jr. within the African-American Community." *Area* 35 (2003): 163–73.

———. "Street Names as Memorial Arenas: The Reputational Politics of Commemorating Martin Luther King Jr. in a Georgia County." In *The Civil Rights Movement in American Memory*, edited by Renee C. Romano and Leigh Raiford, 67–95. Athens: University of Georgia Press, 2006.

———. "Street Names as Memorial Arenas: The Reputational Politics of Commemorating Martin Luther King Jr. in a Georgia County." *Historical Geography* 30 (2002): 99–120.

Ali, Muhammad, with Hana Yasmeen Ali. *The Soul of a Butterfly: Reflections on Life's Journey.* New York: Simon & Schuster, 2004.

Ali, Muhammad, with Herbert Muhammad and Richard Dunham. *The Greatest: My Own Story.* New York: Random House, 1975.

Anderson, J. D. *The Education of Blacks in the South, 1860–1935.* Chapel Hill: University of North Carolina Press, 1988.

Anderson, Jennifer Joline. *Wilma Rudolph: Track & Field Inspiration.* Mankato, MN: ABDO, 2011.

Appy, Christian G., ed. *Cold War Constructions: The Political Culture of US Imperialism, 1945–1956.* Amherst: University of Massachusetts, 2000.

Aronson, Marc. "Selective Memory." *School Library Journal* 54, no. 3 (March 2008): 34.

Ash, Stephen V. "A Community at War; Montgomery County 1861–1865." *Tennessee Historical Quarterly* 36 (1977): 208–21.

Ashe, Arthur, and Arnold Rampersad. *Days of Grace: A Memoir.* New York: Alfred A. Knopf, 1993.

Ashe, Arthur, with Neil Amdur. *Off the Court.* New York: New American Library, 1981.

Ashe, Arthur, with Frank Deford. *Portrait in Motion.* Boston: Houghton Mifflin, 1975.

Assmann, Aleida. "Canon and Archive." In *A Companion to Cultural Memory Studies*, edited by Astrid Erll and Ansgar Nünning, 97–108. Berlin: Walter De Gruyter, 2008.

Assmann, Jan. *Moses the Egyptian: The Memory of Egypt in Western Monotheism.* Cambridge, MA: Harvard University Press, 1997.

Ayala, Emiliano L. "'Poor Little Things' and 'Brave Little Souls': The Portrayal of Individuals with Disabilities in Children's Literature." *Literary Research and Instruction* 39, no. 1 (1999): 103–17.

Azaryahu, Maoz. "German Reunification and the Politics of Street Names: The Case of East Berlin." *Political Geography* 16, no. 6 (1997): 479–93.

Bailey, Beth. "She 'Can Bring Home the Bacon': Negotiating Gender in the 1970s." In *America in the 70s*, edited by Beth Bailey and David Farber, 107–28. Lawrence: University Press of Kansas, 2004.

Baker, Aaron. *Contesting Identities: Sports in American Film.* Urbana: University of Illinois Press, 2003.

Bale, John. *Roger Bannister and the Four-Minute Mile: Sports Myth and Sport History.* London: Taylor & Francis, 2004.

———. *Sports Geography*, 2nd ed. London: Routledge, 2003.

Bates, Daisy. *The Long Shadow of Little Rock: A Memoir.* New York: David McKay, 1962.

Bateson, Mary Catherine. *Composing a Life.* New York: Penguin, 1989.

Baxandall, Rosalyn. "Re-Visioning the Women's Liberation Movement's Narrative: Early Second Wave African American Feminists." *Feminist Studies* 27, no. 1 (2001): 225–45.

Beckett, Angharad, Nick Ellison, Sam Barrett, and Sonali Shah. "'Away with the Fairies?' Disability within Primary-Age Children's Literature." *Journal of Disability and Society* 25, no. 3 (2010): 373–86.

Bell, Ramona J. "Competing Identities: Representations of the Black Female Sporting Body from 1960 to the Present." PhD diss., Bowling Green State University, 2008.

Benstock, Shari, ed. *Feminist Issues in Literary Scholarship.* Bloomington: Indiana University Press, 1987.

Bingham, Dennis. *Whose Lives Are They Anyway? The Biopic as Contemporary Film Genre.* New Brunswick, NJ: Rutgers University Press, 2010.

Biracree, Tom. *Wilma Rudolph: Champion Athlete.* New York: Chelsea House Publishers, 1988.

Birrell, Susan. "Approaching Mt. Everest: On Intertextuality and the Past as Narrative." *Journal of Sport History* 34 (2007): 1–22.

Boamah-Wiafe, Daniel. "Dr. James Emman Kwegyir Aggrey of Achimota: Preacher, Scholar, Teacher, and Gentleman." In *Black Lives: Essays in African American Biography*, edited by James L. Conyers Jr., 182–96. New York: M. E. Sharpe, 1999.

Boggs, Carl, and Tom Pollard. "Postmodern Cinema and the Demise of the Family." *The Journal of American Culture* 26 (2003): 445–453.

Bogle, Donald. *Primetime Blues: African Americans on Primetime Television.* New York: Farrar, Straus and Giroux, 2001.

———. *Toms, Coons, Mulattos, and Bucks: An Interpretive History of Blacks in American Films,* 4th ed. New York: Continuum, 2001.

Booth, Douglas. *The Field: Truth and Fiction in Sport History.* London: Routledge, 2005.

Botelho, Maria Jose. "Reading Class: Disrupting Power in Children's Literature." PhD diss., University of Massachusetts, Amherst, 2004.

Botelho, Maria Jose, and Masha Kabakow Rudman. *Critical Multicultural Analysis of Children's Literature: Mirrors, Windows, and Doors.* New York: Routledge, 2009.

Bowers, Neal. *Out of the South: Poems.* Baton Rouge: Louisiana State University Press, 2002.

Boym, Svetlana. *The Future of Nostalgia*. New York: Basic Books, 2001.

Branch, Taylor. *Parting the Waters: America in the King Years, 1954–1963*. New York: Touchstone Books, 1988.

Braun, Eric. *Wilma Rudolph*. Mankato, MN: Capstone Press, 2006.

Brie, Stephen. "The Land of the Lost Content: Living in the Past with the Waltons." *Americana: The Journal of American Popular Culture (1900–present)* 7, no. 2 (2008). Accessed August 20, 2014. http://www.american popularculture.com/journal/articles/fall_2008/brie.htm.

Brown, Jim, with Myron Cope. *Off My Chest*. Garden City, NY: Doubleday, 1964.

Brown, Jim, with Steve Delsohn. *Out of Bounds*. New York: Zebra Books, Kensington, 1989.

Brundage, W. Fitzhugh. "Introduction: No Deed but Memory." In *Where These Memories Grow: History, Memory, and Southern Identity*, edited by W. Fitzhugh Brundage, 1–28. Chapel Hill: University of North Carolina Press, 2000.

———. *The Southern Past: A Clash of Race and Memory*. Cambridge, MA: Belknap Press of Harvard University Press, 2005.

———, ed. *Where These Memories Grow: History, Memory, and Southern Identity*. Chapel Hill: University of North Carolina Press, 2000.

Buchanan, Scott E. *Some of the People Who Ate My Barbeque Didn't Vote for Me: The Life of Georgia Governor Marvin Griffin*. Nashville, TN: Vanderbilt University Press, 2011.

Buchanan, Thomas C. *Black Life on the Mississippi: Slaves, Free Blacks, and the Western Steamboat World*. Chapel Hill: University of North Carolina Press, 2004.

Butcher, Joni M. "The Bardic Utterance in Situation Comedy Theme Songs, 1960–2000." PhD diss., Louisiana State University and Agriculture and Mechanical College, 2003.

Butterfield, Stephen. *Black Autobiography in America*. Amherst: University of Massachusetts Press, 1974.

Cahn, Susan. *Coming on Strong: Gender and Sexuality in Twentieth-Century Women's Sport*. New York: Free Press, 1994.

Carnes, Mark C. *Past Imperfect: History according to the Movies*. New York: Henry Holt, 1995.

Chafe, William H. *Civilities and Civil Rights: Greensboro, North Carolina, and the Black Struggle for Freedom*. New York: Oxford University Press, 1981.

Clinton, Catherine. *Harriet Tubman: The Road to Freedom*. New York: Little, Brown, 2004.

Cobb, James C. *Away Down South: A History of Southern Identity*. New York: Oxford University Press, 2005.

Coffey, Wayne. *Wilma Rudolph*. Woodbridge, CT: Blackbirch Press, 1993.

Confino, Alon. "Collective Memory and Cultural History: Problems of Method." *The American Historical Review* 102, no. 5 (1997): 1386–403.

Conrad, David. *Stick to It! The Story of Wilma Rudolph*. Minneapolis, MN: Compass Point Books, 2003.

Coontz, Stephanie. *The Way We Never Were: American Families and the Nostalgia Trap*. New York: Basic Books, 1992.

Cooper, Mark, and Carl Johnson. *Chris and Amy Meet Wilma Rudolph, Olympic Gold Medalist: A "Movies in My Mind" Adventure*. Imagination Development Group, 2002. Compact disc.

Couser, G. Thomas. "Autopathography: Women, Illness, and Lifewriting." In *On the Literary Nonfiction of Nancy Mairs: A Critical Anthology*, edited by Merri Lisa Johnson and Susannah B. Mintz, 133–44. New York: Palgrave MacMillan, 2011.

———. "Conflicting Paradigms: The Rhetorics of Disability Memoir." In *Embodied Rhetorics: Disability in Language and Culture*, edited by James C. Wilson, Cynthia Lewiecki-Wilson, Martha Stoddard Holmes, and Catherine Jean Prendergast, 78–91. Carbondale: Southern Illinois University Press, 2001.

———. *Signifying Bodies: Disability in Contemporary Life Writing*. Ann Arbor: University of Michigan Press, 2009.

Craig, Maxine Leeds. *Ain't I a Beauty Queen? Black Women, Beauty, and the Politics of Race*. New York: Oxford University Press, 2002.

Crenshaw, Kimberlee. *Demarginalizing the Intersection of Race and Sex: A Black Feminist Critique of Antidiscrimination Doctrine, Feminist Theory, and Antiracist Politics*. Chicago: University of Chicago Legal Forum, 1989.

Cronin, Mike. "Reflections on the Cultural Paradigm." *Sporting Traditions* 27, no. 2 (2010): 1–13.

Cull, Nicholas J. *The Cold War and the United States Information Agency: American Propaganda and Public Diplomacy, 1945–1989*. Cambridge: Cambridge University Press, 2008.

Custen, George F. *Bio/Pics: How Hollywood Constructed Public History*. New Brunswick, NJ: Rutgers University Press, 1992.

———. "Making History." In *The Historical Film: History and Memory in Media*, edited by Marcia Landy, 67–97. New Brunswick: Rutgers University Press, 2001.

———. "The Mechanical Life in the Age of Human Reproduction: American Biopics, 1961–1980." *Biography* 23, no. 1 (2000): 127–59.

Darke, Paul Anthony. "The Changing Face of Representations of Disability in the Media." In *Disabling Barriers—Enabling Environments*, edited by John Swain, Sally French, Colin Barnes, and Carol Thomas, 100–105. London: Sage, 2004.

Darke, Paul. "Cinematic Representations of Disability." In *The Disability Reader: Social Science Perspectives*, edited by Tom Shakespeare, 181–200. New York: Continuum, 1998.

Davis, Angela. *Angela Davis: Autobiography*. New York: Hutchinson, 1975.

Davis, Lennard J. *Enforcing Normalcy: Disability, Deafness, and the Body*. New York: Verso, 1995.

Davis, Michael D. *Black American Women in Olympic Track & Field*. Jefferson, NC: McFarland, 1992.

"'Definitive' Wilma Rudolph, The." *Journal of Sport Philately* 43, no. 3 (2005): 24–25.

Dennis, Samuel F. "Seeing Hampton Plantation: Race and Gender in a South Carolina Heritage Landscape." In *Landscape and Race in the United States*, edited by Richard Schein, 73–94. New York: Routledge, 2006.

Doss, Erika. *Memorial Mania: Public Feeling in America*. Chicago: University of Chicago Press, 2010.

Doyle, Kegan. "Muhammad Goes to Hollywood: Michael Mann's Ali as Biopic." *The Journal of Popular Culture* 39, no. 3 (2006): 383–406.

Dudziak, Mary L. *Cold War Civil Rights: Race and the Image of American Democracy*. Princeton, NJ: Princeton University Press, 2000.

Duncan, Derek. "Corporeal Histories: The Autobiographical Bodies of Luisa Passerini." *Modern Language Review* 93, no. 2 (1998): 370–83.

Duthie, Christine. "'It's Just Plain Real!': Introducing Young Children to Biography and Autobiography," *The New Advocate* 11, no. 3 (1998): 219–27.

Dwyer, Owen J. "Interpreting the Civil Rights Movement: Contradiction, Confirmation, and the Cultural Landscape." In *The Civil Rights Movement in American Memory*, edited by Renee C. Romano and Leigh Raiford, 5–27. Athens: University of Georgia Press, 2006.

Dwyer, Owen, and Derek H. Alderman, *Civil Rights Memorials and the Geography of Memory*. Chicago: Center for American Places at Columbia College, 2008.

Dyer, Richard. *WHITE*. New York: Routledge, 1997.

Dyreson, Mark. "Icons of Liberty or Objects of Desire? American Women Olympians and the Politics of Consumption." *Journal of Contemporary History* 38 (2003): 435–60.

Eakin, John Paul. *Living Autobiographically: How We Create Identity in Narrative*. Ithaca, NY: Cornell University Press 2008.

Eaton, Gale. *Well-Dressed Role Models: The Portrayal of Women in Biographies for Children*. Oxford: Scarecrow Press, 2006.

Edy, Jill A. *Troubled Pasts: News and the Collective Memory of Social Unrest*. Philadelphia: Temple University Press, 2006.

Engfer, Lee. *Wilma Rudolph: Olympic Track Star*. Mankato, MN: Capstone Press, 2006.

Erll, Astrid. "Cultural Memory Studies: An Introduction." In *A Companion to Cultural Memory Studies*, edited by Astrid Erll and Ansgar Nünning, 1–18. Berlin: Walter De Gruyter, 2008.

Ezra, Michael. *Muhammad Ali: The Making of an Icon*. Philadelphia: Temple University Press, 2009.

Fairclough, Adam. *Better Day Coming: Blacks and Equality, 1890–2000*. New York: Viking, 2001.

Falk, William W., Larry L. Hunt, and Matthew O. Hunt. "Return Migrations of African-Americans to the South: Reclaiming a Land of Promise, Going Home, or Both?" *Rural Sociology* 69, no. 4 (2004): 490–509.

Fertig, Gary. "Using Biography to Help Young Learners Understand the Causes of Historical Continuity and Change." *The Social Studies* 99, no. 4 (2008): 147–54.

Festle, Mary Jo. *Playing Nice: Politics and Apologies in Women's Sports*. New York: Columbia University Press, 1996.

Finch, Jennie, and Ann Killion. *Throw like a Girl: How to Dream Big and Believe in Yourself*. New York: Triumph, 2011.

Finger, Anne. *Elegy for a Disease: A Personal and Cultural History of Polio.* New York: St. Martin's, 2006.

Finney, Nikky. *Head Off and Split: Poems.* Chicago: TriQuarterly, 2011.

Fishbein, Leslie. "*Roots*: Docudrama and the Interpretation of History." In *Why Docudrama? Fact-Fiction on Film and Television*, edited by Alan Rosenthal, 271–95. Carbondale: Southern Illinois Press, 1999.

Flanagan, Alice K. *Wilma Rudolph: Athlete and Educator.* Chicago: Ferguson, 2000.

Fowler, Bridget. *The Obituary as Collective Memory.* New York: Routledge, 2007.

Fox-Genovese, Elizabeth. "To Write My Self: The Autobiographies of Afro-American Women." In *Feminist Issues in Literary Scholarship*, edited by Shari Benstock, 161–80. Bloomington: Indiana University Press, 1987.

Gallagher, Victoria J., and Margaret R. LaWare. "Sparring with Public Memory: The Rhetorical Embodiment of Race, Power, and Conflict in the Monument to Joe Louis." In *Places of Public Memory: The Rhetoric of Museums and Memorials*, edited by Greg Dickinson, Carole Blair, and Brian L. Ott, 87–112. Tuscaloosa: University of Alabama Press, 2010.

Garland-Thomson, Rosemarie. "Disability and Representation." *PMLA* 120, no. 2 (2005): 522–27.

———. *Extraordinary Bodies: Figuring Disability in American Culture and Literature.* New York: Columbia University Press, 1997.

Gartner, Alan, and Tom Joe. "Introduction." In *Images of the Disabled, Disabling Images*, edited by Alan Gartner and Tom Joe, 1–6. New York: Praeger, 1987.

Gates, Henry Louis, Jr., ed. *Bearing Witness: Selections from African-American Autobiography in the Twentieth Century.* New York: Pantheon Books, 1991.

Gergen, Mary M., and Kenneth J. Gergen. "Narratives of the Gendered Body in Popular Autobiography." In *The Narrative Study of Lives*, vol. 1, edited by Ruthellen Josselson and Amia Lieblich, 191–218. Newbury Park, CA: Sage Publications, 1993.

Gibson, Althea, as told to Ed Fitzgerald. *I Always Wanted to Be Somebody.* New York: HarperCollins Publishers, 1958.

Gibson, Bob. *From Ghetto to Glory.* Englewood Cliffs, NJ: Prentice Hall, 1968.

Gilbert, Tiffany. "American Iconoclast: 'Carmen Jones' and the Revolutionary Divadom of Dorothy Dandridge." *Women's Studies Quarterly* 33, no. 3/4 (2005): 234–49.

Gitersos, Terry Valos. "The Sporting Scramble for Africa: GANEFO, the IOC, and the 1965 African Games." *Sport in Society* 14, no. 5 (2011): 645–59.

Gomery, Douglas. "Television, Hollywood, and the Development of Movies Made-for-Television." In *Regarding Television: Critical Approaches—An Anthology*, edited by E. Ann Kaplan, 120–29. Fredericksburg, MD: The University of America Press, 1983.

Gooding-Williams, Robert, ed. *Reading Rodney King: Reading Urban Uprising*. New York: Routledge, 1993.

Goudsouzian, Aram. "Wilma Rudolph: Running for Freedom." In *Tennessee Women: Their Lives and Times*, vol. 1, edited by Sarah Wilkerson Freeman and Beverly Green Bond, 305–32. Southern Women: Their Lives and Times. Athens: University of Georgia Press, 2009.

Gray, Herman. "The Politics of Representation in Network Television." In *Channeling Blackness: Studies on Television and Race in America*, edited by Darnell M. Hunt, 155–74. New York: Oxford University Press, 2005.

Green, Mary Jean. "Structures of Liberation: Female Experience and the Autobiographical Form in Quebec." In *Life/Lines: Theorizing Women's Autobiography*, edited by Bella Brodzki and Celeste Schenck, 189–99. Ithaca, NY: Cornell University Press, 1988.

Greenspan, Bud (director). *Wilma*. DVD. New York: S'more entertainment, 2006.

Grundman, Adolph H. "The Image of Intercollegiate Sports and the Civil Rights Movement: A Historian's View." in *Sport in Higher Education*, edited by Donald Chu, Jeffrey Segrave, and Beverly J. Becker, 339–45. Champaign, IL: Human Kinetics, 1985.

Gudmundsdóttir, Gunnthórunn. *Borderlines: Autobiography and Fiction in Postmodern Life Writing*. Amsterdam: Rodopi, 2003.

Hagen, Joshua. "Parades, Public Space, and Propaganda: The Nazi Culture Parades in Munich." *Geografiska Annaler*: Series B, *Human Geography* 90, no. 4 (2008): 349–67.

Halbwachs, Maurice. *On Collective Memory*. Edited and translated by Lewis A. Coser. Chicago: University of Chicago Press, 1992.

Hall, Stuart, ed. *Representation: Cultural Representations and Signifying Practices*. London: Sage, 1997.

Harper, Jo. *Wilma Rudolph: Olympic Runner*. New York: Aladdin Paperbacks, 2004.

Harris, Duchess. "From the Kennedy Commission to the Combahee Collective: Black Feminist Organizing, 1960–1980." In *Sisters in the Struggle: African American Women in the Civil Rights-Black Power Movement*, edited by Bettye Collier-Thomas and V. P. Franklin, 280–305. New York: New York University Press, 2001.

Harris-Perry, Melissa V. *Sister Citizen: Shame, Stereotypes, and Black Women in America*. New Haven: Yale University Press, 2011.

Hayden, Dolores. *The Power of Place: Urban Landscapes as Public History*. Cambridge, MA: MIT Press, 1995.

Heilbrun, Carolyn G. *Writing a Woman's Life*. New York: Ballantine Books, 1988.

Hixson, Walter L. *Parting the Curtain: Propaganda, Culture, and the Cold War, 1945–1961*. New York: St. Martin's, 1998.

Hofferth, Sandra L., Joan R. Kahn, and Wendy Baldwin. "Premarital Sexual Activity among U.S. Teenage Women over the Past Three Decades." *Family Planning Perspectives* 19, no. 2 (1987): 46–53.

Hollinger, Karen. *In the Company of Women: Contemporary Female Friendship Films*. Minneapolis: University of Minnesota Press, 1998.

Holloway, Jonathan Scott. *Jim Crow Wisdom: Memory and Identity in Black America since 1940*. Chapel Hill: University of North Carolina Press, 2013.

Holloway, Karla. *Passed On: African American Mourning Stories*. Durham, NC: Duke University Press, 2003.

Holte, James Craig. *The Ethnic I: A Sourcebook for Ethnic-American Autobiography*. New York: Greenwood Press, 1988.

Huey, Lynda. *A Running Start: An Athlete, a Woman*. New York: Quadrangle, 1976.

Huggins, Mike. "Gone but Not Forgotten: Sporting Heroes, Heritage and Graveyard Commemoration." *Rethinking History: The Journal of Theory and Practice* 16, no. 4 (2012): 465–77.

Hume, Janice. *Obituaries in American Culture*. Jackson: University Press of Mississippi, 2000.

Hunt, Darnell M. "Black Content, White Control." In *Channeling Blackness: Studies on Television and Race in America*, edited by Darnell M. Hunt, 267–302. New York: Oxford University Press, 2005.

Hurup, Elsebeth. "Bridge over Troubled Water: Nostalgia for the Fifties in Movies of the Seventies and Eighties." In *Cracking the Ike Age: Aspects of Fifties America*, edited by Dale Carter, 56–75. Aarhus, Denmark: Aarhus University Press, 1992.

Huyssen, Andreas. *Twilight Memories: Marking Time in a Culture of Amnesia*. New York: Routledge, 1995.

Inboden, William. *Religion and American Foreign Policy, 1945–1960: The Soul of Containment*. Oxford: Cambridge University Press, 2008.

Irwin-Zarecka, Iwona. *Frames of Remembrance: The Dynamics of Collective Memory*. Piscataway, NJ: Transaction Publishers, 1994.

Jacobs, Linda. *Wilma Rudolph: Run for Glory*. St. Paul, MN: EMC, 1975.

Jacobs, Sylvia M. "James Emman Kwegyir Aggrey: An African Intellectual in the United States." *Journal of Negro History* 81 (1996): 47–61.

Jameson, Fredric. *Postmodernism, or, The Cultural Logic of Late Capitalism*. Durham: Duke University Press, 1991.

Jewell, K. Sue. *From Mammy to Miss America and Beyond: Cultural Images and the Shaping of US Social Policy*. New York: Routledge, 1993.

Johnson, Ann Donegan. *The Value of Overcoming Adversity: The Story of Wilma Rudolph*. La Jolla, CA: Value Communications, 1996.

Joyner-Kersee, Jackie, with Sonja Steptoe. *A Kind of Grace: The Autobiography of the World's Greatest Female Athlete*. New York: Grand Central Publishers, 1997.

Kane, Mary Jo. "Media Coverage of the Female Athlete before, during and after Title IX: *Sports Illustrated* revisited." *Journal of Sport Management* 2, no. 2 (1988): 87–99.

Kane, Mary Jo, and Janet B. Parks. "Mass Media Images as a Reflection of Historical Social Change: The Portrayal of Female Athletes before, during and after Title IX." In *Psychology and Sociology of Sport: Current Selected Research*, vol. 2, edited by Lee Vander Veldenn and James H. Humphrey, 133–50. New York: AMS.

Kansteiner, Wulf. "Meaning in Memory: A Methodological Critique of Collective Memory Studies." *History and Theory* 41, no. 2 (2002): 179–97.

Kearney, Mary Celeste. "Girlfriends and Girl Power: Female Adolescence in Contemporary U.S. Cinema." In *Sugar, Spice, and Everything Nice: The Cinemas of Girlhood*, edited by Frances Gateward and Murray Pomerance, 125–43. Detroit: Wayne State University Press, 2002.

Keys, Barbara J. *Globalizing Sport: National Rivalry and International Community in the 1930s*. Cambridge: Harvard University Press, 2006.

Klarman, Michael J. *From Jim Crow to Civil Rights: The Supreme Court and the Struggle for Racial Equality*. New York: Oxford University Press, 2004.

Klatt, Beverly. "Abraham Lincoln: Deified Martyr, Flesh and Blood Hero, and a Man with Warts." *Children's Literature in Education* 23, no. 3 (1992): 119–29.

Kohl, Herbert. *Should We Burn Babar? Essays on Children's Literature and the Power of Stories*. New York: New Press, 1995.

Kong, Lily, and Brenda S. A. Yeoh. "The Construction of National Identity through the Production of Ritual and Spectacle: An Analysis of National Day Parades in Singapore." *Political Geography* 16, no. 3 (1997): 213–39.

Krull, Kathleen. *Wilma Unlimited: How Wilma Rudolph Became the World's Fastest Woman*. San Diego, CA: Voyager Books, 1996.

Lanker, Brian. *I Dream a World: Portraits of Black Women Who Changed America*. New York: Stewart, Tabori, and Chang, 1989.

Lansbury, Jennifer H. "Alice Coachman: Quiet Champion of the 1940s." In *Out of the Shadows: A Biographical History of African American Athletes*, edited by David K. Wiggins, 147–62. Fayetteville: University of Arkansas, 2006.

Launius, Roger D. "Heroes in a Vacuum: The Apollo Astronaut as Cultural Icon." *The Florida Historical Quarterly* 87, no. 2 (2008): 174–209.

Lechner, Judith V. "Accuracy in Biographies for Children." *The New Advocate* 10, no. 3 (1997): 229–42.

Lee, Taeku. *Mobilizing Public Opinion: Black Insurgency and Racial Attitudes in the Civil Rights Era*. Chicago: University of Chicago Press, 2002.

Leib, Jonathan. "The Witting Autobiography of Richmond, Virginia: Arthur Ashe, the Civil War, and Monument Avenue's Racialized Landscape." In *Landscape and Race in the United States*, edited by Richard Schein, 187–211. New York: Routledge, 2006.

Lejeune, Philippe, Annette Tomarken, and Edward Tomarken. "Autobiography in Third Person." *New Literary History* 9, no. 1 (1977): 27–50.

Levy, Patricia. *Iconic Events: Media, Politics, and Power in Retelling History.* Lanham, MD: Lexington Books, 2007.

Liberti, Rita. "'We Were Ladies, We Just Played Basketball like Boys': African American Womanhood and Competitive Basketball at Bennett College, 1928–1942." *Journal of Sport History* 26, no. 3 (1999): 567–84.

Lintner, Terre. *Wilma Rudolph: A True Winner.* New York: Macmillan/McGraw Hill, 2010.

Long, Judy. *Telling Women's Lives: Subject/Narrator/Reader/Text.* New York: New York University Press, 1999.

Louis, Joe, Chester L. Washington, and Haskell Cohen. *My Life Story, by Joe Louis.* New York: Duell, Sloan and Pearce, 1947.

Louis, Joe, with Edna and Art Rust. *Joe Louis: My Life.* New York: Harcourt Brace Jovanovich, 1978.

Lovett, Bobby L. *America's Historically Black Colleges and Universities: A Narrative History from the Nineteenth Century into the Twenty-First Century.* Macon, GA: Mercer University Press, 2011.

———. *The Civil Rights Movement in Tennessee: A Narrative History.* Knoxville: University of Tennessee Press, 2005.

Lucas, W. Scott. "Beyond Diplomacy: Propaganda and the History of the Cold War." In *Cold War Propaganda in the 1950s,* edited by Gary D. Rawnsley, 11–30. New York: St. Martin's, 1999.

Macceca, Stephanie. *Wilma Rudolph: Against All Odds.* Huntington Beach, CA: Teacher Created Materials, 2010.

Manduziuk, Roseann M., and Suzanne Pullon Fitch. "The Rhetorical Construction of Sojourner Truth." *Southern Communication Journal* 66, no. 2 (2001): 120–38.

Manring, M. M. *Slave in a Box: The Strange Career of Aunt Jemima.* Charlottesville: University Press of Virginia, 1998.

Maraniss, David. *Rome 1960: The Olympics That Changed the World.* New York: Simon & Schuster, 2009.

Marston, Sallie A. "Public Rituals and Community Power: St. Patrick's Day Parades in Lowell, Massachusetts, 1841–1874." *Political Geography Quarterly* 8, no. 3 (1989): 255–69.

McKay, Nellie Y. "Race, Gender, and Cultural Context in Zora Neale Hurston's *Dust Tracks on a Road.*" In *Life/Lines: Theorizing Women's*

Autobiography, edited by Bella Brodzki and Celeste Schenck, 175–88. Ithaca, NY: Cornell University Press, 1988.

McRuer, Robert. *Crip Theory: Cultural Signs of Queerness and Disability*. New York: New York University Press, 2006.

Meyer, Richard E. "Images of Logging on Contemporary Pacific Northwest Gravemarkers." In *Cemeteries and Gravemarkers: Voices of American Culture*, edited by Richard E. Meyer, 61–85. Logan: Utah State University Press, 1989.

Mitchell, David T., and Sharon L. Snyder. "Introduction: Disability Students and the Double Bind of Representation." In *The Body and Physical Difference: Discourses of Disability*, edited by David T. Mitchell and Sharon L. Snyder, 1–34. Ann Arbor: University of Michigan Press, 1997.

———. *Narrative Prosthesis: Disability and the Dependencies of Discourse*. Ann Arbor: University of Michigan Press, 2000.

Moody, Ann. *Coming of Age in Mississippi*. New York: Dial Press, 1962.

Morrison, Toni. *The Bluest Eye*. New York: Holt, Rinehart and Winston, 1970.

———. *Playing in the Dark*. Cambridge, MA: Harvard University Press, 1990.

———. *Sula*. New York: Knopf, 1973.

Moynihan, Daniel Patrick. *The Negro Family: The Case for National Action*. Washington, DC: Office of Policy Planning and Research, US Department of Labor, 1965.

Munslow, Alun. *Narrative and History*. New York: Palgrave Macmillan, 2007.

Naden, Corinne J., and Rose Blue. *Wilma Rudolph*. Chicago: Raintree, 2004.

Nash, Jennifer C. "Re-thinking Intersectionality." *Feminist Review* 89 (June 2008): 1–15.

Nathan, Daniel A. *Saying It's So: A Cultural History of the Black Sox Scandal*. Urbana: University of Illinois Press, 2003.

Nelson, Jack A. "The Invisible Cultural Group: Images of Disability." In *Images That Injure: Pictorial Images in the Media*, 2nd ed., edited by Paul Martin Lester and Susan Dente Ross, 274–92. Westport, CT: Greenwood Press, 2003.

Neuman, Shirley. "Autobiography, Bodies, Manhood." In *Women, Autobiography, Theory*, edited by Sidonie Smith and Julia Watson, 415–28. Madison: University of Wisconsin Press, 1988.

Norkunas, Martha K. *Monuments and Memory: History and Representation in Lowell, Massachusetts*. Washington, DC: Smithsonian Institution Scholarly Press, 2002.

O'Dell, Darlene. *Sites of Southern Memory: The Autobiographies of Katharine Du Pre Lumpkin, Lillian Smith, and Pauli Murray*. Charlottesville: University Press of Virginia, 2001.

O'Reilly, Kathleen, and Michael E. Crutcher. "Parallel Politics: The Spatial Power of New Orleans' Labor Day Parades," *Social and Cultural Geography* 7, no. 2 (2006): 245–65.

Olick, Jeffrey K. *The Politics of Regret: On Collective Memory and Historical Responsibility*. New York: Routledge, 2007.

Olick, Jeffrey K., Vered Vinitzky-Seroussi, and Daniel Levy. "Introduction." In *The Collective Memory Reader*, edited by Jeffrey K. Olick, Vered Vinitzky-Seroussi, and Daniel Levy, 3–62. New York: Oxford University Press, 2011.

Oriard, Michael. "Autobiographies." In *African-Americans in Sport*, vol. 1, edited by David K. Wiggins, 15–17. Armonk, NY: M. E. Sharpe, 2004.

Osmond, Gary. "'Modest Monuments'? Postage Stamps, Duke Kahanamoku and Hierarchies of Social Memory." *The Journal of Pacific History* 43, no. 3 (2008): 313–29.

———. "Photographs, Materiality and Sport History: Peter Norman and the 1968 Mexico City Black Power Salute." *Journal of Sport History* 37, no. 1 (2010): 119–37.

———. "Shimmering Waters: Swimming, Autobiography and Social Memory." *Sporting Traditions* 20, no. 1 (2003): 63–71.

Owens, Jesse, with Paul Niemark. *Blackthink: My Life as Black Man and White Man*. New York: Morrow, 1970.

Paino, Troy D. "Hoosiers in a Different Light: Forces of Change v. the Power of Nostalgia." *Journal of Sport History* 28, no. 1 (2001): 63–80.

Parks, Jenifer. "Verbal Gymnastics: The Soviet Sports Administration and the Decision to Enter the Olympic Games, 1947–1952." In *East Plays West: Sport and the Cold War*, edited by Stephen Wagg and David L. Andrews, 27–44. New York: Routledge, 2007.

Parratt, Catriona. "Wasn't It Ironic? The Haxey Hood and the Great War." In *Deconstructing Sport History: A Postmodern Analysis*, edited by Murray G. Phillips, 131–46. Albany: State University of New York Press, 2006.

Patterson, Floyd, with Milton Gross. *Victory over Myself.* New York: Random House, 1962.

Patterson, James T. *Freedom Is Not Enough: The Moynihan Report and America's Struggle over Black Family Live—From LBJ to Obama.* New York: Basic Books, 2010.

Phillips, Murray G., and Gary Osmond, "Filmic Sports History: Dawn Fraser, Swimming and Australian National Identity." *The International Journal of the History of Sport* 26 (2009): 2126–42.

Phillips, Murray G., Mark E. O'Neill, and Gary Osmond. "Broadening Horizons in Sport History: Films, Photographs, and Monuments." *Journal of Sport History* 34, no. 2 (2007): 271–93.

Pipkin, James W. *Sporting Lives: Metaphor and Myth in American Sports Autobiographies.* Columbia: University of Missouri Press, 2008.

Quayson, Ato. *Aesthetic Nervousness: Disability and the Crisis of Representation.* New York: Columbia University Press, 2007.

Ramshaw, Greg, and Sean Gammon. "More Than Just Nostalgia? Exploring the Heritage/Sport Tourism Nexus." *Journal of Sport Tourism* 10, no. 4 (2005): 229–41.

Reece, Gabrielle, and Karen Karbo. *Big Girl in the Middle.* New York: Three Rivers Press, 1998.

Regester, Charlene B. *African American Women Actresses: The Struggle for Visibility, 1900–1960.* Bloomington: Indiana University Press, 2010.

Remnick, David. *King of the World: Muhammad Ali and the Rise of an American Hero.* New York: Random House, 1998.

Riordan, James. *Sport in Soviet Society: Development of Sport and Physical Education in Russia and the USSR.* Cambridge: Cambridge University Press, 1977.

———. "The USSR and the Olympic Games." *Stadion* 6 (1980): 291–313.

Rippy, Marguerite H. "Commodity, Tragedy, Desire: Female Sexuality and Blackness in the Iconography of Dorothy Dandridge." In *Classic Hollywood, Classic Whiteness*, edited by Daniel Bernardi, 178–209. Minneapolis: University of Minnesota Press, 2001.

Rishoi, Christy. *From Girl to Woman: American Women's Coming-of-Age Narratives*. Albany: State University of New York Press, 2003.

Ritterhouse, Jennifer. *Growing Up Jim Crow: How Black and White Southern Children Learned Race*. Chapel Hill: University of North Carolina Press, 2006.

Roberts, Diane. *The Myth of Aunt Jemima: Representations of Race and Region*. New York: Routledge, 1994.

Roberts, Gene, and Hank Klibanoff. *The Race Beat: The Press, the Civil Rights Struggle and the Awakening of a Nation*. New York: Alfred A. Knopf, 2007.

Robinson, Frank, and Al Silverman. *My Life in Baseball*. New York: Doubleday, 1968.

Robinson, Jackie. *Baseball Has Done It*. Philadelphia: Lippincott, 1964.

Robinson, Jackie, with Alfred Duckett. *Breakthrough to the Big Leagues*. New York: Harper & Row, 1965.

———. *I Never Had It Made*. New York: Putnam, 1972.

Romano, Renee C. "Narratives of Redemption: The Birmingham Church Bombing Trials and the Construction of Civil Rights Memory." In *The Civil Rights Movement in American Memory*, edited by Renee C. Romano and Leigh Raiford, 96–134. Athens: University of Georgia Press, 2006.

Rosenstone, Robert A. *History on Film/Film on History*. Harlow, UK: Pearson Longman, 2006.

———. "In Praise of the Biopic." In *Lights, Camera, History: Portraying the Past in Film*, edited by Richard Francaviglia and Jerry Rodnitzky, 11–29. College Station: Texas A&M University Press, 2007.

———. "Reel History with Missing Reels?" *Perspectives on History* 37 (1999). Accessed online June 30, 2011.

Rubin, Ellen, and Emily Strauss Watson. "Disability Bias in Children's Literature." *The Lion and the Unicorn* 11, no. 1 (1987): 60–67.

Rudolph, Wilma. *Wilma: The Story of Wilma Rudolph*. New York: Signet, 1977.

Russell, Bill, with Taylor Branch. *Second Wind: The Memoirs of an Opinionated Man*. New York: Random House, 1979.

Russell, Bill, with William McSweeney. *Go Up for Glory*. New York: Coward-McCann, 1966.

Ruth, Amy. *Wilma Rudolph*. Minneapolis, MN: Lerner Publications Company, 2000.

Satina, Barbara, and Francine Hultgren, "The Absent Body of Girls Made Visible: Embodiment as the Focus in Education." *Studies in Philosophy & Education* 20 (2001): 521–34.

Saul, Wendy. "Living Proof: Children's Biographies of Marie Curie." In *How Much Truth Do We Tell the Children? The Politics of Children's Literature*, edited by Betty Bacon, 217–28. Minneapolis: MEP, 1988.

Schaefer, Lola M. *Some Kids Use Wheelchairs*. North Mankato, MN: Pebble Books, 2008.

Schein, Richard H., ed. *Landscape and Race in the United States*. New York: Routledge, 2006.

Schraff, Anne. *Wilma Rudolph: The Greatest Woman Sprinter in History*. Berkeley Heights, NJ: Enslow, 2004.

Schulman, Bruce J. *The Seventies: The Great Shift in American Culture, Society, and Politics*. New York: The Free Press, 2001.

Schultz, Jaime. "Contesting the Master Narrative: The Arthur Ashe Statue and Monument Avenue in Richmond, Virginia." *The International Journal of the History of Sport* 28, no. 8–9 (2011): 1235–51.

———. "Leaning into the Turn: Towards A New Cultural Sport History." *Sporting Traditions* 27, no. 2 (2010): 45–59.

———. *Qualifying Times: Points of Change in US Women's Sport*. Champaign: University of Illinois Press, 2014.

Schwartz, Barry. "Collective Forgetting and the Symbolic Power of Oneness: The Strange Apotheosis of Rosa Parks." *Social Psychology Quarterly* 72, no. 2 (2009): 123–42.

Schwenk, Melinda M. "'Negro Stars' and the USIA's Portrait of Democracy." *Race, Gender and Class* 8, no. 4 (2001): 116.

Segel, Elizabeth. "In Biography for Young Readers, Nothing Is Impossible." *The Lion and the Unicorn* 4, no. 1 (1980): 4–14.

Sernett, Milton C. *Harriet Tubman: Myth, Memory, and History*. Durham, NC: Duke University Press, 2007.

Shakespeare, Tom. "Cultural Representation of Disabled People: Dustbins for Disavowal?" *Disability and Society* 9, no. 3 (1994): 283–99.

———. "The Social Model of Disability." In *The Disability Studies Reader*, 2nd ed., edited by Lennard J. Davis, 197–204. New York: Routledge, 2006.

Shaw, Andrea. "The Other Side of the Looking Glass: The Marginalization of Fatness and Blackness in the Construction of Gender Identity." *Social Semiotics* 15, no. 2 (2005): 143–52.

Sherrow, Victoria. *Wilma Rudolph*. Minneapolis: Carolrhoda, 2000.

Shirley, Michael, and George E. Sims. "Introduction." In *Making a New South: Race, Leadership, and Community after the Civil War,* edited by Paul A. Cimbala and Barton C. Shaw, 1–10. Gainesville: University Press of Florida, 2007.

Sibley, David. *Geographies of Exclusion: Society and Difference in the West.* London: Routledge, 1995.

Siegel, Kristi. *Women's Autobiographies, Culture, Feminism.* New York: Peter Lang, 1999.

Sigerman, Harriet. *The Columbia Documentary History of American Women since 1941.* New York: Columbia University Press, 2003.

Sitkoff, Harvard. *The Struggle for Black Equality, 1954–1992.* New York: Hill and Wang, 1993.

Smith, Maureen M. "America's Sport Statues: Myths, Memories, and Meanings: A Case Study of Three Recent Statues." Paper presented at A Mirror of Our Culture, Sport and Society conference, St. Norbert College, De Pere, WI, 2012.

———. "Bill Russell: Pioneer and Champion of the Sixties." In *Out of the Shadows: A Biographical History of African American Athletes,* edited by David K. Wiggins, 223–40. Fayetteville: University of Arkansas Press, 2006.

———. *Wilma Rudolph: A Biography.* Westport, CT: Greenwood Press, 2006.

Smith, Sidonie. "Identity's Body." In *Autobiography and Postmodernism,* edited by Kathleen Ashley, Leigh Gilmore, and Gerald Peters, 266–92. Boston: University of Massachusetts Press, 1994.

———. *Subjectivity, Identity, and the Body: Women's Autobiographical Practices in the Twentieth Century.* Bloomington: Indiana University Press, 1993.

Smith, Sidonie, and Julia Watson. *Reading Autobiography: A Guide for Interpreting Life Narratives.* Minneapolis: University of Minnesota Press, 2010.

———. *Women, Autobiography, Theory: A Reader.* Madison: University of Wisconsin, 1998.

Smith, Tommie, with David Steele. *Silent Gesture: The Autobiography of Tommie Smith*. Philadelphia: Temple University Press, 2007.

Sparkes, Andrew C. "Bodies, Narratives, Selves, and Autobiography: The Example of Lance Armstrong." *Journal of Sport & Social Issues* 28, no. 4 (2004): 397–428.

Spector-Mersel, Gabriela. "Mechanisms of Selection in Claiming Narrative Identities: A Model for Interpreting Narratives." *Qualitative Inquiry* 17, no. 2 (2011): 172–85.

Spivey, Donald. "The Black Athlete in Big-Time Intercollegiate Sports, 1941–1968." *Phylon* 44, no. 2 (1983): 116–25.

Stearns, Peter N. *Fat History: Bodies and Beauty in the Modern West*. New York: New York University Press, 2002.

Steedman, Carolyn Kay. *Landscape for a Good Woman*. New Brunswick, NJ: Rutgers University Press, 1987.

Stites, Richard. "Heaven and Hell: Soviet Propaganda Constructs the World." In *Cold War Propaganda in the 1950s*, edited by Gary Rawnsley, 85–103. New York: St. Martin's, 1999.

Stott, Jon C. "Biographies of Sports Heroes and the American Dream." *Children's Literature in Education* 10, no. 4 (1979): 174–85.

Stover, Johnnie. *Rhetoric and Resistance in Black Women's Autobiography*. Gainesville: University Press of Florida, 2003.

Stratton, W. K. *Floyd Patterson: The Fighting Life of Boxing's Invisible Champion*. Boston: Houghton Mifflin, 2012.

Streissguth, Tom. *Wilma Rudolph*. Minneapolis: Twenty-First Century Books, 2006.

Stride, Chris, Ffion E. Thomas, John P. Wilson, and Josh Pahigian. "Modeling Stadium Statue Subject Choice in U.S. Baseball and English Soccer." *Journal of Quantitative Analysis in Sports* 8, no. 1 (2012): 1–36.

Sydnor, Synthia. "Sport, Celebrity and Liminality." In *Getting into the Game: Anthropological Perspectives on Sport*, edited by Noel Dyck, 221–41. New York: Berg, 2000.

Taylor, Ella G. *Prime-Time Families: Television Culture in Postwar America*. Berkeley: University of California Press, 1989.

Taylor, Ella G., and Andrea S. Walsh. "'And Next Week—Child Abuse': Family Issues in Contemporary TV Movies." In *Culture and Communication: Methodology, Behavior, Artifacts, and Institutions*, edited by Sari Thomas, 168–77. Norwood, NJ: Ablex, 1987.

Temple, Ed, with B'Lou Carter. *Only the Pure in Heart Survive*. Nashville: Broadman Press, 1980.

Theoharis, Jeanne. *The Rebellious Life of Mrs. Rosa Parks*. Boston: Beacon Press, 2013.

Thomas, Damion L. *Globetrotting: African American Athletes and Cold War Politics*. Urbana: University of Illinois Press, 2012.

———. "Let the Games Begin: Sport, US Race Relations and Cold War Politics." *International Journal of the History of Sport* 24, no. 2 (2007): 157–71.

Tice, Karen W. "Queens of Academe: Campus Pageantry and Student Life." *Feminist Studies* 31, no. 2 (2005): 250–83.

Tricard, Louise Mead. *American Women's Track and Field: A History, 1895–1980*. Jefferson, NC: McFarland, 1996.

Turrini, Joseph M. "'It Was Communism versus the Free World': The USA-USSR Dual Track Meet Series and the Development of Track and Field in the United States, 1958–1985." *Journal of Sport History* 28, no. 3 (2001): 403–43.

US Bureau of the Census. *US Census of Population: 1960. Vol. 1, Characteristics of the Population, Part 44, Tennessee*. Washington, DC: US Government Printing Office, 1963.

VanderHaagen, Sara Christine. "So You Will Always Remember: Creating Public Memories and Inventing Agents in Biographical Texts for Children," PhD diss., Northwestern University, 2010.

Verbrugge, Martha H. *Active Bodies: A History of Women's Physical Education in Twentieth-Century America*. New York: Oxford University Press, 2012.

Vertinsky, Patricia, Sherry McKay, and Stephen Petrina. "No Body/ies in the Gym." In *Disciplining Bodies in the Gymnasium: Memory, Monument and Modernism*, edited by Patricia Vertinsky and Sherry McKay, 157–71. London: Routledge, 2004.

Vider, Stephen. "Sanford versus Steinberg: Black Sitcoms, Jewish Writers, and the 1970s Ethnic Revival." *Transition* 105 (2011): 21–29.

Von Eschen, Penny M. *Satchmo Blows Up the World: Jazz Ambassadors Play the Cold War*. Cambridge: Harvard University Press, 2004.

Wade, Mary Dodson. *Wilma Rudolph: Amazing Olympic Athlete*. Berkeley Heights, NJ: Enslow, 2009.

Wagg, Stephen, and David L. Andrews, eds. *East Plays West: Sport and the Cold War*. New York: Routledge, 2007.

Wallach, Jennifer Jensen. *Closer to Truth Than Any Fact: Memoir, Memory, and Jim Crow.* Athens: University of Georgia Press, 2008.

Wang, Ban. "The Cold War, Imperial Aesthetics, and Area Studies." *Social Text* 20, no. 3 (2002): 45–65.

Warner, Marina. *From the Beast to the Blonde: On Fairy Tales and Their Tellers.* New York: Farrar, Straus and Giroux, 1994.

Watkins, Steve. *The Black O: Racism and Redemption in an American Corporate Empire.* Athens: University of Georgia Press, 1997.

Whitfield, Stephen J. *The Culture of the Cold War.* Baltimore: Johns Hopkins University Press, 1996.

Wiggins, David K. "Prized Performers, but Frequently Overlooked Students: The Involvement of Black Athletes in Intercollegiate Sports on Predominantly White University Campuses, 1968–1972." *Research Quarterly for Exercise and Sport* 62, no. 2 (1991): 164–77.

———. "'The Year of Awakening': Black Athletes, Racial Unrest and the Civil Rights Movement of 1968." *The International Journal of the History of Sport* 9, no. 2 (1992): 188–208.

Wiggins, David K., and Patrick B. Miller. *The Unlevel Playing Field: Documentary History of the African American Experience in Sport.* Champaign: University of Illinois Press, 2003.

Willis, Jeanne, and Tony Ross. *Susan Laughs.* New York: Henry Holt, 2000.

Wilma Rudolph: Olympic Champion. Film. (1961). Moving Images Relating to U.S. Domestic and International Activities, compiled 1982–1999, documenting the period 1942–1999. Record Group/Local Identifier: 306-5247, records of the US Information Agency, 1900–2003. College Park, MD: National Archives.

Wilson, Wayne. "Wilma Rudolph: The Making of an Olympic Icon." In *Out of the Shadows: A Biographical History of African American Athletes,* edited by David K. Wiggins, 207–22. Fayetteville: University of Arkansas Press, 2006.

Witt, Doris. *Black Hunger: Food and the Politics of U.S. Identity.* New York: Oxford University Press, 1999.

Woods, Michael. "Performing Power: Local Politics and the Taunton Pageant of 1928." *Journal of Historical Geography* 25, no. 1 (1999): 57–74.

Worsley, Shawan M. *Audience, Agency, and Identity in Black Popular Culture.* New York: Routledge, 2010.

Wright, Roberta Hughes, and Wilber B. Hughes III. *Lay Down Body: Living History in African American Cemeteries.* Detroit: Visible Ink Press, 1996.

Zaharias, Babe Didrikson, as told to Harry Paxton. *This Life I've Led: My Autobiography.* New York: A. S. Barnes, 1955.

Zaretsky, Natasha. *No Direction Home: The American Family and the Fear of National Decline.* Chapel Hill: University of North Carolina Press, 2007.

Zinsser, William. *Extraordinary Lives: The Art and Craft of American Biography.* New York: American Heritage, 1986.

Newspapers and Periodicals Consulted

Amateur Athlete

American Mercury

Appleton (WI) Post-Crescent

Arlington Heights (IL) Daily Herald

Atlanta Constitution

Atlanta Daily World

Atlanta Journal-Constitution

Baltimore Afro-American

Boston Globe

Bulletin du Comité International Olympique

Chicago Defender

Chicago Tribune

Christian Science Monitor

Clarksville (TN) Leaf-Chronicle

Cleveland (OH) Call & Post

Corpus Christi (TX) Times

Daily Graphic (Accra, Ghana)

Dakar (Senegal) Matin

Detroit Free Press

Detroit News

Ebony

Frederick (MD) Post

Independent Press (NJ)

Ironwood (MI) Daily Globe

Jackson (MS) Advocate

Jeannette and Irwin (PA) News-Dispatch

LIFE (magazine)

Long Beach (CA) Independent

Los Angeles Mirror

Los Angeles Sentinel

Los Angeles Times

Louisville (KY) Courier-Journal

Mademoiselle

Maplewood (NJ) Patch

Nashville Banner

Nashville Globe

Nashville Tennessean

Nation, The

Negro Digest

Negro History Bulletin

New Orleans Times-Picayune

New Republic, The

New York Amsterdam News

New York Times

Newsweek

Norfolk (VA) Journal & Guide

Olympic Review

Oneonta (NY) Star

Philately Newsletter

Pittsburgh (PA) Courier

Syracuse (NY) Post-Standard

Rushville (IN) Republican

San Francisco Chronicle

Seattle PI (Post-Intelligencer, online)

Southern Illinoisan (Carbondale, IL)

Sports Illustrated

Newark (NJ) Star-Ledger

Step Inside Design Magazine

Tennessee State Meter

Tennessee State University ACCENT

Time (magazine)

Today's Health

Track and Field News

Urban Journal, The (magazine)

U.S. News and World Report

Washington Post

Index

Italic page number denotes illustration.